Living with the Past

Living with the Past

The Great Books Foundation
A nonprofit educational organization

Published and distributed by

 The Great Books Foundation
A nonprofit educational organization

35 East Wacker Drive, Suite 2300
Chicago, IL 60601-2298

CONTENTS

PREFACE

"So that's why Proust says that voluntary memory preserves nothing of the past!" "Is childhood a time of grace—or terror?" "Why can the Rat Man recognize that he needs help but not change his absurd behavior?"

Anyone who has been in a book discussion group has experienced the joy of new insight. Sometimes an idea or question occurs to us during the group meeting. Often, it is afterward—sometimes much later—that an idea we had overlooked unexpectedly strikes us with new force. A good group becomes a community of minds. We share perspectives, questions, insights, and surprises. Our fellow readers challenge and broaden our thinking as we probe deeply into characters and ideas. They help us resolve questions, and raise new ones, in a creative process that connects literature with life.

It is this kind of experience that makes book discussion groups worthwhile, and that the Great Books Foundation fosters for thousands of readers around the world.

The Great Books Foundation is a pioneer of book discussion groups that bring together dedicated readers who wish to continue to learn throughout their lives. The literature anthologies published by the Foundation have been the focus of many enlightening discussions among people of all educational backgrounds and walks of life. And the *shared inquiry* method practiced by Great Books groups has proven to be a powerful approach to literature that solves many practical concerns of new discussion groups: How can we maintain a flow of ideas? What kinds of questions should we discuss? How can we keep the discussion focused on the reading so that we use our time together to really get at the heart of a work—to learn from it and each other?

With the publication of its 50th Anniversary Series, the Great Books Foundation continues and expands upon its tradition of helping all readers engage in a meaningful exchange of ideas about outstanding works of literature.

ABOUT *LIVING WITH THE PAST*

The reading selections in *Living with the Past* have been chosen to stimulate lively shared inquiry discussions. This collection brings together works from around the world that speak to each other on a theme of universal human significance. In this volume you will find landmark works by Marcel Proust and Sigmund Freud, contemporary fiction by the Polish expatriate Gustaw Herling and the Israeli author David Grossman, and a selection from the poetic memoir of American essayist Annie Dillard. In addition to the prose selections, you will discuss poetry by William Wordsworth, Adrienne Rich, and Robert Lowell.

These are carefully crafted works that readers will interpret in different ways. They portray characters whose lives and motivations are complex, embody concepts that go beyond simple analysis, and raise many questions to inspire extended reflection.

As an aid to reading and discussion, open-ended *interpretive questions* are included with each selection in the volume, and also for the recommended novels *Song of Solomon* by Toni Morrison and *One Hundred Years of Solitude* by Gabriel García Márquez. A fundamental or *basic* interpretive question about the meaning of the selection is printed in boldface, followed by a list of related questions that will help you fully discuss the issue raised by the basic question. Passages for *textual analysis* that you may want to look at closely during discussion are suggested for each set of questions. Questions under the heading "For Further Reflection" can be used at the end of discussion to help your group consider the reading selection in a broader context.

ABOUT SHARED INQUIRY

The success of Great Books discussions depends not only on thought-provoking literature, but also on the *shared inquiry* method of discussion. A shared inquiry discussion begins with a basic interpretive question—a genuine question about the meaning of the selection that continues to be puzzling even after careful reading. As participants offer different possible answers to this question, the discussion leader or members of the group follow up on the ideas that are voiced, asking questions about how responses relate to the original question or to new ideas, and probing what specifically in the text prompted the response.

In shared inquiry discussion, readers think for themselves about the selection, and do not rely on critical or biographical sources outside the text for ideas about its meaning. Discussion remains focused on the text. Evidence for opinions is found in the selection. Because interpretive questions have no single "correct answer," participants are encouraged to entertain a range of ideas. The exchange of ideas is open and spontaneous, a common search for understanding that leads to closer, more illuminating reading.

Shared inquiry fosters a habit of critical questioning and thinking. It encourages patience in the face of complexity, and a respect for the opinions of others. As participants explore the work in depth, they try out ideas, reconsider simple answers, and synthesize interpretations. Over time, shared inquiry engenders a profound experience of intellectual intimacy as your group searches together for meaning in literature.

IMPROVING YOUR DISCUSSIONS

The selections in *Living with the Past* will support six meetings of your discussion group, with each prose selection and the poetry group being the focus of a single meeting. Discussions usually last about two hours, and are guided by a member of the group who acts as leader. Since the leader has no special knowledge or qualification beyond a genuine curiosity about the text, any member of the group may lead discussion. The leader carefully prepares the interpretive questions that he or she wants to explore with the group, and is primarily responsible for continuing the process of questioning that maintains the flow of ideas.

To ensure a successful discussion, we encourage you to make it a policy to read the selection twice. A first reading will familiarize you with the plot and ideas of a selection; on a second reading you will read more reflectively and discover many aspects of the work that deepen your thinking about it. Allowing a few days to pass between your readings will also help you approach a second reading with deeper insight.

Read the selection actively. Make marginal comments that you might want to refer to in discussion. While our interpretive questions can help you think about different aspects of the work, jotting down your own questions as you read is the best way to engage with the selection and bring a wealth of ideas and meaningful questions to discussion.

During discussion, expect a variety of answers to the basic question. Follow up carefully on these different ideas. Refer to and read from the text often—by way of explaining your answer, and to see if the rest of the group understands the author's words the same way you do. (You will often be surprised!) As your group looks closely at the text, many new ideas will arise.

While leaders in shared inquiry discussion strive to keep comments focused on the text and on the basic interpretive question the group is discussing, the entire group can share responsibility for politely refocusing comments that wander from the text into personal anecdotes or issues that begin to sidetrack discussion.

Remember that during shared inquiry discussion you are investigating differing perspectives on the reading, not social issues. Talk should be about characters in the story, not about participants' own lives. By maintaining this focus, each discussion will be new and interesting, with each participant bringing a different perspective to bear on the text. After the work has been explored thoroughly on its own terms, your thinking about important issues of the day or in your own life will be enhanced. We have found that it is best to formally set aside a time—perhaps the last half-hour of discussion, or perhaps over coffee afterward—for members of the group to share personal experiences and opinions that go beyond a discussion of the selection.

DISCUSSING THE POETRY SELECTIONS

Many book groups shy away from the challenge of discussing poetry, but the shared inquiry method will enable you to make poetry a very satisfying part of your discussion group. Poetry, by its very nature, communicates ideas through suggestion, allusion, and resonance. Because meaning in poetry resides in the interaction between author and reader, and is brought to light through the pooling of different perspectives and readers' responses, poems are ideal for shared inquiry discussion.

We suggest that you discuss the three poems in *Living with the Past* in turn, rather than all together as a group. The accompanying interpretive questions will help you focus on each poem individually, and the questions marked "For Further Reflection" will help you consider common and differing elements of the poems.

It is helpful to read each poem aloud before beginning discussion. Because poetry is usually more densely constructed than prose and highly selective in detail, it often lends itself to what we call *textual analysis*—looking closely at particular lines, words, and images as an entryway to discussing the whole work. Having readers share their different associations with a word or image can often help broaden interpretations.

Discussing the Novels

Of course, many novels come to mind that relate to the theme of living with the past. We have recommended *Song of Solomon* and *One Hundred Years of Solitude* as particularly enriching novels on this theme, and have provided interpretive questions that can be a significant aid to the reader. Even readers familiar with these novels will find a shared inquiry discussion of them a new and rewarding experience.

Most shared inquiry groups discuss a novel at a single discussion; some prefer to spread the discussion over more than one session, especially for longer novels. Since it is usually not realistic to expect participants to read a novel twice in full before discussion, we recommend that you at least reread parts of the novel that seemed especially important to you or that raised a number of questions in your mind. Our passages for textual analysis suggest parts of the novel where reading twice might be most valuable. You might even begin your discussion, after posing a basic question, by looking closely at one or two short passages to get people talking about central ideas and offering a variety of opinions that can be probed and expanded into a discussion of the whole work.

How the Great Books Foundation Can Help You

The Great Books Foundation can be a significant resource for you and your discussion group. Our staff conducts shared inquiry workshops throughout the country that will help you or your entire group conduct better discussions. Thousands of people—from elementary school teachers and college professors to those who just love books and ideas—have found our workshops to be an enjoyable experience that changes forever how they approach literature.

The Foundation publishes a variety of reading series that might interest you. We invite you to call us at 1-800-222-5870 or visit our Web site at http://www.greatbooks.org. We can help you start a book group, put you in touch with established Great Books groups in your area, or give you information about many special events—such as poetry weekends or week-long discussion institutes—sponsored by Great Books groups around the country.

Finally, we invite you to inquire about Junior Great Books for students in kindergarten through high school, to learn how you can help develop the next generation of book lovers and shared inquiry participants.

We hope you enjoy *Living with the Past* and that it inaugurates many years of exciting discussions for your group. Great Books programs—for children as well as adults—are founded on the idea that readers discussing together can achieve insight and great pleasure from literature. We look forward, with you, to cultivating this idea through the next century.

OVERTURE

Marcel Proust

MARCEL PROUST (1871–1922) was born
in Paris, the son of wealthy bourgeois
parents. As a child he suffered from delicate
health and was carefully looked after by his
mother. Proust became a popular young man
in the Parisian society he depicted in his
novels, but as his health deteriorated, he
became increasingly withdrawn from this
world. Suffering from asthma and a heart
condition, Proust spent most of his last ten
years in an unventilated, cork-lined room
composing his monumental work, *À la
recherche du temps perdu* (translated
1922–1933 as *Remembrance of Things
Past*), a series of semiautobiographical
novels. The first novel, *Du côté de chez
Swann* (1913, tr. *Swann's Way,* 1928)
went unnoticed by critics, but the second,
À l'ombre des jeunes filles en fleurs (1919,
tr. *Within a Budding Grove,* 1919), won the
Prix Goncourt the year of its publication.
Eccentric and hypersensitive, Proust was
also relentless in the pursuit of his writing,
which he reportedly continued even on
his deathbed.

F OR A LONG TIME I used to go to bed early. Sometimes, when
I had put out my candle, my eyes would close so quickly that I
had not even time to say to myself: "I'm falling asleep." And
half an hour later the thought that it was time to go to sleep
would awaken me; I would make as if to put away the book
which I imagined was still in my hands, and to blow out the
light; I had gone on thinking, while I was asleep, about what I
had just been reading, but these thoughts had taken a rather
peculiar turn; it seemed to me that I myself was the immediate
subject of my book: a church, a quartet, the rivalry between
François I and Charles V. This impression would persist for
some moments after I awoke; it did not offend my reason, but
lay like scales upon my eyes and prevented them from register-
ing the fact that the candle was no longer burning. Then it
would begin to seem unintelligible, as the thoughts of a former
existence must be to a reincarnate spirit; the subject of my book
would separate itself from me, leaving me free to apply myself
to it or not; and at the same time my sight would return and I

would be astonished to find myself in a state of darkness, pleasant and restful enough for my eyes, but even more, perhaps, for my mind, to which it appeared incomprehensible, without a cause, something dark indeed.

I would ask myself what time it could be; I could hear the whistling of trains, which, now nearer and now farther off, punctuating the distance like the note of a bird in a forest, showed me in perspective the deserted countryside through which a traveler is hurrying toward the nearby station; and the path he is taking will be engraved in his memory by the excitement induced by strange surroundings, by unaccustomed activities, by the conversation he has had and the farewells exchanged beneath an unfamiliar lamp, still echoing in his ears amid the silence of the night, by the imminent joy of going home.

I would lay my cheeks gently against the comfortable cheeks of my pillow, as plump and blooming as the cheeks of babyhood. I would strike a match to look at my watch. Nearly midnight. The hour when an invalid, who has been obliged to set out on a journey and to sleep in a strange hotel, awakened by a sudden spasm, sees with glad relief a streak of daylight showing under his door. Thank God, it is morning! The servants will be about in a minute: he can ring, and someone will come to look after him. The thought of being assuaged gives him strength to endure his pain. He is certain he heard footsteps: they come nearer, and then die away. The ray of light beneath his door is extinguished. It is midnight; someone has just turned down the gas; the last servant has gone to bed, and he must lie all night in agony with no one to bring him relief.

I would fall asleep again, and thereafter would reawaken for short snatches only, just long enough to hear the regular creaking of the wainscot, or to open my eyes to stare at the shifting kaleidoscope of the darkness, to savor, in a momentary glimmer of consciousness, the sleep which lay heavy upon the furniture, the room, the whole of which I formed but an insignificant part and whose insensibility I should very soon return to share. Or else while sleeping I had drifted back to an earlier stage in my life, now forever outgrown, and had come under the thrall of one of my childish terrors, such as that old terror of my great-uncle's pulling my curls which was effectually dispelled on the day—the dawn of a new era to me—when they were finally cropped from my head. I had forgotten that event during my sleep, but I remembered it again immediately I had succeeded in waking myself up to escape my great-uncle's fingers, and as a measure of precaution I would bury the whole of my head in the pillow before returning to the world of dreams.

Sometimes, too, as Eve was created from a rib of Adam, a woman would be born during my sleep from some strain in the position of my thighs. Conceived from the pleasure I was on the point of consummating, she it was, I imagined, who offered me that pleasure. My body, conscious that its own warmth was permeating hers, would strive to become one with her, and I would awake. The rest of humanity seemed very remote in comparison with this woman whose company I had left but a moment ago; my cheek was still warm from her kiss, my body ached beneath the weight of hers. If, as would sometimes happen, she had the features of some woman whom I had known in waking hours, I would abandon myself altogether to the sole quest of her, like people who set out on a journey to see with their eyes some city of their desire, and imagine that one can taste in reality what has charmed one's fancy. And then, gradually, the memory of her would dissolve and vanish, until I had forgotten the girl of my dream.

When a man is asleep, he has in a circle round him the chain of the hours, the sequence of the years, the order of the heavenly host. Instinctively, when he awakes, he looks to these, and in an instant reads off his own position on the earth's surface and the time that has elapsed during his slumbers; but this ordered procession is apt to grow confused, and to break its ranks. Suppose that, toward morning, after a night of insomnia, sleep descends upon him while he is reading, in quite a different position from that in which he normally goes to sleep, he has only to lift his arm to arrest the sun and turn it back in its course, and, at the moment of waking, he will have no idea of the time, but will conclude that he has just gone to bed. Or suppose that he dozes off in some even more abnormal and divergent position, sitting in an armchair, for instance, after dinner: then the world will go hurtling out of orbit, the magic chair will carry him at full speed through time and space, and when he opens his eyes again he will imagine that he went to sleep months earlier in another place. But for me it was enough if, in my own bed, my sleep was so heavy as completely to relax my consciousness; for then I lost all sense of the place in which I had gone to sleep, and when I awoke in the middle of the night, not knowing where I was, I could not even be sure at first who I was; I had only the most rudimentary sense of existence, such as may lurk and flicker in the depths of an animal's consciousness; I was more destitute than the cave dweller; but then the memory—not yet of the place in which I was, but of various other places where I had lived and might now very possibly be—would come like a rope let down from heaven to draw me up out of the abyss of not-being, from which I could never have escaped by myself: in a flash I would traverse centuries of civilization, and out of a blurred glimpse of oil lamps, then of shirts with turned-down collars, would gradually piece together the original components of my ego.

Perhaps the immobility of the things that surround us is forced upon them by our conviction that they are themselves and not anything else, by the immobility of our conception of them. For it always happened that when I awoke like this, and my mind struggled in an unsuccessful attempt to discover where I was, everything revolved around me through the darkness: things, places, years. My body, still too heavy with sleep to move, would endeavor to construe from the pattern of its tiredness the position of its various limbs, in order to deduce therefrom the direction of the wall, the location of the furniture, to piece together and give a name to the house in which it lay. Its memory, the composite memory of its ribs, its knees, its shoulder blades, offered it a whole series of rooms in which it had at one time or another slept, while the unseen walls, shifting and adapting themselves to the shape of each successive room that it remembered, whirled round it in the dark. And even before my brain, lingering in cogitation over when things had happened and what they had looked like, had reassembled the circumstances sufficiently to identify the room, it—my body—would recall from each room in succession the style of the bed, the position of the doors, the angle at which the daylight came in at the windows, whether there was a passage outside, what I had had in my mind when I went to sleep and found there when I awoke. The stiffened side on which I lay would, for instance, in trying to fix its position, imagine itself to be lying face to the wall in a big bed with a canopy; and at once I would say to myself, "Why, I must have fallen asleep before Mamma came to say good night," for I was in the country at my grandfather's, who died years ago; and my body, the side upon which I was lying, faithful guardians of a past which my mind should never have forgotten, brought back before my eyes the glimmering flame of the night-light in its urn-shaped bowl of Bohemian glass that hung by chains from the ceiling, and the chimneypiece of Siena marble in my bedroom at Combray, in my grandparents' house, in those far distant days which at this moment I imagined to be in the present without being able to picture them exactly, and which would become plainer in a little while when I was properly awake.

Then the memory of a new position would spring up, and the wall would slide away in another direction; I was in my room in Mme. de Saint-Loup's house in the country; good heavens, it must be ten o'clock, they will have finished dinner! I must have overslept myself in the little nap which I always take when I come in from my walk with Mme. de Saint-Loup, before dressing for the evening. For many years have now elapsed since the Combray days when, coming in from the longest and latest walks, I would still be in time to see the reflection of the sunset glowing in the panes of my bedroom window. It is a very different kind of life that one leads at Tansonville, at Mme. de Saint-Loup's, and a different kind of pleasure that I derive from taking walks only in the evenings, from visiting by moonlight the roads on which I used to play as a child in the sunshine; while the bedroom in which I shall presently fall asleep instead of dressing for dinner I can see from the distance as we return from our walk, with its lamp shining through the window, a solitary beacon in the night.

These shifting and confused gusts of memory never lasted for more than a few seconds; it often happened that, in my brief spell of uncertainty as to where I was, I did not distinguish the various suppositions of which it was composed any more than, when we watch a horse running, we isolate the successive positions of its body as they appear upon a bioscope. But I had seen first one and then another of the rooms in which I had slept during my life, and in the end I would revisit them all in the long course of my waking dream: rooms in winter, where on going to bed I would at once bury my head in a nest woven out of the most diverse materials—the corner of my pillow, the top of my blankets, a piece of a shawl, the edge of my bed, and a copy of a children's paper—which I had contrived to cement together, bird-fashion, by dint of continuous pressure; rooms where, in freezing weather, I would enjoy the satisfaction of being shut in from the outer world (like the sea swallow which builds at the end of a dark tunnel and is kept warm by the surrounding earth), and where, the fire keeping in all night, I would sleep wrapped up, as it were, in a great cloak of snug and smoky air, shot with the glow of the logs intermittently breaking out again in flame, a sort of alcove without walls, a cave of warmth dug out of the heart of the room itself, a zone of heat whose boundaries were constantly shifting and altering in temperature as gusts of air traversed them to strike freshly upon my face, from the corners of the room or from parts near the window or far from the fireplace which had therefore remained cold;—or rooms in summer, where I would delight to feel myself a part of the warm night, where the moonlight striking upon the half-opened shutters would throw down to the foot of my bed its enchanted ladder, where I would fall asleep, as it might be in the open air, like a titmouse which the breeze gently rocks at the tip of a sunbeam;—or sometimes the Louis XVI room, so cheerful that I never felt too miserable in it, even on my first night, and in which the slender columns that lightly supported its ceiling drew so gracefully apart to reveal and frame the site of the bed;—sometimes, again, the little room with the high ceiling, hollowed in the form of a pyramid out of two separate stories, and partly walled with mahogany, in which from the first moment, mentally poisoned by the unfamiliar scent of vetiver, I was convinced of the hostility of the violet curtains and of the insolent indifference of a clock that chattered on at the top of its voice as though I were not there; in which a strange and pitiless rectangular cheval glass, standing across one corner of the room, carved out for itself a site I had not looked to find tenanted in the soft plenitude of my normal field of vision; in which my mind, striving for hours on end to break away from its moorings, to stretch upward so as to take on the exact shape of the room and to reach to the topmost height of its gigantic funnel, had endured many a painful night as I lay stretched out in bed, my eyes staring upward, my ears straining, my nostrils flaring, my heart beating; until habit had changed the color of the curtains, silenced the clock, brought an expression of pity to the cruel, slanting face of the glass, disguised or even completely dispelled the scent of vetiver, and appreciably reduced the apparent loftiness of the ceiling. Habit! that skillful but slow-moving arranger who begins by letting our minds suffer for weeks on end in temporary quarters, but whom our minds are nonetheless only too happy to discover at last, for without it, reduced to their own devices, they would be powerless to make any room seem habitable.

Certainly I was now well awake; my body had veered round for the last time and the good angel of certainty had made all the surrounding objects stand still, had set me down under my bedclothes, in my bedroom, and had fixed, approximately in their right places in the uncertain light, my chest of drawers, my writing table, my fireplace, the window overlooking the street, and both the doors. But for all that, I now knew that I was not in any of the houses of which the ignorance of the waking moment had, in a flash, if not presented me with a distinct picture, at least persuaded me of the possible presence, my memory had been set in motion; as a rule I did not attempt to go to sleep again at once, but used to spend the greater part of the night recalling our life in the old days at Combray with my great-aunt, at Balbec, Paris, Doncières, Venice, and the rest; remembering again all the places and people I had known, what I had actually seen of them, and what others had told me.

At Combray, as every afternoon ended, long before the time when I should have to go to bed and lie there, unsleeping, far from my mother and grandmother, my bedroom became the fixed point on which my melancholy and anxious thoughts were centered. Someone had indeed had the happy idea of giving me, to distract me on evenings when I seemed abnormally wretched, a magic lantern, which used to be set on top of my lamp while we waited for dinnertime to come; and, after the fashion of the master builders and glass painters of Gothic days, it substituted for the opaqueness of my walls an impalpable iridescence, supernatural phenomena of many colors, in which legends were depicted as on a shifting and transitory window. But my sorrows were only increased thereby, because this mere change of lighting was enough to destroy the familiar impression I had of my room, thanks to which, save for the torture of going to bed, it had become quite endurable. Now I no longer recognized it, and felt uneasy in it, as in a room in some hotel or chalet, in a place where I had just arrived by train for the first time.

Riding at a jerky trot, Golo, filled with an infamous design, issued from the little triangular forest which dyed dark green the slope of a convenient hill, and advanced fitfully toward the castle of poor Geneviève de Brabant. This castle was cut off short by a curved line which was in fact the circumference of one of the transparent ovals in the slides which were pushed into position through a slot in the lantern. It was only the wing of a castle, and in front of it stretched a moor on which Geneviève stood lost in contemplation, wearing a blue girdle. The castle and the moor were yellow, but I could tell their color without waiting to see them, for before the slides made their appearance the old-gold sonorous name of Brabant had given me an unmistakable clue. Golo stopped for a moment and listened sadly to the accompanying patter read aloud by my great-aunt, which he seemed perfectly to understand, for he modified his attitude with a docility not devoid of a degree of majesty, so as to conform to the indications given in the text; then he rode away at the same jerky trot. And nothing could arrest his slow progress. If the lantern were moved I could still distinguish Golo's horse advancing across the window curtains, swelling out with their curves and diving into their folds. The body of Golo himself, being of the same supernatural substance as his steed's, overcame every material obstacle—everything that seemed to bar his way—by taking it as an ossature and embodying it in himself: even the door handle, for instance, over which, adapting itself at once, would float irresistibly his red cloak or his pale face, which never lost its nobility or its melancholy, never betrayed the least concern at this transvertebration.

And, indeed, I found plenty of charm in these bright projections, which seemed to emanate from a Merovingian past and shed around me the reflections of such ancient history. But I cannot express the discomfort I felt at this intrusion of mystery and beauty into a room which I had succeeded in filling with my own personality until I thought no more of it than of myself. The anaesthetic effect of habit being destroyed, I would begin to think—and to feel—such melancholy things. The door handle of my room, which was different to me from all the other door handles in the world, inasmuch as it seemed to open of its own accord and without my having to turn it, so unconscious had its manipulation become—lo and behold, it was now an astral body for Golo. And as soon as the dinner bell rang I would hurry down to the dining room, where the big hanging lamp, ignorant of Golo and Bluebeard but well acquainted with my family and the dish of stewed beef, shed the same light as on every other evening; and I would fall into the arms of my mother, whom the misfortunes of Geneviève de Brabant had made all the dearer to me, just as the crimes of Golo had driven me to a more than ordinarily scrupulous examination of my own conscience.

But after dinner, alas, I was soon obliged to leave Mamma, who stayed talking with the others, in the garden if it was fine, or in the little parlor where everyone took shelter when it was wet. Everyone except my grandmother, who held that "It's a pity to shut oneself indoors in the country," and used to have endless arguments with my father on the very wettest days, because he would send me up to my room with a book instead of letting me stay out of doors. "That is not the way to make him strong and active," she would say sadly, "especially this little man, who needs all the strength and willpower that he can get." My father would shrug his shoulders and study the barometer, for he took an interest in meteorology, while my mother, keeping very quiet so as not to disturb him, looked at him with tender respect, but not too hard, not wishing to penetrate the mysteries of his superior mind. But my grandmother, in all weathers, even when the rain was coming down in torrents and Françoise had rushed the precious wicker armchairs indoors so that they should not get soaked, was to be seen pacing the deserted rain-lashed garden, pushing back her disordered gray locks so that her forehead might be freer to absorb the health-giving drafts of wind and rain. She would say, "At last one can breathe!" and would trot up and down the sodden paths—too straight and symmetrical for her liking, owing to the want of any feeling for nature in the new gardener, whom my father had been asking all morning if the weather were going to improve— her keen, jerky little step regulated by the various effects wrought upon her soul by the intoxication of the storm, the power of hygiene, the stupidity of my upbringing and the symmetry of gardens, rather than by any anxiety (for that was quite unknown to her) to save her plum-colored skirt from the mudstains beneath which it would gradually disappear to a height that was the constant bane and despair of her maid.

When these walks of my grandmother's took place after dinner there was one thing which never failed to bring her back to the house: this was if (at one of those points when her circular itinerary brought her back, mothlike, in sight of the lamp in the little parlor where the liqueurs were set out on the card table) my great-aunt called out to her: "Bathilde! Come in and stop your husband drinking brandy!" For, simply to tease her (she had brought so different a type of mind into my father's family that everyone made fun of her), my great-aunt used to make my grandfather, who was forbidden liqueurs, take just a few drops. My poor grandmother would come in and beg and implore her husband not to taste the brandy; and he would get angry and gulp it down all the same, and she would go out again sad and discouraged, but still smiling, for she was so humble of heart and so gentle that her tenderness for others and her disregard for herself and her own troubles blended in a smile which, unlike those seen on the majority of human faces, bore no trace of irony save for herself, while for all of us kisses seemed to spring from her eyes, which could not look upon those she loved without seeming to bestow upon them passionate caresses. This torture inflicted on her by my great-aunt, the sight of my grandmother's vain entreaties, of her feeble attempts, doomed in advance, to remove the liqueur glass from my grandfather's hands—all these were things of the sort to which, in later years, one can grow so accustomed as to smile at them and to take the persecutor's side resolutely and cheerfully enough to persuade oneself that it is not really persecution; but in those days they filled me with such horror that I longed to strike my great-aunt. And yet, as soon as I heard her "Bathilde! Come in and stop your husband drinking brandy," in my cowardice I became at once a man, and did what all we grown men do when face to face with suffering and injustice: I preferred not to see them; I ran up to the top of the house to cry by myself in a little room beside the schoolroom and beneath the roof, which smelt of orrisroot and was scented also by a wild currant bush which had climbed up between the stones of the outer wall and thrust a flowering branch in through the half-opened window. Intended for a more special and a baser use, this room, from which, in the daytime, I could see as far as the keep of Roussainville-le-Pin, was for a long time my place of refuge, doubtless because it was the only room whose door I was allowed to lock, whenever my occupation was such as required an inviolable solitude: reading or daydreaming, secret tears or sensual gratification. Alas! I little knew that my own lack of willpower, my delicate health, and the consequent uncertainty as to my future weighed far more heavily on my grandmother's mind than any little dietary indiscretion by her husband in the course of those endless perambulations, afternoon and evening, during which we used to see her handsome face passing to and fro, half raised toward the sky, its brown and wrinkled cheeks, which with age had acquired almost the purple hue of tilled fields in autumn, covered, if she were "going out," by a half-lifted veil, while upon them either the cold or some sad reflection invariably left the drying traces of an involuntary tear.

My sole consolation when I went upstairs for the night was that Mamma would come in and kiss me after I was in bed. But this good night lasted for so short a time, she went down again so soon, that the moment in which I heard her climb the stairs, and then caught the sound of her garden dress of blue muslin, from which hung little tassels of plaited straw, rustling along the double-doored corridor, was for me a moment of the utmost pain; for it heralded the moment which was bound to follow it, when she would have left me and gone downstairs again. So much so that I reached the point of hoping that this good night which I loved so much would come as late as possible, so as to prolong the time of respite during which Mamma would not yet have appeared. Sometimes when, after kissing me, she opened the door to go, I longed to call her back, to say to her "Kiss me just once more," but I knew that then she would at once look displeased, for the concession which she made to my wretchedness and agitation in coming up to give me this kiss of peace always annoyed my father, who thought such rituals absurd, and she would have liked to try to induce me to outgrow the need, the habit, of having her there at all, let alone get into the habit of asking her for an additional kiss when she was already crossing the threshold. And to see her look displeased destroyed all the calm and serenity she had brought me a moment before, when she had bent her loving face down over my bed, and held it out to me like a host for an act of peace-giving communion in which my lips might imbibe her real presence and with it the power to sleep. But those evenings on which Mamma stayed so short a time in my room were sweet indeed compared to those on which we had guests to dinner, and therefore she did not come at all. Our "guests" were usually limited to M. Swann, who, apart from a few passing strangers, was almost the only person who ever came to the house at Combray, sometimes to a neighborly dinner (but less frequently since his unfortunate marriage, as my family did not care to receive his wife) and sometimes after dinner, uninvited. On those evenings when, as we sat in front of the house round the iron table beneath the big chestnut tree, we heard, from the far end of the garden, not the shrill and assertive alarm bell which assailed and deafened with its ferruginous, interminable, frozen sound any member of the household who set it off on entering "without ringing," but the double tinkle, timid, oval, golden, of the visitors' bell, everyone would at once exclaim "A visitor! Who in the world can it be?" but they knew quite well that it could only be M. Swann. My great-aunt, speaking in a loud voice to set an example, in a tone which she endeavored to make sound natural, would tell the others not to whisper so; that nothing could be more offensive to a stranger coming in, who would be led to think that people were saying things about him which he was not meant to hear;

and then my grandmother, always happy to find an excuse for an additional turn in the garden, would be sent out to reconnoiter, and would take the opportunity to remove surreptitiously, as she passed, the stakes of a rose tree or two, so as to make the roses look a little more natural, as a mother might run her hand through her boy's hair after the barber has smoothed it down, to make it look naturally wavy.

We would all wait there in suspense for the report which my grandmother would bring back from the enemy lines, as though there might be a choice between a large number of possible assailants, and then, soon after, my grandfather would say: "I can hear Swann's voice." And indeed one could tell him only by his voice, for it was difficult to make out his face with its arched nose and green eyes, under a high forehead fringed with fair, almost red hair, done in the Bressant style, because in the garden we used as little light as possible, so as not to attract mosquitoes; and I would slip away unobtrusively to order the liqueurs to be brought out, for my grandmother made a great point, thinking it "nicer," of their not being allowed to seem anything out of the ordinary, which we kept for visitors only. Although a far younger man, M. Swann was very much attached to my grandfather, who had been an intimate friend of Swann's father, an excellent but eccentric man the ardor of whose feelings and the current of whose thoughts would often be checked or diverted by the most trifling thing. Several times in the course of a year I would hear my grandfather tell at table the story, which never varied, of the behavior of M. Swann the elder upon the death of his wife, by whose bedside he had watched day and night. My grandfather, who had not seen him for a long time, hastened to join him at the Swanns' family property on the outskirts of Combray, and managed to entice him for a moment, weeping profusely, out of the death chamber, so that he should not be present when the body was laid in its coffin. They took a turn or two in the park, where there was a little sunshine. Suddenly M. Swann seized my grandfather by the arm and cried, "Ah, my dear old friend, how fortunate we are to be walking here together on such a charming day! Don't you see how pretty they are, all these trees, my hawthorns, and my new pond, on which you have never congratulated me? You look as solemn as the grave. Don't you feel this little breeze? Ah! whatever you may say, it's good to be alive all the same, my dear Amédée!" And then, abruptly, the memory of his dead wife returned to him, and probably thinking it too complicated to inquire into how, at such a time, he could have allowed himself to be carried away by an impulse of happiness, he confined himself to a gesture which he habitually employed whenever any perplexing question came into his mind: that is, he passed his hand across his forehead, rubbed his eyes, and wiped his glasses. And yet he never got over the loss of his wife, but used to say to my grandfather, during the two years by which he survived her, "It's a funny thing, now; I very often think of my poor wife, but I cannot think of her for long at a time." "Often, but a little at a time, like poor old Swann," became one of my grandfather's favorite sayings, which he would apply to all manner of things. I should have assumed that this father of Swann's had been a monster if my grandfather, whom I regarded as a better judge than myself, and whose word was my law and often led me in the long run to pardon offenses which I should have been inclined to condemn, had not gone on to exclaim, "But, after all, he had a heart of gold."

For many years, during the course of which—especially before his marriage—M. Swann the younger came often to see them at Combray, my great-aunt and my grandparents never suspected that he had entirely ceased to live in the society which his family had frequented, and that, under the sort of incognito which the name of Swann gave him among us, they were harboring—with the complete innocence of a family of respectable innkeepers who have in their midst some celebrated highwayman without knowing it—one of the most distinguished members of the Jockey Club, a particular friend of the Comte de Paris and of the Prince of Wales, and one of the men most sought after in the aristocratic world of the Faubourg Saint-Germain.

Our utter ignorance of the brilliant social life which Swann
led was, of course, due in part to his own reserve and discretion,
but also to the fact that middle-class people in those days took
what was almost a Hindu view of society, which they held to
consist of sharply defined castes, so that everyone at his birth
found himself called to that station in life which his parents
already occupied, and from which nothing, save the accident of
an exceptional career or of a "good" marriage, could extract
you and translate you to a superior caste. M. Swann the elder
had been a stockbroker; and so "young Swann" found himself
immured for life in a caste whose members' fortunes, as in a category of taxpayers, varied between such and such limits of
income. One knew the people with whom his father had associated, and so one knew his own associates, the people with
whom he was "in a position to mix." If he knew other people
besides, those were youthful acquaintances on whom the old
friends of his family, like my relatives, shut their eyes all the
more good-naturedly because Swann himself, after he was left
an orphan, still came most faithfully to see us; but we would
have been ready to wager that the people outside our aquain-
tance whom Swann knew were of the sort to whom he would
not have dared to raise his hat if he had met them while he was
walking with us. Had it been absolutely essential to apply to
Swann a social coefficient peculiar to himself, as distinct from
all the other sons of other stockbrokers in his father's position,
his coefficient would have been rather lower than theirs,
because, being very simple in his habits, and having always had
a craze for "antiques" and pictures, he now lived and amassed
his collections in an old house which my grandmother longed to
visit but which was situated on the Quai d'Orléans, a neighborhood in which my great-aunt thought it most degrading to be
quartered. "Are you really a connoisseur, now?" she would say
to him; "I ask for your own sake, as you are likely to have fakes
palmed off on you by the dealers," for she did not, in fact,
endow him with any critical faculty, and had no great opinion
of the intelligence of a man who, in conversation, would avoid

serious topics and showed a very dull preciseness, not only when he gave us kitchen recipes, going into the most minute details, but even when my grandmother's sisters were talking to him about art. When challenged by them to give an opinion, or to express his admiration for some picture, he would remain almost offensively silent, and would then make amends by furnishing (if he could) some fact or other about the gallery in which the picture was hung, or the date at which it had been painted. But as a rule he would content himself with trying to amuse us by telling us about his latest adventure with someone whom we ourselves knew, such as the Combray chemist, or our cook, or our coachman. These stories certainly used to make my great-aunt laugh, but she could never decide whether this was on account of the absurd role which Swann invariably gave himself therein, or of the wit that he showed in telling them: "I must say you really are a regular character, M. Swann!"

As she was the only member of our family who could be described as a trifle "common," she would always take care to remark to strangers, when Swann was mentioned, that he could easily, had he so wished, have lived in the Boulevard Haussmann or the Avenue de l'Opéra, and that he was the son of old M. Swann who must have left four or five million francs, but that it was a fad of his. A fad which, moreover, she thought was bound to amuse other people so much that in Paris, when M. Swann called on New Year's Day bringing her a little packet of *marrons glacés,* she never failed, if there were strangers in the room, to say to him: "Well, M. Swann, and do you still live next door to the bonded vaults, so as to be sure of not missing your train when you go to Lyons?" and she would peep out of the corner of her eye, over her glasses, at the other visitors.

But if anyone suggested to my great-aunt that this Swann, who, in his capacity as the son of old M. Swann, was "fully qualified" to be received by any of the "best people," by the most respected barristers and solicitors of Paris (though he was perhaps a trifle inclined to let this hereditary privilege go by default), had another almost secret existence of a wholly different kind; that when he left our house in Paris, saying that he must go home to bed, he would no sooner have turned the corner than he would stop, retrace his steps, and be off to some salon on whose like no stockbroker or associate of stockbrokers had ever set eyes—that would have seemed to my aunt as extraordinary as, to a woman of wider reading, the thought of being herself on terms of intimacy with Aristaeus and of learning that after having a chat with her he would plunge deep into the realms of Thetis, into an empire veiled from mortal eyes, in which Virgil depicts him as being received with open arms; or—to be content with an image more likely to have occurred to her, for she had seen it painted on the plates we used for biscuits at Combray—as the thought of having had to dinner Ali Baba, who, as soon as he finds himself alone and unobserved, will make his way into the cave, resplendent with its unsuspected treasures.

One day when he had come to see us after dinner in Paris, apologizing for being in evening clothes, Françoise told us after he had left that she had got it from his coachman that he had been dining "with a princess." "A nice sort of princess," retorted my aunt, shrugging her shoulders without raising her eyes from her knitting, serenely sarcastic.

Altogether, my great-aunt treated him with scant ceremony. Since she was of the opinion that he ought to feel flattered by our invitations, she thought it only right and proper that he should never come to see us in summer without a basket of peaches or raspberries from his garden, and that from each of his visits to Italy he should bring back some photographs of old masters for me.

It seemed quite natural, therefore, to send for him whenever a recipe for some special sauce or for a pineapple salad was needed for one of our big dinner parties, to which he himself would not be invited, being regarded as insufficiently important to be served up to new friends who might be in our house for the first time. If the conversation turned upon the princes of the House of France, "gentlemen you and I will never know, will

we, and don't want to, do we?" my great-aunt would say tartly
to Swann, who had, perhaps, a letter from Twickenham in his
pocket; she would make him push the piano into place and turn
over the music on evenings when my grandmother's sister sang,
manipulating this person who was elsewhere so sought after
with the rough simplicity of a child who will play with a collec-
tors' piece with no more circumspection than if it were a cheap
gewgaw. Doubtless the Swann who was a familiar figure in all
the clubs of those days differed hugely from the Swann created
by my great-aunt when, of an evening, in our little garden at
Combray, after the two shy peals had sounded from the gate,
she would inject and vitalize with everything she knew about
the Swann family the obscure and shadowy figure who
emerged, with my grandmother in his wake, from the dark
background and who was identified by his voice. But then, even
in the most significant details of our daily life, none of us can be
said to constitute a material whole, which is identical for everyone, and need only be turned up like a page in an account book
or the record of a will; our social personality is a creation of the
thoughts of other people. Even the simple act which we describe
as "seeing someone we know" is to some extent an intellectual
process. We pack the physical outline of the person we see with
all the notions we have already formed about him, and in the
total picture of him which we compose in our minds those
notions have certainly the principal place. In the end they come
to fill out so completely the curve of his cheeks, to follow so
exactly the line of his nose, they blend so harmoniously in the
sound of his voice as if it were no more than a transparent envelope, that each time we see the face or hear the voice it is these
notions which we recognize and to which we listen. And so, no
doubt, from the Swann they had constructed for themselves my
family had left out, in their ignorance, a whole host of details of
his life in the world of fashion, details which caused other people, when they met him, to see all the graces enthroned in his
face and stopping at the line of his aquiline nose as at a natural
frontier; but they had contrived also to put into this face divested

of all glamour, vacant and roomy as an untenanted house, to plant in the depths of these undervalued eyes, a lingering residuum, vague but not unpleasing—half-memory and half-oblivion—of idle hours spent together after our weekly dinners, round the card table or in the garden, during our companionable country life. Our friend's corporeal envelope had been so well lined with this residuum, as well as various earlier memories of his parents, that their own special Swann had become to my family a complete and living creature; so that even now I have the feeling of leaving someone I know for another quite different person when, going back in memory, I pass from the Swann whom I knew later and more intimately to this early Swann—this early Swann in whom I can distinguish the charming mistakes of my youth, and who in fact is less like his successor than he is like the other people I knew at that time, as though one's life were a picture gallery in which all the portraits of any one period had a marked family likeness, a similar tonality—this early Swann abounding in leisure, fragrant with the scent of the great chestnut tree, of baskets of raspberries, and of a sprig of tarragon.

And yet one day, when my grandmother had gone to ask some favor of a lady whom she had known at the Sacré Coeur (and with whom, because of our notions of caste, she had not cared to keep up any degree of intimacy in spite of several common interests), the Marquise de Villeparisis, of the famous house of Bouillon, this lady had said to her:

"I believe you know M. Swann very well; he's a great friend of my nephews, the des Laumes."

My grandmother had returned from the call full of praise for the house, which overlooked some gardens, and in which Mme. de Villeparisis had advised her to rent a flat, and also for a repairing tailor and his daughter who kept a little shop in the courtyard, into which she had gone to ask them to put a stitch in her skirt, which she had torn on the staircase. My grandmother had found these people perfectly charming: the girl, she said, was a jewel, and the tailor the best and most distinguished man she had ever seen. For in her eyes distinction was a thing wholly independent of social position. She was in ecstasies over some answer the tailor had made to her, saying to Mamma:

"Sévigné would not have put it better!" and, by way of contrast, of a nephew of Mme. de Villeparisis whom she had met at the house:

"My dear, he is so common!"

Now, the effect of the remark about Swann had been, not to raise him in my great-aunt's estimation, but to lower Mme. de Villeparisis. It appeared that the deference which, on my grandmother's authority, we owed to Mme. de Villeparisis imposed on her the reciprocal obligation to do nothing that would render her less worthy of our regard, and that she had failed in this duty by becoming aware of Swann's existence and in allowing members of her family to associate with him. "What! She knows Swann? A person who, you always made out, was related to Marshal MacMahon!" This view of Swann's social position which prevailed in my family seemed to be confirmed later on by his marriage with a woman of the worst type, almost a prostitute, whom, to do him justice, he never attempted to introduce to us—for he continued to come to our house alone, though more and more seldom—but from whom they felt they could establish, on the assumption that he had found her there, the circle, unknown to them, in which he ordinarily moved.

But on one occasion my grandfather read in a newspaper that M. Swann was one of the most regular attendants at the Sunday luncheons given by the Duc de X———, whose father and uncle had been among our most prominent statesmen in the reign of Louis-Philippe. Now my grandfather was curious to learn all the smallest details which might help him to take a mental share in the private lives of men like Molé, the Duc Pasquier, or the Duc de Broglie. He was delighted to find that Swann associated with people who had known them. My great-aunt, on the other hand, interpreted this piece of news in a sense discreditable to Swann; for anyone who chose his associates outside the caste in which he had been born and bred, outside his "proper station," automatically lowered himself in her eyes. It seemed to her that such a one abdicated all claim to enjoy the fruits of the splendid connections with people of good position which prudent parents cultivate and store up for their children's benefit, and she had actually ceased to "see" the son of a lawyer of our acquaintance because he had married a "Highness" and had thereby stepped down—in her eyes—from the respectable position of a lawyer's son to that of those adventurers, upstart footmen or stable boys mostly, to whom, we are told, queens have sometimes shown their favors. She objected, therefore, to my grandfather's plan of questioning Swann, when next he came to dine with us, about these people whose friendship with him we had discovered. At the same time my grandmother's two sisters, elderly spinsters who shared her nobility of character but lacked her intelligence, declared that they could not conceive what pleasure their brother-in-law could find in talking about such trifles. They were ladies of lofty aspirations, who for that reason were incapable of taking the least interest in what might be termed gossip, even if it had some historical import, or, generally speaking, in anything that was not directly associated with some aesthetic or virtuous object. So complete was their negation of interest in anything which seemed directly or indirectly connected with worldly matters that their sense of hearing—having finally come to realize its temporary futility when the tone of the conversation at the dinner table became frivolous or merely mundane without the two old ladies' being able to guide it back to topics dear to themselves—would put its receptive organs into abeyance to the point of actually becoming atrophied. So that if my grandfather wished to attract the attention of the two sisters, he had to resort to some such physical stimuli as alienists adopt in dealing with their distracted patients: to wit, repeated taps on a glass with the blade of a knife, accompanied by a sharp word and a compelling glance, violent methods which these psychiatrists are apt to bring with them into their everyday life among the sane, either from force of professional habit or because they think the whole world a trifle mad.

Their interest grew, however, when, the day before Swann was to dine with us, and when he had made them a special present of a case of Asti, my great-aunt, who had in her hand a copy of the *Figaro* in which to the name of a picture then on view in a Corot exhibition were added the words, "from the collection of M. Charles Swann," asked: "Did you see that Swann is 'mentioned' in the *Figaro?*"

"But I've always told you," said my grandmother, "that he had a great deal of taste."

"You would, of course," retorted my great-aunt, "say anything just to seem different from *us.*" For, knowing that my grandmother never agreed with her, and not being quite confident that it was her own opinion which the rest of us invariably endorsed, she wished to extort from us a wholesale condemnation of my grandmother's views, against which she hoped to force us into solidarity with her own. But we sat silent. My grandmother's sisters having expressed a desire to mention to Swann this reference to him in the *Figaro,* my great-aunt dissuaded them. Whenever she saw in others an advantage, however trivial, which she herself lacked, she would persuade herself that it was no advantage at all, but a drawback, and would pity so as not to have to envy them.

"I don't think that would please him at all; I know very well that I should hate to see my name printed like that, as large as life, in the paper, and I shouldn't feel at all flattered if anyone spoke to me about it."

She did not, however, put any very great pressure upon my grandmother's sisters, for they, in their horror of vulgarity, had brought to such a fine art the concealment of a personal allusion in a wealth of ingenious circumlocution, that it would often pass unnoticed even by the person to whom it was addressed. As for my mother, her only thought was of trying to induce my father to speak to Swann, not about his wife but about his daughter, whom he worshiped, and for whose sake it was understood that he had ultimately made his unfortunate marriage.

"You need only say a word; just ask him how she is. It must be so very hard for him."

My father, however, was annoyed: "No, no; you have the most absurd ideas. It would be utterly ridiculous."

But the only one of us in whom the prospect of Swann's arrival gave rise to an unhappy foreboding was myself. This was because on the evenings when there were visitors, or just M. Swann, in the house, Mamma did not come up to my room. I dined before the others, and afterward came and sat at table until eight o'clock, when it was understood that I must go upstairs; that frail and precious kiss which Mamma used normally to bestow on me when I was in bed and just going to sleep had to be transported from the dining room to my bedroom where I must keep it inviolate all the time that it took me to undress, without letting its sweet charm be broken, without letting its volatile essence diffuse itself and evaporate; and it was precisely on those very evenings when I needed to receive it with special care that I was obliged to take it, to snatch it brusquely and in public, without even having the time or the equanimity to bring to what I was doing the single-minded attention of lunatics who compel themselves to exclude all other thoughts from their minds while they are shutting a door, so that when the sickness of uncertainty sweeps over them again they can triumphantly oppose it with the recollection of the precise moment when they shut the door.

We were all in the garden when the double tinkle of the visitors' bell sounded shyly. Everyone knew that it must be Swann, and yet they looked at one another inquiringly and sent my grandmother to reconnoiter.

"See that you thank him intelligibly for the wine," my grandfather warned his two sisters-in-law. "You know how good it is, and the case is huge."

"Now, don't start whispering!" said my great-aunt. "How would you like to come into a house and find everyone muttering to themselves?"

"Ah! There's M. Swann," cried my father. "Let's ask him if he thinks it will be fine tomorrow."

My mother fancied that a word from her would wipe out all the distress which my family had contrived to cause Swann since his marriage. She found an opportunity to draw him aside for a moment. But I followed her: I could not bring myself to let her out of my sight while I felt that in a few minutes I should have to leave her in the dining room and go up to my bed without the consoling thought, as on ordinary evenings, that she would come up later to kiss me.

"Now, M. Swann," she said, "do tell me about your daughter. I'm sure she already has a taste for beautiful things, like her papa."

"Come along and sit down here with us all on the veranda," said my grandfather, coming up to him. My mother had to abandon her quest, but managed to extract from the restriction itself a further delicate thought, like good poets whom the tyranny of rhyme forces into the discovery of their finest lines.

"We can talk about her again when we are by ourselves," she said, or rather whispered, to Swann. "Only a mother is capable of understanding these things. I'm sure that hers would agree with me."

And so we all sat down round the iron table. I should have liked not to think of the hours of anguish which I should have to spend that evening alone in my room, without being able to go to sleep: I tried to convince myself that they were of no importance since I should have forgotten them next morning, and to fix my mind on thoughts of the future which would carry me, as on a bridge, across the terrifying abyss that yawned at my feet. But my mind, strained by this foreboding, distended like the look which I shot at my mother, would not allow any extraneous impression to enter. Thoughts did indeed enter it, but only on the condition that they left behind them every element of beauty, or even of humor, by which I might have been distracted or beguiled. As a surgical patient, thanks to a local anaesthetic, can look on fully conscious while an operation is being performed upon him and yet feel nothing, I could repeat to myself some favorite lines, or watch my grandfather's efforts to talk to Swann about the Duc d'Audiffret-Pasquier, without being able to kindle any emotion from the one or amusement from the other. Hardly had my grandfather begun to question Swann about that orator when one of my grandmother's sisters, in whose ears the question echoed like a solemn but untimely silence which her natural politeness bade her interrupt, addressed the other with:

"Just fancy, Flora, I met a young Swedish governess today who told me some most interesting things about the cooperative movement in Scandinavia. We really must have her to dine here one evening."

"To be sure!" said her sister Flora, "but I haven't wasted my time either. I met such a clever old gentleman at M. Vinteuil's who knows Maubant quite well, and Maubant has told him every little thing about how he gets up his parts. It's the most interesting thing I ever heard. He's a neighbor of M. Vinteuil's, and I never knew; and he is so nice besides."

"M. Vinteuil is not the only one who has nice neighbors," cried my aunt Céline in a voice that was loud because of shyness and forced because of premeditation, darting, as she spoke, what she called a "significant glance" at Swann. And my aunt Flora, who realized that this veiled utterance was Céline's way of thanking Swann for the Asti, looked at him also with a blend of congratulation and irony, either because she simply wished to underline her sister's little witticism, or because she envied Swann his having inspired it, or because she imagined that he was embarrassed, and could not help having a little fun at his expense.

"I think it would be worthwhile," Flora went on, "to have this old gentleman to dinner. When you get him going on Maubant or Mme. Materna he will talk for hours on end."

"That must be delightful," sighed my grandfather, in whose mind nature had unfortunately forgotten to include any capacity whatsoever for becoming passionately interested in the Swedish cooperative movement or in the methods employed by Maubant to get up his parts, just as it had forgotten to endow my grandmother's two sisters with a grain of that precious salt which one has oneself to "add to taste" in order to extract any savor from a narrative of the private life of Molé or of the Comte de Paris.

"By the way," said Swann to my grandfather, "what I was going to tell you has more to do than you might think with what you were asking me just now, for in some respects there has been very little change. I came across a passage in Saint-Simon this morning which would have amused you. It's in the volume which covers his mission to Spain; not one of the best, little more in fact than a journal, but at least a wonderfully well written journal, which fairly distinguishes it from the tedious journals we feel bound to read morning and evening."

"I don't agree with you: there are some days when I find reading the papers very pleasant indeed," my aunt Flora broke in, to show Swann that she had read the note about his Corot in the *Figaro*.

"Yes," Aunt Céline went one better, "when they write about things or people in whom we are interested."

"I don't deny it," answered Swann in some bewilderment. "The fault I find with our journalism is that it forces us to take an interest in some fresh triviality or other every day, whereas only three or four books in a lifetime give us anything that is of real importance. Suppose that, every morning, when we tore the wrapper off our paper with fevered hands, a transmutation were to take place, and we were to find inside it—oh! I don't know; shall we say Pascal's *Pensées?*" He articulated the title with an ironic emphasis so as not to appear pedantic. "And then, in the gilt and tooled volumes which we open once in ten years," he went on, showing that contempt for worldly matters which some men of the world like to affect, "we should read that the Queen of the Hellenes had arrived at Cannes, or that the Princesse de Léon had given a fancy dress ball. In that way we should arrive at a happy medium." But at once regretting that he had allowed himself to speak of serious matters even in jest, he added ironically: "What a fine conversation we're having! I can't think why we climb to these lofty heights," and then, turning to my grandfather: "Well, Saint-Simon tells how Maulévrier had had the audacity to try to shake hands with his sons. You remember how he says of Maulévrier, 'Never did I find in that coarse bottle anything but ill humor, boorishness, and folly.'"

"Coarse or not, I know bottles in which there is something very different," said Flora briskly, feeling bound to thank Swann as well as her sister, since the present of Asti had been addressed to them both. Céline laughed.

Swann was puzzled, but went on: "'I cannot say whether it was ignorance or cozenage,' writes Saint-Simon. 'He tried to give his hand to my children. I noticed it in time to prevent him.'"

My grandfather was already in ecstasies over "ignorance or cozenage," but Mlle. Céline—the name of Saint-Simon, a "man of letters," having arrested the complete paralysis of her auditory faculties—was indignant:

"What! You admire that? Well, that's a fine thing, I must say! But what's it supposed to mean? Isn't one man as good as the next? What difference can it make whether he's a duke or a groom so long as he's intelligent and kind? He had a fine way of bringing up his children, your Saint-Simon, if he didn't teach them to shake hands with all decent folk. Really and truly, it's abominable. And you dare to quote it!"

And my grandfather, utterly depressed, realizing how futile it would be, against this opposition, to attempt to get Swann to tell him the stories which would have amused him, murmured to my mother: "Just tell me again that line of yours which always comforts me so much on these occasions. Oh, yes: 'What virtues, Lord, Thou makest us abhor!' How good that is!"

I never took my eyes off my mother. I knew that when they were at table I should not be permitted to stay there for the whole of dinnertime, and that Mamma, for fear of annoying my father, would not allow me to kiss her several times in public, as I would have done in my room. And so I promised myself that in the dining room, as they began to eat and drink and as I felt the hour approach, I would put beforehand into this kiss, which was bound to be so brief and furtive, everything that my own efforts could muster, would carefully choose in advance the exact spot on her cheek where I would imprint it, and would so prepare my thoughts as to be able, thanks to these mental preliminaries, to consecrate the whole of the minute Mamma would grant me to the sensation of her cheek against my lips, as a painter who can have his subject for short sittings only prepares his palette, and from what he remembers and from rough notes does in advance everything which he possibly can do in the sitter's absence. But tonight, before the dinner bell had sounded, my grandfather said with unconscious cruelty: "The little man looks tired; he'd better go up to bed. Besides, we're dining late tonight."

And my father, who was less scrupulous than my grandmother or my mother in observing the letter of a treaty, went on: "Yes; run along; off to bed."

I would have kissed Mamma then and there, but at that moment the dinner bell rang.

"No, no, leave your mother alone. You've said good night to one another, that's enough. These exhibitions are absurd. Go on upstairs."

And so I must set forth without viaticum; must climb each step of the staircase "against my heart," as the saying is, climbing in opposition to my heart's desire, which was to return to my mother, since she had not, by kissing me, given my heart leave to accompany me forth. That hateful staircase, up which I always went so sadly, gave out a smell of varnish which had, as it were, absorbed and crystallized the special quality of sorrow that I felt each evening, and made it perhaps even crueler to my sensibility because, when it assumed this olfactory guise, my intellect was powerless to resist it. When we have gone to sleep with a raging toothache and are conscious of it only as of a little girl whom we attempt, time after time, to pull out of the water, or a line of Molière which we repeat incessantly to ourselves, it is a great relief to wake up, so that our intelligence can disentangle the idea of toothache from any artificial semblance of heroism or rhythmic cadence. It was the converse of this relief which I felt when my anguish at having to go up to my room invaded my consciousness in a manner infinitely more rapid, instantaneous almost, a manner at once insidious and brutal, through the inhalation—far more poisonous than moral penetration—of the smell of varnish peculiar to that staircase.

Once in my room I had to stop every loophole, to close the shutters, to dig my own grave as I turned down the bedclothes, to wrap myself in the shroud of my nightshirt. But before burying myself in the iron bed which had been placed there because, on summer nights, I was too hot among the rep curtains of the four-poster, I was stirred to revolt, and attempted the desperate stratagem of a condemned prisoner. I wrote to my mother begging her to come upstairs for an important reason which I could not put in writing. My fear was that Françoise, my aunt's cook who used to be put in charge of me when I was at Combray, might refuse to take my note. I had a suspicion that, in her eyes, to carry a message to my mother when there was a guest would appear as flatly inconceivable as for the doorkeeper of a theater to hand a letter to an actor upon the stage. On the subject of things which might or might not be done she possessed a code at once imperious, abundant, subtle, and uncompromising on points themselves imperceptible or irrelevant, which gave it a resemblance to those ancient laws which combine such cruel ordinances as the massacre of infants at the breast with prohibitions of exaggerated refinement against "seething the kid in his mother's milk," or "eating of the sinew which is upon the hollow of the thigh." This code, judging by the sudden obstinacy which she would put into her refusal to carry out certain of our instructions, seemed to have provided for social complexities and refinements of etiquette which nothing in Françoise's background or in her career as a servant in a village household could have put into her head; and we were obliged to assume that there was latent in her some past existence in the ancient history of France, noble and little understood, as in those manufacturing towns where old mansions still testify to their former courtly days, and chemical workers toil among delicately sculptured scenes from *Le Miracle de Théophile* or *Les quatre fils Aymon.*

In this particular instance, the article of her code which made it highly improbable that—barring an outbreak of fire—Françoise would go down and disturb Mamma in the presence of M. Swann for so unimportant a person as myself was one embodying the respect she showed not only for the family (as for the dead, for the clergy, or for royalty), but also for the stranger within our gates; a respect which I should perhaps have found touching in a book, but which never failed to irritate me on her lips, because of the solemn and sentimental tones in which she would express it, and which irritated me more than usual this evening when the sacred character with which she invested the dinner party might have the effect of making her decline to disturb its ceremonial. But to give myself a chance of success I had no hesitation in lying, telling her that it was not in the least myself who had wanted to write to Mamma, but Mamma who, on saying good night to me, had begged me not to forget to send her an answer about something she had asked me to look for, and that she would certainly be very angry if this note were not taken to her. I think that Françoise disbelieved me, for, like those primitive men whose senses were so much keener than our own, she could immediately detect, from signs imperceptible to the rest of us, the truth or falsehood of anything that we might wish to conceal from her. She studied the envelope for five minutes as though an examination of the paper itself and the look of my handwriting could enlighten her as to the nature of the contents, or tell her to which article of her code she ought to refer the matter. Then she went out with an air of resignation which seemed to imply: "It's hard lines on parents having a child like that."

A moment later she returned to say that they were still at the ice stage and that it was impossible for the butler to deliver the note at once, in front of everybody; but that when the finger-bowls were put round he would find a way of slipping it into Mamma's hand. At once my anxiety subsided; it was now no longer (as it had been a moment ago) until tomorrow that I had lost my mother, since my little note—though it would annoy her, no doubt, and doubly so because this stratagem would make me ridiculous in Swann's eyes—would at least admit me, invisible and enraptured, into the same room as herself, would whisper about me into her ear; since that forbidden and unfriendly dining room, where but a moment ago the ice itself—with burned nuts in it—and the fingerbowls seemed to me to be concealing pleasures that were baleful and of a mortal sadness because Mamma was tasting of them while I was far away, had opened its doors to me and, like a ripe fruit which bursts through its skin, was going to pour out into my intoxicated heart the sweetness of Mamma's attention while she was reading what I had written. Now I was no longer separated from her; the barriers were down; an exquisite thread united us. Besides, that was not all: for surely Mamma would come.

As for the agony through which I had just passed, I imagined that Swann would have laughed heartily at it if he had read my letter and had guessed its purpose; whereas, on the contrary, as I was to learn in due course, a similar anguish had been the bane of his life for many years, and no one perhaps could have understood my feelings at that moment so well as he; to him, the anguish that comes from knowing that the creature one adores is in some place of enjoyment where oneself is not and cannot follow—to him that anguish came through love, to which it is in a sense predestined, by which it will be seized upon and exploited; but when, as had befallen me, it possesses one's soul before love has yet entered into one's life, then it must drift, awaiting love's coming, vague and free, without precise attachment, at the disposal of one sentiment today, of another tomorrow, of filial piety or affection for a friend. And the joy with which I first bound myself apprentice, when Françoise returned to tell me that my letter would be delivered, Swann, too, had known well—that false joy which a friend or relative of the woman we love can give us, when, on his arrival at the house or theater where she is to be found, for some ball or party or "first night" at which he is to meet her, he sees us wandering outside, desperately awaiting some opportunity of communicating with her. He recognizes us, greets us familiarly, and asks what we are doing there. And when we invent a story of having some urgent message to give to his relative or friend, he assures us that nothing could be simpler, takes us in at the door, and promises to send her down to us in five minutes. How we love him—as at that moment I loved Françoise—the good-natured intermediary who by a single word has made supportable, human, almost propitious the inconceivable, infernal scene of gaiety in the thick of which we had been imagining swarms of enemies, perverse and seductive, beguiling away from us, even making laugh at us, the woman we love! If we are to judge of them by him—this relative who has accosted us and who is himself an initiate in those cruel mysteries—then the other guests cannot be so very demoniacal. Those inaccessible and excruciating hours during which she was about to taste of unknown pleasures—suddenly, through an unexpected breach, we have broken into them; suddenly we can picture to ourselves, we possess, we intervene upon, we have almost created, one of the moments the succession of which would have composed those hours, a moment as real as all the rest, if not actually more important to us because our mistress is more intensely a part of it: namely, the moment in which he goes to tell her that we are waiting below. And doubtless the other moments of the party would not have been so very different from this one, would be no more exquisite, no more calculated to make us suffer, since this kind friend has assured us that "Of course, she will be delighted to come down! It will be far more amusing for her to talk to you than to be bored up there." Alas! Swann had learned by experience that the good intentions of a third party are powerless to influence a woman who is annoyed to find herself pursued even into a ballroom by a man she does not love. Too often, the kind friend comes down again alone.

My mother did not appear, but without the slightest consideration for my self-respect (which depended upon her keeping up the fiction that she had asked me to let her know the result of my search for something or other) told Françoise to tell me, in so many words: "There is no answer"—words I have so often, since then, heard the hall porters in grand hotels and the flunkys in gambling clubs and the like repeat to some poor girl who replies in bewilderment: "What! he said nothing? It's not possible. You did give him my letter, didn't you? Very well, I shall wait a little longer." And, just as she invariably protests that she does not need the extra gas which the porter offers to light for her, and sits on there, hearing nothing further except an occasional remark on the weather which the porter exchanges with a bellhop whom he will send off suddenly, when he notices the time, to put some customer's wine on the ice, so, having declined Françoise's offer to make me some tea or to stay beside me, I let her go off again to the pantry, and lay down and shut my eyes, trying not to hear the voices of my family who were drinking their coffee in the garden.

But after a few seconds I realized that, by writing that note to Mamma, by approaching—at the risk of making her angry—so near to her that I felt I could reach out and grasp the moment in which I should see her again, I had cut myself off from the possibility of going to sleep until I actually had seen her, and my heart began to beat more and more painfully as I increased my agitation by ordering myself to keep calm and to acquiesce in my ill fortune. Then, suddenly, my anxiety subsided, a feeling of intense happiness coursed through me, as when a strong medicine begins to take effect and one's pain vanishes: I had formed a resolution to abandon all attempts to go to sleep without seeing Mamma, had made up my mind to kiss her at all costs—even though this meant the certainty of being in disgrace with her for long afterward—when she herself came up to bed. The calm which succeeded my anguish filled me with an extraordinary exhilaration, no less than my sense of expectation, my thirst for and my fear of danger. Noiselessly I opened the window and sat down on the foot of my bed. I hardly dared to move in case they should hear me from below. Outside, things too seemed frozen, rapt in a mute intentness not to disturb the moonlight which, duplicating each of them and throwing it back by the extension in front of it of a shadow denser and more concrete than its substance, had made the whole landscape at once thinner and larger, like a map which, after being folded up, is spread out upon the ground. What had to move—a leaf of the chestnut tree, for instance—moved. But its minute quivering, total, self-contained, finished down to its minutest gradation and its last delicate tremor, did not impinge upon the rest of the scene, did not merge with it, remained circumscribed. Exposed upon this surface of silence which absorbed nothing of them, the most distant sounds, those which must have come from gardens at the far end of the town, could be distinguished with such exact "finish" that the impression they gave of coming from a distance seemed due only to their "pianissimo" execution, like those movements on muted strings so well performed by the orchestra of the Conservatoire that, even though one does not miss a single note, one thinks nonetheless that they are being played somewhere outside, a long way from the concert hall, so that all the old subscribers—my grandmother's sisters too, when Swann had given them his seats—used to strain their ears as if they had caught the distant approach of an army on the march, which had not yet rounded the corner of the Rue de Trévise.

I was well aware that I had placed myself in a position than which none could be counted upon to involve me in graver consequences at my parents' hands; consequences far graver, indeed, than a stranger would have imagined, and such as (he would have thought) could follow only some really shameful misdemeanor. But in the upbringing which they had given me faults were not classified in the same order as in that of other children, and I had been taught to place at the head of the list (doubtless because there was no other class of faults from which I needed to be more carefully protected) those in which I can now distinguish the common feature that one succumbs to them by yielding to a nervous impulse. But such a phrase had never been uttered in my hearing; no one had yet accounted for my temptations in a way which might have led me to believe that there was some excuse for my giving in to them, or that I was actually incapable of holding out against them. Yet I could easily recognize this class of transgressions by the anguish of mind which preceded as well as by the rigor of the punishment which followed them; and I knew that what I had just done was in the same category as certain other sins for which I had been severely punished, though infinitely more serious than they. When I went out to meet my mother on her way up to bed, and when she saw that I had stayed up in order to say good night to her again in the passage, I should not be allowed to stay in the house a day longer, I should be packed off to school next morning; so much was certain. Very well: had I been obliged, the next moment, to hurl myself out of the window, I should still have preferred such a fate. For what I wanted now was Mamma, to say good night to her. I had gone too far along the road which led to the fulfillment of this desire to be able to retrace my steps.

I could hear my parents' footsteps as they accompanied Swann to the gate, and when the clanging of the bell assured me that he had really gone, I crept to the window. Mamma was asking my father if he had thought the lobster good, and whether M. Swann had had a second helping of the coffee-and-pistachio ice. "I thought it rather so-so," she was saying. "Next time we shall have to try another flavor."

"I can't tell you," said my great-aunt, "what a change I find in Swann. He is quite antiquated!" She had grown so accustomed to seeing Swann always in the same stage of adolescence that it was a shock to her to find him suddenly less young than the age she still attributed to him. And the others too were beginning to remark in Swann that abnormal, excessive, shameful, and deserved senescence of bachelors, of all those for whom it seems that the great day which knows no morrow must be longer than for other men, since for them it is void of promise, and from its dawn the moments steadily accumulate without any subsequent partition among offspring.

"I fancy he has a lot of trouble with that wretched wife of his, who lives with a certain Monsieur de Charlus, as all Combray knows. It's the talk of the town."

My mother observed that, in spite of this, he had looked much less unhappy of late. "And he doesn't nearly so often do that trick of his, so like his father, of wiping his eyes and drawing his hand across his forehead. I think myself that in his heart of hearts he no longer loves that woman."

"Why, of course he doesn't," answered my grandfather. "He wrote me a letter about it, ages ago, to which I took care to pay no attention, but it left no doubt as to his feelings, or at any rate his love, for his wife. Hello! you two; you never thanked him for the Asti," he went on, turning to his sisters-in-law.

"What! we never thanked him? I think, between you and me, that I put it to him quite neatly," replied my aunt Flora.

"Yes, you managed it very well; I admired you for it," said my aunt Céline.

"But you did it very prettily, too."

"Yes; I was rather proud of my remark about 'nice neighbors.' "

"What! Do you call that thanking him?" shouted my grandfather. "I heard that all right, but devil take me if I guessed it was meant for Swann. You may be quite sure he never noticed it."

"Come, come; Swann isn't a fool. I'm sure he understood. You didn't expect me to tell him the number of bottles, or to guess what he paid for them."

My father and mother were left alone and sat down for a moment; then my father said: "Well, shall we go up to bed?"

"As you wish, dear, though I don't feel at all sleepy. I don't know why; it can't be the coffee-ice—it wasn't strong enough to keep me awake like this. But I see a light in the servants' hall: poor Françoise has been sitting up for me, so I'll get her to unhook me while you go and undress."

My mother opened the latticed door which led from the hall to the staircase. Presently I heard her coming upstairs to close her window. I went quietly into the passage; my heart was beating so violently that I could hardly move, but at least it was throbbing no longer with anxiety, but with terror and joy. I saw in the well of the stair a light coming upward, from Mamma's candle. Then I saw Mamma herself and I threw myself upon her. For an instant she looked at me in astonishment, not realizing what could have happened. Then her face assumed an expression of anger. She said not a single word to me; and indeed I used to go for days on end without being spoken to, for far more venial offenses than this. A single word from Mamma would have been an admission that further intercourse with me was within the bounds of possibility, and that might perhaps have appeared to me more terrible still, as indicating that, with such a punishment as was in store for me, mere silence and black looks would have been puerile. A word from her then would have implied the false calm with which one addresses a servant to whom one has just decided to give notice; the kiss one bestows on a son who is being packed off to enlist, which would have been denied him if it had merely been a matter of being angry with him for a few days. But she heard my father coming from the dressing room, where he had gone to take off his clothes, and, to avoid the "scene" which he would make if he saw me, she said to me in a voice half-stifled with anger: "Off you go at once. Do you want your father to see you waiting there like an idiot?"

But I implored her again: "Come and say good night to me," terrified as I saw the light from my father's candle already creeping up the wall, but also making use of his approach as a means of blackmail, in the hope that my mother, not wishing him to find me there, as find me he must if she continued to refuse me, would give in and say: "Go back to your room. I will come."

Too late: my father was upon us. Instinctively I murmured, though no one heard me, "I'm done for!"

I was not, however. My father used constantly to refuse to let me do things which were quite clearly allowed by the more liberal charters granted me by my mother and grandmother, because he paid no heed to "principles," and because for him there was no such thing as the "rule of law." For some quite irrelevant reason, or for no reason at all, he would at the last moment prevent me from taking some particular walk, one so regular, so hallowed, that to deprive me of it was a clear breach of faith; or again, as he had done this evening, long before the appointed hour he would snap out: "Run along up to bed now; no excuses!" But at the same time, because he was devoid of principles (in my grandmother's sense), he could not, strictly speaking, be called intransigent. He looked at me for a moment with an air of surprise and annoyance, and then when Mamma had told him, not without some embarrassment, what had happened, said to her: "Go along with him, then. You said just now that you didn't feel very sleepy, so stay in his room for a little. I don't need anything."

"But, my dear," my mother answered timidly, "whether or not I feel sleepy is not the point; we mustn't let the child get into the habit . . ."

"There's no question of getting into a habit," said my father, with a shrug of the shoulders; "you can see quite well that the child is unhappy. After all, we aren't jailers. You'll end by making him ill, and a lot of good that will do. There are two beds in his room; tell Françoise to make up the big one for you, and stay with him for the rest of the night. Anyhow, I'm off to bed; I'm not so nervy as you. Good night."

It was impossible for me to thank my father; he would have been exasperated by what he called mawkishness. I stood there, not daring to move; he was still in front of us, a tall figure in his white nightshirt, crowned with the pink and violet cashmere scarf which he used to wrap around his head since he had begun to suffer from neuralgia, standing like Abraham in the engraving after Benozzo Gozzoli which M. Swann had given me, telling Sarah that she must tear herself away from Isaac.

Many years have passed since that night. The wall of the staircase up which I had watched the light of his candle gradually climb was long ago demolished. And in myself, too, many things have perished which I imagined would last forever, and new ones have arisen, giving birth to new sorrows and new joys which in those days I could not have foreseen, just as now the old are hard to understand. It is a long time, too, since my father has been able to say to Mamma: "Go along with the child." Never again will such moments be possible for me. But of late I have been increasingly able to catch, if I listen attentively, the sound of the sobs which I had the strength to control in my father's presence, and which broke out only when I found myself alone with Mamma. In reality their echo has never ceased; and it is only because life is now growing more and more quiet round about me that I hear them anew, like those convent bells which are so effectively drowned during the day by the noises of the street that one would suppose them to have stopped, until they ring out again through the silent evening air.

Mamma spent that night in my room: when I had just committed a sin so deadly that I expected to be banished from the household, my parents gave me a far greater concession than I could ever have won as the reward of a good deed. Even at the moment when it manifested itself in this crowning mercy, my father's behavior toward me still retained that arbitrary and unwarranted quality which was so characteristic of him and which arose from the fact that his actions were generally dictated by chance expediencies rather than based on any formal plan. And perhaps even what I called his severity, when he sent me off to bed, deserved that title less than my mother's or my grandmother's attitude, for his nature, which in some respects differed more than theirs from my own, had probably prevented him from realizing until then how wretched I was every evening, something which my mother and grandmother knew well; but they loved me enough to be unwilling to spare me that suffering, which they hoped to teach me to overcome, so as to reduce my nervous sensibility and to strengthen my will. Whereas my father, whose affection for me was of another kind, would not, I suspect, have had the same courage, for as soon as he had grasped the fact that I was unhappy he had said to my mother: "Go and comfort him."

Mamma stayed that night in my room, and it seemed that she did not wish to mar by recrimination those hours which were so different from anything that I had had a right to expect, for when Françoise (who guessed that something extraordinary must have happened when she saw Mamma sitting by my side, holding my hand and letting me cry unchided) said to her: "But, Madame, what is young master crying for?" she replied: "Why, Françoise, he doesn't know himself: it's his nerves. Make up the big bed for me quickly and then go off to your own." And thus for the first time my unhappiness was regarded no longer as a punishable offense but as an involuntary ailment which had been officially recognized, a nervous condition for which I was in no way responsible: I had the consolation of no longer having to mingle apprehensive scruples with the bitterness of my tears; I could weep henceforth without sin. I felt no small degree of pride, either, in Françoise's presence at this return to humane conditions which, not an hour after Mamma had refused to come up to my room and had sent the snubbing message that I was to go to sleep, raised me to the dignity of a grown-up person, brought me of a sudden to a sort of puberty of sorrow, a manumission of tears. I ought to have been happy; I was not. It struck me that my mother had just made a first concession which must have been painful to her, that it was a first abdication on her part from the ideal she had formed for me, and that for the first time she who was so brave had to confess herself beaten. It struck me that if I had just won a victory it was over her, that I had succeeded, as sickness or sorrow or age might have succeeded, in relaxing her will, in undermining her judgment; and that this evening opened a new era, would remain a black date in the calendar. And if I had dared now, I should have said to Mamma: "No, I don't want you to, you mustn't sleep here." But I was conscious of the practical wisdom, of what would nowadays be called the realism, with which she tempered the ardent idealism of my grandmother's nature, and I knew that now the mischief was done she would prefer to let me enjoy the soothing pleasure of her company, and not to disturb my father again. Certainly my mother's beautiful face seemed to shine again with youth that evening, as she sat gently holding my hands and trying to check my tears; but this was just what I felt should not have been; her anger would have saddened me less than this new gentleness, unknown to my childhood experience; I felt that I had with an impious and secret finger traced a first wrinkle upon her soul and brought out a first white hair on her head. This thought redoubled my sobs, and then I saw that Mamma, who had never allowed herself to indulge in any undue emotion with me, was suddenly overcome by my tears and had to struggle to keep back her own. When she realized that I had noticed this, she said to me with a smile: "Why, my little buttercup, my little canary boy, he's going to make Mamma as silly as himself if this goes on. Look, since you can't sleep, and Mamma can't either, we mustn't go on in this stupid way; we must do something; I'll get one of your books." But I had none there. "Would you like me to get out the books now that your grandmother is going to give you for your birthday? Just think it over first, and don't be disappointed if there's nothing new for you then."

I was only too delighted, and Mamma went to fetch a parcel of books of which I could not distinguish, through the paper in which they were wrapped, any more than their short, wide format but which, even at this first glimpse, brief and obscure as it was, bade fair to eclipse already the paint box of New Year's Day and the silkworms of the year before. The books were *La Mare au Diable, François le Champi, La Petite Fadette,* and *Les Maîtres Sonneurs.* My grandmother, as I learned afterward, had at first chosen Musset's poems, a volume of Rousseau, and *Indiana;* for while she considered light reading as unwholesome as sweets and cakes, she did not reflect that the strong breath of genius might have upon the mind even of a child an influence at once more dangerous and less invigorating than that of fresh air and sea breezes upon his body. But when my father had almost called her an imbecile on learning the names of the books she proposed to give me, she had journeyed back by herself to Jouy-le-Vicomte to the bookseller's, so that there should be no danger of my not having my present in time (it was a boiling hot day, and she had come home so unwell that the doctor had warned my mother not to allow her to tire herself so), and had fallen back upon the four pastoral novels of George Sand.

"My dear," she had said to Mamma, "I could not bring myself to give the child anything that was not well written."

The truth was that she could never permit herself to buy anything from which no intellectual profit was to be derived, above all the profit which fine things afford us by teaching us to seek our pleasures elsewhere than in the barren satisfaction of worldly wealth. Even when she had to make someone a present of the kind called "useful," when she had to give an armchair or some table silver or a walking stick, she would choose "antiques," as though their long desuetude had effaced from them any semblance of utility and fitted them rather to instruct us in the lives of the men of other days than to serve the common requirements of our own. She would have liked me to have in my room photographs of ancient buildings or of beautiful places. But at the moment of buying them, and for all that the subject of the picture had an aesthetic value, she would find that vulgarity and utility had too prominent a part in them, through the mechanical nature of their reproduction by photography. She attempted by a subterfuge, if not to eliminate altogether this commercial banality, at least to minimize it, to supplant it to a certain extent with what was art still, to introduce, as it were, several "thicknesses" of art: instead of photographs of Chartres Cathedral, of the Fountains of Saint-Cloud, or of Vesuvius, she would inquire of Swann whether some great painter had not depicted them, and preferred to give me photographs of "Chartres Cathedral" after Corot, of the

"Fountains of Saint-Cloud" after Hubert Robert, and of "Vesuvius" after Turner, which were a stage higher in the scale of art. But although the photographer had been prevented from reproducing directly these masterpieces or beauties of nature, and had there been replaced by a great artist, he resumed his odious position when it came to reproducing the artist's interpretation. Accordingly, having to reckon again with vulgarity, my grandmother would endeavor to postpone the moment of contact still further. She would ask Swann if the picture had not been engraved, preferring, when possible, old engravings with some interest of association apart from themselves, such, for example, as show us a masterpiece in a state in which we can no longer see it today (like Morghen's print of Leonardo's *Last Supper* before its defacement). It must be admitted that the results of this method of interpreting the art of making presents were not always happy. The idea which I formed of Venice, from a drawing by Titian which is supposed to have the lagoon in the background, was certainly far less accurate than what I should have derived from ordinary photographs. We could no longer keep count in the family (when my great-aunt wanted to draw up an indictment of my grandmother) of all the armchairs she had presented to married couples, young and old, which on a first attempt to sit down upon them had at once collapsed beneath the weight of their recipients. But my grandmother would have thought it sordid to concern herself too closely with the solidity of any piece of furniture in which could still be discerned a flourish, a smile, a brave conceit of the past. And even what in such pieces answered a material need, since it did so in a manner to which we are no longer accustomed, charmed her like those old forms of speech in which we can still see traces of a metaphor whose fine point has been worn away by the rough usage of our modern tongue. As it happened, the pastoral novels of George Sand which she was giving me for my birthday were regular lumber rooms full of expressions that have fallen out of use and become quaint and picturesque, and are now only to be found in country dialects. And my grandmother had bought them in preference to other books, as she would more readily have taken a house with a Gothic dovecote or some other such piece of antiquity as will exert a benign influence on the mind by giving it a hankering for impossible journeys through the realms of time.

Mamma sat down by my bed; she had chosen *François le Champi,* whose reddish cover and incomprehensible title gave it, for me, a distinct personality and a mysterious attraction. I had not then read any real novels. I had heard it said that George Sand was a typical novelist. This predisposed me to imagine that *François le Champi* contained something inexpressibly delicious. The narrative devices designed to arouse curiosity or melt to pity, certain modes of expression which disturb or sadden the reader, and which, with a little experience, he may recognize as common to a great many novels, seemed to me—for whom a new book was not one of a number of similar objects but, as it were, a unique person, absolutely self-contained —simply an intoxicating distillation of the peculiar essence of *François le Champi.* Beneath the everyday incidents, the ordinary objects and common words, I sensed a strange and individual tone of voice. The plot began to unfold: to me it seemed all the more obscure because in those days, when I read, I used often to daydream about something quite different for page after page. And the gaps which this habit left in my knowledge of the story were widened by the fact that when it was Mamma who was reading to me aloud she left all the love scenes out. And so all the odd changes which take place in the relations between the miller's wife and the boy, changes which only the gradual dawning of love can explain, seemed to me steeped in a mystery the key to which (I readily believed) lay in that strange and mellifluous name of *Champi,* which invested the boy who bore it, I had no idea why, with its own vivid, ruddy, charming color. If my mother was not a faithful reader, she was nonetheless an admirable one, when reading a work in which she found the note of true feeling, in the respectful simplicity of her interpretation and the beauty and sweetness of her voice. Even in ordinary life, when it was not works of art but men and women whom she was moved to pity or admire, it was touching to observe with what deference she would banish from her voice, her gestures, from her whole conversation, now the note of gaiety which might have distressed some mother who had once lost a child, now the recollection of an event or anniversary which might have reminded some old gentleman of the burden of his years, now the household topic which might have bored some young man of letters. And so, when she read aloud the prose of George Sand, prose which is everywhere redolent of that generosity and moral distinction which Mamma had learned from my grandmother to place above all other qualities in life, and which I was not to teach her until much later to refrain from placing above all other qualities in literature too, taking pains to banish from her voice any pettiness or affectation which might have choked that powerful stream of language, she supplied all the natural tenderness, all the lavish sweetness which they demanded to sentences which seemed to have been composed for her voice and which were all, so to speak, within the compass of her sensibility. She found, to tackle them in the required tone, the warmth of feeling which preexisted and dictated them, but which is not to be found in the words themselves, and by this means she smoothed away, as she read, any harshness or discordance in the tenses of verbs, endowing the imperfect and the preterit with all the sweetness to be found in generosity, all the melancholy to be found in love, guiding the sentence that was drawing to a close toward the one that was about to begin, now hastening, now slackening the pace of the syllables so as to bring them, despite their differences of quantity, into a uniform rhythm, and breathing into this quite ordinary prose a kind of emotional life and continuity.

My aching heart was soothed; I let myself be borne upon the current of this gentle night on which I had my mother by my side. I knew that such a night could not be repeated; that the strongest desire I had in the world, namely, to keep my mother in my room through the sad hours of darkness, ran too much counter to general requirements and to the wishes of others for such a concession as had been granted me this evening to be anything but a rare and artificial exception. Tomorrow night my anguish would return and Mamma would not stay by my side. But when my anguish was assuaged, I could no longer understand it; besides, tomorrow was still a long way off; I told myself that I should still have time to take preventive action, although that time could bring me no access of power since these things were in no way dependent upon the exercise of my will, and seemed not quite inevitable only because they were still separated from me by this short interval.

And so it was that, for a long time afterward, when I lay awake at night and revived old memories of Combray, I saw no more of it than this sort of luminous panel, sharply defined against a vague and shadowy background, like the panels which the glow of a Bengal light or a searchlight beam will cut out and illuminate in a building the other parts of which remain plunged in darkness: broad enough at its base, the little parlor, the dining room, the opening of the dark path from which M. Swann, the unwitting author of my sufferings, would emerge, the hall through which I would journey to the first step of that staircase, so painful to climb, which constituted, all by itself, the slender cone of this irregular pyramid; and, at the summit, my bedroom, with the little passage through whose glazed door Mamma would enter; in a word, seen always at the same evening hour, isolated from all its possible surroundings, detached and solitary against the dark background, the bare minimum of scenery necessary (like the decor one sees prescribed on the title page of an old play, for its performance in the provinces) to the drama of my undressing; as though all Combray had consisted of but two floors joined by a slender staircase, and as though there had been no time there but seven o'clock at night. I must own that I could have assured any questioner that Combray did include other scenes and did exist at other hours than these. But since the facts which I should then have recalled would have been prompted only by voluntary memory, the memory of the intellect, and since the pictures which that kind of memory shows us preserve nothing of the past itself, I should never have had any wish to ponder over this residue of Combray. To me it was in reality all dead.

Permanently dead? Very possibly.

There is a large element of chance in these matters, and a second chance occurrence, that of our own death, often prevents us from awaiting for any length of time the favors of the first.

I feel that there is much to be said for the Celtic belief that the souls of those whom we have lost are held captive in some inferior being, in an animal, in a plant, in some inanimate object, and thus effectively lost to us until the day (which to many never comes) when we happen to pass by the tree or to obtain possession of the object which forms their prison. Then they start and tremble, they call us by our name, and as soon as we have recognized their voice the spell is broken. Delivered by us, they have overcome death and return to share our life.

And so it is with our own past. It is a labor in vain to attempt to recapture it: all the efforts of our intellect must prove futile. The past is hidden somewhere outside the realm, beyond the reach of intellect, in some material object (in the sensation which that material object will give us) of which we have no inkling. And it depends on chance whether or not we come upon this object before we ourselves must die.

Many years had elapsed during which nothing of Combray, save what was comprised in the theater and the drama of my going to bed there, had any existence for me, when one day in winter, on my return home, my mother, seeing that I was cold, offered me some tea, a thing I did not ordinarily take. I declined at first, and then, for no particular reason, changed my mind. She sent for one of those squat, plump little cakes called "petites madeleines," which look as though they had been molded in the fluted valve of a scallop shell. And soon, mechanically, dispirited after a dreary day with the prospect of a depressing morrow, I raised to my lips a spoonful of the tea in which I had soaked a morsel of the cake. No sooner had the warm liquid mixed with the crumbs touched my palate than a shudder ran through me and I stopped, intent upon the extraordinary thing that was happening to me. An exquisite pleasure had invaded my senses, something isolated, detached, with no suggestion of its origin. And at once the vicissitudes of life had become indifferent to me, its disasters innocuous, its brevity illusory—this new sensation having had on me the effect which love has of filling me with a precious essence; or rather this essence was not in me, it *was* me. I had ceased now to feel mediocre, contingent, mortal. Whence could it have come to me, this all-powerful joy? I sensed that it was connected with the taste of the tea and the cake, but that it infinitely transcended those savors, could not, indeed, be of the same nature. Whence did it come? What did it mean? How could I seize and apprehend it?

I drink a second mouthful, in which I find nothing more than in the first, then a third, which gives me rather less than the second. It is time to stop; the potion is losing its magic. It is plain that the truth I am seeking lies not in the cup but in myself. The drink has called it into being, but does not know it, and can only repeat indefinitely, with a progressive diminution of strength, the same message which I cannot interpret, though I hope at least to be able to call it forth again and to find it there presently, intact and at my disposal, for my final enlightenment. I put down the cup and examine my own mind. It alone can discover the truth. But how? What an abyss of uncertainty, whenever the mind feels overtaken by itself; when it, the seeker, is at the same time the dark region through which it must go seeking and where all its equipment will avail it nothing. Seek? More than that: create. It is face to face with something which does not yet exist, to which it alone can give reality and substance, which it alone can bring into the light of day.

And I begin again to ask myself what it could have been, this unremembered state which brought with it no logical proof, but the indisputable evidence, of its felicity, its reality, and in whose presence other states of consciousness melted and vanished. I decide to attempt to make it reappear. I retrace my thoughts to the moment at which I drank the first spoonful of tea. I rediscover the same state, illuminated by no fresh light. I ask my mind to make one further effort, to bring back once more the fleeting sensation. And so that nothing may interrupt it in its course I shut out every obstacle, every extraneous idea, I stop my ears and inhibit all attention against the sounds from the next room. And then, feeling that my mind is tiring itself without having any success to report, I compel it for a change to enjoy the distraction which I have just denied it, to think of other things, to rest and refresh itself before making a final effort. And then for the second time I clear an empty space in front of it; I place in position before my mind's eye the still recent taste of that first mouthful, and I feel something start within me, something that leaves its resting place and attempts to rise, something that has been embedded like an anchor at a great depth; I do not know yet what it is, but I can feel it mounting slowly; I can measure the resistance, I can hear the echo of great spaces traversed.

Undoubtedly what is thus palpitating in the depths of my being must be the image, the visual memory which, being linked to that taste, is trying to follow it into my conscious mind. But its struggles are too far off, too confused and chaotic; scarcely can I perceive the neutral glow into which the elusive whirling medley of stirred-up colors is fused, and I cannot distinguish its form, cannot invite it, as the one possible interpreter, to translate for me the evidence of its contemporary, its inseparable paramour, the taste, cannot ask it to inform me what special circumstance is in question, from what period in my past life.

Will it ultimately reach the clear surface of my consciousness, this memory, this old, dead moment which the magnetism of an identical moment has traveled so far to importune, to disturb, to raise up out of the very depths of my being? I cannot tell. Now I feel nothing; it has stopped, has perhaps sunk back into its darkness, from which who can say whether it will ever rise again? Ten times over I must essay the task, must lean down over the abyss. And each time the cowardice that deters us from every difficult task, every important enterprise, has urged me to leave the thing alone, to drink my tea and to think merely of the worries of today and my hopes for tomorrow, which can be brooded over painlessly.

And suddenly the memory revealed itself. The taste was that of the little piece of madeleine which on Sunday mornings at Combray (because on those mornings I did not go out before mass), when I went to say good morning to her in her bedroom, my aunt Léonie used to give me, dipping it first in her own cup of tea or tisane. The sight of the little madeleine had recalled nothing to my mind before I tasted it; perhaps because I had so often seen such things in the meantime, without tasting them, on the trays in pastry cooks' windows, that their image had dissociated itself from those Combray days to take its place among others more recent; perhaps because of those memories, so long abandoned and put out of mind, nothing now survived, everything was scattered; the shapes of things, including that of the little scallop shell of pastry, so richly sensual under its severe, religious folds, were either obliterated or had been so long dormant as to have lost the power of expansion which would have allowed them to resume their place in my con-sciousness. But when from a long-distant past nothing subsists, after the people are dead, after the things are broken and scattered, taste and smell alone, more fragile but more enduring, more unsubstantial, more persistent, more faithful, remain poised a long time like souls, remembering, waiting, hoping, amid the ruins of all the rest; and bear unflinchingly, in the tiny and almost impalpable drop of their essence, the vast structure of recollection.

And as soon as I had recognized the taste of the piece of madeleine soaked in her decoction of lime blossom which my aunt used to give me (although I did not yet know and must long postpone the discovery of why this memory made me so happy) immediately the old gray house upon the street, where her room was, rose up like a stage set to attach itself to the little pavilion opening onto the garden which had been built out behind it for my parents (the isolated segment which until that moment had been all that I could see); and with the house the town, from morning to night and in all weathers, the Square where I used to be sent before lunch, the streets along which I used to run errands, the country roads we took when it was fine. And as in the game wherein the Japanese amuse themselves by filling a porcelain bowl with water and steeping in it little pieces of paper which until then are without character or form, but, the moment they become wet, stretch and twist and take on color and distinctive shape, become flowers or houses or people, solid and recognizable, so in that moment all the flowers in our garden and in M. Swann's park, and the water lilies on the Vivonne and the good folk of the village and their little dwellings and the parish church and the whole of Combray and its surroundings, taking shape and solidity, sprang into being, town and gardens alike, from my cup of tea. ∾

INTERPRETIVE QUESTIONS
FOR DISCUSSION

Why does the narrator consider the state between dreaming and waking to be the source of his creativity?

1. Why doesn't it offend the narrator's reason to see himself as "a church, a quartet, the rivalry between François I and Charles V" in his first moments of waking? Why does this idea grow unintelligible as he becomes conscious of his surroundings? (3)

2. Why, when more fully awake, does the narrator consider the state of darkness in which he finds himself "pleasant and restful" for his mind and, at the same time, "incomprehensible, without a cause, something dark indeed"? (4)

3. Why does the narrator dream of his "childish terrors" but not of their satisfactory resolution? Why does he awaken before he consummates his pleasure with the woman of his dream? (5)

4. What does the narrator mean when he says that "when a man is asleep, he has in a circle round him the chain of the hours, the sequence of the years, the order of the heavenly host"? (5)

5. Why does the narrator feel he has "only the most rudimentary sense of existence" and is "more destitute than the cave dweller" when he awakens in the middle of the night? (6)

6. Why does the narrator experience the early moments of awakening as traversing centuries of civilization, out of which he can "gradually piece together the original components" of his ego?

Why does he think of sleep as "the abyss of not-being" even though he dreams about his past and aspirations of the present? (6)

7. Why do "things, places, years" converge for the narrator during the moments of his awakening? (6)

8. Why does the narrator think of his body as having a more acute memory than his intellect? Why does it matter to him where and in what position he falls asleep? (6–7)

9. Why does the narrator call the process of writing his book "the long course of my waking dream"? (8)

10. Why does the narrator personify the smells, sounds, and appearance of the rooms in which he has slept? (8–9)

11. Why does the narrator state that habit—growing familiar with his surroundings—conquers the agitation he feels in a new place? Does the narrator see habit as the friend or enemy of creativity? (9, 11)

12. Why does the narrator recall his ambivalence toward the magic lantern in his childhood bedroom at Combray, an object which both fed his imagination and artistic sensibility and tortured him by making the room unfamiliar? (10–12)

Suggested textual analysis
Pages 3–10: from the beginning of the selection to "and what others had told me."

Why does the narrator as a child risk disgrace, punishment, and possible banishment in order to receive a good-night kiss from his mother?

1. When he hears his mother in the corridor, why does the young narrator focus on the pain of her eventual departure, rather than anticipate the pleasure of her kiss? (14)

2. Why is the narrator's mother forced to choose between easing the wretchedness of her son and complying with the wishes of her husband who is annoyed by such rituals? (15)

3. Why does the narrator feel that kissing his mother is like an act of communion? Why does she give the narrator the power to sleep? (15, 31)

4. Why is the secretive M. Swann—whom the narrator comes to know intimately later in life and who has suffered like him—the "unwitting author" of the narrator's sufferings? (15, 22, 26, 49) Why does the narrator compare his mother to M. Swann's selfish and rejecting lover? (34–36)

5. Why does the narrator vow to put all his effort into the "brief and furtive" public kiss that he will be allowed to give his mother? Why does he compare himself to a painter who has only short sessions with his model? (31)

6. Why does the narrator feel comforted and connected to his mother just by knowing she will receive and read his note? Why does his resolution to kiss his mother relieve his anxiety and leave him filled with happiness, exhilaration, and a thirst for and fear of danger? (34, 36–37)

7. Why does the narrator imagine that death would be preferable to not pursuing the object of his desire—kissing his mother good night? (38)

8. Why is the narrator given his heart's desire through the unprincipled decision of his father? Why, in this instance, does the father end up being more sensitive to his son's needs than the mother, who respects principles and avoids breaching faith? (41)

9. Why does the narrator compare his father to a work of art in which Abraham exhorts Sarah to tear herself away from Isaac? Why does the narrator recall the image as an engraving of a painting—a work that represents several " 'thicknesses' of art"? (41, 45)

10. Why does the narrator believe that the echo of the sobs he controlled in his father's presence that night never really ceased? Why has the narrator, late in his life, become more attuned to the emotional pain he felt as a child? (42)

11. Why does the narrator call the episode of pursuing and winning his mother a "puberty of sorrow" that raised him to the status of an adult? Did the narrator choose the person he became, or was he fated to unhappiness by his character, frailties, and parents? (43)

12. Why has the moment of being granted his mother endured for the narrator in a way that so many other events in his past have not? (42–43)

Suggested textual analysis
Pages 37–42: beginning, "I was well aware," and ending, "through the silent evening air."

Why are distinct memories of his childhood in Combray lost to the narrator until he tastes a madeleine dipped into his tea?

1. Why, of all the time spent in Combray, does the adult narrator remember only the painful drama of his going to bed? (49–50)

2. Why does the narrator believe that "voluntary memory, the memory of the intellect" preserves nothing of the past? (50)

3. Why isn't the narrator interested in thinking about the "residue of Combray," which would have been prompted by voluntary memory? Why is this Combray "in reality all dead"? (50)

4. Why does the narrator insist that recapturing our past through memory is a matter of chance and "beyond the reach of intellect"? (50)

5. Why does the narrator's profound experience of remembering his past begin with his mechanical, dispirited drinking of a spoonful of tea and cake—a repast of which he normally does not partake? (50)

6. Why does the narrator experience the first moment of his awakening memory as an "exquisite pleasure" invading his senses, "something isolated, detached, with no suggestion of its origin"? (51)

7. Why does the narrator's dawning memory cause him to view the "vicissitudes of life" indifferently? Why does he compare the sensation to being in love? (51)

8. Why does the "potion" gradually lose its "magic"? Why can the narrator only re-create the sensations by making an effort to *think,* to recall the taste of his first mouthful? (51)

9. Why does the narrator conclude that he must do more than seek the truth, he must create it? (51)

10. Why does the "unremembered state" called forth by the tea and cake cause other states of consciousness to disappear? Why does the narrator have trouble identifying what this state is? (51–52)

11. Why can't the narrator compel the memory to the surface of his consciousness? Why does he think it is cowardice that prevents him from recapturing the dead memory? (52–53)

12. Why does the narrator claim that the fragile senses of taste and smell are more enduring than other senses and contain "the vast structure of recollection"? (53)

Suggested textual analysis
Pages 49–54: from "And so it was that," to the end of the selection.

FOR FURTHER REFLECTION

1. Must we all recapture our past, or at least attempt to do so, in order to live fully and happily?

2. Do you agree that "voluntary memory, the memory of the intellect" preserves nothing of the past?

3. Can someone as passionate and hypersensitive as Proust speak to the thoughts and concerns of the average person?

4. Is it a profound or a profane notion to elevate art into a kind of religion, as Proust has done?

5. Does it take an extraordinarily sensitive nature like Proust's to hear the "echoes" of childhood and to understand how they shape the adults we become?

THE RAT MAN

Sigmund Freud

SIGMUND FREUD (1856–1939), the founder of psychoanalysis, was born in Freiberg, Moravia, of Jewish parents. In 1860 his family moved to Vienna, the city where Freud would live most of his life. Freud received his medical degree in 1881 from the University of Vienna. By 1885 he had become noted for his treatment of hysteria using hypnosis. In the following years, Freud postulated that hysteria and neurosis had their origins in repressed sexual energy, a theory that made him a controversial figure throughout his long career. Freud eventually rejected hypnosis as the means of treatment and developed a technique he called "free association" that allows an individual's repressed unconscious thoughts and feelings to emerge as conscious ones. Freud considered the case of the *Rattenmann*—his own affectionate name for his patient—as one of the most instructive and successful of his career. While still treating the Rat Man (1907–1908), Freud began lecturing on the case, introducing his theories and techniques to a wide audience. He found his subject, a twenty-nine-year-old lawyer, as personally entertaining as his symptoms were interesting. Freud even invited the Rat Man to a meal in his home, violating his own strict tenets concerning the proper relationship between analyst and patient.

THE MATTER CONTAINED in the following pages will be
of two kinds. In the first place I shall give some fragmentary
extracts from the history of a case of obsessional neurosis. This
case, judged by its length, the injuriousness of its effects, and the
patient's own view of it, deserves to be classed as a fairly severe
one; the treatment, which lasted for about a year, led to the
complete restoration of the patient's personality, and to the
removal of his inhibitions. In the second place, starting out from
this case, and also taking other cases into account which I have
previously analyzed, I shall make some disconnected statements
of an aphoristic character upon the genesis and finer psychological mechanism of obsessional processes, and I shall thus
hope to develop my first observations on the subject, published
in 1896.

A program of this kind seems to me to require some justifi-
cation. For it might otherwise be thought that I regard this
method of making a communication as perfectly correct and as
one to be imitated; whereas in reality I am only accommodating

myself to obstacles, some external and others inherent in the subject, and I should gladly have communicated more if it had been right or possible for me to do so. I cannot give a complete history of the treatment, because that would involve my entering in detail into the circumstances of my patient's life. The importunate interest of a capital city, focused with particular attention upon my medical activities, forbids my giving a faithful picture of the case. On the other hand I have come more and more to regard the distortions usually resorted to in such circumstances as useless and objectionable. If the distortions are slight, they fail in their object of protecting the patient from indiscreet curiosity; while if they go beyond this they require too great a sacrifice, for they destroy the intelligibility of the material, which depends for its coherence precisely upon the small details of real life. And from this latter circumstance follows the paradoxical truth that it is far easier to divulge the patient's most intimate secrets than the most innocent and trivial facts about him, for, whereas the former would not throw any light on his identity, the latter, by which he is generally recognized, would make it obvious to everyone.

Such is my excuse for having curtailed so drastically the history of this case and of its treatment. And I can offer still more cogent reasons for having confined myself to the statement only of some disconnected results of the psychoanalytic investigation of obsessional neurosis. I must confess that I have not yet succeeded in completely penetrating the complicated texture of a *severe* case of obsessional neurosis, and that, if I were to reproduce the analysis, it would be impossible for me to make the structure, such as by the help of analysis we know or suspect it to be, visible to others through the mass of therapeutic work superimposed upon it. What adds so greatly to the difficulty of doing this is the patients' resistances and the forms in which they are expressed. But even apart from this it must be admitted that an obsessional neurosis is in itself not an easy thing to understand—much less so than a case of hysteria. As a matter of fact we should have expected to find the contrary. The language of an obsessional neurosis—the means by which it expresses its secret thoughts—is, as it were, only a dialect of the language of hysteria; but it is a dialect in which we ought to be able to find our way about more easily, since it is more nearly related to the forms of expression adopted by our conscious thought than is the language of hysteria. Above all, it does not involve the leap from a mental process to a somatic innervation—hysterical conversion—which can never be fully comprehensible to us.

Perhaps it is only because we are less familiar with obsessional neuroses that we do not find these expectations confirmed by the facts. Persons suffering from a severe degree of obsessional neurosis present themselves far less frequently for analytic treatment than hysterical patients. They dissimulate their condition in daily life, too, as long as they possibly can, and often call in a physician only when their complaint has reached such an advanced stage as, had they been suffering, for instance, from tuberculosis of the lungs, would have led to their being refused admission to a sanatorium. I make this comparison, moreover, because, as with the chronic infectious disease which I have just mentioned, we can point to a number of brilliant therapeutic successes in severe no less than in light cases of obsessional neurosis, where these have been taken in hand at an early stage.

In these circumstances there is no alternative but to report the facts in the imperfect and incomplete fashion in which they are known and in which it is legitimate to communicate them. The crumbs of knowledge offered in these pages, though they have been laboriously enough collected, may not in themselves prove very satisfying; but they may serve as a starting point for the work of other investigators, and common endeavor may bring the success which is perhaps beyond the reach of individual effort.

EXTRACTS FROM THE CASE HISTORY

A youngish man of university education introduced himself to me with the statement that he had suffered from obsessions ever since his childhood, but with particular intensity for the last four years. The chief features of his disorder were *fears* that something might happen to two people of whom he was very fond—his father and a lady whom he admired. Besides this he was aware of *compulsive impulses*—such as an impulse, for instance, to cut his throat with a razor; and further he produced *prohibitions,* sometimes in connection with quite unimportant things. He had wasted years, he told me, in fighting against these ideas of his, and in this way had lost much ground in the course of his life. He had tried various treatments, but none had been of any use to him except a course of hydrotherapy at a sanatorium near ———; and this, he thought, had probably only been because he had made an acquaintance there which had led to regular sexual intercourse. Here he had no opportunities of the sort, and he seldom had intercourse and only at irregular intervals. He felt disgust at prostitutes. Altogether, he said, his sexual life had been stunted; onanism had played only a small part in it, in his sixteenth or seventeenth year. His potency was normal; he had first performed coitus at the age of twenty-six.

He gave me the impression of being a clearheaded and shrewd person. When I asked him what it was that made him lay such stress upon telling me about his sexual life, he replied that that was what he knew about my theories. Actually, however, he had read none of my writings, except that a short time before he had been turning over the pages of one of my books and had come across the explanation of some curious verbal associations which had so much reminded him of some of his own "efforts of thought" in connection with his ideas that he had decided to put himself in my hands.

The Beginning of the Treatment

The next day I made him pledge himself to submit to the one and only condition of the treatment—namely, to say everything that came into his head, even if it was *unpleasant* to him, or seemed *unimportant* or *irrelevant* or *senseless*. I then gave him leave to start his communications with any subject he pleased, and he began as follows:[1]

He had a friend, he told me, of whom he had an extraordinarily high opinion. He used always to go to him when he was tormented by some criminal impulse, and ask him whether he despised him as a criminal. His friend used then to give him moral support by assuring him that he was a man of irreproachable conduct, and had probably been in the habit, from his youth onward, of taking a dark view of his own life. At an earlier date, he went on, another person had exercised a similar influence over him. This was a nineteen-year-old student (he himself had been fourteen or fifteen at the time) who had taken a liking to him, and had raised his self-esteem to an extraordinary degree, so that he appeared to himself to be a genius. This student had subsequently become his tutor, and had suddenly altered his behavior and begun treating him as though he were an idiot. At length he had noticed that the student was interested in one of his sisters, and had realized that he had only taken him up in order to gain admission into the house. This had been the first great blow of his life.

He then proceeded without any apparent transition:

---

1. What follows is based upon notes made on the evening of the day of treatment, and adheres as closely as possible to my recollection of the patient's words. I feel obliged to offer a warning against the practice of noting down what the patient says during the actual time of treatment. The consequent withdrawal of the physician's attention does the patient more harm than can be made up for by any increase in accuracy that may be achieved in the reproduction of his case history.

Infantile Sexuality

"My sexual life began very early. I can remember a scene out of my fourth or fifth year. (From my sixth year onward I can remember everything.) This scene came into my head quite distinctly, years later. We had a very pretty young governess called Fräulein Peter.[2] One evening she was lying on the sofa lightly dressed, and reading. I was lying beside her, and begged her to let me creep under her skirt. She told me I might, so long as I said nothing to anyone about it. She had very little on, and I fingered her genitals and the lower part of her body, which struck me as very queer. After this I was left with a burning and tormenting curiosity to see the female body. I can still remember the intense excitement with which I waited at the baths (which I was still allowed to go to with the governess and my sisters) for the governess to undress and get into the water. I can remember more things from my sixth year onward. At that time we had another governess, who was also young and good-looking. She had abscesses on her buttocks which she was in the habit of expressing at night. I used to wait eagerly for that moment, to appease my curiosity. It was just the same at the baths—though Fräulein Lina was more reserved than her predecessor." (In reply to a question which I threw in, "As a rule," the patient told me, "I did not sleep in her room, but mostly with my parents.") "I remember a scene which must have taken place when I was seven years old. We were sitting together one evening—the governess, the cook, another servant-girl, myself, and my brother, who was

---

2. Dr. Alfred Adler, who was formerly an analyst, once drew attention in a privately delivered paper to the peculiar importance which attaches to the *very first* communications made by patients. Here is an instance of this. The patient's opening words laid stress upon the influence exercised over him by men, that is to say, upon the part played in his life by homosexual object-choice; but immediately afterward they touched upon a second *motif*, which was to become of great importance later on, namely, the conflict between man and woman and the opposition of their interests. Even the fact that he remembered his first pretty governess by her surname, which happened to be a man's Christian name, must be taken into account in this connection. In middle-class circles in Vienna it is more usual to call a governess by her Christian name, and it is by that name that she is more commonly remembered.

eighteen months younger than me. The young women were talking, and I suddenly became aware of Fräulein Lina saying: 'It could be done with the little one; but Paul' (that was I) 'is too clumsy, he would be sure to miss it.' I did not understand clearly what was meant, but I felt the slight and began to cry. Lina comforted me, and told me how a girl, who had done something of the kind with a little boy she was in charge of, had been put in prison for several months. I do not believe she actually did anything wrong with me, but I took a great many liberties with her. When I got into her bed I used to uncover her and touch her, and she made no objections. She was not very intelligent, and clearly had very strong sexual cravings. At twenty-three she had already had a child. She afterward married its father, so that today she is a Frau Hofrat. Even now I often see her in the street.

"When I was six years old I already suffered from erections, and I know that once I went to my mother to complain about them. I know too that in doing so I had some misgivings to get over, for I had a feeling that there was some connection between this subject and my ideas and inquisitiveness, and at that time I used to have a morbid idea *that my parents knew my thoughts; I explained this to myself by supposing that I had spoken them out loud, without having heard myself do it.* I look on this as the beginning of my illness. There were certain people, girls, who pleased me very much, and I had a very strong wish *to see them naked.* But in wishing this I had *an uncanny feeling, as though something must happen if I thought such things, and as though I must do all sorts of things to prevent it.*"

(In reply to a question he gave an example of these fears: "For instance, *that my father might die.*") "Thoughts about my father's death occupied my mind from a very early age and for a long period of time, and greatly depressed me."

At this point I learned with astonishment that the patient's father, with whom his obsessional fears were still occupied at that actual time, had died several years previously.

The events in his sixth or seventh year which the patient described in the first hour of his treatment were not merely, as he supposed, the beginning of his illness, but were already the illness itself. It was a complete obsessional neurosis, wanting in no essential element, at once the nucleus and the prototype of the later disorder—an elementary organism, as it were, the study of which could alone enable us to obtain a grasp of the complicated organization of his subsequent illness. The child, as we have seen, was under the domination of a component of the sexual instinct, scoptophilia (the instinct of looking), as a result of which there was a constant recurrence in him of a very intense wish connected with persons of the female sex who pleased him—the wish, that is, to see them naked. This wish corresponds to the later obsessional or compulsive idea; and if the quality of compulsion was not yet present in it, this was because the ego had not yet placed itself in complete opposition to it and did not yet regard it as something foreign to itself. Nevertheless, opposition to this wish from some source or other was already in activity, for its occurrence was regularly accompanied by a painful affect. A conflict was evidently in progress in the mind of this young libertine. Side by side with the obsessive wish, and intimately associated with it, was an obsessive fear: every time he had a wish of this kind he could not help fearing that something dreadful would happen. This something dreadful was already clothed in a characteristic indeterminateness which was thenceforward to be an invariable feature of every manifestation of the neurosis. But in a child it is not hard to discover what it is that is veiled behind an indeterminateness of this kind. If the patient can once be induced to give a particular instance in place of the vague generalities which characterize an obsessional neurosis, it may be confidently assumed that the instance is the original and actual thing which has tried to hide itself behind the generalization. Our present patient's obsessive fear, therefore, when restored to its original meaning, would run as follows: "If I have this wish to see a woman naked, my father will have to die." The painful affect was distinctly colored with a tinge of uncanniness and superstition, and was already beginning to give rise to impulses to do something to ward off the impending evil. These impulses were subsequently to develop into the *protective measures* which the patient adopted.

We find, therefore: an erotic instinct and a revolt against it; a wish which has not yet become compulsive and, struggling against it, a fear which is already compulsive; a painful affect and an impulsion toward the performance of defensive acts. The inventory of the neurosis has reached its full muster. Indeed, something more is present, namely, a kind of *delusional formation* or *delirium* with the strange content that his parents knew his thoughts because he spoke them out loud without his hearing himself do it. We shall not go far astray if we suppose that in making this attempt at an explanation the child had some inkling of those remarkable mental processes which we describe as unconscious and which we cannot dispense with if we are to throw any scientific light upon this obscure subject. "I speak my thoughts out loud, without hearing them" sounds like a projection into the outer world of our own hypothesis that he had thoughts without knowing anything about them; it sounds like an endopsychic perception of the repressed.

For the situation is clear. This elementary neurosis of childhood already involved a problem and an apparent absurdity, like any complicated neurosis of maturity. What can have been the meaning of the child's idea that if he had this lascivious wish his father would have to die? Was it sheer nonsense? Or are there means of understanding the words and of looking upon them as a necessary consequence of earlier events and premises?

If we apply knowledge gained elsewhere to this case of childhood neurosis, we shall not be able to avoid the suspicion that in this instance as in others, that is to say, before the child had reached his sixth year, there had been conflicts and repressions, which had themselves been overtaken by amnesia, but had left behind them as a residuum the particular content of this obsessive fear. Later on we shall learn how far it is possible for us to rediscover those forgotten experiences or to reconstruct them with some degree of certainty. In the meantime stress may be laid on the fact, which is probably more than a mere coincidence, that the patient's infantile amnesia ended precisely with his sixth year.

To find a chronic obsessional neurosis beginning like this in early childhood, with lascivious wishes of this sort connected with uncanny apprehensions and an inclination to the performance of defensive acts, is no new thing to me. I have come across it in a number of other cases. It is absolutely typical, although probably not the only possible type. Before proceeding to the events of the second sitting, I should like to add one more word on the subject of the patient's early sexual experiences. It will hardly be disputed that they may be described as having been considerable both in themselves and in their consequences. But it has been the same with the other cases of obsessional neurosis that I have had the opportunity of analyzing. Such cases, unlike those of hysteria, invariably possess the characteristic of premature sexual activity. Obsessional neuroses make it much more obvious than hysterias that the factors which go to form a psychoneurosis are to be found in the patient's infantile sexual life and not in his present one. The current sexual life of an obsessional neurotic may often appear perfectly normal to a superficial observer; indeed, it frequently offers to the eye far fewer pathogenic elements and abnormalities than in the instance we are now considering.

The Great Obsessive Fear

"I think I shall begin today with the experience which was the direct occasion of my coming to you. It was in August during the maneuvers at ———. I had been suffering before, and tormenting myself with all kinds of obsessional thoughts, but they had quickly passed off during the maneuvers. I was keen to show the regular officers that people like me had not only learned a good deal but could stand a good deal too. One day we started from ——— on a short march. During a halt I lost my pince-nez, and, although I could easily have found them,

I did not want to delay our start, so I gave them up. But I wired to my opticians in Vienna to send me another pair by the next post. During that same halt I sat between two officers, one of whom, a captain with a Czech name, was to be of no small importance to me. I had a kind of dread of him, *for he was obviously fond of cruelty.* I do not say he was a bad man, but at the officers' mess he had repeatedly defended the introduction of corporal punishment, so that I had been obliged to disagree with him very sharply. Well, during this halt we got into conversation, and the captain told me he had read of a specially horrible punishment used in the East . . ."

Here the patient broke off, got up from the sofa, and begged me to spare him the recital of the details. I assured him that I myself had no taste whatever for cruelty, and certainly had no desire to torment him, but that naturally I could not grant him something which was beyond my power. He might just as well ask me to give him the moon. The overcoming of resistances was a law of the treatment, and on no consideration could it be dispensed with. (I had explained the idea of "resistance" to him at the beginning of the hour, when he told me there was much in himself which he would have to overcome if he was to relate this experience of his.) I went on to say that I would do all I could, nevertheless, to guess the full meaning of any hints he gave me. Was he perhaps thinking of impalement?—"No, not that; . . . the criminal was tied up . . ."—he expressed himself so indistinctly that I could not immediately guess in what position—". . . a pot was turned upside down on his buttocks . . . some *rats* were put into it . . . and they . . ."—he had again got up, and was showing every sign of horror and resistance—" . . . *bored their way in* . . ."—Into his anus, I helped him out.

At all the more important moments while he was telling his story his face took on a very strange, composite expression. I could only interpret it as one of *horror at pleasure of his own of which he himself was unaware.* He proceeded with the greatest difficulty: "At that moment the idea flashed through my mind *that this was happening to a person who was very dear to me.*"

In answer to a direct question he said that it was not he himself who was carrying out the punishment, but that it was being carried out as it were impersonally. After a little prompting I learned that the person to whom this "idea" of his related was the lady whom he admired.

He broke off his story in order to assure me that these thoughts were entirely foreign and repugnant to him, and to tell me that everything which had followed in their train had passed through his mind with the most extraordinary rapidity. Simultaneously with the idea there always appeared a "sanction," that is to say, the defensive measure which he was obliged to adopt in order to prevent the fantasy from being fulfilled. When the captain had spoken of this ghastly punishment, he went on, and these ideas had come into his head, by employing his usual formulas (a "But" accompanied by a gesture of repudiation, and the phrase "Whatever are you thinking of?") he had just succeeded in warding off *both* of them.

This "both" took me aback, and it has no doubt also mystified the reader. For so far we have heard only of one idea—of the rat punishment being carried out upon the lady. He was now obliged to admit that a second idea had occurred to him simultaneously, namely, the idea of the punishment also being applied to his father. As his father had died many years previously, this obsessive fear was much more nonsensical even than the first, and accordingly it had attempted to escape being confessed to for a little while longer.

That evening, he continued, the same captain had handed him a packet that had arrived by the post and had said: "Lieutenant A has paid the charges for you. You must pay him back." The packet had contained the pince-nez that he had wired for. At that instant, however, a "sanction" had taken shape in his mind, namely, *that he was not to pay back the money* or it would happen—(that is, the fantasy about the rats would come true as regards his father and the lady). And immediately, in accordance with a type of procedure with which he was familiar, to combat this sanction there had arisen a command in the shape of a vow: *"You must pay back the 3.80 crowns to Lieutenant A."* He had said these words to himself almost half aloud.

Two days later the maneuvers had come to an end. He had spent the whole of the intervening time in efforts at repaying Lieutenant A the small amount in question; but a succession of difficulties of an apparently *external* nature had arisen to prevent it. First he had tried to effect the payment through another officer who had been going to the post office. But he had been much relieved when this officer brought him back the money, saying that he had not met Lieutenant A there, for this method of fulfilling his vow had not satisfied him, as it did not correspond with the wording, which ran: *"You* must pay back the money to Lieutenant A." Finally, he had met Lieutenant A, the person he was looking for; but he had refused to accept the money, declaring that he had not paid anything for him, and had nothing whatever to do with the post, which was the business of Lieutenant B. This had thrown my patient into great perplexity, for it meant that he was unable to keep his vow, since it had been based upon false premises. He had excogitated a very curious means of getting out of his difficulty, namely, that he should go to the post office with both the men, A and B, that A should give the young lady there the 3.80 crowns, that the young lady should give them to B, and that then he himself should pay back the 3.80 crowns to A according to the wording of his vow.

It would not surprise me to hear that at this point the reader had ceased to be able to follow. For even the detailed account which the patient gave me of the external events of these days and of his reactions to them was full of self-contradictions and sounded hopelessly confused. It was only when he told the story for the third time that I could get him to realize its obscurities and could lay bare the errors of memory and the displacements in which he had become involved. I shall spare myself the trouble of reproducing these details, the essentials of which we shall easily be able to pick up later on, and I will only add that at the end of this second sitting the patient behaved as though he were dazed and bewildered. He repeatedly addressed me as "Captain," probably because at the beginning of the hour I had told him that I myself was not fond of cruelty like Captain M., and that I had no intention of tormenting him unnecessarily.

The only other piece of information that I obtained from him during this hour was that from the very first, on all the previous occasions on which he had had a fear that something would happen to people he loved no less than on the present one, he had referred the punishments not only to our present life but also to eternity—to the next world. Up to his fourteenth or fifteenth year he had been devoutly religious, but from that time on he had gradually developed into the freethinker that he was today. He reconciled the contradiction between his beliefs and his obsessions by saying to himself: "What do you know about the next world? Nothing *can* be known about it. You're not risking anything—so do it." This form of argument seemed unobjectionable to a man who was in other respects particularly clearheaded, and in this way he exploited the uncertainty of reason in the face of these questions to the benefit of the religious attitude which he had outgrown.

At the third sitting he completed his very characteristic story of his efforts at fulfilling his obsessional vow. That evening the last gathering of officers had taken place before the end of the maneuvers. It had fallen to him to reply to the toast of "The Gentlemen of the Reserve." He had spoken well, but as if he were in a dream, for at the back of his mind he was being incessantly tormented by his vow. He had spent a terrible night. Arguments and counterarguments had struggled with one another. The chief argument, of course, had been that the premise upon which his vow had been based—that Lieutenant A had paid the money for him—had proved to be false. However, he had consoled himself with the thought that the business was not yet finished, as A would be riding with him next morning part of the way to the railway station at P——, so that he would still have time to ask him the necessary favor. As a matter of fact he had not done this, and had allowed A to go off without him; but he had given instructions to his orderly to let A know that he intended to pay him a visit that afternoon. He himself had reached the station at half past nine in the morning. He had deposited his luggage there and had seen to various things he had to do in the small town, with the intention of afterward paying his visit to A. The village in which A was stationed was about an hour's drive from the town of P——. The railway journey to the place where the post office was would take three hours. He had calculated, therefore, that the execution of his complicated plan would just leave him time to catch the evening train from P—— to Vienna. The ideas that were struggling within him had been, on the one hand, that he was simply being cowardly and was obviously only trying to save himself the unpleasantness of asking A to make the sacrifice in question and of cutting a foolish figure before him, and that that was why he was disregarding his vow; and, on the other hand, that it would, on the contrary, be cowardly of him to fulfill his vow, since he only wanted to do so in order to be left in peace by his obsessions. When in the course of his deliberations, the patient added, he found the arguments so evenly balanced as these, it was his custom to allow his actions to be decided by chance events as though by the hand of God. When, therefore, a porter at the station had addressed him with the words, "Ten o'clock train, sir?" he had answered "Yes," and in fact had gone off by the ten o'clock train. In this way he had produced a *fait accompli* and felt greatly relieved. He had proceeded to book a seat for luncheon in the restaurant car. At the first station they had stopped at it had suddenly struck him that he still had time to get out, wait for the next down train, travel back in it to P——, drive to the place where Lieutenant A was quartered, from there make the three hours' train journey with him to the post office, and so forth. It had only been the consideration that he had booked his seat for luncheon with the steward of the restaurant car that had prevented his carrying out this design. He had not abandoned it, however; he had only put off getting out until a later stop. In this way he had struggled through from station to station, till he had reached one at which it had seemed to him impossible to get out because he had relatives living there. He had then determined to travel through to Vienna, to look up his friend there and lay the whole matter before him, and then, after his friend had made his decision, to catch the night train back to P——. When I expressed a doubt whether this would have been feasible, he assured me that he would have had half an hour to spare between the arrival of the one train and the departure of the other. When he had arrived in Vienna, however, he had failed to find his friend at the restaurant at which he had counted on meeting him, and had not reached his friend's house till eleven o'clock at night. He told him the whole story that very night. His friend had held up his hands in amazement to think that he could still be in doubt whether he was suffering from an obsession, and had calmed him down for the night, so that he had slept excellently. Next morning they had gone together to the post office, to dispatch the 3.80 crowns to ——, the post office at which the packet containing the pince-nez had arrived.

It was this last statement which provided me with a starting point from which I could begin straightening out the various distortions involved in his story. After his friend had brought him to his senses he had dispatched the small sum of money in question neither to Lieutenant A nor to Lieutenant B, but direct to the post office. He must therefore have known that he owed the amount of the charges due upon the packet *to no one but the official at the post office,* and he must have known this before he started on his journey. It turned out that in fact he had known it before the captain made his request and before he himself made his vow; for he now remembered that a few hours *before* meeting the cruel captain he had had occasion to introduce himself to another captain, who had told him how matters actually stood. This officer, on hearing his name, had told him that he had been at the post office a short time before, and that the young lady there had asked him whether he knew a

Lieutenant H. (the patient, in fact), for whom a packet had arrived, to be paid for on delivery. The officer had replied that he did not, but the young lady had been of opinion that she could trust the unknown lieutenant and had said that in the meantime she would pay the charges herself. It had been in this way that the patient had come into possession of the pince-nez he had ordered. The cruel captain had made a mistake when, as he handed him over the packet, he had asked him to pay back the 3.80 crowns to A, and the patient must have known it was a mistake. In spite of this he had made a vow founded upon this mistake, a vow that was bound to be broken. In so doing he had suppressed to himself, just as in telling the story he had suppressed to me, the episode of the other captain and the existence of the trusting young lady at the post office. I must admit that when this correction has been made his behavior becomes even more senseless and unintelligible than before.

After he had left his friend and returned to his family his doubts had overtaken him afresh. His friend's arguments, he saw, had been no different from his own, and he was under no delusion that his temporary relief was attributable to anything more than his friend's personal influence. His determination to consult a doctor was woven into his delirium in the following ingenious manner. He thought he would get a doctor to give him a certificate to the effect that it was necessary for him, in order to recover his health, to perform some such action as he had planned in connection with Lieutenant A; and the lieutenant would no doubt let himself be persuaded by the certificate into accepting the 3.80 crowns from him. The chance that one of my books happened to fall into his hands just at that moment directed his choice to me. There was no question of getting a certificate from me, however, all that he asked of me was, very reasonably, to be freed of his obsessions. Many months later, when his resistance was at its height, he once more felt a temptation to travel to P—— after all, to look up Lieutenant A and to go through the farce of returning him the money.

Initiation into the Nature of the Treatment

The reader must not expect to hear at once what light I have to throw upon the patient's strange and senseless obsessions about the rats. The true technique of psychoanalysis requires the physician to suppress his curiosity and leaves the patient complete freedom in choosing the order in which topics shall succeed each other during the treatment. At the fourth sitting, accordingly, I received the patient with the question: "And how do you intend to proceed today?"

"I have decided to tell you something which I consider most important and which has tormented me from the very first." He then told me at great length the story of the last illness of his father, who had died of emphysema nine years previously. One evening, thinking that the condition was one which would come to a crisis, he had asked the doctor when the danger could be regarded as over. "The evening of the day after tomorrow," had been the reply. It had never entered his head that his father might not survive that limit. At half past eleven at night he had lain down for an hour's rest. He had woken up at one o'clock, and had been told by a medical friend that his father had died. He had reproached himself with not having been present at his death; and the reproach had been intensified when the nurse told him that his father had spoken his name once during the last days, and had said to her as she came up to the bed: "Is that Paul?" He had thought he noticed that his mother and sisters had been inclined to reproach themselves in a similar way; but they had never spoken about it. At first, however, the reproach had not tormented him. For a long time he had not realized the fact of his father's death. It had constantly happened that, when he heard a good joke, he would say to himself: "I must tell Father that." His imagination, too, had been occupied with his father, so that often, when there was a knock at the door, he would think: "Here comes Father," and when he walked into a room he would expect to find his father in it. And although he had never forgotten that his father was dead, the prospect of seeing a ghostly apparition of this kind had had no terrors for him; on the contrary, he had greatly desired it. It had not been until eighteen months later that the recollection of his neglect had recurred to him and begun to torment him terribly, so that he had come to treat himself as a criminal. The occasion of this happening had been the death of an aunt by marriage and of a visit of condolence that he had paid at her house. From that time forward he had extended the structure of his obsessional thoughts so as to include the next world. The immediate consequence of this development had been that he became seriously incapacitated from working. He told me that the only thing that had kept him going at that time had been the consolation given him by his friend, who had always brushed his self-reproaches aside on the ground that they were grossly exaggerated. Hearing this, I took the opportunity of giving him a first glance at the underlying principles of psychoanalytic therapy. When there is a *mésalliance,* I began, between an affect and its ideational content (in this instance, between the intensity of the self-reproach and the occasion for it), a layman will say that the affect is too great for the occasion—that it is exaggerated—and that consequently the inference following from the self-reproach (the inference, that is, that the patient is a criminal) is false. On the contrary, the physician says: "No. The affect is justified. The sense of guilt cannot in itself be further criticized. But it belongs to another content, which is unknown (*unconscious*), and which requires to be looked for. The known ideational content has only got into its actual position owing to a mistaken association. We are not used to feeling strong affects without their having any ideational content, and therefore, if the content is missing, we seize as a substitute upon another content which is in some way or other suitable, much as our police, when they cannot catch the right murderer, arrest a wrong one instead. Moreover, this fact of there being a mistaken association is the only way of accounting for the powerlessness of logical processes in combating the tormenting idea." I concluded by admitting that this new way of looking at the matter gave immediate rise to some hard problems; for how could he admit that his self-reproach of being a criminal toward his father was justified, when he must know that as a matter of fact he had never committed any crime against him?

At the next sitting the patient showed great interest in what I had said, but ventured, so he told me, to bring forward a few doubts.—How, he asked, could the information that the self-reproach, the sense of guilt, was justified have a therapeutic effect?—I explained that it was not the information that had this effect, but the discovery of the unknown content to which the self-reproach was really attached.—Yes, he said, that was the precise point to which his question had been directed.—I then made some short observations upon *the psychological differences between the conscious and the unconscious,* and upon the fact that everything conscious was subject to a process of wearing-away, while what was unconscious was relatively unchangeable; and I illustrated my remarks by pointing to the antiques standing about in my room. They were, in fact, I said, only objects found in a tomb, and their burial had been their preservation: the destruction of Pompeii was only beginning now that it had been dug up.—Was there any guarantee, he next inquired, of what one's attitude would be toward what was discovered? One man, he thought, would no doubt behave in such a way as to get the better of his self-reproach, but another would not.—No, I said, it followed from the nature of the circumstances that in every case the affect would for the most part be overcome during the progress of the work itself. Every effort was made to preserve Pompeii, whereas people were anxious to be rid of tormenting ideas like his.—He had said to himself, he went on, that a self-reproach could only arise from a breach of a person's own inner moral principles and not from that of any external ones.—I agreed, and said that the man who merely breaks an external law often regards himself as a hero.—Such an occurrence, he continued, was thus only possible where a *disintegration of the personality* was already present. Was there a possibility of his effecting a reintegration of his personality? If this could be done, he thought he would be able to make a success of his life, perhaps a better one than most people.—I replied that I was in complete agreement with this notion of a splitting of his personality. He had only to assimilate this new contrast, between a moral self and an evil one, with the contrast I had already mentioned, between the conscious and the unconscious. The moral self was the conscious, the evil self was the unconscious.—He then said that, though he considered himself a moral person, he could quite definitely remember having done things in his *childhood* which came from his other self. —I remarked that here he had incidentally hit upon one of the chief characteristics of the unconscious, namely, its relation to the *infantile*. The unconscious, I explained, *was* the infantile; it was that part of the self which had become separated off from it in infancy, which had not shared the later stages of its development, and which had in consequence become *repressed*. It was the derivatives of this repressed unconscious that were responsible for the involuntary thoughts which constituted his illness. He might now, I added, discover yet another characteristic of the unconscious; it was a discovery which I should be glad to let him make for himself.—He found nothing more to say in this immediate connection, but instead he expressed a doubt whether it was possible to undo modifications of such long standing. What, in particular, could be done against his idea about the next world, for it could not be refuted by logic?—I told him I did not dispute the gravity of his case nor the significance of his pathological constructions; but at the same time his youth was very much in his favor as well as the intactness of his personality. In this connection I said a word or two upon the good opinion I had formed of him and this gave him visible pleasure.

At the next sitting he began by saying that he must tell me an event in his childhood. From the age of seven, as he had already told me, he had had a fear that his parents guessed his thoughts, and this fear had in fact persisted all through his life. When he was twelve years old he had been in love with a little girl, the sister of a friend of his. (In answer to a question he said that his love had not been sensual; he had not wanted to see her naked for she was too small.) But she had not shown him as much affection as he had desired. And thereupon the idea had come to him that she would be kind to him if some misfortune were to befall him; and as an instance of such a misfortune his father's death had forced itself upon his mind. He had at once rejected the idea with energy. And even now he could not admit the possibility that what had arisen in this way could have been a "wish"; it had clearly been no more than a "connection of thought."—By way of objection I asked him why, if it had not been a wish, he had repudiated it.—Merely, he replied, on account of the content of the idea, the notion that his father might die.—I remarked that he was treating the phrase as though it were one that involved lèse-majesté; it was well known, of course, that it was equally punishable to say "The Emperor is an ass" or to disguise the forbidden words by saying "If anyone says, etc., . . . then he will have me to reckon with." I added that I could easily insert the idea which he had so energetically repudiated into a context which would exclude the possibility of any such repudiation; for instance, "If my father dies, I shall kill myself upon his grave."—He was shaken, but did not abandon his objection. I therefore broke off the argument with the remark that I felt sure this had not been the first occurrence of his idea of his father's dying; it had evidently originated at an earlier date, and some day we should have to trace back its history.—He then proceeded to tell me that a precisely similar thought had flashed through his mind a second time, six months before his father's death. At that time he had already been in love with his lady, but financial obstacles made it impossible to think of an alliance with her. The idea had then occurred to him that *his father's death might make him rich enough to marry her.* In defending himself against this idea he had gone to the length of wishing that his father might leave him nothing at all so that he might have no compensation for his terrible loss. The same idea, though in a much milder form, had come to him

for a third time, on the day before his father's death. He had
then thought: "Now I may be going to lose what I love most";
and then had come the contradiction: "No, there is someone
else whose loss would be even more painful to you."[3] These
thoughts surprised him very much, for he was quite certain that
his father's death could never have been an object of his desire
but only of his fear.—After his forcible enunciation of these
words I thought it advisable to bring a fresh piece of theory to
his notice. According to psychoanalytical theory, I told him,
every fear corresponded to a former wish which was now
repressed; we were therefore obliged to believe the exact contrary of what he had asserted. This would also fit in with
another theoretical requirement, namely, that the unconscious
must be the precise contrary of the conscious.—He was much
agitated at this and very incredulous. He wondered how he
could possibly have had such a wish, considering that he loved
his father more than anyone else in the world; there could be no
doubt that he would have renounced all his own prospects of
happiness if by so doing he could have saved his father's life.
—I answered that it was precisely such intense love as his that
was the condition of the repressed hatred. In the case of people
to whom he felt indifferent he would certainly have no difficulty
in maintaining side by side inclinations to a moderate liking and
to an equally moderate dislike: supposing, for instance, that he
were an official, he might think that his chief was agreeable as
a superior, but at the same time pettifogging as a lawyer and
inhuman as a judge. Shakespeare makes Brutus speak in a similar way of Julius Caesar: "As Caesar loved me, I weep for him;
as he was fortunate, I rejoice at it; as he was valiant, I honor
him; but as he was ambitious, I slew him." But these words
already strike us as rather strange, and for the very reason that
we had imagined Brutus's feeling for Caesar as something deeper.
In the case of someone who was closer to him, of his wife for

---

3. There is here an unmistakable indication of an opposition between the two objects of his love,
his father and the "lady."

instance, he would wish his feelings to be unmixed, and consequently, as was only human, he would overlook her faults, since they might make him dislike her—he would ignore them as though he were blind to them. So it was precisely the intensity of his love that would not allow his hatred—though to give it such a name was to caricature the feeling—to remain conscious. To be sure, the hatred must have a source, and to discover that source was certainly a problem; his own statements pointed to the time when he was afraid that his parents guessed his thoughts. On the other hand, too, it might be asked why this intense love of his had not succeeded in extinguishing his hatred, as usually happened where there were two opposing impulses. We could only presume that the hatred must flow from some source, must be connected with some particular cause, which made it indestructible. On the one hand, then, connection of this sort must be keeping his hatred for his father alive, while on the other hand, his intense love prevented it from becoming conscious. Therefore nothing remained for it but to exist in the unconscious, though it was able from time to time to flash out for a moment into consciousness.

He admitted that all of this sounded quite plausible, but he was naturally not in the very least convinced by it.[4] He would venture to ask, he said, how it was that an idea of this kind could have remissions, how it could appear for a moment when he was twelve years old, and again when he was twenty, and then once more two years later, this time for good. He could not believe that his hostility had been extinguished in the intervals, and yet during them there had been no sign of self-reproaches. —To this I replied that whenever anyone asked a question like that, he was already prepared with an answer; he needed only to be encouraged to go on talking.—He then proceeded, some-

---

4. It is never the aim of discussions like this to create conviction. They are only intended to bring the repressed complexes into consciousness, to set the conflict going in the field of conscious mental activity, and to facilitate the emergence of fresh material from the unconscious. A sense of conviction is only attained after the patient has himself worked over the reclaimed material, and so long as he is not fully convinced the material must be considered as unexhausted.

what disconnectedly as it seemed, to say that he had been his father's best friend, and that his father had been his. Except on a few subjects, upon which fathers and sons usually hold aloof from one another.—(What could he mean by that?)—there had been a greater intimacy between them than there now was between him and his best friend. As regards the lady on whose account he had slighted his father in that idea of his, it was true that he had loved her very much, but he had never felt really sensual wishes toward her, such as he had constantly had in his childhood. Altogether, in his childhood his sensual impulses had been much stronger than during his puberty.—At this I told him I thought he had now produced the answer we were waiting for, and had at the same time discovered the third great characteristic of the unconscious. The source from which his hostility to his father derived its indestructibility was evidently something in the nature of *sensual desires,* and in that connection he must have felt his father as in some way or other an *interference.* A conflict of this kind, I added, between sensuality and childish love was entirely typical. The remissions he had spoken of had occurred because the premature explosion of his sensual feelings had had as its immediate consequence a considerable diminution of their violence. It was not until he was once more seized with intense erotic desires that his hostility reappeared again owing to the revival of the old situation. I then got him to agree that I had not led him on to the subject either of childhood or of sex, but that he had raised them both of his own free will. —He then went on to ask why he had not simply come to a decision, at the time he was in love with the lady, that his father's interference with that love could not for a moment weigh against his love of his father.—I replied that it was scarcely possible to destroy a person *in absentia.* Such a decision would only have been possible if the wish that he took objection to had made its first appearance on that occasion; whereas, as a matter of fact, it was *a long-repressed wish,* toward which he could not behave otherwise than he had formerly done, and which was consequently immune from destruction. This wish (to get rid of his father as being an interference) must have originated at a time when circumstances had been very different—at a time, perhaps, when he had not loved his father more than the person whom he desired sensually, or when he was incapable of making a clear decision. It must have been in his very early childhood, therefore, before he had reached the age of six, and before the date at which his memory became continuous; and things must have remained in the same state ever since.—With this piece of construction our discussion was broken off for the time being.

At the next sitting, which was the seventh, he took up the same subject once more. He could not believe, he said, that he had ever entertained such a wish against his father. He remembered a story of Sudermann's, he went on, that had made a deep impression upon him. In this story there was a woman who, as she sat by her sister's sickbed, felt a wish that her sister should die so that she herself might marry her husband. The woman thereupon committed suicide, thinking she was not fit to live after being guilty of such baseness. He could understand this, he said, and it would be only right if his thoughts were the death of him, for he deserved nothing less.[5]—I remarked that it was well known to us that patients derived a certain satisfaction from their sufferings, so that in reality they all resisted their own recovery to some extent. He must never lose sight of the fact that a treatment like ours proceeded to the accompaniment of a *constant resistance;* I should be repeatedly reminding him of this fact.

He then went on to say that he would like to speak of a criminal act, in the author of which he did not recognize himself, though he quite clearly recollected doing it. He quoted a saying of Nietzsche's: " 'I did this,' says my Memory. 'I cannot have done this,' says my Pride and remains inexorable. In the end— Memory yields." "Well," he continued, "my memory has *not*

5. This sense of guilt involves the most glaring contradiction of his opening denial that he had ever entertained such an evil wish against his father. This is a common type of reaction to repressed material which has become conscious: the "No" with which the fact is first denied is immediately followed by a confirmation of it, though, to begin with, only an indirect one.

yielded on this point."—"That is because you derive pleasure from your reproaches as being a means of self-punishment." —"My younger brother—I am really very fond of him now, and he is causing me a great deal of worry just at present, for he wants to make what I consider a preposterous match; I have thought before now of going and killing the person so as to prevent his marrying her—well, my younger brother and I used to fight a lot when we were children. We were very fond of one another at the same time, and were inseparable; but I was plainly filled with jealousy, as he was the stronger and better-looking of the two and consequently the favorite."—"Yes. You have already given me a description of a scene of jealousy in connection with Fräulein Lina."—"Very well then, on some such occasion (it was certainly before I was eight years old, for I was not going to school yet, which I began to do when I was eight)—on some such occasion, this is what I did. We both had toy guns of the usual make. I loaded mine with the ramrod and told him that if he looked up the barrel he would see something. Then, while he was looking in, I pulled the trigger. He was hit on the forehead and not hurt; but I had meant to hurt him very much indeed. Afterward I was quite beside myself, and threw myself on the ground and asked myself how ever I could have done such a thing. But I *did* do it."—I took the opportunity of urging my case. If he had preserved the recollection of an action so foreign to him as this, he could not, I maintained, deny the possibility of something similar, which he had now forgotten entirely, having happened at a still earlier age in relation to his father.—He then told me he was aware of having felt other vindictive impulses, this time toward the lady he admired so much, of whose character he painted a glowing picture. It might be true, he said, that she could not love easily; but she was reserving her whole self for the one man to whom she would some day belong. She did not love him. When he had become certain of that, a conscious fantasy had taken shape in his mind of how he should grow very rich and marry someone else, and should then take her to call on the lady in order to hurt her feelings. But at that point the fantasy had broken down, for he had been obliged to own to himself that the other woman, his wife, was completely indifferent to him; then his thoughts had become confused, till finally it had been clearly borne in upon him that this other woman would have to die. In this fantasy, just as in his attempt upon his brother, he recognized the quality of *cowardice* which was so particularly horrible to him.—In the further course of our conversation I pointed out to him that he ought logically to consider himself as in no way responsible for any of these traits in his character; for all of these reprehensible impulses originated from his infancy, and were only derivatives of his infantile character surviving in his unconscious; and he must know that moral responsibility could not be applied to children. It was only by a process of development, I added, that a man, with his moral responsibility, grew up out of the sum of his infantile predispositions.[6] He expressed a doubt, however, whether all his evil impulses had originated from that source. But I promised to prove it to him in the course of the treatment.

He went on to adduce the fact of his illness having become so enormously intensified since his father's death; and I said I agreed with him insofar as I regarded his sorrow at his father's death as the chief source of the *intensity* of his illness. His sorrow had found, as it were, a pathological expression in his illness. Whereas, I told him, a normal period of mourning would last from one to two years, a pathological one like his would last indefinitely.

This is as much of the present case history as I am able to report in a detailed and consecutive manner. It coincides roughly with the expository portion of the treatment; this lasted in all for more than eleven months.

---

6. I only produced these arguments so as once more to demonstrate to myself their inefficacy. I cannot understand how other psychotherapists can assert that they successfully combat neuroses with such weapons as these.

Some Obsessional Ideas and Their Explanation

Obsessional ideas, as is well known, have an appearance of being either without motive or without meaning, just as dreams do. The first problem is how to give them a sense and a status in the mental life of the individual, so as to make them comprehensible and even obvious. The problem of translating them may seem insoluble; but we must never let ourselves be misled by that illusion. The wildest and most eccentric obsessional or compulsive ideas can be cleared up if they are investigated deeply enough. The solution is effected by bringing the obsessional ideas into temporal relationship with the patient's experiences, that is to say, by inquiring when a particular obsessional idea made its first appearance and in what external circumstances it is apt to recur. When, as so often happens, an obsessional idea has not succeeded in establishing itself permanently, the task of cleaning it up is correspondingly simplified. We can easily convince ourselves that, when once the interconnections between an obsessional idea and the patient's experiences have been discovered, there will be no difficulty in obtaining access to whatever else may be puzzling or worth knowing in the pathological structure we are dealing with—its meaning, the mechanism of its origin, and its derivation from the preponderant motive forces of the patient's mind.

As a particularly clear example I will begin with one of the *suicidal impulses* which appeared so frequently in our patient. This instance almost analyzed itself in the telling. He had once, he told me, lost some weeks of study owing to his lady's absence: she had gone away to nurse her grandmother, who was seriously ill. Just as he was in the middle of a very hard piece of work the idea had occurred to him: "If you received a command to take your examination this term at the first possible opportunity, you might manage to obey it. But if you were commanded to cut your throat with a razor, what then?" He had at once become aware that this command had already been given, and was hurrying to the cupboard to fetch his razor when he thought: "No, it's not so simple as that. You must go and kill the old woman." Upon that, he had fallen to the ground, beside himself with horror.

In this instance the connection between the compulsive idea and the patient's life is contained in the opening words of his story. His lady was absent, while he was working very hard for an examination so as to bring the possibility of an alliance with her nearer. While he was working he was overcome by a longing for his absent lady, and he thought of the cause of her absence. And now there came over him something which, if he had been a normal man, would probably have been some kind of feeling of annoyance against her grandmother: "Why must the old woman get ill just at the very moment when I'm longing for *her* so frightfully?" We must suppose that something similar but far more intense passed through our patient's mind—an unconscious fit of rage which could combine with his longing and find expression in the exclamation: "Oh, I should like to go and kill that old woman for robbing me of my love!" Thereupon followed the command: "Kill yourself, as a punishment for these savage and murderous passions!" The whole process then passed into the obsessional patient's consciousness accompanied by the most violent affect and *in a reverse order*—the punitive command coming first, and the mention of the guilty outburst afterward. I cannot think that this attempt at an explanation will seem forced or that it involves many hypothetical elements.

Another impulse, which might be described as indirectly suicidal and which was of longer duration, was not so easily explicable. For its relation to the patient's experiences succeeded in concealing itself behind one of those purely external associations which are so repellent to our consciousness. One day while he was away on his summer holidays the idea suddenly occurred to him that he was too fat [German *"dick"*] and that he must *make himself thinner.* So he began getting up from table before the pudding came round and tearing along the road without a hat in the blazing heat of an August sun. Then he would dash up a mountain at the double, till, dripping with perspiration, he was forced to come to a stop. On one occasion his suicidal intentions actually emerged without any disguise from behind this mania for getting thinner: as he was standing on the edge of a steep precipice he suddenly received a command to jump over, which would have been certain death. Our patient could think of no explanation of this senseless obsessional behavior until it suddenly occurred to him that at that time his lady had also been stopping at the same resort; but she had been in the company of an English cousin, who was very attentive to her and of whom the patient had been very jealous. This cousin's name was Richard, and, according to the usual practice in England, he was known as *Dick*. Our patient, then, had wanted to kill this Dick; he had been far more jealous of him and enraged with him than he could admit to himself, and that was why he had imposed on himself this course of banting by way of a punishment. This obsessional impulse may seem very different from the directly suicidal command which was discussed above, but they have nevertheless one important feature in common. For they both arose as reactions to a tremendous feeling of rage, which was inaccessible to the patient's consciousness and was directed against someone who had cropped up as an interference with the course of his love.

Some other of the patient's obsessions, however, though they too were centered upon his lady, exhibited a different mechanism and owed their origin to a different instinct. Besides his banting mania he produced a whole series of other obsessional activities at the period during which the lady was stopping at his summer resort; and, in part at least, these directly related to her. One day, when he was out with her in a boat and there was a stiff breeze blowing, he was obliged to make her put on his cap, because a command had been formulated in his mind that *nothing must happen to her*. This was a kind of *obsession for protecting,* and it bore other fruit besides this. Another time, as they were sitting together during a thunderstorm, he was obsessed, he could not tell why, with the necessity *for counting* up to forty or fifty between each flash of lightning and its accompanying thunderclap. On the day of her departure he knocked his foot against a stone lying in the road, and was *obliged* to put it out of the way by the side of the road, because the idea struck him that her carriage would be driving along the same road in a few hours' time and might come to grief against this stone. But a few minutes later it occurred to him that this was absurd, and he was *obliged* to go back and replace the stone in its original position in the middle of the road. After her departure he became a prey to an *obsession for understanding,* which made him a curse to all his companions. He forced himself to understand the precise meaning of every syllable that was addressed to him, as though he might otherwise be missing some priceless treasure. Accordingly he kept asking: "What was it you said just then?" And after it had been repeated to him he could not help thinking it had sounded different the first time, so he remained dissatisfied.

All of these products of his illness depended upon a certain circumstance which at that time dominated his relations to his lady. When he had been taking leave of her in Vienna before the summer holidays, she had said something which he had construed into a desire on her part to disown him before the rest of the company; and this had made him very unhappy. During her stay at the holiday resort there had been an opportunity for discussing the question, and the lady had been able to prove to him that these words of hers which he had misunderstood had on the contrary been intended to save him from being laughed at. This made him very happy again. The clearest allusion to this incident was contained in the obsession for understanding. It was constructed as though he were saying to himself: "After such an experience you must never misunderstand anyone again, if you want to spare yourself unnecessary pain." This resolution was not merely a generalization from a single occasion, but it was also displaced—perhaps on account of the lady's absence—from a single highly valued individual onto all the remaining inferior ones. And the obsession cannot have arisen solely from his satisfaction at the explanation she had given him; it must have expressed something else besides, for it ended in an unsatisfying doubt as to whether what he had heard had been correctly repeated.

The other compulsive commands that had been mentioned put us upon the track of this other element. His obsession for protecting can only have been a reaction—as an expression of remorse and penitence—to a contrary, that is, a hostile, impulse which he must have felt toward his lady before they had their *éclaircissement*. His obsession for counting during the thunderstorm can be interpreted, with the help of some material which he produced, as having been a defensive measure against fears that someone was in danger of death. The analysis of the obsessions which we first considered has already warned us to regard our patient's hostile impulses as particularly violent and as being in the nature of senseless rage; and now we find that even after their reconciliation his rage against the lady continued to play a part in the formation of his obsessions. His doubting mania as to whether he had heard correctly was an expression of the doubt still lurking in his mind as to whether he had really understood his lady correctly this time and as to whether he had been justified in taking her words as a proof of her affection for him. The doubt implied in his obsession for understanding was a doubt of her love. A battle between love and hate was raging in the lover's breast, and the object of both these feelings was one and the same person. The battle was represented in a plastic form by his compulsive and symbolic act of removing the stone from the road along which she was to drive, and then of undoing this deed of love by replacing the stone where it had lain, so that her carriage might come to grief against it and she herself be hurt. We shall not be forming a correct judgment of this second part of the compulsive act if we take it at its face value as having merely been a critical repudiation of a pathological action. The fact that it was accompanied by a sense of compulsion betrays it as having itself been a part of the pathological action, though a part which was determined by a motive contrary to that which produced the first part.

Compulsive acts like this, in two successive stages, of which the second neutralizes the first, are a typical occurrence in obsessional neuroses. The patient's consciousness naturally misunderstands them and puts forward a set of secondary motives to account for them—*rationalizes* them, in short. But their true significance lies in their being a representation of a conflict between two opposing impulses of approximately equal strength: and hitherto I have invariably found that this opposition has been one between love and hate. Compulsive acts of this sort are theoretically of special interest, for they show us a new type of symptom-formation. What regularly occurs in hysteria is that a compromise is arrived at which enables both the opposing tendencies to find expression simultaneously— which kills two birds with one stone; whereas here each of the two opposing tendencies finds satisfaction singly, first one and then the other, though naturally an attempt is made to establish some sort of logical connection (often in defiance of all logic) between the antagonists.[7]

The conflict between love and hatred showed itself in our patient by other signs as well. At the time of the revival of his piety he used to make up prayers for himself, which took up more and more time and eventually lasted for an hour and a half. The reason for this was that he found, like an inverted Balaam, that something always inserted itself into his pious phrases and turned them into their opposite. For instance, if he said, "May God protect him," an evil spirit would hurriedly

7. Another obsessional patient once told me the following story. He was walking one day in the park at Schönbrunn [the imperial palace on the outskirts of Vienna] when he kicked his foot against a branch that was lying on the ground. He picked it up and flung it into the hedge that bordered the path. On his way home he was suddenly seized with uneasiness that the branch in its new position might perhaps be projecting a little from the hedge and might cause an injury to someone passing by the same place after him. He was obliged to jump off his tram, hurry back to the park, find the place again, and put the branch back in its former position—although anyone else but the patient would have seen that, on the contrary, it was bound to be more dangerous to passersby in its original position than where he had put it in the hedge. The second and hostile act, which he carried out under compulsion, had clothed itself to his conscious view with the motives that really belonged to the first and philanthropic one.

insinuate a "not." On one such occasion the idea occurred to him of cursing instead, for in that case, he thought, the contrary words would be sure to creep in. His original intention, which had been repressed by his praying, was forcing its way through in this last idea of his. In the end he found his way out of his embarrassment by giving up the prayers and replacing them by a short formula concocted out of the initial letters or syllables of various prayers. He then recited this formula so quickly that nothing could slip into it.

He once brought me a dream which represented the same conflict in relation to his transference onto the physician. He dreamed that my mother was dead; he was anxious to offer me his condolences, but was afraid that in doing so he might break into *an impertinent laugh,* as he had repeatedly done on similar occasions in the past. He preferred, therefore, to leave a card on me with "p. c." written on it; but as he was writing them the letters turned into "p. f."[8]

The mutual antagonism between his feelings for his lady was too marked to have escaped his conscious perception entirely, although we may conclude from the obsessions in which it was manifested that he did not rightly appreciate the depth of his negative impulses. The lady had refused his first proposal, ten years earlier. Since then he had to his own knowledge passed through alternating periods, in which he either believed that he loved her intensely, or felt indifferent to her. Whenever in the course of the treatment he was faced by the necessity of taking some step which would bring him nearer the successful end of his courtship, his resistance usually began by taking the form of a conviction that after all he did not very much care for her—though this resistance, it is true, used soon to break down. Once when she was lying seriously ill in bed and he was most deeply concerned about her, there crossed his mind as he looked at her

---

8. [The customary abbreviations for *"pour condoler"* and *"pour féliciter"* respectively.] This dream provides the explanation of the compulsive laughter which so often occurs on mournful occasions and which is regarded as such an unaccountable phenomenon.

a wish that she might lie like that forever. He explained this idea by an ingenious piece of sophistry: maintaining that he had only wished her to be permanently ill so that he might be relieved of his intolerable fear that she would have a repeated succession of attacks. Now and then he used to occupy his imagination with daydreams, which he himself recognized as "fantasies of revenge" and felt ashamed of. Believing, for instance, that the lady set great store by the social standing of a suitor, he made up a fantasy in which she was married to a man of that kind, who was in some government office. He himself then entered the same department, and rose much more rapidly than her husband, who eventually became his subordinate. One day, his fantasy proceeded, this man committed some act of dishonesty. The lady threw herself at his feet and implored him to save her husband. He promised to do so; but at the same time informed her that it had only been for love of her that he had entered the service, because he had foreseen that such a movement would occur; and now that her husband was saved, his own mission was fulfilled and he would resign his post.

He produced other fantasies in which he did the lady some great service without her knowing that it was he who was doing it. In these he only recognized his affection, without sufficiently appreciating the origin and aim of his magnanimity, which was designed to repress his thirst for revenge, after the manner of Dumas' Count of Monte Cristo. Moreover he admitted that occasionally he was overcome by quite distinct impulses to do some mischief to the lady he admired. These impulses were mostly in abeyance when she was there, and only appeared in her absence.

The Exciting Cause of the Illness

One day the patient mentioned quite casually an event which I could not fail to recognize as the exciting cause of his illness, or at least as the immediate occasion of the attack which had begun some six years previously and had persisted to that day.

He himself had no notion that he had brought forward anything of importance. He could not remember that he had ever attached any importance to the event; and moreover he had never forgotten it. Such an attitude on his part calls for some theoretical consideration.

In hysteria it is the rule that the exciting causes of the illness are overtaken by amnesia no less than the infantile experiences by whose help the exciting causes are able to transform their affective energy into symptoms. And where the amnesia cannot be complete, it nevertheless subjects the recent traumatic exciting cause to a process of erosion and robs it at least of its most important components. In this amnesia we see the evidence of the repression which has taken place. The case is different in obsessional neuroses. The infantile preconditions of the neurosis may be overtaken by amnesia, though this is often an incomplete one; but the immediate occasions of the illness are, on the contrary, retained in the memory. Repression makes use of another, and in reality a simpler, mechanism. The trauma, instead of being forgotten, is deprived of its affective cathexis; so that what remains in consciousness is nothing but its ideational content, which is perfectly colorless and is judged to be unimportant. The distinction between what occurs in hysteria and in an obsessional neurosis lies in the psychological processes which we can reconstruct behind the phenomena; the *result* is almost always the same, for the colorless mnemonic content is rarely reproduced and plays no part in the patient's mental activity. In order to differentiate between the two kinds of repression we have on the surface nothing to rely upon but the patient's assurance that he has a feeling in the one case of having always known the thing and in the other of having long ago forgotten it.

For this reason it not uncommonly happens that obsessional neurotics, who are troubled with self-reproaches but have connected their affects with the wrong causes, will also tell the physician the true causes, without any suspicion that their self-reproaches have simply become detached from them. In relating such an incident they will sometimes add with astonishment or even with an air of pride: "But I think nothing of that." This happened in the first case of obsessional neurosis which gave me an insight many years ago into the nature of the malady. The patient, who was a government official, was troubled by innumerable scruples. He was the man whose compulsive act in connection with the branch in the park at Schönbrunn I have already described. I was struck by the fact that the florin notes with which he paid his consultation fees were invariably clean and smooth. (This was before we had a silver coinage in Austria.) I once remarked to him that one could always tell a government official by the brand-new florins that he drew from the State treasury, and he then informed me that his florins were by no means new, but that he had them ironed out at home. It was a matter of conscience with him, he explained, not to hand anyone dirty paper florins; for they harbored all sorts of dangerous bacteria and might do some harm to the recipient. At that time I already had a vague suspicion of the connection between neuroses and sexual life, so on another occasion I ventured to ask the patient how he stood in regard to that matter. "Oh, that's quite all right," he answered airily, "I'm not at all badly off in that respect. I play the part of a dear old uncle in a number of respectable families, and now and then I make use of my position to invite some young girl to go out with me for a day's excursion in the country. Then I arrange that we shall miss the train home and be obliged to spend the night out of town. I always engage two rooms—I do things most handsomely; but when the girl has gone to bed I go in to her and masturbate her with my fingers."—"But aren't you afraid of doing her some harm, fiddling about in her genitals with your dirty hand?"—At this he flared up: "Harm? Why, what harm should it do her? It hasn't done a single one of them any harm yet, and they've all of them enjoyed it. Some of them are married now, and it hasn't done them any harm at all."—He took my remonstrance in very bad part, and never appeared again. But I could only account for the contrast between his fastidiousness with the paper florins and his unscrupulousness in abusing the girls entrusted to him by supposing that the self-reproachful affect had become *displaced*. The aim of this displacement was obvious enough: if his self-reproaches had been allowed to remain where they belonged he would have had to abandon a form of sexual gratification to which he was probably impelled by some powerful infantile determinants. The displacement therefore ensured his deriving a considerable advantage from his illness [*paranosic gain*].

But I must now return to a more detailed examination of the exciting cause of our patient's illness. His mother had been brought up in a wealthy family with which she was distantly connected. This family carried on a large industrial concern. His father, at the time of his marriage, had been taken into the business, and had thus by his marriage made himself a fairly comfortable position. The patient had learned from some chaff exchanged between his parents (whose marriage was an extremely happy one) that his father, some time before making his mother's acquaintance, had made advances to a pretty but penniless girl of humble birth. So much by way of introduction. After his father's death the patient's mother told him one day that she had been discussing his future with her rich relations, and that one of her cousins had declared himself ready to let him marry one of his daughters when his education was completed; a business connection with the firm would offer him a brilliant opening in his profession. This family plan stirred up in him a conflict as to whether he should remain faithful to the lady he loved in spite of her poverty, or whether he should follow in his father's footsteps and marry the lovely, rich, and well-connected girl who had been assigned to him. And he resolved this conflict, which was in fact one between his love and the persisting influence of his father's wishes, by falling ill; or, to put it more correctly, by falling ill he avoided the task of resolving it in real life.

The proof that this view was correct lies in the fact that the chief result of his illness was an obstinate incapacity for work, which allowed him to postpone the completion of his education for years. But the results of such an illness are never unintentional; what appears to be the consequence of the illness is in reality the cause or motive of falling ill.

As was to be expected, the patient did not, to begin with, accept my elucidation of the matter. He could not imagine, he said, that the plan of marriage could have had any such affects: it had not made the slightest impression on him at the time. But in the further course of treatment he was forcibly brought to believe in the truth of my suspicion, and in a most singular manner. With the help of a transference fantasy, he experienced, as though it were new and belonged to the present, the very episode from the past which he had forgotten, or which had only passed through his mind unconsciously. There came an obscure and difficult period in the treatment; eventually it turned out that he had once met a young girl on the stairs in my house and had on the spot promoted her into being my daughter. She had pleased him, and he pictured to himself that the only reason I was so kind and incredibly patient with him was that I wanted to have him for a son-in-law. At the same time he raised the wealth and position of my family to a level which agreed with the model he had in mind. But his undying love for his lady fought against the temptation. After we had gone through a series of the severest resistances and bitterest vituperations on his part, he could no longer remain blind to the overwhelming effect of the perfect analogy between the transference fantasy and the actual state of affairs in the past. I will repeat one of the dreams which he had at this period, so as to give an example of his manner of treating the subject. He dreamed that *he saw my daughter in front of him with two patches of dung instead of eyes.* No one who understands the language of dreams will find much difficulty in translating this one: it declared that *he was marrying my daughter not for her "beaux yeux" but for her money.*

The Father Complex and the Solution of the Rat Idea

From the exciting cause of the patient's illness in his adult years there was a thread leading back to his childhood. He had found himself in a situation similar to that in which, as he knew or suspected, his father had been before *his* marriage; and he had thus been able to identify himself with his father. But his dead father was involved in his recent attack in yet another way. The conflict at the root of his illness was in essentials a struggle between the persisting influence of his father's wishes and his own amatory predilections. If we take into consideration what the patient reported in the course of the first hours of his treatment, we shall not be able to avoid a suspicion that this struggle was a very ancient one and had arisen as far back as in his childhood.

By all accounts our patient's father was a most excellent man. Before his marriage he had been a noncommissioned officer, and, as relics of that period of his life, he had retained a straightforward soldierly manner and a penchant for using downright language. Apart from those virtues which are celebrated upon every tombstone, he was distinguished by a hearty sense of humor and a kindly tolerance toward his fellowmen. That he could be hasty and violent was certainly not inconsistent with his other qualities, but was rather a necessary complement to them; but it occasionally brought down the most severe castigations upon the children, while they were young and naughty. When they grew up, however, he differed from other fathers in not attempting to exalt himself into a sacrosanct authority, but in sharing with them a knowledge of the little failures and misfortunes of his life with good-natured candor. His son was certainly not exaggerating when he declared that they had lived together like the best of friends, except upon a single point. And it must no doubt have been in connection with that very point that thoughts about his father's death had occupied his mind when he was a small boy with unusual and undue intensity, and that those thoughts made their appearance in the wording of the obsessional ideas of his childhood; and it can only have been in that same connection that he was able to wish for his father's death, in order that a certain little girl's sympathy might be aroused and that she might become kinder toward him.

There can be no question that there was something in the sphere of sexuality that stood between the father and son, and that the father had come into some sort of opposition to the son's prematurely developed erotic life. Several years after his father's death, the first time he experienced the pleasurable sensations of copulation, an idea sprang into his mind: "This is glorious! One might murder one's father for this!" This was at once an echo and an elucidation of the obsessional ideas of his childhood. Moreover his father, shortly before his death, had directly opposed what later became our patient's dominating passion. He had noticed that his son was always in the lady's company, and had advised him to keep away from her, saying that it was imprudent of him and that he would only make a fool of himself.

To this unimpeachable body of evidence we shall be able to add fresh material, if we turn to the history of the onanistic side of our patient's sexual activities. There is a conflict between the opinions of doctors and patients on this subject which has not hitherto been properly appreciated. The patients are unanimous in their belief that onanism, by which they mean masturbation during puberty, is the root and origin of all their troubles. The doctors are, upon the whole, unable to decide what line to take; but, influenced by the knowledge that not only neurotics but most normal persons pass through a period of onanism during their puberty, the majority of them are inclined to dismiss the patients' assertions as gross exaggerations. In my opinion the patients are once again nearer to a correct view than the doctors; for the patients have some glimmering notion of the truth, while the doctors are in danger of overlooking an essential point. The thesis propounded by the patients certainly does not correspond to the facts in the sense in which they themselves construe it, namely, that onanism during puberty (which may almost be described as a typical occurrence) is responsible for all neurotic disturbances. Their thesis requires interpretation. The onanism of puberty is in fact no more than a revival of the onanism of infancy, a subject which has hitherto invariably been neglected. Infantile onanism reaches a kind of climax, as a rule, between the ages of three and four or five; and it is the clearest expression of a child's sexual constitution, in which the etiology of subsequent neuroses must be sought. In this disguised way, therefore, the patients are putting the blame for their illnesses upon their infantile sexuality; and they are perfectly right in doing so. On the other hand, the problem of onanism becomes insoluble if we attempt to treat it as a clinical unit, and forget that it can represent the discharge of every variety of sexual component and of every sort of fantasy to which such components can give rise. The injurious effects of onanism are only in a very small degree autonomous—that is to say, determined by its own nature. They are in substance merely part and parcel of the pathogenic significance of the sexual life as a whole. The fact that so many people can tolerate onanism—that is, a certain amount of it—without injury merely shows that their sexual constitution and the course of development of their sexual life have been such as to allow them to exercise the sexual function within the limits of what is culturally permissible; whereas other people, because their sexual constitution has been less favorable or their development has been disturbed, fall ill as a result of their sexuality,—they cannot, that is, achieve the necessary suppression or sublimation of their sexual components without having recourse to inhibitions or substitute-formations.

Our present patient's behavior in the matter of onanism was most remarkable. He did not indulge in it during puberty to an extent worth mentioning, and therefore, according to one set of views, he might have expected to be exempt from neurosis. On the other hand, an impulsion toward onanistic practices came over him in his twenty-first year, *shortly after his father's death*. He felt very much ashamed of himself each time he gave way to this kind of gratification, and soon foreswore the habit. From that time onward it reappeared only upon rare and extraordinary occasions. It was provoked, he told me, when he experienced especially fine moments or when he read especially fine passages. It occurred once, for instance, on a lovely summer's afternoon when, in the middle of Vienna, he heard a postilion blowing his horn in the most wonderful way, until a policeman stopped him, because blowing horns is not allowed in the center of the town. And another time it happened, when he read in *Dichtung und Wahrheit* how the young Goethe had freed himself in a burst of tenderness from the effects of a curse which a jealous mistress had pronounced upon the next woman who should kiss his lips after her; he had long, almost superstitiously, suffered the curse to hold him back, but now he broke his bonds and kissed his love joyfully again and again.

It seemed to the patient not a little strange that he should be impelled to masturbate precisely upon such beautiful and uplifting occasions as these. But I could not help pointing out that these two occasions had something in common—a prohibition, and the defiance of a command.

We must also consider in the same connection his curious behavior at a time when he was working for an examination and toying with his favorite fantasy that his father was still alive and might at any moment reappear. He used to arrange that his working hours should be as late as possible in the night. Between twelve and one o'clock at night he would interrupt his work, and open the front door of the flat as though his father were standing outside it; then, coming back into the hall, he would take out his penis and look at it in the looking glass. This crazy conduct becomes intelligible if we suppose that he was acting as though he expected a visit from his father at the hour when ghosts are abroad. He had on the whole been idle at his work during his father's lifetime, and this had often been a cause of annoyance to his father. And now that he was returning as a ghost, he was to be delighted at finding his son hard at work. But it was impossible that his father should be delighted at the other part of his behavior; in this therefore he must be defying him. Thus, in a single unintelligible obsessional act, he gave expression to the two sides of his relation with his father, just as he did subsequently with regard to his lady by means of his obsessional act with the stone.

Starting from these indications and from other data of a similar kind, I ventured to put forward a construction to the effect that when he was a child of under six he had been guilty of some sexual misdemeanor connected with onanism and had been soundly castigated for it by his father. This punishment, according to my hypothesis, had, it was true, put an end to his onanism, but on the other hand it had left behind it an ineradicable grudge against his father and had established him for all time in his role of an interferer with the patient's sexual enjoyment. To my great astonishment the patient then informed me that his mother had repeatedly described to him an occurrence of this kind which dated from his earliest childhood and had evidently escaped being forgotten by her on account of its remarkable consequences. He himself, however, had no recollection of it whatever. The tale was as follows. When he was very small—it became possible to establish the date more exactly owing to its having coincided with the fatal illness of an elder sister—he had done something naughty, for which his father had given him a beating. The little boy had flown into a terrible rage and had hurled abuse at his father even while he was under his blows. But as he knew no bad language, he had called him all the names of common objects that he could think of, and had screamed: "You lamp! You towel! You plate!" and so on. His father, shaken by such an outburst of elemental fury, had stopped beating him, and had declared: "The child will be either a great man or a great criminal!"[9] The patient believed that the scene made a permanent impression upon himself as well as upon his father. His father, he said, never beat him again; and he also attributed to this experience a part of the change which came over his own character. From that time forward he was a

---

9. These alternatives did not exhaust the possibilities. His father had overlooked the commonest outcome of such premature passions—a neurosis.

coward—out of fear of the violence of his own rage. His whole life long, moreover, he was terribly afraid of blows, and used to creep away and hide, filled with terror and indignation, when one of his brothers or sisters was beaten.

The patient subsequently questioned his mother again. She confirmed the story, adding that at the time he had been between three and four years old and that he had been given the punishment because he had *bitten* someone. She could remember no further details, except for a very uncertain idea that the person the little boy had hurt might have been his nurse. In her account there was no suggestion of his misdeed having been of a sexual nature.[10]

A discussion of this childhood scene will be found in a footnote, and here I will only remark that its emergence shook the patient for the first time in his refusal to believe that at some prehistoric period in his childhood he had been seized with fury (which had subsequently become latent) against the father

---

10. In psychoanalyses we frequently come across occurrences of this kind, dating back to the earliest years of the patient's childhood, in which his infantile sexual activity appears to reach its climax and often comes to a catastrophic end owing to some misfortune or punishment. Such occurrences are apt to appear in a shadowy way in dreams. Often they will become so clear that the analyst thinks he has a firm hold of them, and will nevertheless evade any final elucidation; and unless he proceeds with the greatest skill and caution he may be compelled to leave it undecided whether the scene in question actually took place or not. It will help to put us upon the right track in interpreting it, if we recognize that more than one version of the scene (each often differing greatly from the other) may be detected in the patient's unconscious fantasies. If we do not wish to go astray in our judgment of their historical reality, we must above all bear in mind that people's "childhood memories" are only consolidated at a later period, usually at the age of puberty; and that this involves a complicated process of remodeling, analogous in every way to the process by which a nation constructs legends about its early history. It at once becomes evident that in his fantasies about his infancy the individual as he grows up *endeavors to efface the recollection of his autoerotic activities;* and this he does by exalting their memory-traces to the level of object-love, just as a real historian will view the past in the light of the present. This explains why these fantasies abound in seductions and assaults, where the facts will have been confined to autoerotic activities and the caresses or punishments that stimulated them. Furthermore, it becomes clear that in constructing fantasies about his childhood the individual *sexualizes his memories;* that is, he brings commonplace experiences into relation with his sexual activity, and extends his sexual interest to them—though in doing this he is probably following upon the traces of a really existing connection. . . .

whom he loved so much. I must confess that I had expected it
to have a greater effect, for the incident had been described to
him so often—even by his father himself—that there could be
no doubt of its objective reality. But, with that capacity for
being illogical which never fails to bewilder one in such highly
intelligent people as obsessional neurotics, he kept urging
against the evidential value of the story the fact that he himself
could not remember the scene. And so it was only along the
painful road of transference that he was able to reach a conviction that his relation to his father really necessitated the
postulation of this unconscious complement. Things soon
reached a point at which, in his dreams, his waking fantasies,
and his associations, he began heaping the grossest and filthiest
abuse upon me and my family, though in his deliberate actions
he never treated me with anything but the greatest respect. His
demeanor as he repeated these insults to me was that of a man
in despair. "How can a gentleman like you, sir," he used to ask,

---

It is seldom that we are in the fortunate position of being able, as in the present instance, to
establish the facts upon which these tales of the individual's prehistoric past are based, by recourse
to the unimpeachable testimony of a grown-up person. Even so, the statement made by our
patient's mother leaves the way open to various possibilities. That she did not proclaim the sexual
character of the offense for which the child was punished may have been due to the activity of
her own censorship; for with all parents it is precisely this sexual element in their children's past
that their own censorship is most anxious to eliminate. But it is just as possible that the child was
reproved by his nurse or by his mother herself for some commonplace piece of naughtiness of a
nonsexual nature, and that his reaction was so violent that he was castigated by his father. In fantasies
of this kind nurses and servants are regularly replaced by the superior figure of the mother.
A deeper interpretation of the patient's dreams in relation to this episode revealed the clearest
traces of the presence in his mind of an imaginative production of a positively epic character.
In this his sexual desires for his mother and sister and his sister's premature death were linked
up with the young hero's chastisement at his father's hands. It was impossible to unravel this
tissue of fantasy thread by thread; the therapeutic success of the treatment was precisely what
stood in the way of this. The patient recovered, and his ordinary life began to assert its claims:
there were many tasks before him, which he had already neglected far too long, and which
were incompatible with a continuation of the treatment. I am not to be blamed, therefore,
for this gap in the analysis. The scientific results of psychoanalysis are at present only a
by-product of its therapeutic aims, and for that reason it is often just in those cases where
treatment fails that most discoveries are made.

"let yourself be abused in this way by a low, good-for-nothing wretch like me? You ought to turn me out: that's all I deserve." While he talked like this, he would get up from the sofa and roam about the room, a habit which he explained at first as being due to delicacy of feeling: he could not bring himself, he said, to utter such horrible things while he was lying there so comfortably. But soon he himself found a more cogent explanation, namely, that he was avoiding my proximity for fear of my giving him a beating. If he stayed on the sofa he behaved like someone in desperate terror trying to save himself from castigations of boundless dimensions; he would bury his head in his hands, cover his face with his arm, jump up suddenly and rush away, his features distorted with pain, and so on. He recalled that his father had had a passionate temper, and sometimes in his violence had not known where to stop. Thus, little by little, in this school of suffering, the patient won the sense of conviction which he had lacked—though to any disinterested mind the truth would have been almost self-evident. And now the path was clear to the solution of his rat idea. The treatment had reached its turning point, and a quantity of material information which had hitherto been withheld became available, and so made possible a reconstruction of the whole concatenation of events.

In my description I shall, as I have already said, content myself with the briefest possible summary of the circumstances. Obviously the first problem to be solved was why the two speeches of the Czech captain—his rat story, and his request to the patient that he should pay back the money to Lieutenant A—should have had such an agitating effect on him and should have provoked such violently pathological reactions. The presumption was that it was a question of "complexive sensitiveness," and that the speeches had jarred upon certain hyperaesthetic spots in his unconscious. And so it proved to be. As always happened with the patient in connection with military matters, he had been in a state of unconscious identification with his father, who had seen many years' service and had been full of stories of his soldiering days. Now it happened by chance—for chance may play a part in the formation of a symptom, just as the wording may help in the making of a joke—that one of his father's little adventures had an important element in common with the captain's request. His father, in his capacity as noncommissioned officer, had control over a small sum of money and had on one occasion lost it at cards. (Thus he had been a *"Spielratte."*[11]) He would have found himself in a serious position if one of his comrades had not advanced him the amount. After he had left the army and become well-off, he had tried to find this friend in need so as to pay him back the money, but had not managed to trace him. The patient was uncertain whether he had ever succeeded in returning the money. The recollection of this sin of his father's youth was painful to him, for, in spite of appearances, his unconscious was filled with hostile strictures upon his father's character. The captain's words, "You must pay back the 3.80 crowns to Lieutenant A," had sounded to his ears like an allusion to this unpaid debt of his father's.

But the information that the young lady at the post office at Z—— had herself paid the charges due upon the packet, with a complimentary remark about himself, had intensified his identification with his father in quite another direction. At this stage in the analysis he brought out some new information, to the effect that the landlord of the inn at the little place where the post office was had had a pretty daughter. She had been decidedly encouraging to the smart young officer, so that he had thought of returning there after the maneuvers were over and of trying his luck with her. Now, however, she had a rival in the shape of the young lady at the post office. Like his father in the tale of his marriage, he could afford now to hesitate upon which of the two he should bestow his favors when he had finished his military service. We can see at once that his singular indecision whether he should travel to Vienna or go back to the place where the post office was, and the constant temptation he felt to turn back while he was on the journey, were not so senseless

---

11. [Literally, "play-rat." Colloquial German for "gambler." —Trans.]

as they seemed to us at first. To his conscious mind, the attraction exercised upon him by Z——, the place where the post office was, was explained by the necessity for seeing Lieutenant A and fulfilling the vow with his assistance. But in reality what was attracting him was the young lady at the post office, and the lieutenant was merely a good substitute for her, since he lived at the same place and had himself been in charge of the military postal service. And when subsequently he heard that it was not Lieutenant A but another officer, B, who had been on duty at the post office that day, he drew him into his combination as well; and he was then able to reproduce in his deliria in connection with the two officers the hesitation he felt between the two girls who were so kindly disposed toward him.

In elucidating the effects produced by the captain's rat story we must follow the course of the analysis more closely. The patient began by producing an enormous mass of associative material, which at first, however, threw no light upon the circumstances in which the formation of his obsession had taken place. The idea of the punishment carried out by means of rats had acted as a stimulus to a number of his instincts and had called up a whole quantity of recollections; so that, in the short interval between the captain's story and his request to him to pay back the money, rats had acquired a series of symbolical meanings, to which, during the period which followed, fresh ones were continually being added. I must confess that I can only give a very incomplete account of the whole business. What the rat punishment stirred up more than anything else was his *anal erotism,* which had played an important part in his childhood and had been kept in activity for many years by a constant irritation due to worms. In this way rats came to have the meaning of *"money."* The patient gave an indication of this connection by reacting to the word *"Ratten"* ["rats"] with the association *"Raten"* ["installments"]. In his obsessional deliria he had coined himself a regular rat currency. When, for instance, in reply to a question, I told him the amount of my fee for an hour's treatment, he said to himself (as I learned six months later), "So many florins, so many rats." Little by little he translated into this language the whole complex of money interests which centered round his father's legacy to him; that is to say, all his ideas connected with that subject were, by way of the verbal bridge *"Raten—Ratten,"* carried over into his obsessional life and became subjected to his unconscious. Moreover, the captain's request to him to pay back the charges due upon the packet served to strengthen the money significance of rats, by way of another verbal bridge *"Spielratte,"* which led back to his father's gambling debt.

But the patient was also familiar with the fact that rats are carriers of dangerous infectious diseases; he could therefore employ them as symbols of his dread (justifiable enough in the army) of *syphilitic infection.* This dread concealed all sorts of doubts as to the kind of life his father had led during his term of military service. Again, in another sense, the *penis* itself is a carrier of syphilitic infection; and in this way he could consider the rat as a male organ of sex. It had a further title to be so regarded; for a penis (especially a child's penis) can easily be compared to a *worm,* and the captain's story had been about rats burrowing in someone's anus, just as the large round-worms had in his when he was a child. Thus the penis significance of rats was based, once more, upon anal eroticism. And apart from this, the rat is a dirty animal, feeding upon excrement and living in sewers.[12] It is perhaps unnecessary to point out how great an extension of the rat delirium became possible owing to this new meaning. For instance, "So many rats, so many florins," could serve as an excellent characterization of a certain female profession which he particularly detested. On the other hand, it is certainly not a matter of indifference that the substitution of a penis for a rat in the captain's story resulted in a situation of intercourse *per anum,* which

---

12. If the reader feels tempted to shake his head at the possibility of such leaps of imagination in the neurotic mind, I may remind him that artists have sometimes indulged in similar freaks of fancy. Such, for instance, are Le Poitevin's *Diableries érotiques.*

could not fail to be especially revolting to him when brought into connection with his father and the woman he loved. And when we consider that the same situation was reproduced in the compulsive threat which had formed in his mind after the captain had made his request, we shall be forcibly reminded of certain curses in use among the Southern Slavs. Moreover, all of this material, and more besides, was woven into the fabric of the rat discussions behind the screen-association *"heiraten"* ["to marry"].

The story of the rat punishment, as was shown by the patient's own account of the matter and by his facial expression as he repeated the story to me, had fanned into a flame all of his prematurely suppressed impulses of cruelty, egoistic and sexual alike. Yet, in spite of all this wealth of material, no light was thrown upon the meaning of his obsessional idea until one day the Rat-Wife in Ibsen's *Little Eyolf* came up in the analysis, and it became impossible to escape the inference that in many of the shapes assumed by his obsessional deliria rats had another meaning still—namely, that of *children*.[13] Inquiry into the origin of this new meaning at once brought me up against some of the earliest and most important roots. Once when the patient was visiting his father's grave he had seen a big beast, which he had taken to be a rat, gliding along over the grave. He assumed that it had actually come out of his father's grave, and had just been having a meal off his corpse. The notion of a rat is inseparably bound up with the fact that it has sharp teeth with which it gnaws and bites. But rats cannot be sharp-toothed, greedy, and dirty with impunity: they are cruelly persecuted and mercilessly put to death by man, as the patient had often observed with horror. He had often pitied the poor creatures. But he himself

13. Ibsen's Rat-Wife must certainly be derived from the legendary Pied Piper of Hamelin, who first enticed away the rats into the water, and then, by the same means, lured the children out of the town never to return. So too, Little Eyolf threw himself into the water under the spell of the Rat-Wife. In legends generally the rat appears not so much as a disgusting creature but as something uncanny—as a chthonic animal, one might almost say, and it is used to represent the souls of the dead.

had been just such a nasty, dirty little wretch, who was apt to bite people when he was in a rage, and had been fearfully punished for doing so. He could truly be said to find "a living likeness of himself" in the rat. It was almost as though Fate, when the captain told him his story, had been putting him through an association test: she had called out a "complex stimulus-word," and he had reacted to it with his obsessional idea.

According, then, to his earliest and most momentous experiences, rats were children. And at this point he brought out a piece of information which he had kept away from its context long enough, but which now fully explained the interest he was bound to feel in children. The lady, whose admirer he had been for so many years, but whom he had nevertheless not been able to make up his mind to marry, was condemned to childlessness by reason of a gynecological operation which had involved the removal of both ovaries. This indeed—for he was extraordinarily fond of children—had been the chief reason for his hesitation.

It was only then that it became possible to understand the inexplicable process by which his obsessional idea had been formed. With the assistance of our knowledge of infantile sexual theories and of symbolism (as learned from the interpretation of dreams) the whole thing could be translated and given a meaning. When, during the afternoon halt (upon which he had lost his pince-nez), the captain had told him about the rat punishment, the patient had only been struck at first by the combined cruelty and lasciviousness of the situation depicted. But immediately afterward a connection had been set up with the scene from his childhood in which he himself had bitten someone. The captain—a man who could defend such punishments—had been substituted by him for his father, and had thus drawn down upon himself a part of the reviving exasperation which had burst out, upon the original occasion, against his cruel father. The idea which came into his consciousness for a moment, to the effect that something of the sort might happen to someone he was fond of, is probably to be translated into a wish such as "You ought to have the same thing done to you!" aimed at the teller of the story, but through him at his father. A day and a half later, when the captain had handed him the packet upon which the charges were due and had requested him to pay back the 3.80 crowns to Lieutenant A, he had already been aware that his "cruel superior" was making a mistake, and that the only person he owed anything to was the young lady at the post office. It might easily, therefore, have occurred to him to think of some derisive reply, such as, "Will I, though?" or "Pay your grandmother!" or "Yes! You bet I'll pay him back the money!"—answers which would have been subject to no compulsive force. But instead, out of the stirrings of his father-complex and out of his memory of the scene from his childhood, there formed in his mind some such answer as: "Yes! I'll pay back the money to A when my father or the lady have children!" or "As sure as my father or the lady can have children, I'll pay him back the money!" In short, a derisive asseveration coupled with an absurd condition which could never be fulfilled.

But now the crime had been committed; he had insulted the two persons who were dearest to him—his father and his lady. The deed had called for punishment, and the penalty had consisted in his binding himself by a vow which it was impossible for him to fulfil and which entailed literal obedience to his superior's ill-founded request. The vow ran as follows: *"Now you must really pay back the money to A."* In his convulsive obedience he had repressed his better knowledge that the captain's request had been based upon erroneous premises: "Yes, you must pay back the money to A, as your father's surrogate has required. Your father cannot be mistaken." So too the king cannot be mistaken; if he addresses one of his subjects by a title which is not his, the subject bears that title ever afterward.

Only vague intelligence of these events reached the patient's consciousness. But his revolt against the captain's order and the sudden transformation of that revolt into its opposite were both represented there. First had come the idea that he was *not* to pay back the money, or it (that is, the rat punishment) would happen; and then had come the transformation of this idea into a vow to the opposite effect, as a punishment for his revolt.

Let us, further, picture to ourselves the general conditions under which the formation of the patient's great obsessional idea occurred. His libido had been increased by a long period of abstinence coupled with the friendly welcome which a young officer can always reckon upon receiving when he goes among women. Moreover, at the time when he had started for the maneuvers, there had been a certain coolness between himself and his lady. This intensification of his libido had inclined him to a renewal of his ancient struggle against his father's authority, and he had dared to think of having sexual intercourse with other women. His loyalty to his father's memory had grown weaker, his doubts as to his lady's merits had increased; and in that frame of mind he let himself be dragged into insulting the two of them, and had then punished himself for it. In doing so he had copied an old model. And when at the end of the maneuvers he had hesitated so long whether he should travel to Vienna or whether he should stop and fulfil his vow, he had represented in a single picture the two conflicts by which he had from the very first been torn—whether or not he should remain obedient to his father and whether or not he should remain faithful to his beloved.

I may add a word upon *the interpretation of the "sanction"* which, it will be remembered, was to the effect that "otherwise the rat punishment will be carried out on both of them." It was based upon the influence of two infantile sexual theories, which I have discussed elsewhere. The first of these theories is that babies come out of the anus; and the second, which follows logically from the first, is that men can have babies just as well as women. According to the technical rules for interpreting dreams, the notion of coming out of the rectum can be represented by the opposite notion of creeping into the rectum (as in the rat punishment), and *vice versa.*

We should not be justified in expecting such severe obsessional ideas as were present in this case to be cleared up in any simpler manner or by any other means. When we reached the solution that has been described above, the patient's rat delirium disappeared.

THEORETICAL

Some Psychological Peculiarities of Obsessional Neurotics: Their Attitude toward Reality, Superstition, and Death

In this section I intend to deal with a few mental characteristics of obsessional neurotics which, though they do not seem important in themselves, nevertheless lie upon the road to a comprehension of more important things. They were strongly marked in our present patient; but I know that they are not attributable to his individual character, but to his disorder, and that they are to be met with quite typically in other obsessional patients.

Our patient was to a high degree superstitious, and this although he was a highly educated and enlightened man of considerable acumen, and although he was able at times to assure me that he did not believe a word of all this rubbish. Thus he was at once superstitious and not superstitious; and there was a clear distinction between his attitude and the superstition of uneducated people who feel themselves at one with their belief. He seemed to understand that his superstition was dependent upon his obsessional thinking, although at times he gave way to it completely. The meaning of this inconsistent and vacillating behavior can be most easily grasped if it is regarded in the light of a hypothesis which I shall now proceed to mention. I did not hesitate to assume that the truth was not that the patient still had an open mind upon this subject, but that he had two separate and contradictory convictions upon it. His oscillation between these two views quite obviously depended upon his momentary attitude toward his obsessional disorder. As soon as he had got the better of one of these obsessions, he used to smile in a superior way at his own credulity, and no events occurred that were calculated to shake his firmness; but the moment he came under the sway of another obsession which had not been cleared up—or, what amounts to the same thing, of a resistance—the strangest coincidences would happen to support him in his credulous belief.

His superstition was nevertheless that of an educated man, and he avoided such vulgar prejudices as being afraid of Friday or of the number thirteen, and so on. But he believed in premonitions and in prophetic dreams; he would constantly meet the very person of whom, for some inexplicable reason, he had just been thinking; or he would receive a letter from someone who had suddenly come into his mind after being forgotten for many years. At the same time he was honest enough—or rather, he was loyal enough to his official conviction—not to have forgotten instances in which the strangest forebodings had come to nothing. On one occasion, for instance, when he went away for his summer holidays, he had felt morally certain that he would never return to Vienna alive. He also admitted that the great majority of his premonitions related to things which had no special personal importance to him, and that, when he met an acquaintance of whom, until a few moments previously, he had not thought of for a very long time, nothing further took place between himself and the miraculous apparition. And he naturally could not deny that all the important events of his life had occurred without his having had any premonition of them, and that, for instance, his father's death had taken him entirely by surprise. But arguments such as these had no effect upon the discrepancy in his convictions. They merely served to prove the obsessional nature of his superstitions, and that could already be inferred from the way in which they came and went with the increase and decrease of his resistance.

I was not in a position, of course, to give a rational explanation of all the miraculous stories of his remoter past. But as regards the similar things that happened during the time of his treatment, I was able to prove to him that he himself invariably had a hand in the manufacture of these miracles, and I was able to point out to him the methods that he employed. He worked by means of indirect vision and reading, forgetting, and, above all, errors of memory. In the end he used himself to help me in discovering the little sleight of hand tricks by which these wonders were performed. I may mention one interesting infantile root of his belief that forebodings and premonitions came true. It was brought to light by his recollection that very often, when a date was being fixed for something, his mother used to say: "I shan't be able to on such-and-such a day. I shall have to stop in bed then." And in fact when the day in question arrived she had invariably stayed in bed!

There can be no doubt that the patient felt a need for finding experiences of this kind to act as props for his superstition, and that it was for that reason that he occupied himself so much with the inexplicable coincidences of everyday life with which we are all familiar, and helped out their shortcomings with unconscious activity of his own. I have come across a similar need in many other obsessional patients and have suspected its presence in many more besides. It seems to me easily explicable in view of the psychological characteristics of the obsessional neurosis. In this disorder, as I have already explained, repression is effected not by means of amnesia but by a severance of causal connections brought about by a withdrawal of affect. These repressed connections appear to persist in some kind of shadowy form (which I have elsewhere compared to an entopic perception), and they are thus transferred, by a process of projection, into the external world, where they bear witness to what has been effaced from consciousness.

Another mental need, which is also shared by obsessional neurotics and which is in some respects related to the one just mentioned, is the need for *uncertainty* in their life, or for *doubt*. An inquiry into this characteristic leads deep into the investigation of instinct. The creation of uncertainty is one of the methods employed by the neurosis for drawing the patient away from *reality* and isolating him from the world—which is among the objects of every psychoneurotic disorder. Again, it is only too obvious what efforts are made by the patients themselves in order to be able to avoid certainty and remain in doubt. Some of them, indeed, give a vivid expression to this tendency in a dislike of clocks and watches (for they at least make the time of day certain), and in the unconscious artifices which they employ in order to render these doubt-removing instruments innocuous. Our present patient had developed a peculiar talent for avoiding a knowledge of any facts which would have helped him in deciding his conflict. Thus he was in ignorance upon those matters relating to his lady which were the most relevant to the question of his marriage: he was ostensibly unable to say who had operated upon her and whether the operation had been unilateral or bilateral. He had to be forced into remembering what he had forgotten and into finding out what he had overlooked.

The predilection felt by obsessional neurotics for uncertainty and doubt leads them to turn their thoughts by preference to those subjects upon which all mankind are uncertain and upon which our knowledge and judgments must necessarily remain open to doubt. The chief subjects of this kind are paternity, length of life, life after death, and memory—in the last of which we are all in the habit of believing, without having the slightest guaranteee of its trustworthiness.

In obsessional neuroses the uncertainty of memory is used to the fullest extent as a help in the formation of symptoms; and we shall learn directly the part played in the actual content of the patients' thoughts by the questions of length of life and life after death. But as an appropriate transition I will first consider one particular superstitious trait in our patient to which I have already alluded and which will no doubt have puzzled more than one of my readers.

I refer to the *omnipotence* which he ascribed to his thoughts and feelings, and to his wishes, whether good or evil. It is, I must admit, decidedly tempting to declare that this idea was a delusion and that it oversteps the limits of obsessional neurosis. I have, however, come across the same conviction in another obsessional patient; and he was long ago restored to health and is leading a normal life. Indeed, all obsessional neurotics behave as though they shared this conviction. It will be our business to throw some light upon these patients' overestimation of their powers. Assuming, without more ado, that this belief is a frank acknowledgment of a relic of the old megalomania of infancy, we will proceed to ask the patient for the grounds of his conviction. In reply, he adduces two experiences. When he returned for a second visit to the hydropathic establishment at which his disorder had been relieved for the first and only time, he asked to be given his old room, for its position had facilitated his relations with one of the nurses. He was told that the room was already taken and that it was occupied by an old professor. This piece of news considerably diminished his prospects of successful treatment, and he reacted to it with the unamiable thought: "I wish he may be struck dead for it!" A fortnight later he was woken up from his sleep by the disturbing idea of a corpse; and in the morning he heard that the professor had really had a stroke, and that he had been carried up into his room at about the time he himself had woken up. The second experience related to an unmarried woman, no longer young, though with a great desire to be loved, who had paid him a great deal of attention and had once asked him point-blank whether he could not love her. He had given her an evasive answer. A few days afterward he heard that she had thrown herself out of the window. He then began to reproach himself, and said to himself that it would have been in his power to save her life by giving her his love. In this way he became convinced of the omnipotence of his love and of his hatred. Without denying the omnipotence of love we may point out that both of these instances were concerned with death, and we may adopt the obvious explanation that, like other obsessional neurotics, our patient was compelled to overestimate the effects of his hostile feelings upon the external world, because a large part of their internal, mental effects escaped his conscious knowledge. His love—or rather his hatred—was in truth overpowering; it was precisely they that created the obsessional thoughts, of which he could not understand the origin and against which he strove in vain to defend himself.

Our patient had a quite peculiar attitude toward the question of death. He showed the deepest sympathy whenever anyone died, and religiously attended the funeral; so that among his brothers and sisters he earned the nickname of "bird of ill omen." In his imagination, too, he was constantly making away with people so as to show his heartfelt sympathy for their bereaved relatives. The death of an elder sister, which took place when he was between three and four years old, played a great part in his fantasies, and was brought into intimate connection with his childish misdemeanors during the same period. We know, moreover, at what an early age thoughts about his father's death had occupied his mind, and we may regard his illness itself as a reaction to that event, for which he had felt an obsessional wish fifteen years earlier. The strange extension of his obsessional fears to the "next world" was nothing else than a compensation for these death wishes which he had felt against his father. It was introduced eighteen months after his father had died, at a time when there had been a revival of his sorrow at the loss, and it was designed—in defiance of reality, and in deference to the wish which had previously been showing itself in fantasies of every kind—to undo the fact of his father's death. We have had occasion in several places to translate the phrase "in the next world" by the words "if my father were still alive."

But the behavior of other obsessional neurotics does not differ greatly from that of our present patient, even though it has not been their fate to come face to face with the phenomenon of death at such an early age. Their thoughts are unceasingly occupied with other people's length of life and possibility of death; their superstitious propensities have, to begin with, had no other content and have perhaps no other source whatever. But these neurotics need the help of the possibility of death chiefly in order that it may act as a solution of conflicts they have left unsolved. Their essential characteristic is that they are incapable of coming to a decision, especially in matters of love; they endeavor to postpone every decision, and, in their doubt which person they shall decide for or what measures they shall take against a person, they are obliged to choose as their model the old German courts of justice, in which the suits were usually brought to an end, before judgment had been given, by the death of the parties to the dispute. Thus in every conflict which enters their lives they are on the look out for the death of someone who is of importance to them, usually of someone they love—such as one of their parents, or a rival, or one of the objects of their love between which their inclinations are wavering. But at this point our discussion of the death-complex in obsessional neuroses touches upon the problem of the instinctual life of obsessional neurotics. And to this problem we must now turn.

The Instinctual Life of Obsessional Neurotics, and the Origins of Compulsion and Doubt

If we wish to obtain a grasp of the psychical forces whose interplay built up this neurosis, we must turn back to what we have learned from the patient on the subject of the exciting causes of his falling ill as a grown-up man and as a child. He fell ill when he was in his twenties on being faced with a temptation to marry another woman instead of the one whom he had loved so long; and he avoided a decision of this conflict by postponing all the necessary preliminary actions. The means for doing this was given him by his neurosis. His hesitation between the lady he loved and the other girl can be reduced to a conflict between his father's influence and his love for his lady, or, in other words, to a conflicting choice between his father and his sexual object, such as had already subsisted (judging from his recollections and obsessional ideas) in his remote childhood. All through his life, moreover, he was unmistakably victim to a conflict between love and hatred, in regard both to his lady and to his father. His fantasies of revenge and such obsessional phenomena as his obsession for understanding and his exploit with the stone in the road bore witness to his discordant feelings; and they were to a certain degree comprehensible and normal, for the lady by her original refusal and subsequently by her coolness had given him some excuse for hostility. But his relations with his father were dominated by a similar discordance of feeling, as we have seen from our translation of his obsessional thoughts; and his father too must have given him an excuse for hostility in his childhood, as indeed we have been able to establish almost beyond question. His attitude toward the lady—a compound of tenderness and hostility—came to a great extent within the scope of his conscious knowledge; at most he deceived himself over the degree and strength of his negative feelings. But his hostility toward his father, on the contrary, though he had once been acutely conscious of it, had long since vanished from his ken, and it was only in the teeth of the most violent resistance that it could be brought back into his consciousness. We may regard the repression of his infantile hatred of his father as the event which brought his whole subsequent career under the dominion of the neurosis.

The conflicts of feeling in our patient which we have here enumerated separately were not independent of each other, but were bound together in pairs. His hatred of his lady was inevitably coupled with his attachment to his father, and inversely his hatred of his father with his attachment to his lady. But the two conflicts of feeling which result from this simplification—namely, the opposition between his relation to his father and to his lady, and the contradiction between his love and his hatred within each of these relations—had no connection whatever with each other, either in their content or in their origin. The first of these two conflicts corresponds to the normal vacillation between male and female which characterizes everyone's choice of a love-object. It is first brought to the child's notice by the time-honored question: "Which do you love most, Papa or Mamma?" and it accompanies him through his whole life, whatever may be the relative intensity of his feelings to the two sexes or whatever may be the sexual aim upon which he finally becomes fixed. But normally this opposition soon loses the character of a hard-and-fast contradiction, of an inexorable either/or. Room is found for satisfying the unequal demands of both sides, although even in a normal person; the higher estimation of one sex is always thrown into relief by a depreciation of the other.

The other conflict, that between love and hatred, strikes us more strangely. We know that incipient love is often perceived as hatred, and that love, if it is denied satisfaction, may easily be partly converted into hatred, and poets tell us that in the more tempestuous stages of love the two opposed feelings may subsist side by side for a while as though in rivalry with each other. But the chronic coexistence of love and hatred, both directed toward the same person and both of the highest degree of intensity, cannot fail to astonish us. We should have expected that the passionate love would long ago have conquered the hatred or been devoured by it. And in fact such a protracted survival of two opposites is only possible under quite peculiar psychological conditions and with the cooperation of the state of affairs in the unconscious. The love has not succeeded in extinguishing the hatred but only in driving it down into the unconscious; and in the unconscious the hatred, safe from the danger of being destroyed by the operations of consciousness, is able to persist and even to grow. In such circumstances the conscious love attains as a rule, by way of reaction, an especially high degree of intensity, so as to be strong enough for the perpetual task of keeping its opponent under repression. The necessary condition for the occurrence of such a strange state of affairs in a person's erotic life appears to be that at a very early age, somewhere in the prehistoric period of his infancy, the two opposites should have been split apart and one of them, usually the hatred, have been repressed.

If we consider a number of analyses of obsessional neurotics we shall find it impossible to escape the impression that a relation between love and hatred such as we have found in our present patient is among the most frequent, the most marked, and probably, therefore, the most important characteristics of the obsessional neurosis. But however tempting it may be to bring the problem of the "choice of neurosis" into relation with the instinctual life, there are reasons enough for avoiding such a course. For we must remember that in every neurosis we come upon the same suppressed instincts behind the symptoms. After all, hatred, kept suppressed in the unconscious by love, plays a great part in the pathogenesis of hysteria and paranoia. We know too little of the nature of love to be able to arrive at any definite conclusion here; and, in particular, the relation between the *negative factor*[14] in love and the sadistic components of the libido remains completely obscure. What follows is therefore to be regarded as no more than a provisional explanation. We may suppose, then, that in the cases of unconscious hatred with which we are concerned the sadistic components of love have, from constitutional causes, been exceptionally strongly developed, and have consequently undergone a premature and all too thorough suppression, and that the neurotic phenomena we have observed arise on the one hand from conscious feelings of affection which have become exaggerated as a reaction, and on the other hand from sadism persisting in the unconscious in the form of hatred.

But in whatever way this remarkable relation of love and hatred is to be explained, its occurrence is established beyond any possibility of doubt by the observations made in the present case; and it is gratifying to find how easily we can now follow the puzzling processes of an obsessional neurosis by bringing them into relation with this one factor. If an intense love is opposed by an almost equally powerful hatred, and is at the same time inseparably bound up with it, the immediate

---

14. Alcibiades says of Socrates in the Symposium: "Many a time have I wished that he were dead, and yet I know that I should be much more sorry than glad if he were to die: so that I am at my wits' end."

consequence is certain to be a partial paralysis of the will and an incapacity for coming to a decision upon any of those actions for which love ought to provide the motive power. But this indecision will not confine itself for long to a single group of actions. For, in the first place, what actions of a lover are not brought into relation with his one principal motive? And secondly, a man's attitude in sexual things has the force of a model to which the rest of his reactions tend to conform. And thirdly, it is an inherent characteristic in the psychology of an obsessional neurotic to make the fullest possible use of the mechanism of *displacement.* So the paralysis of his powers of decision gradually extends itself over the entire field of the patient's behavior.

And here we have the domination of *compulsion* and *doubt* such as we meet with in the mental life of obsessional neurotics. The doubt corresponds to the patient's internal perception of his own indecision, which, in consequence of the inhibition of his love by his hatred, takes possession of him in the face of every intended action. The doubt is in reality a doubt of his own love—which ought to be the most certain thing in his whole mind; and it becomes diffused over everything else, and is especially apt to become displaced onto what is most insignificant and trivial. A man who doubts his own love may, or rather *must,* doubt every lesser thing.

It is this same doubt that leads the patient to uncertainty about his protective measures, and to his continual repetition of them in order to banish that uncertainty; and it is this doubt, too, that eventually brings it about that the patient's protective acts themselves become as impossible to carry out as his original inhibited decision in connection with his love. At the beginning of my investigations I was led to assume another and more general origin for the uncertainty of obsessional neurotics and one which seemed to be nearer the normal. If, for instance, while I am writing a letter someone interrupts me with questions, I afterward feel a quite justifiable uncertainty as to what I may not have written under the influence of the disturbance, and, to make sure, I am obliged to read the letter over after I have finished it. In the same way I might suppose that the uncertainty of obsessional neurotics, when they are praying, for instance, is due to unconscious fantasies constantly mingling with their prayers and disturbing them. This hypothesis is correct, but it may be easily reconciled with our earlier statement. It is true that the patient's uncertainty whether he has carried through a protective measure is due to the disturbing effect of unconscious fantasies; but the content of these fantasies is precisely the contrary impulse—which it was the very aim of the prayer to ward off. This became clearly evident in our patient on one occasion, for the disturbing element did not remain unconscious but made its appearance openly. The words he wanted to use in his prayer were, *"May God protect her,"* but a hostile *"not"* suddenly darted out of his unconscious and inserted itself into the sentence; and he understood that this was an attempt at a curse. If the "not" had remained mute, he would have found himself in a state of uncertainty, and would have kept on prolonging his prayers indefinitely. But since it became articulate he eventually gave up praying. Before doing so, however, he, like other obsessional patients, tried every kind of method for preventing the opposite feeling from insinuating itself. He shortened his prayers, for instance, or said them more rapidly. And similarly other patients will endeavor to *"isolate"* all such protective acts from other things. But none of these technical procedures are of any avail in the long run. If the impulse of love achieves any success by displacing itself onto some trivial act, the impulse of hostility will very soon follow it onto its new ground and once more proceed to undo all that it has done.

And when the obsessional patient lays his finger on the weak spot in the security of our mental life—on the untrustworthiness of our memory—the discovery enables him to extend his doubt over everything, even over actions which have already been performed and which have so far had no connection with the love-hatred complex, and over the entire past. I may recall the instance of the woman who had just bought a comb for her little daughter in a shop, and, becoming suspicious of her husband, began to doubt whether she had not as a matter of fact been in possession of the comb for a long time. Was not this woman saying point-blank: "If I can doubt your love" (and this was only a projection of her doubt of her own love for him), "then I can doubt this too, then I can doubt everything"—thus revealing to us the hidden meaning of neurotic doubt?

The *compulsion* on the other hand is an attempt at a compensation for the doubt and at a correction of the intolerable conditions of inhibition to which the doubt bears witness. If the patient, by the help of displacement, succeeds at last in bringing one of his inhibited intentions to a decision, then the intention *must* be carried out. It is true that this intention is not his original one, but the energy dammed up in the latter cannot let slip the opportunity of finding an outlet for its discharge in the substitutive act. Thus this energy makes itself felt now in commands and now in prohibitions, according as the affectionate impulse or the hostile one snatches control of the pathway leading to discharge. If it happens that a compulsive command cannot be obeyed, the tension becomes intolerable and is perceived by the patient in the form of extreme anxiety. But the pathway leading to a substitutive act, even where the displacement has been onto a triviality, is so hotly contested, that such an act can as a rule be carried out only in the shape of a protective measure intimately associated with the very impulse which it is designed to ward off.

Furthermore, by a sort of *regression,* preparatory acts become substituted for the final decision, thinking replaces acting, and, instead of the substitutive act, some thought preliminary to it asserts itself with all the force of compulsion. According as this regression from acting to thinking is more or less marked, a case of obsessional neurosis will exhibit the characteristics of obsessive thinking (that is, of obsessional ideas) or of obsessive acting in the narrower sense of the word. True obsessional acts such as these, however, are only made possible because they constitute a kind of reconciliation, in the shape of a compromise formation, between the two antagonistic impulses. For obsessional acts tend to approximate more and more—and the longer the disorder lasts the more evident does this become—to infantile sexual acts of an onanistic character. Thus in this form of the neurosis acts of love are carried out in spite of everything, but only by the aid of a new kind of regression; for such acts no longer relate to another person, the object of love and hatred, but are autoerotic acts such as occur in infancy.

The first kind of regression, that from acting to thinking, is facilitated by another factor concerned in the production of the neurosis. The histories of obsessional patients almost invariably reveal an early development and premature repression of the sexual instinct of looking and knowing (the scoptophilic and epistemophilic instinct); and, as we know, a part of the infantile sexual activity of our present patient was governed by that instinct.[15]

We have already mentioned the important part played by the sadistic instinctual components in the genesis of obsessional neuroses. Where the epistemophilic instinct is a preponderating feature in the constitution of an obsessional patient, brooding becomes the principal symptom of the neurosis. The thought process itself becomes sexualized, for the sexual pleasure which is normally attached to the content of thought becomes shifted onto the act of thinking itself, and the gratification derived from reaching the conclusion of a line of thought is experienced as a *sexual* gratification. In the various forms of obsessional neurosis in which the epistemophilic instinct plays a part, its relation to thought processes makes it particularly well adapted to attract the energy which is vainly endeavoring to make its way forward into action, and divert it into the sphere of thought, where there is a possibility of its obtaining pleasurable gratification of another sort. In this way, with the help of the epistemophilic instinct, the substitutive act may in its turn be replaced by preparatory acts of thought. But procrastination in action is

---

15. The very high average of intellectual capacity among obsessional patients is probably also connected with this fact.

soon replaced by dilatoriness in thought, and eventually the whole process, together with all its peculiarities, is transferred into the new sphere, just as in America an entire house will sometimes be moved from one site to another.

I may now venture, upon the basis of the preceding discussion, to determine the psychological characteristic, so long sought after, which lends to the products of an obsessional neurosis their "obsessive" or compulsive quality. A thought process is obsessive or compulsive when, in consequence of an inhibition (due to a conflict of opposing impulses) at the motor end of the psychical system, it is undertaken with an expenditure of energy which (as regards both quality and quantity) is normally reserved for actions alone; or, in other words, *an obsessive or compulsive thought is one whose function it is to represent an act regressively.* No one, I think, will question my assumption that processes of thought are ordinarily conducted (on grounds of economy) with smaller displacements of energy, probably at a higher level, than are acts intended to discharge an affect or to modify the external world.

The obsessive thought which has forced its way into consciousness with such excessive violence has next to be secured against the efforts made by conscious thought to resolve it. As we already know, this protection is afforded by the *distortion* which the obsessive thought has undergone before becoming conscious. But this is not the only means employed. In addition, each separate obsessional idea is almost invariably removed from the situation in which it originated and in which, in spite of its distortion, it would be most easily comprehensible. With this end in view, in the first place *an interval of time is inserted* between the pathogenic situation and the obsession that arises from it, so as to lead astray any conscious investigation of its causal connections; and in the second place the content of the obsession is taken out of its particular setting by being *generalized.* Our patient's "obsession for understanding" is an example of this. But perhaps a better one is afforded by another patient. This was a woman who prohibited herself from wearing any sort of personal adornment, though the exciting cause of the prohibition related only to one particular piece of jewelry: she had envied her mother the possession of it and had had hopes that one day she would inherit it. Finally, if we care to distinguish verbal distortion from distortion of content, there is yet another means by which the obsession is protected against conscious attempts at solution. And that is the choice of an indefinite or ambiguous wording. After being misunderstood, the wording may find its way into the patient's "deliria," and whatever further processes of development or substitution his obsession undergoes will then be based upon the misunderstanding and not upon the proper sense of the text. Observation will show, however, that the deliria constantly tend to form new connections with that part of the matter and wording of the obsession which is not present in consciousness.

I should like to go back once more to the instinctual life of obsessional neurotics and add one more remark upon it. It turned out that our patient, besides all his other characteristics, was a *renifleur* (or osphresiolagniac). By his own account, when he was a child he had recognized everyone by their smell, like a dog; and even when he was grown up he was more susceptible to sensations of smell than most people. I have met with the same characteristic in other neurotics, both in hysterical and in obsessional patients, and I have come to recognize that a tendency to osphresiolagnia, which has become extinct since childhood, may play a part in the genesis of neurosis. And here I should like to raise the general question whether the atrophy of the sense of smell (which was an inevitable result of man's assumption of an erect posture) and the consequent organic repression of his osphresiolagnia may not have had a considerable share in the origin of his susceptibility to nervous disease. This would afford us some explanation of why, with the advance of civilization, it is precisely the sexual life that must fall a victim to repression. For we have long known the intimate connection in the animal organization between the sexual instinct and the function of the olfactory organ.

In bringing this paper to a close I may express a hope that, though my communication is incomplete in every sense, it may at least stimulate other workers to throw more light upon the obsessional neurosis by a deeper investigation of the subject. What is characteristic of this neurosis—what differentiates it from hysteria—is not, in my opinion, to be found in instinctual life but in psychological relations. I cannot take leave of my patient without putting on paper my impression that he had, as it were, disintegrated into three personalities: into one unconscious personality, that is to say, and into two preconscious ones between which his consciousness could oscillate. His unconscious comprised those of his impulses which had been suppressed at an early age and which might be described as passionate and evil impulses. In his normal state he was kind, cheerful, and sensible—an enlightened and superior kind of person, while in his third psychological organization he paid homage to superstition and asceticism. Thus he was able to have two different creeds and two different outlooks upon life. This second preconscious personality comprised chiefly the reaction-formations against his repressed wishes, and it was easy to foresee that it would have swallowed up the normal personality if the illness had lasted much longer. I have at present an opportunity of studying a lady suffering severely from obsessional acts. She has become similarly disintegrated into an easygoing and lively personality and into an exceedingly gloomy and ascetic one. She puts forward the first of them as her official ego, while in fact she is dominated by the second. Both of these psychical organizations have access to her consciousness, but behind her ascetic personality may be discerned the unconscious part of her being—quite unknown to her and composed of ancient and long-repressed conative impulses.[16] ᔦ

---

16. (*Additional Note, 1923.*)—The patient's mental health was restored to him by the analysis which I have reported upon in these pages. Like so many other young men of value and promise, he perished in the Great War.

INTERPRETIVE QUESTIONS
FOR DISCUSSION

Why is Freud able to cure the Rat Man?

1. Why is the Rat Man able to recognize that he needs help but not that his attempts to repay Lieutenant A are an absurd "farce"? (68, 81)

2. Why does Freud consider the "patient's own view" of his condition in classifying the Rat Man's case as "fairly severe"? (65)

3. Why does Freud take note of the intelligence of his patient? Does he think intelligent people are more inclined to obsessive neurosis, or that they are more able to be cured through psychoanalysis? (111, 133)

4. Why does Freud insist that the Rat Man "pledge himself to submit to the one and only condition" of psychoanalytic treatment—to say everything that comes into his head, even if it is unpleasant, or seemingly unimportant, irrelevant, or senseless? (69)

5. Why does the Rat Man begin his treatment by telling Freud how he was duped by his tutor? (69)

6. Why does Freud interpret his patient's expression as he details the rat punishment as one of "horror at pleasure of his own of which he himself was unaware"? (75)

7. Why does Freud develop a good opinion of the Rat Man so early in the treatment, and then express this opinion to his patient? (85)

8. According to Freud, why does having a severe obsessional neurosis destroy an individual's personality? (84, 136)

9. In response to the Rat Man's question about the "remission" of his self-reproaches, why does Freud say that the answers will be found if the patient continues talking? (88)

10. Why does Freud say that the Rat Man had to become ill—that he "could not behave otherwise"—when his love for the lady was weighed against his love for his father? (89)

11. Why must Freud prove, rather than simply tell his patient, that he is in no way responsible for the reprehensible impulses in his character? (92)

12. Why does the transference fantasy finally convince the Rat Man that Freud is correct—that he harbors hatred toward his father for interfering with his sexual gratification? (104, 111)

Suggested textual analyses
Pages 84–85: beginning, "At the next sitting," and ending, "and this gave him visible pleasure."

Pages 88–90: beginning, "He admitted that all of this sounded quite plausible," and ending, "our discussion was broken off for the time being."

What does Freud want other therapists to learn from his case study?

1. Does Freud think that his technique for curing the Rat Man can be copied or taught? (65–66)

2. If Freud was so successful in treating the Rat Man, why does he suggest that his case study only contains "crumbs of knowledge"? (67)

3. Are we to conclude that the Rat Man's feeling that he and his father were best friends contributed to his neurosis? (89)

4. Why does Freud reiterate that aspects of this extraordinary case are common or typical? (74, 90, 101, 129)

5. According to Freud, why do neurotics derive "a certain satisfaction from their sufferings" and so to some extent resist their own recovery? (90)

6. Why does Freud conclude that discovering when obsessional ideas first occurred and what brought them on will lead to a cure? (93, 120)

7. Does Freud adequately explain how therapists can recognize the exciting cause of an obsessional neurotic's illness if the patients are themselves unaware of the event's importance? (100–104)

8. Why does Freud grant little importance to the death of the Rat Man's sister in his analysis of the "exciting event" of his neurosis? (110–111, 125)

9. Why does Freud stress that many of the conclusions reached during the analysis were the work of the patient?

10. Why does Freud say that it is "easily explicable" why superstition is a characteristic of obsessional neurotics, and that it "is only too obvious" that their need for uncertainty is a wish to withdraw from reality? (122, 123)

11. Why does Freud link the neurotic's obsession with death to the inability to come to a decision in matters of love? (125–126, 129–130)

12. Why does Freud believe he needs to know more about "the nature of love" in order to fully understand obsessive neuroses? Why does he postulate that premature and thorough suppression of the sadistic components of love might cause neurosis? (129)

Suggested textual analysis
Pages 128–135: beginning, "If we consider a number of analyses," and ending, "which is not present in consciousness."

Why does Freud look to infantile sexuality as the cause of adult neurosis?

1. Why is an obsessional neurosis easier to treat at an early stage? (67)

2. Why does the Rat Man fear for his father and his lady friend, when his impulse is to cut his own throat? (68)

3. Why does the Rat Man think that a diminution of his obsessions, impulses, and prohibitions was due to having sexual intercourse on a regular basis? (68)

4. Why does the Rat Man think his illness began with the "morbid idea" that his parents knew his thoughts? (71)

5. Are we meant to conclude that if the premature sexual activity came after the end of infantile amnesia, the neurosis would be less severe or that it would not have developed into a neurosis at all? (73)

6. Why did the Rat Man's sensual impulses subside during puberty? (89, 107)

7. Why did the Rat Man repress his infantile anger toward his father rather than overcome it or forgive him? (110)

8. How do other typical characteristics of the obsessional neurotic—superstition, uncertainty, and omnipotence—originate in infantile sexuality? (120–126)

9. Why does Freud conclude that the Rat Man's repression of his infantile hatred of his father was what caused his neurosis? (127)

10. According to Freud, how does one reconcile the sadistic or negative aspect of infantile love so that it doesn't manifest itself in adult neurosis? (129)

11. Why does the thought process become sexualized in highly intelligent obsessional neurotics? (133)

12. Why does Freud speculate that the loss of a keen sense of smell is somehow responsible for nervous diseases associated with sexual repression and the advance of civilization? (135)

Suggested textual analysis
Pages 70–74: beginning, "My sexual life began very early," and ending, "the patient's infantile amnesia ended precisely with his sixth year."

FOR FURTHER REFLECTION

1. How can we avoid giving our children "an excuse for hostility" in their childhood?

2. Why is the notion that children are sexual beings difficult for many people to accept?

3. Is it "only human" to have repressed hatred for those whom we love intensely?

4. Is conflict between one's parents and one's sexual object inevitable?

5. How can anyone escape being neurotic, given how susceptible we are to random events in childhood?

6. Can a mildly neurotic person make him or herself healthier by reading "The Rat Man"?

7. Why is analysis a "school of suffering"? (112)

8. Does Freud's "Rat Man" help to explain the boyhood neurosis of Proust's narrator in "Overture"?

THE ISLAND

Gustaw Herling

GUSTAW HERLING (1919–   ) was born
near Kielce, Poland. During World War II,
he helped to found an anti-Nazi
underground organization in Warsaw.
After his arrest in 1940, he was imprisoned
in a Soviet slave labor camp in northern
Russia. Herling's experiences from this
two-year period are described in his memoir
A World Apart. After the war, he lived in
England and then settled in Naples, Italy,
where he continues to live and write.

We are forsaken like children lost in the woods. When you stand before me and look at me, what do you know of my sufferings and what do I know of yours? And if I fell at your feet and cried and told you, would you know any more about me than you know about hell when they say it is hot and sets one shivering? Therefore we men should stand before each other with as much awe, thoughtfulness, and love as before the gates of hell.

FRANZ KAFKA
From a letter to Oscar Pollak (1903)

1

ALTHOUGH IT WAS the middle of May 1950, there still were not many tourists. Once a day when the boat came from Naples, the funicular, like a trawl, would haul a group of people up from the harbor below and unload them in the square. They would stop for a moment among the tables of the only café, take a quick glance around at the people, look up at the clock tower as if they wanted to remember the precise hour of their arrival, and then disappear down the narrow streets and paths into the depths of the island.

The weather was sunny and cool. Between late afternoon and dusk, as the sun withdrew behind the cover of Monte del Sole, the people around the tables of the café slowly emerged from the shadow of their reveries and looked around the square for the still-warm patches of sunset luster. In the morning some of the tourists from the northern countries went down to the sea, but even they returned to the town right after their swim and waited patiently, not hurrying the season.

Spring came late that year. It had been hot, almost scorching, in January and February, and then the winter rains fell. In March and April the sky hid behind low clouds, the air turned sooty like the glass of a kerosene lamp, and a fire burned on the hearth of more than one house on the island. The sea, the color of bluing in dirty soapsuds, pounded monotonously against the rocky shore. Occasionally the hazy outlines of the mainland and the neighboring islands were visible.

At the beginning of May a clear dry wind brought the island's overdue spring. The sea calmed; lightly wrinkled in the morning, splashed with sun at noon, it seemed to paste translucent flakes of blue-green along the shore. The vegetation of gardens and vineyards, of pine woods and fruit trees, glowed against the tawny yellow background of rocky cliffs and naked mountain ridges. All the magic of the water, the stone, and the secret filters of the sky oozing in from the outside came to life again in the island's grottoes—the Green Grotto, the Azure Grotto, the Violet Grotto. And the church bells chimed as if they were alloyed of glass and metal.

The island is a three-hour boat ride from Naples, and has no tourist sights other than the paltry ruins of a few Roman villas and the Certosa, a medieval Carthusian monastery. But tourists do not bring history texts or guide books with them to the island. For the tourists the island is, above all, "the pearl of the Mediterranean" of the travel posters, where the sea is clearer and more beautiful than anywhere else in the bay of Naples; where the summer sun toasts the skin for ten hours a day; where the rose wine quickens the blood; where the little houses are plastered white, their brightly colored shutters standing out boldly in the glittering light; where wooden sandals click pleasantly along the pavement; where a little rowboat carries one into a kingdom of silver shadows in the underground grottoes; where songs are full of tender words; where the lights of Naples glitter on the far horizon and the *lampare* of fishing boats twinkle around the island on sultry lazy nights; and where the stars quiver like cooling cinders around the full moon, red as the heart of a volcano. When there is nothing to do in the two hours between sunset and nightfall, the tourists sometimes climb up to the remains of the Roman past, a vantage point from which they have the most extensive view of the island and the bay; or they circle the Certosa in a lazy stroll on the only plateau of any size between the sea and the town.

It is different for the inhabitants of the island. Making their living primarily from tourism, they have adapted the rhythm of their lives, rather than to farming or fishing, to the trawl that during the season hauls tourists up by the hundreds from the harbor to the square. Besides, the soil is barren. Here and there, after removing the surface layer of building stone, the islanders have made the land support small vineyards, little fields, vegetable gardens, olive trees, and lemon and orange; the nets cast out near the shore sparkle grudgingly with the scanty catch. And that is why not only the two hours between sunset and nightfall but all the long months after the end of the season are empty for the inhabitants. Then they live alone with their island.

In their minds its history does not really reach back as far as the time when the sovereigns and patricians of Rome built their villas on the two extremities of the island, known today as Monte della Madonna dei Marini and Monte del Faro. If the inhabitants like to visit these places it is not merely for the remains of ancient walls dug up by archaeologists, or for the fragments of friezes, armless statues, and marble baths lying in the grass; they also like to look at the tall slender Madonna who stands on the brink of the precipice facing the sea and watches over seafarers with her arms raised against storm and gale, and near her, the tiny church where in the summer Padre Rocca says mass in the presence of scarcely a single person; and on the other end of the island the lighthouse, which, with its reflectors, performs in a different way the same function as the Madonna of Seafarers with her outstretched arms and her sweet eyes.

More vivid in the minds and feelings of the inhabitants of the island is the medieval Certosa. Every year on the nineteenth of September the large, polychrome wood sculpture of the *Pietà dell'Isola*—the Mother holding in her drooping arms the Son taken from the Cross—emerges from the Certosa in a litter borne on the shoulders of four Certosini. Beyond the gate the waiting crowd joins the four monks and, amid the flowers and paper streamers thrown by children dressed in white, to the chanting and ringing of bells, the procession moves along slowly in time to the strained step of the monks down to the main church in the square. At night the whole square is illuminated with colored lamps. The day the *Pietà dell'Isola* makes the trip down to the main church and back is the island's greatest holiday and at the same time the culmination of the season. Soon after, the tourists begin to leave the island and many of them, particularly those from the northern countries, carry away with them like a parting souvenir of their vacation the memory of that strange *festa,* unable either to understand or accept the contrast between the gay humor of the faithful and the symbol of suffering and pain borne with such difficulty by the four monks.

The history of the Certosa and of this ceremony, however, is worth closer examination.

2

The Certosa was founded in the fourteenth century. A representative of the most powerful family on the island, a man who served as secretary to Joan I of Anjou in nearby Naples, built it at his own expense to celebrate the birth of his first son. He endowed it with land, money, papal bulls, religious preroga-

tives, and numerous privileges to ensure for all time its temporal and spiritual inheritance.

The site could not have been better selected. In accordance
with the monastic rule and with a view to preserving the spirit,
the monks in their cells could not see beyond the arched line of
the shore and a hardly perceptible strip of sea beyond it on the
horizon; on the sides, two hills overgrown with pine and olive
cut them off from the world. In accordance, too, with the rule
of pirate warfare and with a view to preserving the flesh, the
low and rather hidden location of the Certosa screened it from
observation and from the weapons of the Saracens.

But it did not reward its founder with the good fortune he
expected. After the dethronement and murder of Joan of Anjou,
he was banished, his possessions were confiscated, and only by
an act of exceptional grace was he permitted to await his death
as a penitent and pilgrim behind the same walls he had had
erected years before out of gratitude for his firstborn and to the
greater glory of Heaven among his descendants. Having ran-
somed his son from captivity, the monks gave their indirect
benefactor, as well, refuge in the Certosa.

Thus, as the founder of the Certosa had formerly repaid
Providence for his short-lived good fortune on this earth, so the
Certosa settled accounts with him later, when wise Providence
neglected his worldly affairs in order to press him, along with
his son, into the service of that power and glory which are more
enduring than that which he had hitherto served. It led him onto
the road of happiness—not the road that glows with worldly
splendor and immediate reward, but the road that is more genuine and less ephemeral.

If one can believe the chroniclers who were his contemporaries, the founder of the Certosa, once he had exchanged his
princely mantle for the penitent's habit, understood this lesson
better than his protectors and hosts; he was the only great and
sincere penitent behind the wall. The wealth of the Certosa, considerable even at the time of its founding, grew continuously,

and it did not remain without influence—fatal in the opinion of the chronicles—on the life of several monks. Surrounded by servants, excited by their ever-increasing earnings from the cultivated land (particularly the vineyards), they gradually forgot the object of their cloistered isolation from the world and in the end became the gentlemen landlords of the island. The monks squeezed it like a cluster of grapes in the press of taxes and leases and only rarely came to the aid of the needy. Again the hand of God intervened, but almost two centuries had to pass before that happened. In spite of its apparently safe and secure location, the Certosa was burned and completely plundered by Dragut the corsair in the middle of the sixteenth century. It took ten years to rebuild it, and this time a tower was added, from which at last one could see the whole seashore. The Certosa returned to its former affluence after the plague of 1656, having received the inheritance of all those island families who died out without heirs. Again there began a period of material prosperity, fatal to all hermits, together with the sometimes open warfare that the poor clergy of the island waged against the monks. Thus when Joseph Bonaparte abolished the monasteries and confiscated their possessions in 1807, no one on the island (with the probable exception of the monks themselves) shed tears over the condemned Certosa. The sentence was not revoked, even upon the restoration of the Bourbons. An unusual sign of Providence marked the end of the Certosa's splendor: when the Certosini abandoned the island in 1808, the tower, which had been built in the sixteenth century to defend them from the pirates, collapsed. This reminded the island chroniclers that, a few days before the death of the Roman emperor in the villa on what is now Monte della Madonna dei Marini, another tower had collapsed—a signal tower in the place where today the Madonna watches over seafarers.

The island's aversion for the Certosa was not, however, fed exclusively by the monks' greed and material egotism; it went deeper, to the events of 1656, which revealed other aspects of their egotism a hundred times more incompatible with the calling of knights of the legions of God.

The plague had been reaping an abundant harvest in Naples for some months. Abandoned corpses lay scattered under the walls of buildings in the streets and alleys; the burial carts came for them ever less frequently; the people passed by at a distance; the churches were deserted; a funeral lament mingled in the air with the black smoke of burning beds, straw mattresses, and clothes of those who had died from the pestilence. The black columns of smoke, floating freely in the windless, limpid Neapolitan sky, often assumed ominous shapes, neither altogether human nor altogether bestial. Perhaps it was only these columns of smoke that kept the inhabitants of the island, as they looked out at the vault of the bay, from forgetting the scourge that was mercilessly lashing the city on the mainland. Although the smoke brought the news of the plague, fortunately, it was unable to bring the plague itself. The island lived in continual alarm, but the passing days, sluggish like those funeral banners of a smoky shroud, slowly strengthened the conviction that one could, after all, trust in the buckler of the sea, although how flimsy and weak it had been against enemy attacks! One may well imagine that in spite of the islanders' age-old intimacy with the sea, in spite of the many good turns for which they had been indebted to it in the past, only then did the habitants of the island really come to love it.

But the sea did not withstand the assault of the plague. The sea failed the islanders and cracked at the beginning of June. There are two contradictory accounts of the stratagem the pestilence used to breach the island's sea armor and to penetrate the camp of the besieged. In both accounts, however, the figure of the betrothed—the immortal Italian *promesso sposo*—plays the leading role. According to one version the betrothed stole to the island from Naples in order to examine at first hand the dowry of his bride-to-be, and along with his own bacillus of avarice he dragged with him the Neapolitan bacillus of the plague. The other betrothed was the hero of a much more romantic story. Even before the outbreak of the plague he had been banished from Naples to the island for his part in the popular revolt led by Masaniello against the Spaniards, and during the period of the pestilence the young man received from the family of his beloved, who had died in Naples, a letter with a lock of her hair. Beside its romanticism, which appeals more immediately to the imagination, this version seems more in keeping with the nature of plagues and cataclysms in which the fate of thousands of people always hangs by a thread.

June 1. Three days before the appearance of the plague the census of the island, still preserved in the local archives, mentioned the figure of 1,588 inhabitants. By November 1, when no incident of death or illness had been noted for a week and the epidemic was considered extinguished, the island's revised sad census counted 1,023 inhabitants. The greatest mortality occurred in the scorching month of August, which entered 137 victims in the archival registers.

On June 4, at the news of the arrival of the plague, eighteen monks locked the gate of the Certosa and cut themselves off from the world, creating an island sheltered by thick walls within the island. The inhabitants of the island were stunned with horror: if the cloistered rule of isolation and turning one's back on earthly matters was sometimes more a flight from the Cross than its acceptance, it was certainly so in that time of calamity. It was not only a matter of the resources of the Certosa, although in view of the gradually paralyzed agriculture and fishing on the island, that too must have had its weight. It was also, and perhaps that above all, a matter of human solidarity in suffering, peril, and death. Nothing so exasperates human hearts as the sight of shoulders that refuse to bear the common fate. At best, Naples could look on the island, still untouched by the pestilence, with bitterness and envy; with the tightening of the ring of misfortune, the island must have looked at its *own* island beyond the walls of the Certosa with altogether unbridled hatred.

At the beginning, the island revealed its hatred in oblique glances at that immense mass of gray stone, like an impregnable fortified castle, silent in its detached contempt for the surrounding pestilence. But in July enraged despair drove the island to a more glaring demonstration of feelings hitherto forcibly repressed. The chronicles report that after sunset on July 13, unidentified persons threw the corpses of two of the plague-stricken over the wall into the Certosa. This newly discovered practice continued in a sporadic and covert manner until the end of the month. In August, when the number of deaths suddenly increased, the attack of corpses was intensified and no longer took place under cover of night, but openly in the full blaze of the *solleone*, the most violent sun of the south. From the Chiostro Grande the handful of monks, surrounded by death, moved to the Chiostro Piccolo. In vain. The column of dead besiegers reached them there too, by way of a narrow path between the side wall and the steep slope of one of the hills.

The retreating monks had one remaining bastion that was relatively protected: the Giardino del Priore, the Prior's Garden, on the edge of an escarpment that fell steeply down to the sea and was inaccessible from without. But who could be sure that the plague would not reach from the dead, decomposing under the sun in the courtyards of the cloisters, to the living, crouching fearfully in the Prior's Garden—carried there by flies, birds, and lizards? Or, what was worse, by means of the age-old carriers of the plague—rats, which nested in the granaries and larders and in the basements crowded with vats and barrels of wine between the garden and the Chiostro Piccolo. The lookout tower, built a hundred years before, after the Certosa's destruction by the pirates, was useless now. The new invader would not approach from the sea, nor was there any way to observe its approach from the interior of the island. It had been within the precinct of the fortress itself for a month.

Only pride, that enemy of humility with which the tunic is sewn, prevented the monks, backed against their own wall of defense, from admitting their error, opening the gates of the Certosa, and crossing with heads bent in repentance the bulwark of corpses that divided them from the flood of tears and suffering that had inundated the island. The monks waited for an excuse. It came in the second half of September. The number of deaths had diminished in the first days of September, and the islanders had taken heart at the sight of two new wayside chapels, which on the advice of the bishop of the island had been built in honor of Saint Boche and Saint Sebastian, patrons of the plague-stricken. But immediately afterward, a terrible thing happened: the only three priests on the island died one after the other in the course of a week. Terror gripped the faithful and froze the blood in their veins. Was it a sign of Providence warning of new devastations to come? Had they not already paid a high enough price for their sins, that now they could not even hear the church bells, that now they would have to die without the sacraments and reveal without the sacraments this atrocious world to the newborn?

It was then that the bishop of the island wrote a letter to the prior of the Certosa humbly imploring him to let three or four monks come out to take the place of the dead priests. The prior's reply is preserved in the archives. In succinct terms (how insatiable pride is when it has a chance to hide its secret weakness and save itself!) he consented in the name of the brothers entrusted to his care *di ponere la vita per il prossimo nonostante che sia ministerio repugnante alla nostra professione,* "to offer their lives for their neighbors even though it be a ministry repugnant to the order."

The morning of September 19, the gates of the Certosa opened. Four monks slowly crossed the threshold. Swaying above their heads on a hastily built wooden litter was the famous *Pietà dell'Isola,* the work of an unknown Sienese master acquired by the monastery in the sixteenth century to commemorate an anniversary of its foundation. In the kinder September sun every color of the worn polychrome acquired its full tone: the golden tresses of the Mater Dolorosa shone, and only the long thin body of the Son seemed grayer, as if it had been sprinkled with ashes before coming into the light of day. In the chapel of the Certosa echoed the silvery thin voice of the little bell. The Certosini stopped for a moment and glanced at the malevolent faces of the group of passersby that stopped suddenly. But seeing that it was vain to hope someone would take the sacred weight from their shoulders in sign of reconciliation, the monks moved on toward the main church, often stopping along the way and drying the rivulets of perspiration on their foreheads with the sleeves of their habits. When they reached the end of their Calvary, they celebrated mass and remained among the inhabitants of the island. In October, as the last embers of the plague were extinguished, two of the monks really "offered their lives for their neighbors." But neither then nor later was anything able to erase in the islanders' eyes the ignominy of "the order that had found that ministry repugnant." And more than one brick was added to the wall that was to separate the Certosa from the island for centuries to come by the fact that those whose hearts had trembled in helpless fear in the face of the scourge now found courage enough in those same hearts to reach out their hands when there was an opportunity for material gain: by virtue of the ancient Angevin grant, the Certosa received all the island possessions that had been deprived by the contagion of their legal proprietors and natural heirs.

Thus the Certosa reached the end of its glorious and tempestuous history, the end decreed by Joseph Bonaparte and accepted with relief by the island. All attempts to restore it failed, and the slow decadence that the new epoch prepared for it truly could not have been sadder: first it was turned into a prison, then into an asylum for invalids and cripples, and, finally, in 1860, into a barracks for a discipline company of the army. Where the quiet of prayer and cloistered abundance had once existed for centuries, there now sounded, in succession, the rosaries of convicts, the din of wooden legs tapping and the hissing of imprecations, the metallic clatter of arms and the rustling sound of soldiers' curses. And perhaps those sounds were more pleasing to the God of the plague, the God who sent ill fortune to man constantly to remind his disaccustomed feet of the thorns and sharp stones of our terrestrial wandering, than the click of monastic sandals in the shade of the porticoes of the Chiostro Grande and the Chiostro Piccolo, the jingle of ducats in the moneybags of the Certosa, and the terrified whispers of whitened lips in the refuge of the Giardino del Priore.

But the Certosa was restored—not, to be sure, in its former splendor, but it was restored—on the eve of the First World War. With the consent of the island authorities four monks came from a monastery between Pisa and Lucca. Having become acquainted with the history of the Certosa, they decided of their own free will that every year on September 19, they would humbly bend their shoulders under the sculpture of the *Pietà dell'Isola* and carry it in procession to the church and back again, as if in symbolic atonement for the sin of their predecessors of 1656. There was a tacit understanding that no one except the monks was to touch the handles of the litter on which the Mother of Sorrows held in her arms the inanimate body of the Redeemer. If one of the monks died, another came from the mainland to take his place. The *festa* of September 19 quickly established itself and became an indivisible part of the life of the inhabitants of the island. In the first years, because of the war, perhaps one saw in the sculpture of the Sienese master not only a reminder of the episode that had taken place two-and-a-half centuries before but also the image of a woman lifting from the battlefield the mortal remains of a father, husband, or son. Later the islanders certainly discovered the attraction to tourists of that ceremony, which stamped an exotic seal on the end of the visitors' season in the island. The Second World War probably renewed that eloquence which the *Pietà dell'Isola* had had during the preceding war. But to all these elements must be added the most important one. In the south of Italy, where human solitude before God and Nature, in the presence of the secret of Life and Death, finds its delight in miracles, and in the folk magic of the Lucanian and Calabrian countryside, in the power of the *iettatura,* of the *malocchio,* of the breaking of spells, in the miraculous skulls of the Neapolitan catacombs of Santa Maria della Sanità, in the dramatic processions of the Passion, in the gloomy realism of the instruments of the Passion of Our Lord carried about on Easter eve in Sicily and Sardinia—in this south, a singular coincidence of date must have caught the attention of the island, because every year on September 19 the miracle of San Gennaro takes place in nearby Naples. It is tempting to imagine that above the bay a kind of signal immediately passed between the crowd on the island that followed the procession from the Certosa and the crowd that cheered and applauded the same day in Naples at the news that the coagulated blood of the martyr saint of Pozzuoli had again liquefied.

The Certosa was poor now and had lost all its former wealth. With difficulty its new residents planted a small vineyard in the wild and ruined Prior's Garden. Every day one of the monks took an alms-bag and went begging among the passengers of the boat that ran between the island and Naples, and among the passersby on the streets of Naples as well. The monks did not have even the means to remove the ruins inside the walls of the Certosa. Only the wall itself, cracked and broken in so many places, was more or less restored to its original state in 1933 (seventeen years before the events with which the present narrative will be concerned) by the best *mastro* on the island, Sebastiano. It was Sebastiano's last major work: shortly before completing it the tragedy occurred, and for some time, under the influence of Immacolata, the inhabitants of the island again looked on the Certosa with superstitious rancor.

What else is there to describe? The Certosa, its famous sculpture, and, at the end of this chapter, the island itself seen from on high, from the summit of Monte della Madonna dei Marini.

From a distance the Certosa suggests a gray fortress, heavy and massive, but from nearby, there is little, except its size, that distinguishes it from the architecture of the whole island. All the roofs on the island are vaults that look like wooden shovel faces turned upside-down—a memento of the times when water was provided by the rains and conducted through drains laid out around the vaults of the roofs into receptacles on the ground. Today only a second function is served by the hemispherical vaults of the roofs: the sun's heat is diffused over the largest possible surface. The clock tower, like the other little turrets on the island, is topped by a triangular slanted hood.

The unknown sculptor of the *Pietà dell'Isola* must have carefully studied the sculptures and pictures of his predecessors and contemporaries on the same theme before he applied his chisel to wood. The *Pietà* has no originality. The position of the Mother at once suggests the classicizing Michelangelo of the Basilica of St. Peter, before he created the dramatic forms of the Palestrina *Pietà* and the *Pietà* of the Cathedral of Florence. In the figure of Christ, instead of the tradition of the body bent delicately like a ribbon between the outstretched arms, an older tradition is preserved: the body is rigid and tense in an almost abstract plane. The face of the Madonna framed in golden tresses slipping out from under the black kerchief that falls to her shoulders is sad and yet strangely serene, as in Perugino's San Giusto *Pietà*. Her eyes and mouth seem to unite in a kiss on the lips of the Son, half open in pain and thirst. One would like to believe that the Sienese master had read the *Laudi* of the thirteenth-century Jacopone da Todi, and that while he worked he often repeated to himself these two verses: *una han sepoltura . . . mate e filio affocato* and *de dura morte afferrate . . . mate e filio a un cruciato:* "Mother and Son have the same tomb" and "grasped by one cruel death . . . together in the Crucifixion of pain."

When Padre Rocca, who comes from Mantua, looks out over the island in the last rays of the setting sun from the belvedere near his little church and parish, he always makes the same mental observation (even though he has already spent thirty years on the island): "On the surface it is the typical Mediterranean landscape, just as the Romantic painters and poets of the beginning of the last century saw it and represented it; but if you look for a while at the sweet, ripe shadows of the rocks and trees and houses sprinkled with a gilding of light, and trembling in the brief purple reflection of the sea, you realize that there is something of the classical in it as well."

3

Sebastiano was thirty years old when he was commissioned to repair the wall of the Certosa. He was born on the island, the only son of a fisherman who rowed tourists to the Green Grotto during the season. Both of his parents died when he was young, and Sebastiano inherited his father's boat and two professions. After he finished his military service in Livorno and Florence, he sold the boat and the nets, rented out his parents' house near Monte del Faro, and moved to Naples to learn the mason's craft. He stayed there five years, working first as an assistant mason and later as a young *mastro* on the removal of the baroque adornments of the Flemish-Gothic church of Santa Maria Donnaregina in the old quarter of the city.

Sebastiano returned to the island and soon became famous for his skill in his craft and for his conscientiousness in the execution of his work. Although the building boom on the island (which had lasted throughout the preceding century, when English and German travelers "discovered" the island) had long since entered a phase of gradual decline, Sebastiano never waited long for a job while he passed his time in the house at the foot of the lighthouse or in the bar in the square. The modest local commissions, however, did not much attract him. He had seen the churches of Florence during his military service, and he had worked in Naples, where he would pass his lunch hour in the cool nave of Donnaregina—with his eyes ecstatically fixed on the tomb of Maria of Hungary, the work of the chisel of Tino di Camaino, and on Cavallini's frescoes—or in the Loffredo Chapel, adorned with frescoes by followers of Giotto and Cimabue. Then Sebastiano had dreamed of another kind of work. But there was probably no expecting it on the island, so in his free moments he would sit in the courtyard of his house and carve bas-reliefs from the stone that was so common on the island. For the most part he sculptured fruit-laden *carrettini* with two enormous wheels drawn by oxen, or strange fish shapes and smaller boats, or figures of archers and centaurs like those he had seen many times on the metopes of Thesauros sul Sele and at Paestum, and he would carve scenes of the Passion. The imaginative world of the self-taught sculptor, who barely knew how to read and write, was stretched like a tent on these four pegs: the ancient methods of fruit harvesting still practiced here and there in the Sorrentine peninsula and in the Salernitano, as well as in Sicily and Sardinia; fishing; the Greek representations of war and history; and the pictures that, in Florentine and Neapolitan churches, in the church in the square, and in the little chapel on Monte della Madonna dei Marini, made people kneel and bend their heads to their breasts as the sweet breeze bends the heavy ears of grain in their sheaves. In a certain way that was the instinctive world of imagination of the whole island.

But as soon as Sebastiano returned from Naples and set his string-tied suitcase on his native soil, all his thoughts turned toward the Certosa.

The monks were in no position to consider any kind of restoration; their money barely sufficed to provide for the most urgent daily needs. Sebastiano visited them often. He would silently caress the wounded columns of the Chiostro Grande, expertly measure the damage to the walls of the buildings, sit thoughtfully on the little mounds of rubbish swept under the porticoes, and, before leaving, slowly make the circuit of the outer walls. He was loved at the Certosa, perhaps because he was the only person on the island who loved the Certosa.

In the meantime he waited patiently, and again he became attached to the places of his childhood and youth.

Below his house, which seemed almost to be glued to the declivity of Monte del Faro, there was a little green valley with enough grass to attract the nearby flocks of black goats and sheep. The three shepherd boys slept when it was hot, and when there was a breeze they played *morra,* screeching like hoot owls as they sat under a large nut tree in a hollow of the valley. Above, on the rocky heights that cut off the view of the sea, the stone remains of one of the Roman villas bleached in the sun like the calcified bones of a skeleton. A path leads to the ruins through scattered rye patches dotted with poppies, a path bordered at every step by a living hedgerow of aloe and by dead cactus leaves. Hunters sat motionless in some of the dips of the path with dogs that hunted with their eyes for quail in the vicinity of Monte del Faro; more often the dogs' gaze caught the gulls that skimmed the surface of the water in rapid descent and sometimes rebounded in a single motion above the high line of the shore. The island was beautiful, more beautiful now than when as a boy Sebastiano had known all its secret hiding places. It lulled itself to the sound of the crickets. It lazily followed the strips of shadow across the face of the sundial. At dawn it shone with freshness. In full day it put on a thin veil of heat. In the late afternoon it revealed itself in all the sharpness of its outline as far as distant Naples. At night the island was full of secret rustlings, chattering, loud bursts of laughter, murmurings, and echoes. It breathed continually in a tepid atmosphere of the past: it had preserved the echoes of past epochs in nature and in its ruins. Returning home at night Sebastiano would pass beside the deep cavern where the moon had once shone on the mysteries of the Romans: the dance of those naked boys and girls whose image was immortalized in the scene of the cavalcade in the bas-relief discovered at Monte della Madonna dei Marini. Hurrying and feeling his way along the path that wound around the back wall of the Certosa, Sebastiano automatically made the sign of the cross at the thought of the bodies of the plague-stricken that had been thrown into the cloister from there.

Then there was Immacolata who lived on the island.

4

Immacolata was the daughter of the widow of a stone quarrier at Capo Scogliera. Soon after Sebastiano returned from Naples to the island, he went to the quarry near her house to look for building stone. It was then that he saw Immacolata for the first time. She was eighteen.

He paid little attention to the blocks of stone torn out of the walls of the promontory and rolled to the edge of the road, he was so absorbed by the sight of the young woman who led him to her two brothers, who continued the trade of their father. How was it that he had never noticed her before, when she was still a girl or at the funeral of her father, crushed to death by the premature explosion of a dynamite charge at the bottom of the quarry? She was not genuinely beautiful, but there was something elementally physical in her whole being. She moved with the ease and grace of a young animal, as if she were fully aware of arousing desire in men at every agile and slightly somnolent movement of her body. Most of all Sebastiano liked her hair, which glittered like bronze and was so rare on the island, where women vied with each other only in their various shades of raven-black hair.

After that, he went to see Immacolata every Sunday after sunset, and in the summer they would disappear among the *ginestra* bushes that formed a broad plain sloping up beyond the quarry and grew halfway up Monte del Sole. She knew every stone there, every crevice in the ground, for since the death of her father she had come this way every day to do the cleaning for Padre Rocca. In the hot evenings they would lie in the grass mouth to mouth with their arms around each other; or they would lie on their backs next to each other, their gaze wandering among the stars, hard and glassy over their heads, pale lower in the sky, and glimmering with an uncertain light over the distant glow of Naples. Then they would go to her house for a glass of wine. One morning Sebastiano woke earlier than usual; he got up before dawn, opened the front door, sat down on the stoop, and looked at the last stars, like morning dew on the leaves of trees and flowers. And he regretted that he was not watching them with Immacolata. He talked to her mother, and the wedding was arranged for three years later.

That year, 1933, life seemed to smile on him from two sides at once: in a couple of months, on the holiday of the *Pietà dell'Isola,* he would lead Immacolata to the altar, and in April the monks had finally decided on the restoration of the Certosa, beginning with the walls.

It was an unforgettable moment on the island when Sebastiano nailed up the planks of a movable scaffolding under the wall of the Certosa and dug a pit outside the Chiostro Grande to slake lime. A crowd of men dressed in black and women with colored scarves on their heads gathered at a distance, commenting in whispers on the event. Four monks wearing dark brown habits tied with white cords at the waist, with their hoods hanging halfway down their backs, followed all of Sebastiano's movements in silent attention. Step by step the children accompanied little Tonino, whom Sebastiano had long since taken as his helper from the poorest village at the port. So many years had passed since the duel between the Certosa and the island, yet the restoration of that wall made a greater and somehow more real impression on the islanders than had the return of the monks before the First World War. The new inhabitants of the Certosa secretly nurtured the hope that the trowel of the best *mastro* on the island would also heal, in addition to the breaches and cracks in the wall, the still-open wound of the past; and this is surely why the Certosa, although it had always been proud of its gray-green color, like the patina of the rocks along the shore, chose to see the restored walls painted the calcium white of all the houses and fences on the island. For almost three centuries the generations of inhabitants of the island had been unwilling to abandon to the winds of forgetfulness the last crumbs of mistrust that local history had passed down from father to son and son to grandson to their hands, outstretched over the abyss of time.

Sebastiano stood alone on his scaffolding, out of reach of these waves of ancient wrath and equally ancient prayers for pardon that turned and rebounded from each other. At last he could look as much as he liked at the rays of sunlight playing in and out of the colonnades. And somewhere above him he heard music such as no human ears had ever heard. He gazed at the panes in the windows of the chapel, and he saw pictures that human eyes had never seen; at the palms in the Prior's Garden, which beat the sky with their green fronds, and he remembered the Chiostro del Paradiso from his two-day pilgrimage to Amalfi; and at the cracks in the half-closed little windows of four cells of the cloister building, through which only God could catch and gather up to Himself the slender thread of a prayer. Sebastiano often turned back in memory to the years he had spent at Donnaregina. Again he felt like a mason in the service of centuries that he could never understand and before which his spirit trembled. Had it not been for centuries the destiny and glory of man to leave behind him as enduring as possible a sign of his hand? And although it would not have been difficult for Sebastiano to finish the wall of the Certosa in three months' time, he had already conceived the idea of prolonging the work at least till the middle of September.

Similarities of human destinies are deceptive. Yet it is impossible to resist the impression that Sebastiano, driven by an unknown force, had entered on a trail carved out several hundred years before by the history of the unfortunate founder of the Certosa and buried all these centuries in the sand of a world that rolls ever onward. For both of them, though for different reasons and in different circumstances, the Certosa was to have been a crown of triumph. And for both of them, still in different circumstances, it became a crown of thorns. Since time immemorial philosophers have debated whether life repeats itself, like an unimaginative needleworker embroidering the same patterns over and over again, and the issue is still unresolved. Whether the inscrutable sentences of God are written in thousands of copies and modified only in the smallest details, or whether, in the opposite view, each of us is reflected in the immense eye of Providence and receives from the infallible hand of the Judge a different fate tailored exclusively to his measure is a question that troubles believers and theologians. But even though Immacolata burdened the Certosa with too much responsibility for the misfortune that befell her and Sebastiano, the poor mason of Monte del Faro seems at a certain point to have entered a path covered over for ages and to have stumbled on the petrified bones of the prince-secretary of Joan of Anjou hidden in the sand.

That moment came in July, the twenty-fifth to be exact. The wall was just about finished, and Sebastiano was working unhurriedly on the last section. Built behind the Prior's Garden right over the declivity of the plateau on the sea side, it was the most difficult section. The sun blazed mercilessly, its heat unrelieved by even a breath of wind, and permitted the trees to throw no more leaf shadow on the scorched ground than there are dots stamped on summer percales. From afar the shore rocks looked as dry as pumice. The sky was undone by the heat, like tissue paper stuck to a heated pot. There was nothing extraordinary in the fact that Sebastiano set about slaking fresh lime during his lunch break. The dust and white smoke over the pit blended with the milky-white atmosphere that enveloped the island. There was no one around; Tonino had taken the funicular down to the port. From time to time the wooden click of sandals on the stone walks of the nearby cloister could be heard.

In that solitude and quiet, broken only by the hissing of the lime, Sebastiano suddenly looked up and saw Immacolata at a bend in the road above, coming toward him from town.

A half-hour later the clock in the square struck one. The lonely sound floated over the island, describing ever larger and more muffled circles; Tonino hurried off from the funicular station toward the Certosa. The last vibration of the clock's echo had barely died out when the air, motionless again, resounded to a man's heart-rending scream, which gave way at once to a howl or a whine, not exactly like a wild beast's but not human either, a long, drawn-out, and painful wail. Then a weakening pause and the wail, quieter now, was overpowered by another sound, as if suddenly torn from all the cords—the piercing scream of a woman. When Tonino finally emerged from the path in front of the Certosa, he saw Immacolata staggering toward him. She had buried her hands in her magnificent bronze hair and was pressing them to her temples. When she saw Tonino she screamed twice, *"Aiuto, aiuto!"* She stopped suddenly, clutched her stomach, and sank to a sitting position on the ground. Tonino stopped by her only a fraction of a second and then ran on. By the lime pit two monks were kneeling over a figure twisted in convulsions, a human tatter soaked with white powder and lying face down on the ground frantically jabbing his hands into his eyes. The three of them finally managed to turn him over on his back: small cracked flecks of lime still stuck to his hands, his cheeks, and his forehead. Sebastiano's face was swollen and red; locked like claws his fingers continually tried to cover his eyes; he pressed them with a panting groan down into the orbits. Finally the monks and Tonino managed (Sebastiano did not offer much resistance) to carry him to the cloister *ambulatorio* in the Chiostro Piccolo. Running to town for the doctor, Tonino passed Immacolata still sitting on the ground, rhythmically swaying back and forth and softly repeating, *"Aiuto, aiuto!"* But it was not clear whether she was repeating that cry for help to herself or to the little crowd of people around her that her shout had brought from their houses in the most violent heat of the afternoon.

Slowly Immacolata calmed herself enough to utter something more than her monotonous call for help. She told the *carabinieri* sergeant that Sebastiano had tripped and struck his knee on the long handle of the shovel he used to slake the lime: the curved shovel, shallowly immersed in the pit, had snapped back like a bolt of lightning and splashed its entire contents in his face. The two monks listened to this account with lowered eyelids—eyelids under which obstinately persisted the sight of the wooden handle not leaning on the side of the square pit where

Sebastiano had writhed in pain. But could one be sure that the shovel, forcefully struck by his knee, had not bounced to the opposite side of the pit? Then the rotation of the shovel face in the direction of Sebastiano's head would have been even more comprehensible. For the moment the matter would have to stand there, until Sebastiano could speak. But days and weeks passed, and Sebastiano lay motionless in the penumbra of what had once been a monk's cell with the upper part of his head bandaged and a bandage over his eyes and mouth, as if gagged.

The procession of the *Pietà dell'Isola* was sad that year. Fewer fireworks were set off, and those grudgingly. The crowd of people on the road from the Certosa to the church watched with embarrassment the little group bearing the statue; the children tossed flowers and streamers less abundantly than usual, and then hid behind the row of adults. The procession itself tried to move along as fast as it could. At sunset only the facade of the church in the square was illuminated. Had the old shadow come back to life? Did people believe the accusations made by Immacolata, who ever since the accident had cursed the Certosa from afar? Did they think of the gray patch in the white-plastered wall of the Certosa that was visible from the sea behind the Prior's Garden? Did they look at the Madonna, with her glance suspended over the lips of the tortured Son, and remember that only a week before Immacolata had given birth to a dead child, which Padre Rocca (although she belonged to a different parish) baptized, christened Giovanni, and buried in the cemetery at the foot of Monte della Madonna dei Marini?

On the way back the procession broke up before reaching the gate of the Certosa. Beyond the gate, in the courtyard of the Chiostro Grande, the four monks stopped dumbfounded and set down their load at what they saw. Between the columns of the portico, barefoot and wearing only trousers and a shirt and with his head bandaged, walked Sebastiano. He did not answer when called, nor did he make even the slightest movement of his head. As he walked he touched the columns with outstretched hands, as if he were groping. The monks were sure he was deaf. Perhaps he was mute. And he was probably blind.

5

The four monks were mistaken. When Sebastiano emerged from the cell on September 19, 1933, after eight weeks of mortal torpor, he was not altogether deaf, nor altogether mute, nor altogether blind. The shock of the accident by the Certosa wall had only robbed him of hearing and speech to such a degree that the words imprisoned in his throat were too weak to break out and preferred to silence their timidly beating little hearts rather than to break into flight with the despairing hum of broken wings. And the sounds of the world around him were not altogether dead and incomprehensible, but reduced to the buzz of a seashell held up to the ear; they seemed to reach him as if through a thick pane of glass. His left eye was forever covered by an immovable membrane, but there remained a little crack in the corner of his right eye. If he lifted his head at an angle he saw persons and objects in an incessant vibration, as they are when you turn from an afternoon nap and look at the sun from under blinking eyelashes: even the fluctuating shadows are split into an infinite number of smaller shadows, leading one's shattered attention even farther from its real source.

One may wonder whether these three faculties of human existence, of which Sebastiano had been in large measure deprived, were of any use to him at all. For Sebastiano had lost something else more important then hearing, speech, or sight: his memory. The last and only sensation that he salvaged from the world was pain. Pain so horrible that the mere recollection of it raised the empty lump of a moan in his throat and shook him for a long time, as if he were hiccuping. He was frightened by everything; the mere touch of a tree, a house, or a passerby drove him to panic. Somewhere deep inside him, under the lowest stratum of this pain, there crawled a grim suffering without a face, without a name, and without associations. There were moments when he was oppressed, rather than by the suffering itself, by its insinuation, never identified and in its dark formlessness constantly eluding his outstretched arms. How much more painful is the blindness of his memory than the blindness of his eyes! And how much more tormenting was the shadow of a shadow of his memory fleeing farther and farther from its source than the half-mute apparitions, the tattered fragments and fleeting forms that sparkled and whirled in an eternal dance before his half-closed eyelid!

For the first two or three days a curious group, mostly children, kept him company in his wanderings far and wide over the island. They quickly realized that every effort to bring him back to the past was useless, but they feared that on the treacherous narrow paths along the edge of the precipice he might step into that future from which there is no return. He always walked barefoot ahead of them, and sometimes he broke into a short dash if he sensed that he were being followed. Then he would stop, listen intently, and, unable to distinguish the human voices from the murmur of the sea, sit down peacefully. Then his escort too would stop behind him; they discussed whether they should leave him to his fate; they wondered (although the September sun was milder) whether they should put a fisherman's straw hat on his head.

Although Sebastiano had no determined goal, he rarely rested, constantly driven on by an obtuse perseverance that was an end in itself. But the island had no straight roads: they all ran around it or crossed it, returning like rope knots to where they had begun. So he appeared several times a day in the same places, everywhere received by the silent gaze of the men and the tearful compassion of the women. The first day toward evening he fell exhausted on a bench in the village at the foot of Monte della Madonna dei Marini and began moving his lips voicelessly like a fish thrown up on the sand. A kettle of milk was brought to him, a plate of soup, and a half loaf of bread. From then on, whenever he stopped at that hour near human habitation, he did not lack for food.

The bird of misfortune that soars over the immense world had singled out a victim on the island; and the island, as accustomed to misfortune as it was to the algae that settle on the seashore after low tide and dry in the sun until they decay, bent in silent resignation over the victim abandoned half-alive by his celestial assailant.

The curious abandoned the wanderer when the sun set behind a nearby island and the fan of night, still slightly reddened along the broad shore, rose from the sea. Sebastiano slept in the open air, and even the darkness, suddenly whisking away the tremor of light and shadow before his half-open lid, startled him. He bedded himself as he could: on the hard, naked earth under a hanging rock, in the cool caverns, in the grass between the roots of trees, in the hard stubble of the *ginestra,* or, more happily than elsewhere, on the fine, warm sand of the beaches, but never within the orbit of human habitation. At dawn he took to the beaten paths and looked for the nearest spring.

He never avoided the Certosa in his wanderings, and when he went around it and seemed to touch the wall with aversion, it was at first taken as a sign that innumerable fragments of memory rattled around inside him. To all appearances, however, he did not recognize his own house by Monte del Faro, and the first time he passed through the village of the stonecutters and Immacolata ran out into the road and fell down with loud sobs at his knees, vainly calling him by name, he was so frightened that he fled and ran off with long leaps in the direction of Capo Scogliera. Only at the entrance to the stone quarry did he recover from his fright, and walking more slowly then, he turned into a path leading to the ruins of the Roman villa. That day Immacolata joined his sad retinue. She returned home that evening overcome by what she had seen. From then on, every time she noticed him from a distance, a rapid sign of the cross that ended with her thumb timidly held to her lips was the only acknowledgment she made of their former engagement.

It could be said that Sebastiano had retained more memory of all the roads and paths on the island in his naked feet than in that relic of sight which fate had spared him. He remembered every irregularity, every smooth and even stretch of stone paving, every rock, every tree stump and every grassy zone in the valleys, every rise and every hollow in the mule paths that traversed the slopes of the uplands. In the chaos of his mind and heart only one sensation—feeling again and so well recognizing the earth under his feet—sometimes touched his mouth with a cheerful smile. Then he would walk straight ahead without fatigue, and he seemed to hear through the humming in his ears a pure and reassuring note from somewhere below. Perhaps in some mysterious way the blood in his veins picked up the rhythm of the secret pulsation of the island on which he had been born and which he had once loved with a conscious love.

After those first few days the group that accompanied him slowly began to disperse, until they altogether deserted him. Assured that he had at least retained the sensitivity of his feet after the accident and that life was dearer to him than death, the inhabitants of the island entrusted him to the protection of God and Providence. He remained alone then with his nameless suffering and his blinded memory, which only once roused him with a sudden expressiveness like the lightning puncture of a needle: the first night from his lair at the foot of Monte della Madonna dei Marini, he saw a luminous spot vibrating in the distance.

It was the facade of the church in the square, illuminated in honor of the feast of the *Pietà dell'Isola*.

6

Months passed, and then years, and the island became accustomed to its solitary wanderer. With the passing of time Sebastiano was seen even more rarely. Often he disappeared and several days would pass before he unexpectedly re-emerged as if from underground, now here, now there, with his little sack of belongings, sewn from old sailcloth. Autumn and winter, always barefoot, he paid no attention to the cold or to the rain as he waited patiently on the edge of some inhabited zone until someone finally noticed him from the window. But in bad weather he sought a different refuge for the night: under a surviving piece of roof in the Roman ruins, under the covered verandas of villas empty after the season, in the entrance hall of a square dwelling by the lighthouse. The *carabinieri*'s attempt to put him in the little hospice on the island ended unsuccessfully; that was the only time that anyone had seen him angry, and fragments of a strange stutter came from his mouth. Since he was not a threat to public order, the next day the door to that sad liberty of wandering was again opened for him. The first winter the question of his memory was again briefly raised (in a negative manner this time), for even the cold was unable to drive him at night either behind the walls of the Certosa or to his own little house, which the authorities finally turned over indefinitely to a school of ornamental crafts. Slowly, no one knew how or when, the moment arrived when it seemed that the former Sebastiano had never existed—only, from time immemorial, that miserable creature into whose hands tourists, newly arrived and still unfamiliar with the life of the island, slid an offering that he immediately rejected. *"Er ist verrückt,"* the Germans said in horror. "He doesn't seem to be in need," said the English, shrugging their shoulders. Slowly, too, the feast that ended the season regained its former splendor.

It is time to describe Sebastiano's appearance. Before the accident he was of average height. He had broad shoulders and a square angular head that might have been carved from some hard wood. Like a visor his low forehead covered large greenish eyes in which calm and vigor were mixed with a childlike ingenuousness. Eight weeks in bed at the Certosa aged him ten years. He came out thin and flabby, as if the bones were trying to break through the envelope of skin. That abrupt advance in age had changed him in two ways: Sebastiano seemed taller than before, but at the same time strangely bent forward because of the vulture-like curve of his back and neck. The features of his face were drawn and pulled from the burn, especially on the right side. His eyes, one sealed and the other underscored by an oblique crack, gave him an expression of feigned or impotent ferocity. He had become partially bald in those two months. His sparse hair seemed longer and wilder and had to he confined in a round knot at the back of his neck. In compensation he had a thick curly beard like the ancient busts of Greek sages or the Apostles in Byzantine frescoes. Now and then the shepherds cut Sebastiano's hair while he slept, when he came to the little green valley where the sheep and goats fattened. He liked to sleep to the barely perceptible sound of the little Abruzzi hornpipe that the shepherds sometimes carried with them. Other than the secret voice of the earth beneath the soles of his feet, this was the only clear, distinct, and pain-relieving note that penetrated his consciousness.

Among the places he particularly favored during his roaming about the island were these: the rarely frequented slopes of Monte della Madonna dei Marini, to the east; Capo Scogliera, on the sea side; and a shallow pool between the twin-peaked rock rising from the bottom of the sea just offshore and the western slope of Monte del Faro. On the wild slope of the mountain, the holly growing in thin layers of soil on the rocks, the high-stemmed flowers, and the soft networks of bindweed formed a spot in which a seated man was completely covered. There the sunrise struck the island with its first rays and powdered the air with a dew of light. The breath coursed through the body like a fresh stream, and it was like pressing lips to a cool spring before turning again to the dry burst of solar heat. On a mound of sand by the sea at Capo Scogliera, covered halfway up by stones, a black cross commemorated the death of nine fishermen in a storm at the beginning of the century. Few people reached here from the mainland, for the only access meant frequent sliding over the rocks, while the black monument of the catastrophe held boats at bay. Like Sebastiano, the seagulls that roosted on the arms of the cross, indifferent to the explosions from the stone quarries, preferred this secluded spot to all others. In the summer Sebastiano bathed in the pool between the two-peaked rock and Monte del Faro. Without undressing he entered the water above his waist and immersed his head. The emerald-green spots of stones, the dark-red marine musk, the roses and blues of algae branches, laces to which little shells were glued, the silver flashes of tiny sardines—he saw everything through the crack in his eye with such clarity, as if only the underwater kingdom were unveiled to him. Perhaps it was for this that he preferred that pool above all else. He would dry himself on the flat protuberance of the rock wall, and sometimes he would still be lying there long after sunset, when the revolving fire began its nightly rotation in the glass tower of the lighthouse. Sebastiano's world, the island he traversed unceasingly, was like a clock the two hands of which advanced together around the quadrant and innumerable times crossed the same segments of division, subject only to the rhythms of the toothed cogs in the covered mechanism. A clock does not ask if it is night or day, spring or autumn. Its time is dead, the skeleton of time. Unless it is filled like modeled clay with living hours, months, and years, it remains immobile despite all appearance of motion. It is like a river dried up by drought: it winds along the ribbon of its desiccated bed, it keeps its former shape and direction, it still courses around the sharp turns and sweet meanderings, but it has already forgotten what water is—talking with tens of voices, changing into tens of colors, reflecting the sky in its passage, and reflecting the trees and clouds.

If Sebastiano had been able to consider his own life, he would have discovered that he really never knew when he awoke from sleep: at dawn, when the luminous ray before his right eye lifted his body from his mat; or past the threshold of night, when darkness and fatigue laid him on the ground and made him impotent with their weight. During the day he wandered about the island as if asleep. And he sank into the expanses of nocturnal dreams as if in waking. Under the wings of night and sleep, his blind eyes opened and found in the desert of memory a few oases in the hardened lava crust: Maria of Hungary, lying carved in stone on her tomb in the Church of Donnaregina, leaned on one elbow and drew her face toward his; Cavallini's Madonna, wearing the medallion of the Infant on her breast and to her right the angel that defends her from the assault of the dragon; golden-haired cherubim that fly down from the walls and circle so closely that they fill him with terror as well as excitement; fruit-laden carts pulled by oxen with human heads; a black cross torn from a mound of earth and carried by someone up a mountain. A casual witness leaning over the sleeping man would also have heard sounds that resembled words and short sobs or sighs. At daybreak everything disappeared without the slightest trace, like the flame on the altar when it is extinguished by the tin cone of the snuffer.

One day at the beginning of summer 1939, he woke up at dawn on the slope of Monte della Madonna dei Marini and, instead of going as usual to the well by the gate of the little cemetery where Padre Rocca had buried Immacolata's son, he began to climb up toward the top. The holly branches hurt him as he went. The hard thistle stalks and the bending flower stems struck him like whips, but he did not stop. Gripping the protruding ridges of the slope, he climbed upward, driven on by a strange sense of exaltation and urgency. Until then he had always instinctively gone around the place where the Madonna of Seafarers watched, although on rainy nights he might venture as far as the lower floors of Roman villas. That day, however, instinct guided his steps another way. The sun had already emerged from its marine covering when he appeared from behind the last projection perpendicular to the wall and stood up on the flat level of the peak. The animated statue with arms bent at the elbow and lifted toward the sky, like a two-armed candlestick, seemed to long for the brightness of dawn. The regular path on the plateau was sufficiently wide and safe that the islanders and the tourists often followed it to the little church or to the ancient ruins. The door of the chapel was half open; the dark crack quivered with a luminous reflection from inside. The coarse cloth curtain hanging in the doorway swelled with a breath of wind.

Sebastiano approached the entrance cautiously and pushed the door open. At first the darkness enveloped him. Then, tilting his head up at an angle, he perceived through a fog two little flaming tongues that quivered against a background of dark, narrow windows. Farther down, to one side, was the small figure of a kneeling boy. At that moment the priest turned from the altar toward the empty nave and lifted his arms. The movement was instantaneous. It should have been only part of a rapid, complete circle, but noticing the new arrival, Padre Rocca turned pale and froze. In that position he resembled the Madonna dei Marini, with his arms still stretched above the bright forms of the candles in the corners. It lasted so long that the boy stepped up to the altar with a questioning gesture. Sebastiano let his head fall on his chest and sank again into darkness. It was a pure black this time, as if the limpid water of the pool under Monte del Faro where he bathed had come up from the darkness to refresh him. Suddenly something came free in him; it seemed as if something had loosened the knot in his throat. A kind of short and fugitive gleam, far away and without rejection, acute and altogether unnerving, penetrated him like a ray of hot and invisible light. Tears slowly fell from his right eye, and he felt their burning rivulet on his cheek until they rolled from his skin into his beard. Suddenly the inseparable companion of his existence disappeared: the memory of pain and beneath it that suffering without a name and without a face. No, he had not returned to the past; the past had been torn from him without a trace. When Padre Rocca approached him after the mass and said, "Welcome to the house of God! Don't you recognize me? I'm the parish priest of the Madonna dei Marini," Sebastiano only heard the usual hum and did not even nod his head. He finally rose from his knees and without noticing the figure standing before him he left the church, again pushing the door open cautiously.

But a certain change had taken place in him: he saw better. Going down the path to the island, he stopped on two different occasions, each time drawn by a patch of landscape. For a long time he gazed at the yellow, sun-scorched hill as if he had never seen it before, with the thin, contorted trunks and dust-faded leaves of its dwarf olives. And later he noticed a little pine forest, where occasional rays of sunlight fell between the thin, light columns of the trees. The second scene suddenly reawakened in him an inexplicable emotion, and he selected the pine forest as his resting place for the night.

From then on Sebastiano was a regular morning visitor (and in the summer the only visitor other than the boy who served at the mass) at the church on Monte della Madonna dei Marini.

7

The Second World War barely touched the island. But in the first years its existence might have been guessed from the nature of the new arrivals: the French and English tourists stopped coming; among the Italians from the mainland men in uniform predominated; and there were Germans. Italian Jews with sufficient funds, apprehension, and the gift of foresight settled in some of the more deserted parts of the island to wait out the storm in that relatively out-of-the-way place. One of these, Dr. Filippo Sacerdote of Mantua, discovered his old friend and countryman in Padre Rocca and went to live with him in the parish house, spending his time looking after the health of the village at the foot of the mountain. People talked very little and then in whispers of these unusual newcomers, as if they already knew that the Jews' fate would depend on silence.

Thus, the sea again became a protective shield, as it had been almost three centuries before. This time it endured to the end—even when the bombs fell on Naples and, as in the year of the plague, black columns of smoke, trimmed at the bottom by a scissor-edge of fire, rose in the calm Neapolitan sky; when the

moon and stars disappeared at night in the scarlet and black
sky; the island remained untouched by the fire of destruction.
When the war ended in the south of Italy, the funicular began to
carry up from the port—instead of Italians and Germans—
American, English, French, and Polish officers. And the Jewish
fugitives returned to the mainland. When Vesuvius suddenly
awakened in April 1944 after a long sleep, the rain of ash was
greeted as a sign of expiation; and the last glow of fire over the
crater, like a nocturnal brother of the rainbow, was taken as a
sign of the reconciliation of heaven and earth. The only mark
that the war left behind on the island appeared in the square
some time later: a marble slab in honor of the inhabitants of the
island who had fallen in the First World War was enriched by a
dozen new names. Immacolata's two brothers headed the funeral
list, both cited as *caduto per la Patria in Africa,* and their dates
were given.

During these four years, when the world was covered with
blood and tears and encompassed by fire and suffering, life on
the island followed its usual course. Sebastiano still walked the
paths barefoot, turned his head up at an angle toward the sun
when he stopped to rest, passed the now more numerous groups
of passersby, and by his mere presence seemed to prove that
nothing had changed there, and that nothing would change as
long as the empty blue space cut off on all sides the disturbing
human spectacle. Sebastiano's heart was full of a sweet calm
since the morning visits to the little church on Monte della
Madonna dei Marini had come to be a clear reference point in
his wanderings. Since his accident Immacolata had aged prematurely and become ugly (as only southern women can grow old
and turn ugly while still young). She had gone to work again
when her brothers were called into service, and now worked in
back of the bar in the square. The Certosini looked in vain for
a chance to erase the shame of their seventeenth-century predecessors in this new, bellicose intervention of God. Nothing
happened that could confer more than a symbolic value on the
statue the monks carried out of the Certosa every September 19.

Nevertheless they could not but notice with a sense of satisfaction that, just as during the First World War, the danger in the air evoked a flicker of frightened and prayerful invocation in the eyes of the crowd when the *Pietà dell'Isola* passed above their heads.

Only to the life of Padre Rocca had the war brought a great change. When Dr. Sacerdote knocked on the door of the parish house in 1942, for a moment the priest did not believe his eyes. His whole youth, everything that over the years had fallen day after day to the bottom of the deep well of memory, returned to him like a long-held breath. "Is it you, Filippo? Is it you?" he stammered, and touched the shoulders and face of his guest with trembling hands. At the end he broke into a weak and moaning sob like the crying of a baby. Leaning his forehead on the doctor's breast, first hugging him close, then pushing him away, he finally abandoned himself, with no more resistance or fear, to images that sprang up from a dark abyss. Their native Mantua with the oblong opening of the square in front of the Palazzo Ducale and the loggias facing it, the maze of streets downtown and the school in the Corso Giulio Romano, the flat lakes like spring floods, the orphan home near the Gonzaga Palazzo del Tè, and Mantegna's greyhounds—Mantua lighted up and slowly went dark before his eyes in the intoxicating perfume of spring, in the weak glimmer of the streetlamps under the dark, high cupola of the night, in the gray-green icy light of Lombard mornings. Padre Rocca had never gone back; shortly after he was ordained, he was sent to the island. That was in 1920. Besides nostalgia and the feeling that he was an outsider, it was the solitude that caused him the most suffering in the eagle's roost of the Roman emperors, where along with the silent Madonna he looked at the sea and the island immersed in the solar heat. Although he was not yet old, nor was it time for him to think of death, he repeated often and willingly a phrase of La Rochefoucauld that he had read somewhere: *Le soleil ni la mort ne se peuvent regarder fixement.* And yet for years and years he had stared at the one and the other and never saw another living soul except the boy who brought provisions up to him and served at the morning mass and Immacolata, who came in the afternoon. Only on Sunday was the church filled with the faithful. Sometimes tourists came up toward sunset to visit the ruins, and Padre Rocca would accompany them just to exchange a couple of words. After the season the inhabitants of the island sometimes came up to take a look at the Madonna of Seafarers. An ailment that made his legs swollen and heavy like barrels kept him from ever going farther than the village at the foot of the mountain when the last sacrament or a funeral required his presence. "Solitude," he murmured, "what an awful thing it is, Filippo. God gives grace, but not company." And suddenly Padre Rocca realized two things: that the Italian word itself, *sole,* the sun, is a part of "solitude"; and, as he rested his head on the breast of a man of another faith, that he had blasphemed.

Dr. Sacerdote was moved too and, taller than his friend, he put his arms around the priest's neck. Persecuted rather by fear of humiliation and insult than by a real and immediate menace to life and liberty, Dr. Sacerdote had found not only an evidently safe haven but the most important thing of all, esteem and friendship. He was an old bachelor and had left no one other than some distant relatives behind in Mantua.

The two men lived together in the parish house. They rarely saw each other during the day, but in the evening they would walk among the ruins, silently admire the panorama from the belvedere, or chat far into the night in the little room that served as a library, where the guest slept. Gradually the doctor got into the habit of sitting in the last row at morning mass; Sebastiano often knelt not far from him. Like the two candles burning on the altar, like the outstretched arms of the gentle Madonna, they both looked down the little nave and found a solace for their wandering feet.

In the deepest recess of his heart, while in shame imploring God's pardon, Padre Rocca prayed that the war would last as long as possible.

8

One day in June 1944, Padre Rocca woke as usual before dawn, but instead of getting up at the first sign of consciousness, as was his habit, he fell at once into a half sleep. Under the thin, cracked skin of consciousness he could feel the enormous weight of his body, which sank no further into sleep, however, for it seemed to be bound and held to the surface as if by a dense growth of algae.

The white light of day poured through the window curtain like milk into a glass bowl. The priest made desperate efforts to free himself from the bonds of sleep, but the more he struggled with that unknown force that had immobilized him in the moment of waking, the weaker and more resigned he felt. His perspiration-soaked shirt stuck to his skin and suffocated him; it seemed to crush his chest with an unbearable weight. As he struggled, half-awake, impotent, and breathing heavily, terror gripped him. It was an indefinable terror, not at all specific but sufficiently menacing and deep to wring from his throat a scream that sounded like a deep breath. He had one desperate wish, to open his eyes. At last he succeeded, and the first thing he saw under his opened lids was the little black crucifix on the sunlit wall. He felt even greater terror. He suddenly lost even that minimal sense of time and place which he had found when he broke through the surface of reality. The cross seemed a spider on the wall. He could not distinguish the end of life from the unfathomable depths of death. Free of the mesh that had bound him so tightly, he lost his breath, and with a terror beyond the limits of an agony that allowed neither time nor place for a scream, he began to sink, floating in the last gleams of consciousness like a body carried by underwater currents in no particular direction.

Half an hour later Dr. Sacerdote was beside him. "He must rest," he said to the boy who served the mass, who had come to get him. The boy helped him give the priest an injection. "He'll have to spend a week in bed." "He could have had a long life," the doctor said to himself, "if it hadn't been for this solitude. It's destroying him bit by bit like a cancer."

Dr. Sacerdote pushed the curtain aside and looked out the window. Sebastiano was sitting on the church steps as if waiting for something. Finally he got up, turned his head around, and went off in the direction of the path along which he had climbed at dawn.

The doctor pulled the chair up to the sick man's bed and looked around the room with interest. Beside the wardrobe of lightly polished wood, the kneeling-bench that looked like a child's school desk, and a white iron washbowl with a pitcher under the basin, there was no furniture. An oil lamp was suspended by little chains from the lower frame of a large picture of the Nativity hanging above the bed. There was a small crucifix on the opposite wall. And on the side walls there were two faded little postcards, pinned at the four corners, with brick-colored withered leaves stuffed under their worn edges. One was a scene of Mantua at night, and the other was a cheap reproduction of the *Pietà dell'Isola*.

The weather was sultry, but with no sign of rain. It was one of those mornings on the island that are clear but somehow leaden at the same time, when you can sit for a long time without moving, and for lack of anything better you turn back to your own neglected and incoherent thoughts, which have been obscured as if by low-floating clouds that darken the landscape and only rarely allow you a glimpse of some hitherto unnoticed or unobserved detail.

Dr. Sacerdote suddenly recalled a scene he had witnessed several months earlier. He had given it slight importance at the time, but just as in a narrow space between wandering clouds you notice with so much more distinctness a patch of the landscape barely glanced at before because the rest of the view is so obscured by dark gray veiling, so the doctor saw the scene again with unusual clarity.

It was almost dark as he returned from delivering a baby in the village. A fine drizzle fell, and the drops were scattered in the air like the little jets of the rotating water taps that irrigated the island's vineyards during the drought. Every few minutes he had to clean his glasses, fogged by the dew of the humid spray. It was a winter day, sad and mournful. Just in front of him he saw a stretch of path and, farther up, the woolly tatters in which the mountain—with the Roman ruins, the church, and the watchful Madonna—wrapped itself when the bitter cold came. At a distance the sea murmured in a hushed voice. As the doctor left the village with its yellow window panes glowing and dripping, a bent shadow wrapped in rags passed him going in the opposite direction. The doctor recognized his companion of the morning masses. *"Buona sera,"* he shouted. He knew it was useless to expect a reply. He only shouted to drive away the wintry atmosphere, but the silence in which his words were drowned seemed gloomy and numbing and failed to quicken his lonely steps.

Before reaching the crossroad from which the proper pathway up the mountain turned off, the little road ran alongside the cemetery. It was girdled by a low, thick wall, white like all the enclosed places on the island, and looked something like a bastion or a dam. Walking with his eyes fixed straight ahead, he often had the feeling, particularly at dusk, that the crosses on the tombstones were a row of silent figures standing on tiptoe to watch passersby. But there had never been anything in that little cemetery to cause a shiver. All country cemeteries are like that: when people pass by, they make the sign of the cross with the natural familiarity of a greeting made to the living and a thought consecrated to the dead.

The doctor reached the end of the wall and was about to turn off to the left when a rustle of foliage too distinct in the silence to be merely a breath of wind attracted his attention. He stopped and glanced toward the cemetery. Some time passed before he succeeded in distinguishing through his cleaned glasses the figure of his friend in the dark gloom. Padre Rocca stood over a small tomb overgrown with grass and marked by a small cross. With one hand, probably because of his failing legs, he held onto a young tree and shook it back and forth. He held his other hand closed in a fist on his breast, as if he were holding the edges of his unbuttoned coat. For an instant it seemed to the doctor that the tree was shaking the man who leaned against it, and the rustle of the dead leaves was in fact a human sob. Dr. Sacerdote remembered that a visit to the parish cemetery was, in a certain sense, a part of the daily occupations of his friend, and although it seemed a strange hour and unsuitable weather for such a visit, he passed on without making his presence known.

But halfway up, perhaps held back by some obscure fear, he decided to wait. He stopped under a protruding ledge and sat on a bench that had been set in the shade for tourists; he tried to overcome the cold that penetrated him, pulling his hands inside his sleeves. He had to wait a long time for his friend. The two men covered the remaining piece of road together, both reluctant to talk. Several times the breathless priest had to lean for support on the companion who held his arm, and at one point the doctor dragged him along as if he were bearing a wounded man from a battlefield. For the first time then, the enemy that had been furtively insinuating itself into the heart of the priest of the Madonna dei Marini revealed itself openly.

Now the face of the sick man turned a waxen color. Padre Rocca's breath was almost imperceptible; now and then a weak bubble of air formed in front of his gums like the small bubbles that rise from time to time from the bottom of a pond. Sleep again drove him to the limit of consciousness.

The doctor bathed his face, leaden with heat, in the basin, but no sooner had he dried himself and sat down again in the chair than he felt the beating in his temples increase, and again he surrendered to his slow meditations.

What attracted the doctor's attention most of all, as he remembered that scene several months later, was the shadow that passed him near the entrance to the cemetery. Only God, and perhaps no one else, could ever understand why. Looking back he realized that all the time the two men were climbing up the mountain he had been oppressed by the idea that Sebastiano was following them. Where could he have got that idea? He knew almost nothing about that poor wretch. From the beginning he had taken a professional interest in the case, but the unbalanced cripple would not let him come near. Later the doctor became accustomed to Sebastiano's frequent presence at morning mass. The priest spoke of him with reluctance. Once or twice he had muttered, "What does he always come here for?" The doctor had replied jokingly that Sebastiano was simply trying to preserve the honor of the temple that everyone else had forgotten. But the doctor had another, more serious theory on the subject: he believed that the mason saw the two lighted candles on the altar in the darkness of the little church better than he saw anything else, and so he was involuntarily drawn there.

Why then had the doctor imagined that the shadow was following them, unless it was that Padre Rocca had seemed to be fleeing from something and had run ahead without stopping to the very limit of his forces. *Andiamo Filippo, andiamo . . .*

The doctor opened his lids a crack and suddenly had a strange illusion (one of those strange associations of thought that one should never try to explain by the casual affinity of related elements): the pale torso of a naked man pierced by arrows, beads of coagulated blood dripping from their points, the head bent under long hair that fell to the shoulders, and an expression of pain and, at the same time, of celestial rapture in clear upturned eyes. The vision so startled him that he shook himself as if he were waking from a dream.

Some time passed before he realized that the picture that memory, by some strange caprice, had thrust before his eyes was Saint Sebastian as Mantegua had depicted him.

Toward afternoon a bit of color appeared in the priest's cheeks, and he fell into a calm and refreshing sleep. But soon he began to be delirious. He raised himself and tried to lean on his elbows but immediately fell back again on the pillows. He stammered incomprehensible words that finally turned into a prolonged groan and burst from time to time in short sobs. The worried doctor bent over him, but it was merely the somnolent reaction of a long period of unconsciousness that must have been full of bad dreams. Although he had no fever, the sick man sometimes seemed to be on fire. His face and neck and the chest exposed by his open shirt burned to the touch.

Padre Rocca's sleep had that wealth of content that only comes in moments of mortal illness or danger.

Although we know little of the essence of dreams, we know at least that they let us observe the past without those empty interludes, those clamorous or simply insignificant blank passages of the stream of time. So we often see reality compressed in an instantaneous flash, instead of the authentic, diluted version of the past that, no matter how dramatic at the moment, loses much of its drama with the passing of the years. For this reason, what we see in dreams sometimes seems more real than the actual events that we have seen with our open eyes assuring us of that tangible consistency which is altogether incomparable to the volatile substance of dreams. A dream extracts what is essential from the disordered chaos of life, and even if its unravelling takes only a few minutes on the clock of our existence, a dream gives such a larger sense of continuity, of consistency, of logical sequence, of clarity and precision; in short, of those characteristics which the world lacks, tottering as it does on the edge of nonsense and compared by the poet to a story told by an idiot, full of sound and fury. But in order that the secret of the great moment of contact between life and death will never be revealed, and so that no one may boast (even at the end or at the threat of the end) that he has been allowed to observe his own life from the other shore, he returns at daybreak from the world of dreams with his tongue torn out, as if returned from the slavery of an enemy jealous of his secrets. No one has ever succeeded in recounting his dream with precision. Awakening reduces the illusion of the dream to the level of the illusion of reality in the tale of the idiot, full of sound and fury. One returns with a disordered impression that is impossible to straighten out and explain; it vanishes like a puff of smoke, which can never regain its lost form. Once the dream is over, its richness, its logic, its clarity become the nothing after an explosion—mere fragments of an immaterial and surprising structure.

So it was with Padre Rocca. Much later, when he had regained his strength, he remembered his crisis in a calmer mind. And from the ruins of that dream he could exhume only a few relatively clear fragments. He was certain that there was an enormous range in the picture, yet he stood perplexed before it, like a man who has seen the whole picture in a flash for a moment but has only retained one or two isolated fragments of the whole—too casual and vaguely related to form the basis of a total reconstruction.

Padre Rocca saw Immacolata just as she had been that day, but somehow changed. It was that afternoon when solitude had clutched his throat (for only solitude, and not the hunger of the body he had long since dominated, stole his reason and demanded that simple contact with life and with the world) and had driven him to that madness whose sinful fruit lay at the foot of Monte della Madonna dei Marini. In reality he had knelt before Immacolata and begged her consent, trembling with emotion, certainly ludicrous in his stammering, his heart flooded with self-hatred and hatred for her and all the cruel work of creation. Repulsed by Immacolata, he became enraged at the thought of his own humiliation and used violence. But all that appeared in a completely different way in the dream.

In the dream Immacolata was standing by the open window, and the rays of the sun caressed her bronze-colored hair. A sudden gust of wind blew through her thick tresses, and hundreds of golden glints seemed to fan out against the blue background of the sky. She did not look at him. She was looking up, with her hands joined in the hollow under her breast. The joy of life, as he had never before so fully sensed it, filled him with a sense of sweet impotence. It seemed, if he remembered correctly, that there was no one on the island but Immacolata and himself. He heard a strange song without words, as if all the colors of the gulf had been transformed into glass bubbles of different tones and were struck against each other in all directions by an invisible hand. He approached her, fell to his knees, and threw his arms about her waist, but she fell over a precipice like a statue toppled from a high rock, screaming *"Aiuto, aiuto!"* That scream was doubly linked to reality. It had broken from her lips that afternoon, and she had come to him with the same cry the evening of that July day when Sebastiano, after hearing her confession, had leapt at her by the Certosa wall with his eyes full of blood, only to cover them a minute later with outstretched fingers, screaming in pain.

"You have to get away from here," Dr. Sacerdote said when the sick man finally awoke, opened his eyes with difficulty, and asked for water. "You must ask for a transfer."

The priest smiled melancholically. "What else do I have in life besides my habits?" he replied.

It was the priest's friend who, two months later, left the island forever.

9

Thus, although it was the middle of May 1950, there still were not many tourists. Once a day when the boat came from Naples, the funicular, like a trawl, would haul a group of people up from the harbor below and unload them in the square. They would stop for a moment among the tables of the only café, take a quick glance around at the people, look up at the clock tower as if they wanted to remember the precise hour of their arrival, and then disappear down the narrow streets and paths into the depths of the island.

The weather was sunny and cool. Between late afternoon and dusk, as the sun withdrew behind the cover of Monte del Sole, the people around the tables of the café slowly emerged from the shadow of their reveries and looked around the square for the still-warm patches of sunset luster. In the morning some of the tourists from the northern countries went down to the sea, but even they returned to the town right after their swim and waited patiently, not hurrying the season.

Spring came late that year. It had been hot, almost scorching, in January and February, and then the winter rains fell. In March and April the sky hid behind low clouds, the air turned sooty like the glass of a kerosene lamp, and a fire burned on the hearth of more than one house on the island. The sea, the color of bluing in dirty soapsuds, pounded monotonously against the rocky shore. Occasionally the hazy outlines of the mainland and the neighboring islands were visible.

At the beginning of May a clear, dry wind brought the island's overdue spring. The sea calmed; lightly wrinkled in the morning, splashed with sun at noon, it seemed to paste translucent flakes of blue-green along the shore. The vegetation of gardens and vineyards, of pine woods and fruit trees glowed against the tawny yellow background of rocky cliffs and naked mountain ridges. All the magic of the water, the stone, and the secret filters of the sky oozing in from the outside came to life again in the island's grottoes—the Green Grotto, the Azure Grotto, the Violet Grotto. And the church bells chimed as if they were alloyed of glass and metal.

In the morning concert of the bells, the little bell on Monte della Madonna dei Marini sounded weakest of all. There was a pause after the first strong knell, broken by the dying heartbeats of iron on bronze; they were strung out like broken pearls, smaller and ever quieter, until they melted in their own echoes. Then a few more knells, but violent and rapid as if the bell-ringer hoped to overcome his fatigue with sheer obstinacy, like a traveler on the last stretch of road before the peak. Again a chaotic sequence of broken sounds and echoes filled the air, bouncing off each other, suffocating, going off in all directions, and gradually vanishing in the commotion of a new day and in the cries of the fishermen. There was one final knell, deep, prolonged, and abruptly cut off. The silence that followed was so long that it seemed that the bell-ringer must still be hanging onto the rope.

Listening to the music of the bell in the church on Monte della Madonna dei Marini, it seemed as if a human heart and not one of iron was talking about itself to the island. In the village at the foot of the mountain, people shrugged their shoulders: "Poor Padre Rocca, he's sick. He's growing old."

And, in fact, the priest had aged greatly in those last six years; he submitted to his illness without a struggle. His short figure was bent rather than hunched. He performed the mass on quivering, swollen legs, and when he raised his arms in the gesture of the offertory, his legs trembled like the flames of the candles on the altar. He still went down to the village under his own power to minister to the dead and dying, seldom as that was, but he always required two persons to help him back up the mountain.

Besides this, his solitude had been put to a new test for more than six months. Although Sebastiano had not been very well received when he first came to Monte della Madonna dei Marini, the priest had become so used to him (particularly after Dr. Sacerdote's departure) that whenever the mason failed to appear at morning mass, the priest of the Madonna of Seafarers felt rather like an abandoned orphan. Such is the secret bond that links human destinies: in solitude, the rope that chokes the throat becomes a life belt. Even the shadow of guilt slowly vanishes and at the end disappears; a hand with blood flowing in its veins finds nothing in the glow of the sun but its own shadow. After mass Sebastiano would rest on the steps of the church. Padre Rocca would sit down beside him and tell him what he had never been able to confide to any human ear or even to the silence of the tomb—perhaps because Sebastiano was neither one nor the other, and at the same time both. Perhaps the priest had long felt the need of confession. And as he retreated fearfully from the world, he may have found a desperate courage in the presence of a man whose only link to the world was his infirmity and spiritless existence. Whether it was right or wrong, the priest was greatly relieved to find a confidant in the man who was the principal subject of his sad story.

But as hard as he tried, he could not or would not reveal the whole truth even to his deaf confidant. Who, after all, can tell the whole truth about himself? We are forsaken like children lost in the woods. When you stand before me and look at me, what do you know of my sufferings and what do I know of yours? And if I fell at your feet and cried and told you, would you know any more about me than you know about hell when they say it is hot and sets one shivering? No, Padre Rocca could find no words to express his deeply hidden suffering other than those, inept and shameful, that blamed all his error and sorrow on solitude. Although he was an articulate man, he was as mute as his listener. And Sebastiano? He could not find a fictitious refuge from his sorrow in words. Perhaps he understood nothing or too little of it; he did not, luckily for him, have to look blindly into its cold eyes. Often at the most touching moment of the priest's monologue, Sebastiano would unexpectedly get up and, as if he were altogether unaware of the speaker's presence, he would drag his weary legs toward the path that led to the lower part of the island.

Sebastiano had stopped going to Monte della Madonna dei Marini at the beginning of the preceding November. One rainy morning at dawn the youngest monk at the Certosa, Fra Giacomo, found Sebastiano lying motionless in a ditch at the foot of the wall behind the Prior's Garden, near the edge of the plateau over the sea—under that same piece of wall which Sebastiano had left unrestored years before and which (like a perennial memento of the event) had remained gray-green like the patina of the rocks, in marked contrast with the white of the rest of the girdle of the Certosa. Who knows if the young monk—only recently transferred to the island from the monastery of Altamura, in Apulia, to take the place of a dead companion—knew the story of the Certosa well enough to wonder for a moment, as he looked at the man lying face down (it could have been a dead man wrapped in rags), if the seventeenth-century invaders of that terrified fortress had not looked like that, when the column of the plague-ridden reached the last bastion of the Prior's Garden. But the Certosa was free of its former faintheartedness, and only wanted to redeem itself and extirpate the past shame forever, so a moment after he was discovered, Sebastiano found himself being carried by all four brothers toward the Chiostro Piccolo. One of the monks had lifted Sebastiano's body before, on July 25, 1933.

It was an acute inflammation of the lungs, a serious threat to an organism so enfeebled by wandering; and the struggle to drive the specter of death from the little cell where the vagabond had been laid lasted several weeks. The day before Christmas Eve the convalescent crossed the threshold of his enforced confinement and, meeting no obstacles, headed slowly for the Chiostro Grande. He seemed to want to leave the Certosa, and Fra Giacomo even carried the sailcloth bag, hurriedly filled with provisions, as far as the gate. An unexpected thing happened: after making a circuit of the arcades of the portico, lightly touching the columns with his right hand as if they were the strings of a stone harp, Sebastiano returned to his cell by the same path he had taken when he came into the large courtyard of the monastery.

Neither the next day nor any day following did Sebastiano leave the Certosa. Its four inhabitants glowed with a silent joy. In the eyes of the whole island, the man who had driven his naked, scarred feet back and forth across the island for sixteen years, as if he could no longer find a place for himself in the rude and sun-scorched soil of his native land, had finally found a spot where he could rest. Had Sebastiano's aimless wandering finally exhausted and undone him? Had two months of illness rooted out his desire to live in the roads and paths of the little world surrounded on all sides by the sea? No one expected an answer to these questions, and who could answer them except the man who had settled into a new existence in the Certosa, and his lips were firmly sealed. But similarities again suggested themselves, because, like children lost in the woods, we seek in comparison a sense of continuity and existence, like signs carved in the bark of trees by the hand of our predecessors. Once before, the Certosa had received a benefactor into its hands, so that he might meet death within the walls that, in gratitude for the birth of his first heir, he had constructed to the greater glory of Heaven among the generations to come. Although it had been no fault of his own, Sebastiano had been unable to complete the restoration of the Certosa walls. Could one be sure that it was not for this reason (as the inhabitants of the island believed) that his first offspring, born out of wedlock, now lay in the little cemetery at the foot of Monte della Madonna dei Marini? It was up to the Certosa to balance the accounts of its erstwhile restorer; Sebastiano had not managed by himself to repay Providence for that miserable crumb of happiness which had been his on this earth. And so, contrary to the hopes and expectations of the monks, the old note of aversion again marked the island's relations with the Certosa.

The Certosa acquired a new penitent. What sins could he have to atone for, Sebastiano, who had exchanged a vagabond's mat for a monastery cell and a cloak of rags for the habit of a penitent? Why renounce his vagabond liberty and submit to the severe code of contrition? No one knew (and who could have known?) that, before pain ripped a scream from the mason's throat that hot afternoon, the life of the pregnant woman standing before him had hung for a moment by a thread. Even the medieval chroniclers did not know in what circumstances and by whose hand the wife of the prince-secretary of Joan of Anjou had died shortly before the success of the plot against the throne.

Sebastiano did not replace his ragged garments with an expiatory habit, but with the tunic of the monastery. He donned the habit, in conformity with local usage (although it is dying out), of the *monaco di casa,* whereby lay people who do not take monastic orders can live in their own homes withdrawn from worldly interests. Actually Sebastiano had been much more of a monk when he wandered about the island with the patient step of a pilgrim than he was after he found home and refuge within the Certosa. Although no one urged him or obliged him to do so, he worked in the Prior's Garden in the morning. And by spring it already seemed that the Garden, grown wild except for the little vineyard by the wall, had by the grace of God regained part of its former magnificence. One could rack one's brain to figure out how Sebastiano managed to work with such precision. He must have been able to see something, because no sooner had he pulled up the weeds than he brought forth a lawn so symmetrical that a gardener stringing lines on pegs would have been proud of it. The monks were even more astonished when he began helping Fra Giacomo in his workshop in the evenings.

Before entering the monastery of Altamura, Fra Giacomo (who came from Benevento) had done a bit of carving and after the war had won a certain renown for a wood reproduction of the famous bronze doors of the cathedral in his hometown, which were almost completely destroyed in a bombing in 1943. When he arrived on the island, not only did he immediately appreciate the beauty of what, besides the Roman excavations, was its principal treasure, the *Pietà dell'Isola,* but he also took it into his head to make it one of the sources of income of the impoverished Certosa. Counting on the tourist trade, Fra Giacomo began to copy the work of the anonymous Sienese master in the form of little altars to be sold as souvenirs of the island. When he had been brought to the workshop by the young monk, Sebastiano sandpapered the sculptures before they were painted: the work required only a normal sense of touch. Very soon, however, Sebastiano was reaching for the chisel, and with astounding precision he corrected Fra Giacomo's hurried work. While he worked he held his head in the position in which he used to look for the sun in the sky. It was useless to wonder whether he saw something through the crack in the corner of the right eye, or whether it was necessary to see at all with those hands, every nerve of which had remembered since childhood the forms of the *Pietà dell'Isola.* In May Sebastiano fell ill again. This time the cause of the suffering was not clear, and it was feared that he would die. He lay in his cell with his face to the wall, he refused food because he had obvious difficulty in swallowing, he slept continuously, and he only awoke to reach into the shadows for a cup of camomile or punch on the little trunk by his bed. As he slept, there was a hoarse rattle in his throat in which only the monk who had witnessed the accident seventeen years before detected a familiar note. Sometimes during his sleep he would bend his arms and cover his cheeks, forehead, and eyes as if he were shielding them, or as if he were defending himself from some menacing phantom.

The news of the danger that threatened his life quickly spread throughout the island. Although they had known during the preceding illness of his lungs that the chances of saving him hung in a delicate balance, it was only now that the islanders wondered what they would do without him. He had become as inseparable a part of the island as the slopes of the rocks, the naked crests of the mountains, the colored grottoes, the Madonna dei Marini with her arms raised on high, the black cross that commemorated the death of the nine fishermen, and the lighthouse on Monte del Faro. The gate of the Certosa was open all day, and people were continually gathering to talk in whispers (a superfluous courtesy, alas) as they waited for some news from the monks who took turns at the bedside of the mortally tired pilgrim. Baskets of fruit, fish, fresh bread, and wine were brought from the farthest villages. Since Sebastiano had scarcely touched food in his waking moments, there was something about it all that suggested a pagan sacrifice to the hesitant and pensive god that slowly weighed the poor man's fate in his hands. Never had such close bonds of cordial intimacy linked the island and the Certosa as in the second half of May 1950, dispersing the shadows of the ancient and the recent past. Two or three times a day Immacolata came up from the bar in the square. Toward the end of the month the boy who served at the mass in the church of the Madonna dei Marini led Padre Rocca down on muleback. Intrigued by the continual traffic to the Certosa, the first tourists on the island entered the gates of the Certosa. "Our Sebastiano is dying," they were informed in a tone that precluded the thought that someone might not know who the dying man was.

In the end life tipped the balance. June came, the weather suddenly turned warmer, and the season began in earnest, attracting hundreds of new arrivals every day, foreigners and Italians. It was then that Sebastiano raised himself on his elbows and indicated that he wanted to sit up. A bowl of soup was brought to him at once. The courtyard of the monastery resounded with loud shouts. A couple of hours later the whole island—from Monte della Madonna dei Marini to Monte del Faro, from the harbor to Capo Scogliera—had heard the joyous news. The island had no idea for what purpose the Supreme Judge had destined him, when, at the end of June, Sebastiano returned to work in the Prior's Garden and in Fra Giacomo's workshop.

10

Although summer arrived late, it was hotter than it had ever been. The older people on the island could not remember a hotter summer.

Early in the morning it seemed as if the sun had already reached its zenith at double or triple speed. Like an unchecked fire, drawn from ignited tinder to an enormous pile of hay so dry that it crumbled between the fingers, the heat enveloped the island in one long hot breath. The tourists who followed the winding paths down to the sea were careful not to touch the rocks in the narrow passes, they were so hot. The blue of the sky took on a shading of ashen color, and a solar fog in the air veiled the horizon with white smoke, so that at most a mile or so of the water surrounding the island was visible. Naked bodies throbbed in every corner of the island, even on the unfrequented dunes of Capo Scogliera; the water along the shore bubbled as it does when nets full of fish are hauled up. The gulls hung over the water in tired flight. The daily pauses to irrigate the fields and vineyards were always briefer. The heat killed the perfumes of the island, absorbing everything in the sharp, brackish smell of algae putrefying on the beaches. Only toward nightfall the sweet-sour perfume of the fruit trees and the flowers filled the air. And farther up, toward the peaks of the highlands, waves of mint and sage mingled in the air. After only a couple of hours, the initials that tourists carved in the cactus leaves and on the agaves looked as if they had been impressed with iron bands heated in coals. Colors, white and green in particular, no longer belonged to objects but were simply the abstract intensity of the essence of color. The same was true of the forms of objects. The houses bunched together on the slopes and the palms strung across the rocky terrain looked like flat designs on glass that owe the illusion of solidity and a third dimension only to the play of the rays of the sun.

One could best get an idea of the heat of the island when people could no longer hold their heads up—in the hours of siesta. From one to four, and sometimes even till five, life stopped. In the sultry and heavy silence every hammer blow, every human voice or click of wooden sandals had in its sound and echo something viscous and slow. In the emptiness, whitened to incandescence, every solitary walker hesitated with a drunken step in the bondage of his own dark shadow.

The sweltering heat did not disappear at night, but the horizon cleared. The solar fog evaporated shortly before sunset. As the sun began to descend behind the nearby island and shot out its last sanguine beams, all along the line that separated sky and sea the horizon seemed to burst into flames that consumed the opaque white veil. Red and pink bands, in various shades that gradually darkened at the edges as if they were trimmed with Spanish lace, marked the limits of vision, and oblong clouds, whose existence no one would have suspected in those hot and windless days, sprang into sight. Not the slightest breeze blew from the sea. But the air gradually became more transparent; and scarcely had the last strip of sky darkened after sunset than Naples, invisible by day, appeared covered with a network of little lights.

Sunset was the sign of truce. In the little streets near the square, and in the square itself, the people came together in turbulent, uneasy crowds. There was something in the evening strolls that suggested the prudent moderation and hesitancy of a convalescent's steps. Tents rose on the beaches, and motionless groups of tourists stood out on those points from which guides insist one must admire the beauty of the island, their glances caressing the silvery water that sweetly and lazily brushed against the rocks.

Only the late hours disbanded and scattered that crowd looking for a breath of lighter air. When twelve strokes rang from the clock tower, the silence of the island deepened as it did during the siesta. The air remained hot with the vapor of the daylong heat but acquired a silken delicacy toward dawn. During the full moon, until long after midnight, a strange, phosphorescent luminosity pervaded the island and gave everything prodigiously expressive outlines, as if they were engraved in dark glass. To someone observing this panorama from a ship, it would have seemed that the sea, suffused with moonlight, did not separate the island from the surrounding islands and from the mainland, but that it preserved the island from the fate of the rest of the world submerged in darkness—solitary and asleep, looking like a kneeling hooded monk with his head bent forward to the earth.

July and August passed. In September there was still no indication that summer had passed its apogee and that nature would begin to fold up the outspread fan of sun, shortening the days and freshening the wind.

11

Because the air was clear at night, the fireworks of the Piedigrotta festival and the lights of the city of Naples were visible during the first half of September. From sunset till two in the morning the entire Neapolitan shore glowed, and its reflection rose above the horizon in a thin, multicolored skein. At first the fireworks were set off timidly and sporadically in anticipation of the culminating moment of the *festa*: they exploded high in the sky like flowers that had suddenly bloomed, and then poured out purple and blue streams that were extinguished halfway down over the ashen sea front.

Among the many pairs of eyes on the island that watched the distant reflections of the lights of the Neapolitan festival, one pair stared with unusual persistence. Early in the evening Fra Giacomo had stolen out of the Certosa and climbed the pine-and-olive-covered hill that blocked the Certosa from the Naples side of the island. He sat leaning his head against a tree trunk with his face toward the mainland city. Not even the sound of midnight from the clock tower in the square moved him. He lost all sense of time and, although night had long since darkened all the illuminations, he remained in a kind of torpor until dawn, when the morning chill aroused him.

It is not easy to say what it is that awakens the inexpressible reveries and nostalgia that slowly rise within the soul like birds in flight: a fragment of landscape, a single lighted window in a darkened house front, a glimmer on a distant shore, the smell of the earth, a heavy rain, or the murmur of the wind. Such thoughts seem to have their source in something concrete, yet they elude the tongue and never show themselves in full light; they slip through fingers too clumsy to catch and hold them. They seem to evoke the sensation of a continuous but vain approach to something unattainable—to the very root of consciousness, overgrown with sterile and emotionless years—as if they sprang forth in those regions (near the dreams of delirium perhaps) where everything is somehow known but condemned to indistinct existence. And examined in detail they still do not reveal all of their secret nature, yet sometimes they can suddenly drive a man to an act that no one can understand.

Fra Giacomo had been on the island less than a year. And in that time he had rarely thought of the monastery of Altamura in the sad dead plain of Apulia, with its countless naked hills sinking into lime bogs, its dwarf olives clinging to the reluctant earth like the roots of some enormous tree that has not been altogether uprooted, and its peasants barely distinguishable from monks in their black and dark-brown cloaks. For Fra Giacomo the Certosa had been a change for the better, for he had not sought in the monk's tunic the severity and poverty that strengthen faith, but merely oblivion from war; and where besides the island, barely grazed by the war, would it have been easier to forget the churches and homes in flame, the burned corpses of one's closest relatives, children dismembered by the exploding bombs, a masterpiece of art reduced to dust? Having abandoned the world as he had seen it in his youth, he found the grace of a memory without pain among the white walls of the Certosa and the beauties of the island.

Perhaps the world had returned to him now in the lights of the Neapolitan festival that brightened the mainland shore with a strip of colored light, or in the murmur of the sea's converse with the moon, or in the hot, sweet air that wound around the leaves of the olive and the needles of the pine. Fra Giacomo closed his eyes, and from his childhood the sounds of those holidays celebrated everywhere in Campania, with their songs alternately mournful and gay and the sound of broken glass and fireworks crackling in the air, came back to him. But it was not this that plumbed the source of his nostalgia and vague longing. Not this, but a feeling to which he had vainly struggled to attach a name or face, a feeling that embraced everything around him but lingered nowhere. When he folded his hands on his knees he seemed to touch one of the statuettes that he had carved in the Certosa and to read its forms with the fingers of a blind man. He mused: since the world has been, someone has always fallen only to be lifted in arms of mercy; since the beginning, the sea has patiently washed away the blood of the dead, the moon has imperturbably illuminated the houses of the living deep in sleep, while the sun-lashed island rests and refreshes itself in the arms of the night. How to repel that world and withdraw from it forever?

The last night of the Neapolitan *festa* there was a veritable storm of fireworks. They rose suddenly on all sides like a confused antiaircraft barrage, they burst open at the same altitude and traced ever-new patterns on the vaults of heaven—flowers, then a rain of incandescent ash, scattered comets, then necklaces and rings, and gushing fountains. No corner of the sky was empty, and the whole gulf shook with the cannonade. Delirium gripped the mainland city: hardly had one wave of shouts subsided when another began. The sea sparkled like a mirror reflecting countless chandeliers. The stars had all been blown away, who knows where, and the moon shone through a crack in the luminous clouds no brighter than a modest streetlamp. The Castel dell'Ovo was submerged in a flood of fireworks: the ancient fortress of the Normans and Angevins glowed brilliantly for a moment and then waved a black banner of smoke. Perhaps the island remembered not only the recent war but also the funeral signs of the plague year.

It was only a few days till September 19 and the festival of the *Pietà dell'Isola,* which was to fall on a Thursday that year. That Wednesday after sunset, unbeknown to his three fellow monks at the Certosa, Fra Giacomo boarded the vaporetto to the mainland that brought provisions every month to the lighthouse at the foot of Monte del Faro. He did not regret that step which no one except himself—on the island nor in Benevento, nor in the monastery of Altamura—could have understood. He felt some regret as the island swiftly receded against the clear gray sky. And he felt regret for the one person on the island to whom he had felt close, the man whose friendship he could never repay with even a single miserable word. If the young monk had only known what his flight would mean to the vagabond guest of the Certosa!

12

Fra Giacomo was missed at the Certosa the next morning at dawn. One of the brothers knocked at the door of his cell after matins; there was no answer. Inside, the folded bed and the empty shelf left no room for doubt.

In the chapel the three remaining monks looked at each other, and then at the sculpture of the *Pietà dell'Isola* by the side altar. Together they managed to lift the sculpture onto the litter and drag it—setting it down every few steps and changing positions at the front handles—as far as the portico of the Chiostro Grande. The gate of the Certosa was still closed. Again day had broken with a bright sun and without wind, but a wave of fresher air seemed to be coming toward the island from the sea: nature itself was coming to the *festa* that marked the decline of summer and the end of the season. Although the procession never left the Certosa before ten, when the last gong of the clock tower was answered by the two bells of the church in the square, the sound of preparations could already be heard beyond the walls: thin voices of children, shouts of men and women, fragments of hymns that were to be sung in procession by choirs of children. Someone fired off two trial fireworks: like pennons of lamb's wool they hung suspended in the brilliant blue of the sky.

Shortly before the designated time the three monks bearing the statue emerged from the portico into the open courtyard near the gate. Between the dark tunics and the milky glow of the morning light, the sun sank into the black of the Madonna's kerchief and sparkled over her golden tresses. The garment that covered the bent figure was as blue as the sea at night. On the rigid ashen figure of the Son, the rays of the sun seemed to resculpture the curling hair and the knotted beard, the spikes of the crown of thorns, the sharp cheekbones, and the tight cleft of the mouth. Perhaps God Himself wished to end the old tradition and unite the island and the Certosa in a supremely simple gesture of mutual help and humility in the presence of that sculptured representation of pain and mercy? Perhaps He had already chosen the man behind the walls to take the place of the fugitive and to open the way to a final reconciliation.

Just then Sebastiano made his appearance at the end of the arcade that led to the Prior's Garden. He set his pails down, closed the door behind him, and, picking up the pails again, walked to the well in the center of the courtyard. After two illnesses he was thinner and weaker than ever. His step acknowledged a decay of the body for which there is no medicine. Sebastiano let the bucket on the chain all the way down; it cost him an obvious effort to wind the chain back, and several times he stopped to hold the handle for a moment in his bony hand. He drank deeply and immersed his head in the bucket. Then he filled the pails and sat down on the edge of the well, his wet face turned toward the sun. The three monks exchanged a glance, and one of them went to the well. Sebastiano made no objections to the monks' proposal. At the sound of the church bells the gate was opened, and the *Pietà* emerged on the shoulders of four bearers.

Sebastiano walked in front on the right so that anyone could see at once that the Certosa had no intention of hiding the sad truth, and so that Sebastiano would carry less weight as the bearers walked along. The crowd opened wide and stopped in silence. "Where is Fra Giacomo?" someone shouted, then cut himself short as if he were ashamed of his own voice. The children, dressed in white, unaware of what had happened, decked the statue with flowers, confetti, and colored paper streamers; the little girls timidly intoned the first hymn. But the funereal silence of the older people broke the usual order of the procession. Slowly, with four pairs of sandals shuffling, the procession moved forward as the stunned crowd looked on. Even the sound of the bells seemed alarmed, their solitary tolling unaccompanied by cheering voices. Above hundreds of heads the Madonna turned her serene but suffering glance not toward the Son but toward the neck with the knot of hair. As the procession went downhill, the head of the Redeemer hung so near the bent head of the bearer on the right that they could have touched at any moment. The procession stopped before the steps that led up to the square and the followers reassembled behind it.

It was obvious by now that Sebastiano was bearing a weight beyond his powers. His feet, which had known every inch of the island for years, stiffened for a moment in mid-step and trembled lightly in the air as if searching for a level spot on the ground. His knees trembled, and the veins in his calves rose and swelled. He struggled to breathe, with a hoarse and asthmatic wheezing; sweat rolled down his forehead and temples, and, catching the bits of confetti stuck to his cheeks, bore them down to his beard; he clawed his fingers into the coarse shaft of wood. But in his face, under the contracted membranes and particularly in the crack in his right eye, the feverish labor of thought seemed to be reawakening from a long torpor; as if he remembered something, as if every step took him farther back into time, as if he were traversing an enormous distance with those cautious steps, as if he were recognizing piece by piece the burden he was bearing—and in the September sun Sebastiano did not bleed, he liquefied.

At the foot of the stairs, when the procession stopped to catch its breath, the people nearest the front pair of bearers saw that the blind man's lids had opened slightly and that tears were flowing down his cheeks.

As the procession climbed the stairs, most of the weight of the sculpture was borne by the two bearers in the rear, but Sebastiano suddenly betrayed signs of distress. Either he had lost his grip on the pole on his shoulder, or his feet had lost their almost dance-like rhythm and touched the steps too soon. In any case, something like panic gripped him and seemed to pull him forward as a horse drags forward with an overloaded cart on a slippery road. At one point the *Pietà dell'Isola* tilted perilously to one side, and a murmur of horror rose from the crowd. Sebastiano straightened up, readjusted the pole on his shoulder, and moved forward with a calmer step. His face was as wet as it had been when he sat on the well and looked up at the sun.

Farther along, the road was straighter and smoother. But that piece seemed to give him more difficulty than the stairs. The previous exertion must have brought him to the limit of his endurance, for in the heavy and sometimes wavering movements of his body there was more of a mechanical trance than a muscular effort. The sun shone with greater force. The crowd was altogether silent, and the only sound beside the bells was the shuffle of feet behind the statue. The procession reached a point where the road narrowed. *"Lasciate passare,"* "Let us pass," the monk in front cried vainly at those who stood on both sides. Jostled by someone, Sebastiano fell abruptly to one side. His knees buckled and his feet spun out of his sandals, as if he wanted to kneel. *"Aiutatelo,"* "Help him," a woman cried. It was impossible to recognize whose voice it was in the noise.

But the whole scene lasted only a few seconds. Sebastiano straightened himself again and took the next step with confidence. The procession was nearing the second ramp of stairs, beyond which the road arched between the little houses of the town and led easily into the square.

13

Padre Rocca suffered the first seizure of choking and the typical attack of fear that accompanies it when he knelt at the altar after mass and could not rise. The boy who served at mass grabbed the priest's elbow with both hands. Padre Rocca struggled to his feet, and glanced around the nave as he went into the sacristy. Ten or fifteen people had come to mass from the village at the foot of Monte della Madonna dei Marini before going to the *festa* of the *Pietà dell'Isola*. Padre Rocca would have given much if someone had stayed behind at least through the afternoon. Solitude threw him into a particular panic in such moments and disturbed the clarity of his mind. What frightened him most was the idea that God was ready to let him die alone. Returning to the parish house he saw the heads of the departing communicants at a bend in the road. He patted the boy's head and pushed him in the direction of people who were going away.

In his room Padre Rocca felt weak and choked again, but he did not have the courage to lie down. He was afraid of getting drowsy and exposing his sick heart to a blow in his sleep, without ever noticing the aggressor's approach or attack; there were hope and help if only he remained awake. So he walked around the room like a caged animal, stopping to look at the postcards on the walls and out the window at the deserted courtyard of the church. He stopped before the little black crucifix and cracked the knuckles of his locked fingers or closed his eyes and pressed his fingers to his lips in a rapid prayer: "Dear God, I ask very little: Thy will be done, but don't let me die alone." He decided to go out to the belvedere near the statue of the Madonna of Seafarers but then recoiled in terror from the idea. He realized that from the edge of the high rock wall he would see the immense deserted world and the motionless sea. And the waves beating in the grottoes at the foot of the mountain would surge in his brain.

He all but ran from the parish house, and only beyond the bend in the road, where he almost slipped, did he realize that he was headed down toward the village.

With his feet still gripping the ground, he leaned back, half lying against the slope of the hill and turned his head so as not to look down. His heart seemed to be tearing itself from his chest, and then it would contract as if it were being squeezed, while he desperately gasped for air. Again he murmured his prayer, "Dear God . . . ," each time emphasizing the word "alone." Even if he had to drag himself on all fours he felt that he must reach the village. He had never felt such terror; he almost leapt over the precipice. But the impulse passed in a moment. He did not expect that anyone in the village could help him. But the sun, the sun, *il sole*! He burned with the desire to see human faces around him.

When he had regained his strength and his calm, he began the descent very cautiously and very slowly. Oh, if someone would see him! He instinctively cupped his hands under his heart and bent over almost to the ground, as if he were holding a precious and fragile object that, at the slightest jar, would fall from his hands and shatter into tiny pieces. But it was unlikely that anyone would see him before he reached the village. The path was deserted except for the lizards basking in the sun, who fled before him and disappeared with a rapid swish into the holly that bordered the path. There were no trees, and the cracked leaves of the agave and cactus that seemed glued to the rock offered no shade at all.

He reached the point where a crevice opened up and the path turned for about a hundred yards along the back of the hill that blocked the sea view from both sides of the island—far away to the right, almost straight off to the left. Two persons could barely walk abreast at this point in the path, and every time Padre Rocca had been accompanied from the village, one of his escorts had had to let go of his arm and walk behind. When the priest went down to the village alone, it was only here that he slowed his pace and avoided looking to the left. Now he stood as if rooted to the ground and was afraid to move. Yet only a few minutes before he had been ready to throw himself over the precipice! How many faces the hidden fear of a sick heart shows!

From where he stood one could see the little road below that led along the cemetery wall: it seemed farther and more unattainable than ever. At most he was half a mile from the little bench set up for tourists at the halfway point from the peak. He remembered that winter evening almost seven years before when he had found relief in the sight of a friend sitting on that bench.

After Dr. Sacerdote left the island, he sent the priest a picture postcard from Mantua twice a year, at Christmas and Easter, with a couple of lines of greetings and inquiries after his health. But Padre Rocca had never answered them, and in the end the thread that bound him to his past and his hometown was broken. The cards adorned one wall of the room in the parish house, making the discolored and worn reproduction of the *Pietà dell'Isola* on the opposite wall seem even lonelier. Thus his life passed, leaving traces no larger than the footprints left by a lost traveler in the sands of the desert. So little remained on Monte della Madonna dei Marini when the flood of the war subsided. Life, real life, was down there where, after the footpath turned off, the little road led past the cemetery to the village. In the course of thirty years, thousands of men and women had whispered through the confessional grating the story of a life he could never know, even though he had the power of condemning or absolving that life. Once he too had gone astray, and a low cross planted in the cemetery was the eternal marker. Nevertheless he absolved himself in the depths of his soul, like all those over whom the Madonna on the hill watched—because there was no other life. There was no other life beyond that from which he gave absolution and toward which he sinfully aspired. There had never been any sin other than this, that men are born, defend themselves from solitude, and fear death. "Dear God, forgive me, have mercy on Your lost servant!"

Padre Rocca's swollen legs constantly ached. He let himself fall onto a rock by the side of the road, looking first at the road up the hill and then at the steep slope of the rock wall. No, he could not decide. At the mere thought of that narrow pass he clenched his fists against his chest and felt his head spin. He looked toward the peak of the mount, with the fragile statue erect as a lightning rod. He could be back in no time if he had not had to pace his heart so cautiously. Now he regretted his impulse to flee the solitude of the parish house. He smiled bitterly as he remembered that he had sworn to reach the village, even on all fours. There was no chance of any inhabitant or tourist appearing before nightfall. Only Sebastiano might happen by at any hour. But Sebastiano had not emerged from the Certosa for several weeks.

Padre Rocca tried to master his terror and pull together the remains of his troubled mind. Was it possible, he wondered, that age and illness had so weakened him that after thirty years, knowing every inch of that pass, he was suddenly afraid of a few minutes of nervous apprehension. But Padre Rocca tried in vain. He looked down at the sea far below the escarpment and, as if he were seeing it for the first time, he marveled that never before had he had such a clear and distinct sense of its peril. He got up from the rock and tried to climb back up the mountain. He did not even get ten yards. Pallid and barely able to stand, the priest returned to the rock.

The sun rose higher now and shone directly in his face. He had left his hat in the parish house, so he put his sweaty handkerchief on his head and unbuttoned his cassock. At first he felt almost well in the lazy heat that enveloped him. But for fear of falling asleep, he kept his eyes open. He knew he could not endure the duel for long, but he did not surrender, and with lids only slightly lowered he stared with an obstinate courage at the yellow disk that throbbed so hard in its heart it seemed it must burst from the sky. Finally Padre Rocca gave in and clamped the handkerchief over his eyes. It was hard to keep his eyes open under the rosy glow.

When he awoke a sharp breeze burned his face. The torn handkerchief hung stiffly on the branches of a bush under the edge of the precipice. Some little time passed before he remembered where he was and why, and before he became aware of the sound of bells. "*E uscita la Pietà dell'Isola,*" he murmured, "The procession has begun." So it must have been ten o'clock; at least an hour had passed since he sat down. He listened again, and again he felt a strange sense of happiness: the echoes of the bells were like the tinkling of little glass spheres.

He did not know how much time had passed when he woke again. The air shook with explosions. The sound of the bells was almost lost in the din, but he could hear clearly, though smothered by the distance, the shout or song that rose from hundreds of human throats.

Padre Rocca got up and, as if enchanted or unconscious, staggered on without looking down at his feet.

14

Before the rockets shot off into the blue, and before the bells of the church in the square pealed a sweeter sound, shouts and songs rose from the crowd ahead as the procession reached the top of the second set of stairs and entered the last, almost flat stretch of road.

The road was wider now. After the exertion of the narrow crowded passage of the second set of stairs, Sebastiano felt a freer space around him and a flat surface under his feet. He seemed to have regained all his energy, and it appeared that he would reach his goal. But it only seemed so for a brief moment. At first he walked with the lightness and agility he had had when, still a young man, he wandered about the island in the first years after his accident. But he soon realized that he could no longer sustain himself, that he had nothing more to give in that last stretch before the end. Something in him had cracked and refused to obey him. Unable to get a new foothold, he swayed back and forth in one spot, as if he were standing on a sand dune. Suddenly, and everyone saw it, he began looking feverishly in all directions, as if he needed help, and his face was strangely excited. It was another four hundred yards at most to the church. *"Aiutatelo!"* "Help him!" Immacolata began to scream. This time her call was heard. Men's hands tore the pole from Sebastiano's convulsively clenched fists and set the litter with the statue on the ground. Freed of his burden, Sebastiano bent over, dropped his head to his chest, took a step forward, and fell heavily, like a tree sawn through that needs only a slight push to be toppled.

Immacolata rushed to him first. She turned him over on his back, and, kneeling over him, she carefully slid her shoulders under his neck and the upper part of his rigid body. He seemed dead or immersed in a deep sleep. The bells stopped ringing. The bright sun was nearing its zenith, and the people stood silent and motionless, while above the fruit trees and vineyards and gardens and the little white houses the blue sky rose like a bell of blue glass over the island and the sea in the distance. And it was hard to decide which of the two pairs of figures side by side on the ground was the sculpture of the Sienese master, and which more deserved to be called the *Pietà dell'Isola!* But only one came to life: Immacolata raised her head, the black kerchief fell from her gold-bronze hair, and her lament broke the silence.

No one who was there will ever forget Immacolata's lamentation. It was the lamentation of the south, penetrating in its primitive violence, half aggressive and half supplicating. It was not composed of words. Detached sounds, neither shouts nor sobs, formed a guttural litany. There were curses and humble prayers in that litany, guilt and redemption, despair and faith, the misery of the fall and the hope of resurrection, a curse on fate and submission to its judgment. Compressed into a few dense minutes, it evoked the sterile nights and vain sleep of seventeen years. It appealed to the sun, to the earth, to the sea, to the sky, to the crowd, to anything that could move mercy, anything that could grant a crumb of kindness to life. Its last penetrating note hung above the man she held in her arms, and its softer echo vanished in the direction of Monte della Madonna dei Marini. And, like a bird tired of flying, perhaps it fell into the cemetery at the foot of the mountain.

Those who remembered Immacolata right after the accident, when she cursed the Certosa, sensed that they were listening to the same lament they had heard then.

When she ran out of breath she let her head fall and looked into Sebastiano's face with dry eyes. She did not have to bend lower, to his lips, for one to see that she made a superhuman effort to rouse a spark of life. The seconds dragged by like hours. Sebastiano moved, and through the crack in his right eye he could see: not a quivering shadow broken into an infinite number of lesser shadows, but distinct colors and sharp outlines. For a moment he thought he was looking at the Madonna of Donnaregina, and he was amazed at the change. He did not see the medallion of the Infant on her breast, nor the angel to her right who defended her with his sword from the dragon; nor did he see the dark tomb of the Son on the other side. Then Sebastiano froze for a moment. A shiver ran through that body exhausted by the climb and by the weight of its burden, and that shiver seemed to free him from the last bonds that held him.

"Immacolata," he said. "Immacolata," he repeated, almost shouting. Only now was his real suffering to begin.

A single word rang out, "*Miracolo,*" a shout mixed with song. Fireworks were shot off in all directions, and flowers, paper stars and streamers, and a cloud of colored confetti filled the air. The rockets began to beat at the gates of heaven, and the bells, drowned by the exploding fireworks, rang out again. Then the monks stepped aside; other hands lifted the statue and carried it triumphantly to the church in the square, ending forever the island's aversion for the Certosa.

15

That same evening the news passed from mouth to mouth on the island that at the very moment in which Sebastiano was resurrected (that word was used to describe the epilogue to the procession of the *Pietà dell'Isola* of September 19, 1950: *Quando è risorto il nostro Sebastiano*) the coagulated blood of the martyr of Pozzuoli liquefied in the Cathedral of Naples. But that was not exactly true—according to the Cathedral register for 1950, the miracle of San Gennaro had occurred even before the procession left the Certosa. But nothing has ever been able to persuade islanders that the two miracles were not simultaneous. The south is as addicted to miracles as lonely people are to dreams, and will not allow a single detail to detract from its miracles, even when they fail to withstand the simple checking of facts. For the people of the south find in miracles, in longing for them and waiting for them (like the lonely man in dreams), the hope that when reality is too cruel there can be deliverance from it.

The next day, however, a sad note disturbed the island's joy. Only a few tourists had gone up to Monte della Madonna dei Marini toward sunset on the day of the *festa,* and they had noticed nothing along the road. The next morning the boy who served mass for Padre Rocca did not find the priest of the Seafarers' Madonna in the church or in the parish house. As he was returning to the village he saw a handkerchief caught in a *ginestra* bush just over the edge of the precipice. He looked down and hurried on.

The remains of Padre Rocca, head split open and chest deeply gashed on a sharp point of rock, were found on a promontory about fifty yards above the level of the sea. It was a difficult job to drag the body to the narrow strip of beach where the boats came with the police and the fisherman who had been sent for help. It was impossible to establish the circumstances of death. Suicide was rejected, out of respect for the dead man's profession. But opinion wavered between sunstroke and a fainting spell brought on by his heart. The fact that the priest had left his hat behind in the parish house seemed to confirm the former verdict. But there was no reason why both possibilities could not be mentioned in the death certificate, and so they were. "He was sick, poor Padre Rocca," the inhabitants of the village at the foot of the mountain testified. "He had suddenly grown very old." Because he only came down in case of urgent need, and because it had been five months since the boy who served at mass had led him all the way to the Certosa, they decided that some vision or presentiment must have drawn him toward the procession of the *Pietà dell'Isola*. Everything, in those moments of joy and transport, was turned to the praise of the miracle.

Toward the end of September the season began to wane. The departing tourists watched the island diminish gradually in the distance, and in the transparent sky of the last days of summer it seemed to break away from the background of sky, sea, and setting sun like the relief carving of a kneeling monk with his hooded head bent to the ground. Some of the tourists, as a memento of the scene of which they had been involuntary witnesses, carried away miniature carved altars, souvenirs of the island. As the boat neared the port of Naples the island disappeared behind the curtain of sunset, and the lighthouse on Monte del Faro began its ceaseless blinking. ∽

INTERPRETIVE QUESTIONS
FOR DISCUSSION

Why is Sebastiano the one who heals the ancient wound between the Certosa and the islanders?

1. Nearly three centuries later, why are the inhabitants of the island still unable to forgive the Certosa monks for the sin of their predecessors during the plague of 1656? (165)

2. When Sebastiano returns to the island after his training in Naples, why do all his thoughts turn toward restoring the Certosa? (162)

3. Does Sebastiano's dedicated work on the Certosa spring from a wish to praise God or from personal pride? Why does Sebastiano wish to leave behind him "as enduring as possible a sign of his hand"? (166)

4. Why does the author compare the fate of Sebastiano, a poor mason, to that of the prince-secretary of Joan of Anjou? (167)

5. After the accident, why does Sebastiano become a solitary wanderer of the island, rarely resting and "constantly driven on by an obtuse perseverance"? (171)

6. Why does Immacolata, who threw the lime in Sebastiano's face, blame the Certosa for Sebastiano's "accident" by the Certosa wall? (169)

7. After his illness, why does Sebastiano don the tunic of the monks and stay on to live and work in the Certosa? (194–196)

8. Why does the wandering Sebastiano become an inseparable part of the island for its inhabitants? Why do they call him "our Sebastiano" and rejoice at his recovery from his second serious illness? (197)

9. Why does it turn out that it is the monks' and the islanders' mutual concern for Sebastiano that forges new bonds of "cordial intimacy" between the Certosa and the island? (197)

10. Why does the "miracle" of Sebastiano regaining his speech and sight end forever the island's ancient aversion for the Certosa? (213–214)

Suggested textual analyses

Pages 161–167: beginning, "Sebastiano was thirty years old," and ending, "the prince-secretary of Joan of Anjou hidden in the sand."

Pages 193–198: beginning, "Sebastiano had stopped going to Monte della Madonna dei Marini," and ending, "in the Prior's Garden and in Fra Giacomo's workshop."

Why is Padre Rocca slowly destroyed by his solitary life, "bit by bit like a cancer"?

1. Why is Padre Rocca's heart flooded with hate for "all the cruel work of creation" when he begs Immacolata for sexual contact? (189)

2. Why does the appearance of his old friend Dr. Sacerdote cause Padre Rocca to break into a moaning sob like that of a baby? Up until then, why had he not allowed himself to remember images of life in his native Mantua? (181)

3. As Padre Rocca struggles to maintain consciousness during his attack, why does the black crucifix on his wall look like a spider to him? (183)

4. Why is Padre Rocca's hate-filled, violent rape of Immacolata transformed in his dream into a beatific image? Why does Padre Rocca's dream end with Immacolata falling over a precipice "like a statue toppled from a high rock" when he embraces her? (190)

5. Why does Padre Rocca refuse to heed Dr. Sacerdote's advice to request a transfer, replying, "What else do I have in life besides my habits?" (190) Why doesn't Padre Rocca respond to the postcards that Dr. Sacerdote sends him? (209)

6. Why is Padre Rocca unable to express his deep suffering and shame? Why does he confess over and over again to Sebastiano but never tell him the whole truth? (192–193)

7. Why does Fra Giacomo, unlike Padre Rocca, decide to flee the island? Does Fra Giacomo return to the mainland because he wishes to withdraw from or embrace the age-old pain of the world? (201–203)

8. Why is Padre Rocca terrified—to the point of almost leaping over the precipice—by the idea that God might let him die alone? (208)

9. Why does Padre Rocca absolve himself "in the depths of his soul" for the sin of raping Immacolata? What does he mean when he tells himself that there "had never been any sin other than this, that men are born, defend themselves from solitude, and fear death"? (210)

10. Why is the story told so that Padre Rocca dies at the same time that Sebastiano is "resurrected"? (214–215)

Suggested textual analyses

Pages 188–190: beginning, "Padre Rocca's sleep had that wealth of content," and ending, "left the island forever."

Pages 207–211: beginning, "Padre Rocca suffered the first seizure," and ending, "without looking down at his feet."

Why does the author suggest that Sebastiano's suffering might be fated by a God who "embroiders the same patterns over and over again"?

1. When he works on the Certosa wall, why does Sebastiano feel like "a mason in the service of centuries that he could never understand"? Why does his spirit tremble before these centuries? (166)

2. Why does Sebastiano's "grim suffering without a face, without a name, and without associations" lack memory? (170–171) Why is he overcome by a "chaos of his mind and heart"? (173)

3. Six years after his accident, why does Sebastiano suddenly change his daily pattern and go to the chapel on Monte della Madonna dei Marini, a place that up until then he had always instinctively avoided? (177–178)

4. Why is the memory of pain and suffering torn from Sebastiano after he sees Padre Rocca standing with his arms outstretched above the brightly lit candles? (178)

5. Why does Dr. Sacerdote have a sudden vision of Saint Sebastian as painted by Mantegna when he recalls the evening that he discovered Padre Rocca in the cemetery and felt oppressed by the idea that they were being followed by Sebastiano? (187)

6. When Sebastiano is gravely ill for the second time, why are we told that the baskets of food the islanders bring him suggest a pagan sacrifice? (197)

7. Why does carrying the *Pietà dell'Isola*—"that sculptured representation of pain and mercy"—cause Sebastiano's memory to reawaken? (204–206)

8. Why are Sebastiano and Immacolata described as a living version of the *Pietà dell'Isola* when she cradles her former lover's rigid body in her arms? (212)

9. Why does Sebastiano's "real suffering" begin when he regains his memory and calls Immacolata by name? (213)

10. Why does the author refer to the "miracle" of Sebastiano's reawakening with irony, stating that the south is "addicted to miracles" and will not allow a single detail to detract from them? (214)

Suggested textual analyses

Pages 203–207: beginning, "Fra Giacomo was missed at the Certosa," and ending, "led easily into the square."

Pages 211–215: from, "Before the rockets shot off," to the end of the selection.

FOR FURTHER REFLECTION

1. Do the interlocking fates of Sebastiano, Immacolata, and Padre Rocca form a universal paradigm of human suffering, or do they represent a specifically Christian vision of human existence?

2. Was Padre Rocca's life of self-imposed suffering pointless or did it enrich him spiritually?

3. Do you think that life repeats itself "like an unimaginative needleworker embroidering the same patterns over and over again"?

4. Should Padre Rocca have absolved himself of the sin of raping Immacolata? What was Padre Rocca's greatest sin?

5. Do pain and suffering bring humanity closer to the divine realm?

Momik

David Grossman

DAVID GROSSMAN (1954–), one of
Israel's most highly regarded young writers,
was born in Jerusalem. His works include
the novels *The Yellow Wind* (1988), *See
Under: Love* (1989), *The Smile of the Lamb*
(1991), and *The Book of Intimate Grammar*
(1994), and the nonfiction *Sleeping on a
Wire: Conversations with Palestinians in
Israel* (1992). He is also the author of
a collection of short stories and three
children's books. He is fluent in Arabic,
and his interest in the relations between
Palestinians and Jews informs his works.
Awards that he has won include the Prime
Minister's Prize for Hebrew Literature (1984)
and the Israel Publishers Association's Prize
for the best novel in Hebrew (1985). This
selection, "Momik," is the first chapter of
See Under: Love. The Herrneigel story that
fascinates Momik is the subject of the
third chapter, "Wasserman."

I T WAS LIKE THIS, a few months after Grandma Henny was buried in her grave, Momik got a new grandfather. This grandfather arrived in the Hebrew month of Shebat in the year 5317 of the Creation, which is 1959 by the other calendar, not through the special radio program *Greetings from New Immigrants* which Momik had to listen to every day at lunch between 1:20 and 1:30, keeping his ears open in case they called out one of the names on the list Papa wrote down for him on a piece of paper; no, Grandfather arrived in a blue Mogen David ambulance that pulled up in front of Bella Marcus's café– grocery store in the middle of a rainstorm, and this big fat man, dark but like us, not a shvartzer, stepped out and asked Bella if she knew anyone around here called Neuman, and Bella got scared and wiped her hands on her apron and said, Yes, yes, did something happen, God forbid? And the man said, Don't get excited, lady, nothing happened, what can happen. No, I bring them a relative, see, and he thumbed backward over his shoul- der at the ambulance in the street which seemed empty and

quiet, and Bella suddenly turned as white as this wall and everybody knows she isn't scared of anything, but she wouldn't go
anywhere near the ambulance, she only edged closer to Momik,
who was doing Bible homework at one of the little tables, and
said, "Vay iz mir," a relative now? And the man said, "Nu, lady,
we don't got all day, so if you know these people maybe you can
tell me where they are, because is nobody home." He talked
broken Hebrew like that even though he didn't look so much
like a newcomer, and Bella said to him, Sure, what did you
expect, sure nobody's home, because these people are not para-
sites, these people work plenty hard for their bread, morning to
night they're working in the lottery booth two streets down,
and this little boy here, he's theirs, so just you wait a minute,
mister, I'm going to run get them. And she ran out with her
apron still on and then the man winked at Momik, and when
Momik didn't do anything because he knows how you're supposed to behave around strangers, the man shrugged his
shoulders and started reading the newspaper Bella left there and
he said to the air, Even with this rain we're having, seems like
it's going to be a drought year, yeah, that's all we need. And
Momik who is usually well mannered didn't hang around for
more but ran outside to the ambulance and climbed up on the
back step, wiped the rain from the little round window, and
peered inside where the oldest man in the world was swimming
like maybe a fish in an aquarium. He wore blue-striped pajamas
and was all wrinkled like Grandma before she died. His skin
was yellowish-brown, like a turtle's, sagging down around his
skinny neck and arms, his head was bald, and his eyes were
blank and blue. He was swimming hard through the ambulance
air, and Momik remembered the sad Swiss farmer from Aunt
Idka and Uncle Shimmik in the little glass ball with the
snowflakes which he had accidentally broken once, and he
opened the door without a second thought, but then he jumped
back when he heard the old man talking to himself in a weird
voice that went up and down excitedly, and then sounded
almost like crying, as if he were in some play or telling a tall

tale, but at the same time, and this is what's so hard to understand, Momik was one thousand percent sure that this old man
was Anshel, Grandma Henny's little brother, Mama's uncle, the
one everybody said Momik looked like, especially around the
chin and forehead and nose, the one who wrote children's stories for magazines in Europe, but didn't Anshel die by the Nazis,
may-their-name-be-blotted-out, and this one is alive all right
and Momik hoped his parents would agree to keep him in the
house because after Grandma Henny died Mama said that all
she wanted now was to live out her life in peace, and suddenly
there was Mama with Bella hobbling after her on ailing legs,
lucky break for Marilyn Monroe, and she yelled at Mama in
Yiddish to calm down, you shouldn't upset the child, and
behind them trudged the great giant his papa, panting and red
in the face, and Momik thought it really must be serious for
both of them to leave the booth together. Anyway, the ambulance driver calmly folded the newspaper and asked if they were
the Neumans, the family from the late Henny Wasserman, rest
her soul, and Mama said, Yes she was my mother, what happened? and the fat driver smiled a big fat smile and said,
Nothing happened, why are always people expecting something
happened; no we came to deliver just the grandfather to you, a
mazel tov. And they all went around to the back of the ambulance and the driver opened the door and climbed in and lifted
the old man lightly in his arms and Mama cried, Oy, no, it can't
be, it's Anshel, and first she sort of swayed and Bella ran to the
café and brought a chair back just in time and the driver said,
There, there, we didn't bring to you bad news, God forbid, and
after setting the old man down on his feet he gave him a friendly
slap on the back which was bony and crooked and he said, Nu,
Mr. Wasserman, so here's the mishpocheh,[1] and to Mama and
Papa he said, Ten years he's been with us at the insane house in
Bat Yam, and you never know what he's talking to himself like
now, maybe praying or who knows, and he doesn't hear what

---

1. The immediate family.

you say like a deaf man nebuch,[2] so here's the mishpocheh! he screamed in Grandfather's ear to prove to everyone that he really was deaf, ach, like a stone, who knows what they did to him there, may-their-name-be-blotted-out! and nu, we don't even know which camp he was by or what, there came out people in a worse condition, you should see, no, better you shouldn't see, but now one month ago he all of a sudden opens his mouth and says the names of people, like Mrs. Henny Mintz, and our boss, he made like a detective and so he found out that those names he says are the names of people dead, may-they-rest-in-peace, and the list shows Mrs. Mintz here in this house, but she's dead too now, may-she-rest-in-peace, so you are the only family left, and it doesn't look like Mr. Wasserman will be getting any healthier and he can eat by himself already and, you should pardon the expression, make his duty by himself, and this country nebuch isn't so rich, and the doctors say in his condition he can be looked after in the home, family is family right? So here are his clothes and his papers and things and his prescriptions too for medicines that he takes, he's a sweet old man, and quiet too, except for the noises and all the moving around, but not too bad, nothing serious, everybody likes him, they call him the Malevsky family, because he all the time sings, that's a joke, see, now say hello to the children! he shouted in the old man's ear. Ach nothing, like a stone, here, Mr. Neuman, you sign here and here that I bring him to you, maybe you got an ID or something with you? No? Never mind, I believe you anyway. Nu, shoin, well, a mazel tov, this is a happy day like a new baby coming to you, oh sure, you get used to him, so now we better be heading back to Bat Yam, plenty of work waiting there, so goodbye, Mr. Wasserman, don't forget us! And he smiled cheerfully in the old man's face, though Grandfather didn't seem to notice, and got into the ambulance and drove away, fast.

---

2. Poor thing.

Bella ran to fetch Mama a piece of lemon to give her some strength. Papa stood still and stared at the rain running into the empty gully where the city was supposed to have planted a pine tree. The rain trickled down Mama's face as she sat on the chair with her eyes shut. She was so short her feet didn't touch the ground. Momik took the old man by his bony hand and gently led him under the awning of Bella's grocery store. Momik and the old man were about the same height because the old man was all hunched over and had a little hump at the back of his neck. And then all of a sudden Momik noticed there was a number on the new grandfather's arm, like Papa's and Aunt Idka's and Bella's, although Momik could see right away it was a different kind of number and he tried to memorize it but Bella came back with the lemon meanwhile and started rubbing Mama's temples with it and the air smelled good but Momik kept waiting because he knew Mama wouldn't wake up so soon.

And who should come walking down the street just then but Max and Moritz, whose real names were Ginzburg and Zeidman, though nobody remembers that anymore except for Momik who remembers everything. They were inseparable, those two. They lived together in the storeroom at Building Number 12, where they kept the rags and all the junk they collected. Once when city inspectors came to kick them out of the storeroom, Bella screamed so loud they beat it out of there. Max and Moritz never talked to anyone outside of each other. Ginzburg who was filthy and smelly always walked around saying, Who am I who am I, but that's because he lost his memories on account of those Nazis, may-their-name-be-blotted-out, and the small one, Zeidman, just smiled at everyone all the time and they said he was empty inside. They never went anywhere without each other, Ginzburg the dark one leading, Zeidman behind him carrying the old black briefcase you could smell a mile away, grinning at the air. Whenever Mama used to see them coming she would mutter, Oif alle poste palder, oif alle viste valder, a calamity in the empty fields and the empty woods, and of course she told Momik never to go anywhere near the two of them, but he knew they were all right, because Bella didn't let the city inspectors kick them out of the storeroom, although she did call them funny names like Mupim and Chupim and Pat and Patashon, who were these cartoon characters back where they all came from.

So it was pretty weird how this time the two of them walked slowly by and didn't seem to be afraid of anyone and they stepped right up to Grandfather and looked him over and as Momik watched Grandfather he noticed his nose twitching as though he could smell them, which doesn't mean a whole lot since Ginzburg you could smell even without a nose, but this was something else because all of a sudden Grandfather stopped singing his tune and stared at the two dodos, which is another name Mama called them, and Momik saw the three of them stiffening as if they all had the same feeling, and then the new grandfather suddenly swerved around like he was angry he'd wasted his time which he had no business wasting and he sang that stupid tune again as if he couldn't see anything and paddled through the air like he was swimming or talking to someone who wasn't there, and Max and Moritz stared at him, and the small one, Zeidman, started making noises and moving around the way Grandfather does, he's always copying people, and Ginzburg growled and started to walk away, with Zeidman following in his trail. And you also always see them together on the stamps Momik draws for the royal kingdom.

So anyway, meanwhile Mama stood up white as this wall, all weak and wobbly, and Bella braced her and said, Lean on me, Gisella, and Mama wouldn't even look at the new grandfather and she said to Bella, This will kill me, mark my words, why doesn't God just leave us in peace and let us live a little, and Bella said, Tfu, tfu, Gisella, what are you saying, this is not a cat, this is a live human being, you shouldn't talk that way, and Mama said, It's not enough I'm an orphan, not enough we had so much suffering from my mother, now this, now everything all over again, look at him, look how he looks, he's coming here to die, that's what, and Bella said, Sha sha, and held her hand and they huddled together next to Grandfather but Mama wouldn't look at him and then Papa coughed, Nu, why are you standing there, and he bravely put his hand on the old man's shoulder and looked at Momik with a shy expression and led the old man away, and Momik, who already knew he would call the old man Grandfather even though he wasn't his real grandfather, told himself that if the old man didn't die when Papa touched him, that must mean a person from Over There is safe from harm.

The same day, Momik went to search in the cellar. He'd always been afraid to go down to the cellar because of the dark and the dirt, but this time he had to. There, together with the big brass beds and the mattresses with straw sticking out and the bundles of clothes and the piles of shoes, was Grandma Henny's kifat, a kind of box you tie up, with all the clothes and stuff she brought from Over There and this book called a *Teitsh Chumash* and also the *Tzena u-Rena,* and the bread board Grandma Henny used there for making pastry dough and three bags full of goose feathers she had dragged halfway around the world in boats and trains braving terrible dangers just so she could make herself a feather quilt in Eretz Yisrael to keep her feet warm, but when she arrived it turned out that Aunt Idka and Uncle Shimmik, who got here first and quickly made a lot of money, had already bought a double feather quilt, so the feathers stayed in the cellar where pretty soon they caught mildew and other cholerias, but you don't throw out a thing like that around here. So anyway, the point is that at the bottom of the kifat was a notebook with Grandma's Yiddish notes, all her memories like from the days when she still had a memory, but then Momik remembered that a long time ago before he could even read, before he'd turned into an alter kopf, which means the head of a smart old man, Grandma showed him a page from an old, old magazine, and in it was a story by Grandma Henny's brother, this Anshel, written one hundred years ago, but Mama got mad at Grandma for upsetting the boy with things that are no more and shouldn't be mentioned, and sure enough the magazine page was still in the notebook but when Momik picked it up it started to crumble, so he carried it between the pages of the notebook with a fluttering heart and sat down on the kifat to tie it back up with the ropes but he was too light so he left it open because he wanted to get out fast but suddenly he had an idea that was so strange he just stood still and forgot what he wanted to do next, but his thingy knew and he made it out just in time to piss under the stairwell, which is what always happens to him when he goes down to the cellar.

So anyway, he sneaked the notebook into the house without anyone noticing, and ran to his room and opened it and saw that the page had crumbled a little more on the way and the top corner was torn off. The page was yellow and cracked like the earth after a long time without rain and Momik knew right away he'd have to copy what it said on another piece of paper, otherwise, kaput. He found his spy notebook under the mattress and, wild with excitement, he wrote out the story on the torn page, word for word.

The Children of the Heart Rescue the Red Sk
A story in fifty chapters by the popular auth
Anshel Wasserman-Scheheraz
Chapter the Twenty-seventh

> *O Constant Reader! In our previous episode, we saw the*
> *Children of the Heart swiftly borne upon the wings of the*
> *"Leap in Time" machine: destination—the lesser luminary*
> *called the moon. This machine was the product of the*
> *craft and intelligence of the wise Sergei, whose mastery of*
> *technics and the currents of electricality in the case of the*
> *magnificent machine we did so fully elucidate in our foregoing*
> *chapter, whither we refer our Constant Reader for the*
> *sundry particulars effaced from memory. And so, aboard the*
> *machine, arm in arm with the Children of the Order, were*
> *Red Men of the Navajo tribe and their proud king, who*
> *rejoiced in the name: Red Slipper (mayhap our Amiable*
> *Reader knows of the Red Skin's predilection for suchlike*

*names fantastical, though we may smile to hear them!).
And together they fled the truculence of the martial men
who would drive them from the land of their fathers, chief
among these the sanguineous native of the country of
England, John Lee Stewart. Thus they betook themselves to
the moon for shelter and succor in their distress, in the hope
likewise of turning a new leaf in the copybook of their
wretched lives. Lo! The wondrous machine traverses the
stars, and breaches the rings of Saturn, streaked with
gossamer, swift as light! And on they venture while the
amiable Otto Brig, first and foremost among the Children of
the Heart, to soothe the spirits of the Red Skins (so lately
delivered from the hands of their enemies, and whisked aloft
in the chariot of fire) rehearsed for them the glorious deeds
of the Children of the Heart, anent our Faithful Reader is
informed to the last letter and with which we shall not tire
him at this time. And Otto's young sister, blithe Paula of the
golden hair, prepared a repast for the company to refresh
their troubled minds and flagging spirits. And Albert Fried,
the silent boy, was just then sitting privily at the helm, nobly
pondering whether humankind should ever set foot upon the
moon, since as the Amiable Reader knows so well, Albert
Fried was conversant with every sort of creature from lice
eggs to horned buffaloes, and likewise the language of each,
as was King Solomon of yore, and he hastened to find his
small copybook in which to record the scientific facts he
would observe in short order, for our friend Albert Fried is
a lover of order, and it well behooves the younger readers
amongst us to follow his example in this and other matters.
And as he was writing, the dulcet murmur of a flute fell
upon his ears, and this so astonished him that he rose to his
feet and approached the hall of passage. In the doorway
he stood, bewildered by the sight which met his eyes: for
there stood Harotian, the small Armenian fellow, a wizard
skilled in every work of wonder and of sorcery, piping for
the company, whilst the melody he played so nimbly upon*

*his flute becalmed the anxious hearts of the Red Skins and
allayed their fears. The piping was balm to them, and small
wonder: for little Harotian himself had long ago been
rescued by the Children of the Heart when the Turks of
Turkestan plundered a village in the hills of Armenia,
and Harotian alone was spared, as fully recounted in the
adventuresome tale entitled "The Children of the Heart
Rescue the People of Armenia," and the young Harotian
was touched to the heart by the sadness of these voyagers.
And meanwhile, as Sergei was standing watch on deck, a
heavy cloud descended, for he grasped in his hand the horn
of vision that magnifies two-hundred-fold, and screamed:
"Woe is he who faces such calamity! Flee! To the moon!"
And they beheld it, and were filled with horror. Otto their
leader looked through the horn of vision, and his heart
stopped, his face turned ashen, while Paula clasped his
hand, screaming: "For God's sake, Otto, what is it that you
saw?" But Otto's tongue was pinched and doughlike, and
no reply could he make, though his face bore testimony
to the evil which had befallen them all, and horror, perhaps
Death, lurked at the window.*

Continued in next week's issue of
Little Lights***

This was the story Momik found in the magazine, and as soon
as he started copying it down in his spy notebook he knew it was
the most exciting story ever written, and the paper smelled about
a thousand years old and seemed to come out of a Bible with
all those biblical-looking words Momik knew he would never
understand no matter how many thousands of times he read
the page over, because to get the meaning of a story like this
you need a commentary by Rashi or somebody because people
don't talk that way anymore except maybe Grandfather Anshel,
though even without understanding every word in it you could
tell this story was the origin of every book and work of literature

ever written, and the books that came later were merely imita-
tions of this page Momik had been lucky enough to find like a
hidden treasure, and he felt that once he knew this he would
know just about everything, and then he wouldn't have to go to
school anymore, so right away he started to memorize it because
brains he's got, bless him, and it only took him a week to learn
it all by heart, and he would recite while getting ready for bed:
"Harotian, the small Armenian fellow, a wizard skilled in every
work of wonder and of sorcery, piping for the company," etc.,
or on his way to school the next morning, till he got so caught
up in the story he couldn't stop wondering what that awful thing
they saw on the moon through the horn of vision was, and
sometimes he would try to guess how the story ended, though
he knew a real Bible ending was something only Grandfather
Anshel could invent, but Grandfather Anshel hadn't.

Mama and Papa decided Grandfather should have the small
room Grandma Henny used to live in, but he wasn't anything
like Grandma Henny. He couldn't sit still for one minute and
even in his sleep he twitched and gabbled and flapped his arms
around. Whenever they locked him in the house he would cry
and make such a scene they had to let him out. In the morning
after Mama and Papa left for the lottery booth and Momik had
gone off to school, Grandfather Anshel would walk up and
down the street till he was tired and then he would go sit on the
green bench outside Bella's grocery–café and talk to himself.
Grandfather stayed with Momik and his parents for a total of
five months before he disappeared. The first week of his stay,
Momik started drawing pictures of him on the imperial stamps,
with the legend "Anshel Wasserman: Hebrew Writer Who
Perished in the Holocaust." Bella brought a weak glass of tea
out for Grandfather. She reminded him gently, "Mendarf
pishen, Mr. Wasserman," and led him to her toilet like a child.
Bella is a real angel from heaven. Her husband, Hezkel Marcus,
died a very long time ago and left her all alone with Joshua,
a difficult child and a bit meshuggeneh, and with these ten
fingers here Bella made an army officer out of him and a college

graduate too. Besides Joshua, Hezkel left her his own father, old Mr. Aaron Marcus—zal er zein gezunt und shtark, may he be healthy and strong—who was sick and weak and feeble-minded and hardly ever left his bed anymore, and Bella, whom Hezkel used to treat like a real queen—and he wouldn't even let her move a glass from here to here—did not sit around the house with her feet up all day long after Hezkel died but went out to work in the little grocery store so as not to lose the regular customers at least, and she even expanded and brought in three more tables and a soda fountain and an espresso machine, and Bella was on her feet from dawn till dusk spitting blood, only her pillow knows how many tears she cried, but Joshua never went hungry, and nobody ever died of hard work.

Bella's café served breakfast specials and home-cooked meals for people of taste. Momik remembered the words "people of taste" because he was the one who wrote the menus three times (for Bella's three tables), and decorated them with drawings of people looking all fat and smily after eating such a good meal at Bella's. And she served home-baked cookies too, fresher than Bella, as she would tell anyone who asked her, though not too many people asked these days, because hardly anyone ever came in besides the Moroccan construction workers from the new housing developments at Beit Mazmil who showed up around ten in the morning for a quart of milk, a loaf of bread, and a cup of yogurt, or the few neighborhood customers and then of course Momik. Only Momik didn't pay. The other regulars stopped shopping there when the new modern supermarket opened at the shopping center where they gave a free set of cork coasters for buying thirty pounds' worth of groceries, as if people always had a glass of tea on a coaster with the princess, and now they rush over like maybe they're going to find gold there instead of smoked fish and radishes, and also because everyone gets to push a solid-steel shopping cart around, says Bella, not really angry, and whenever she mentions the supermarket, Momik blushes and looks the other way, because he goes there too sometimes to see the lights and all the stuff they sell and the cash registers that ring, and how they kill the carp in the fish tank, but she doesn't mind so much about her regular customers leaving (says Bella), or that rich she'll never be, tell me, does Rockefeller eat two dinners, does Rothschild sleep on two beds, no, what bothers her most is the tedium, the boredom, and if things go on like this much longer she'll go out and scrub floors rather than sit around here all day, because to Hollywood she won't be going, not this year, because of her legs maybe, so Marilyn Monroe can relax with that new Jewish husband of hers. Bella sits at one of the empty tables all day long reading *Woman's Own* and *Evening News,* smoking one Savyon cigarette after another. Bella isn't afraid of anything, and she always says exactly what she thinks, which is why when the city inspectors came to throw Max and Moritz out of the storeroom, she gave them such a piece of her mind they had a conscience for the rest of their lives, and she wasn't even afraid of Ben-Gurion and called him "the Little Dictator from Plonsk," but she didn't always talk that way, because don't forget that like all the grownups Momik knew Bella came from Over There, a place you weren't supposed to talk about too much, only think about in your heart and sigh with a drawn-out krechtz,[3] oyyyy, the way they always do, but Bella is different from the others somehow and Momik heard some really important things from her about it, and even though she wasn't supposed to reveal any secrets, she did drop hints about her parents' home Over There, and it was from her that Momik first heard about the Nazi Beast.

The truth is, in the beginning Momik thought Bella meant some imaginary monster or a huge dinosaur that once lived in the world which everyone was afraid of now. But he didn't dare ask anyone who or what. And then when the new grandfather showed up and Momik's mama and papa screamed and suffered at night worse than ever, and things were getting impossible, Momik decided to ask Bella again, and Bella snapped back that

3. [Plaintive moan.]

there are some things, thank God, a nine-year-old boy doesn't have to know yet, and she undid his collar button with a frown, saying it choked her just to see him buttoned up like that, but Momik decided to persist this time and he asked her straight out what kind of animal is the Nazi Beast (since he knew there weren't any imaginary animals in the world and surely no dinosaurs either), and Bella took a long puff on her cigarette and stubbed it out in the ashtray and gave a krechtz, and looked at him, and screwed her mouth up and didn't want to say, but she let it slip out that the Nazi Beast could come out of any kind of animal if it got the right care and nourishment, and then she quickly lit another cigarette, and her fingers shook a little, and Momik saw he wasn't going to get any more from her this time, and he went out to the street, thoughtfully dragging his school-bag along the wet pavement, buttoning his collar absent-mindedly, and then he stood contemplating that Grandfather Anshel of his, sitting on the green bench across the street as usual, lost in his own world, waving his hands while he argued with the invisible somebody who never gave him a moment's rest, but the interesting thing is that Grandfather wasn't alone on the bench anymore.

It seems that in the past few days, without his noticing, Grandfather had started to collect all kinds of people around him. In fact they were these very old people nobody had noticed in the neighborhood before, or if anyone did notice them, they tried not to talk about them, people like Ginzburg and Zeidman for example, who'd walk up and stare in his face, and Zeidman would start making signs like Grandfather right away, because he always does what other people do, and then came Yedidya Munin who sleeps in the empty synagogue with all the martyred saints. Yedidya Munin is the one who walks bowlegged because of his hernia, and wears two pairs of glasses one on top of the other, one for the sun and the other not, and children are absolutely forbidden to go anywhere near him because he's obscene, but Momik knows Munin is really a good person, that all he wants in life is to love someone from a fine, distinguished family, and to make children with her in his own special way, which is why every Friday Momik secretly takes Bella's newspapers and clips out the personal ads of the famous Mrs. Esther Levine, modern matchmaker and leading expert in arranging contacts with visitors from overseas, but no one is allowed to know this, God forbid. And then came Mr. Aaron Marcus, father of Bella's Hezkel, whom nobody had seen for ten years and all the neighbors said Kaddish over him already, and here he was, alive, looking nice and all dressed up (well, Bella wasn't about to let him go out to the street looking like a shlumper), only his face, God help him, was twitching and cracking into a thousand-and-one faces you wouldn't want to see. And then came Mrs. Hannah Zeitrin, whose husband the tailor deserted her, may-his-name-be-blotted-out, and now she is a living widow, that's what she's always hollering and screaming, and it was lucky the compensation money came in, because otherwise she would have died of starvation, God forbid, because the tailor, pshakrev,[4] didn't even leave her the dirt under his fingernails, everything he took with him choleria,[5] and Mrs. Zeitrin is a very good woman, but she's also a whore and she mates with shvartzers, a shvartz yar oif ir, a black year on her, as Mama says whenever she walks by, and Mrs. Zeitrin really does do that with Sasson Sasson, a fullback on the Jerusalem Ha Poel soccer team, and with Victor Arussi, who's a taxi driver, and also with Azura, the butcher from the shopping center whose hair is full of feathers, and who looks like a nice guy actually, the kind that wouldn't mate, but everyone knows he does. At first Momik hated Hannah with a black hatred, and he swore he would only marry somebody from a fine, distinguished family, like the women in the ads of Esther Levine the matchmaker, somebody who would love him for his handsomeness and intelligence and shyness, and who would never mate with others, but once when he said something about

---

4. Scoundrel.

5. A Polish curse, meaning "bright cholera."

Hannah Zeitrin to Bella, Bella got angry with him and said what a poor woman Hannah Zeitrin is, and you should pity her, the way you should pity everyone, and you don't know everything about what happened to Hannah Over There, she never dreamed when she was born that this is how she would end up, sure everyone has hopes and dreams in the beginning, that's what Bella said, so then Momik started to understand Hannah a little differently, and he saw that she was very beautiful kind of, with her big blond wig like Marilyn Monroe, and her big red face with the nice little mustache, and her swollen legs all bandaged up; she's pretty in a way, only she hates her body and she scratches herself with her fingernails, and calls her body my furnace, my tragedy, and it was Munin who explained to him that she screams like that because she needs to mate all the time, because otherwise she'll go out somewhere or something, and that's the reason the tailor ran away from her, because he isn't made of steel you know, and also he had some kind of problem with horns, and that was something Momik would have to find out about from Bella, and these stories began to worry him a little, because what if someday none of her maters showed up and she happened to see Momik walking up the street? But thank God it didn't happen, and another thing is that Mrs. Zeitrin is also angry with God, and she shakes her fists at Him and makes all kinds of not-so-nice gestures, and she screams and curses at Him in Polish, which is bad enough, but then she starts swearing in Yiddish too, which you can be sure He understands. And all she wants is for Him to dare show His face, just once, to a simple woman from Dinov, but anyway, He hasn't dared so far, and every time she starts screaming that way and running up and down the street Momik dashes to the window for a view of the meeting, because how long will God be able to control Himself with all her insults, and everyone listening yet; what, is He made of steel? And now Mrs. Zeitrin has also been turning up at the bench and sitting next to Grandfather, but nicely, like a good little girl, still scratching herself all over, but quietly, without screaming or fighting with anyone, because even she could see that, deep inside, Grandfather is a very gentle man.

Momik is too shy to walk up to them, so instead he kind of moseys by, dragging his schoolbag along the sidewalk, till all of a sudden there he is, casually standing beside the bench where he can hear what they're saying in Yiddish, which is a slightly different Yiddish from the kind Mama and Papa speak, though in fact he understands every word: Our rabbi, whispers little Zeidman, was such a smart man even the top doctors declared he had two brains! And Yedidya Munin says, Eht! (a noise they all make). Our rebbeleh in Neustadt, the "yanukeh," they called him, he met his end There too, nebuch, he didn't want to write his commentaries in a book, nu, sure, the greatest Hasidim didn't always want to, so what happens? I tell you what happens: three things the little rebbe of blessed memory had to realize were signs from Above! You hear me, Mr. Wasserman? From Above! And in Dinov, says Mrs. Zeitrin to no one in particular, in Dinov where I come from, Jagiello's monument in the square was fifty meters high maybe and all marble! Imported marble!

Momik is so excited he forgets to shut his mouth! Because they're talking freely about Over There! It's almost dangerous the way they let themselves talk about it, but he has to make the most of this opportunity and remember everything, everything, and then run home and write it down in his notebook, and draw pictures too, because some things it's better to draw. So that when they talk about certain places Over There, for instance, he can sketch them in the secret atlas he's preparing. Like that mountain Mr. Marcus talks about, he can draw it in now, that huge mountain the goyim Over There call Jew Mountain, which is a magic mountain, so help us both, Mr. Wasserman, if you happened to find something up there, it disappeared before you got it home, a terrible sight! *Schrecklich!* And wood you gathered on the mountain, it wouldn't catch fire! It burned but was not consumed! That's what Mr. Marcus said, changing faces at incredible speed, God help us, but Mr. Munin tugs Grandfather's coat sleeve like a child and says, Another thing,

Mr. Wasserman, in Neustadt where I come from there was a man called Weintraub, Shaya Weintraub, they called him. A young fellow. A boy. But such a genius! Even in Warsaw they heard of him! He received a special award from the Minister of Education himself! Imagine that, the Pole gave him an award! Now listen to this, says Mr. Munin, digging deeper than usual in his pocket (searching for a treasure any beggar can find, says Bella), this Weintraub, if you asked him in the month of Tammuz, Tammuz shall we say, Please, Shaya, tell me how many minutes to go, God willing, before next Passover, you hear that, minutes, not days, not weeks, and then, just like that, may we both live to see our children married, Mr. Wasserman, he gives you the exact answer, like a regular robot. And Mrs. Hannah Zeitrin stops scratching and hitching her skirt up to scratch the top of her legs, and she looks at Munin and asks with a sneer, Would this Weintraub be the one with a head like an ear of corn by any chance, God forbid, the one that moved to Krakov? And Mr. Munin who seems kind of annoyed suddenly says in a quieter voice, Yes, that's the fellow, a genius like no other . . . and Hannah Zeitrin throws her head back, with a screechy-sounding laugh and says, And what became of him? Shaya Weintraub played the stock market and sank down down down. A genius, ha!

And they talk on and on this way, never stopping or listening to each other, to a singsong Momik has heard before somewhere, though he can't remember where exactly, speaking the language of Over There, the top-secret codes and passwords, recklessly, brashly saying: District of Lubov, Bzjozov Province, and the old cattle market, the big fire at the Klauiz, army work, protection, apostate out of spite, Red Feige Lea and Black Feige Lea, and the Goldeneh Bergel, the golden hill outside Zeidman's town where the King of Sweden buried caskets filled with gold when he fled the Russian Army, ach, and Momik swallows hard and remembers it all, for this kind of thing he has an excellent mind, a real alter kopf head, okay, so a Shaya Weintraub, a regular robot, he isn't yet, but Momik too can tell you on the spot how many gym classes to go before summer vacation, and how many hours of school (minutes too), not to mention some of the other things he knows, like his prophecies, because Momik is practically a prophet, a kind of Merlin the Magician, why he can guess when the next surprise quiz in arithmetic is going to be, and Miss Aliza, the teacher, actually did walk in and say, Please put away your notebooks, boys and girls, and take out paper and pencil. And the children stared at Momik in amazement, but that prophecy was a cinch because three months earlier when Papa went to have his heart checked at Bikkur Cholim Hospital they had a quiz, and Momik gets a bit nervous whenever Papa goes for his heart checkup, which is why he remembered, and next time Papa went they had another surprise quiz, so after that Momik guessed that four weeks from Monday Miss Aliza would give another quiz, but the other children don't understand this type of thing, for them four weeks is too long a time to measure, so they think Momik is a magician, but anyone who has a spy notebook and writes down everything that happens can tell that things that happen once will happen again, so Momik drives the children crazy with his accurate, spylike prediction about the tank column crossing the Malcha road once every twenty-one days at ten o'clock in the morning, and he can also tell (it spooks him too) the next time those ugly pimples are going to pop out all over Netta the science teacher's face, but these are silly prophecies, hocus-pocus stuff to make the kids respect him and stop teasing him, because the really big prophecies are for Momik alone, there's no one he can tell them to, like spying on his parents, and all the spy work to put together the vanished land of Over There like a jigsaw puzzle, there's still a lot of work left on this, and he's the only one in the whole wide world who can do it, because who else can save Mama and Papa from their fears and silences and krechtzes, and the curse, which was even worse after Grandfather Anshel turned up and made them remember all the things they were trying so hard to forget and not tell anyone.

Momik intends to rescue Grandfather Anshel too of course, only he doesn't quite know how yet. He's tried one or two methods already, but so far, nothing works. First, when Momik used to sit with Grandfather and give him his lunch, he would accidentally knock on the table sometimes the way Raphael Blitz and Nachman Farkash the convicts did when they were planning their prison break. He couldn't tell whether the knocking meant anything or not, but he had this hunch, this hope actually, that someone inside Grandfather would knock back. But nothing happened. Then Momik tried to figure out the secret code on Grandfather's arm. He'd tried this before with Papa's and Bella's and Aunt Idka's code numbers, but he didn't get anywhere that time either. The numbers drove him crazy because they weren't written in ink and they couldn't be washed off with water or spit. Momik tried everything to wash Grandfather's arm, but the number stayed fixed, which gave Momik an idea that maybe the number wasn't written from the outside but from the inside, and that convinced him more than ever that there was somebody there inside Grandfather, and the others too maybe, which is how they call out for help, and Momik racked his brains to understand what it could be, and he wrote down Grandfather's number in his spy notebook next to Papa's and Bella's and Idka's, and did all kinds of calculations, and then luckily in school they learned about gematria and the numerical values of the alphabet which naturally Momik was the first in his class to understand, and when he got home he tried to turn the numbers into letters in different ways, but all he got was a bunch of strange words he didn't understand, and still Momik would not give up, and once in the middle of the night he had an Einsteiny idea, he remembered there are things called safes where rich people hide their money and diamonds, and these safe things will only open if you turn seven dials in a certain secret way, and you can bet Momik spent half the night experimenting, and the next day, as soon as he picked Grandfather up at the bench on his way home from school and gave him his lunch and sat down across the table from him, he called out various combinations of the numbers from Grandfather's arm in a slow, solemn voice. He sounded kind of like the guy on the radio who announces the numbers that won the thirty-thousand-pound prize in the lottery, and he had a peculiar feeling that any minute now his grandfather would split down the middle like a yellow string bean, and a smily little chick of a grandfather who loves children would pop out, only it didn't happen, and suddenly Momik felt strangely sad, and he got up and went over to old Grandfather, and hugged him tight, and felt how warm he was, like an oven, and Grandfather stopped talking to himself, and for maybe half a minute he was quiet, and kept his face and hands still, and sort of listened to what was going on inside, but he could never stop talking for very long.

Then Momik used his systematic approach, the kind he's really good at. Whenever he and Grandfather were left alone in the house together, Momik would start following him around with a notebook and pen, recording Grandfather's gibberish in Hebrew letters. Okay, he didn't write down every single word he said, not every single word, that would be too dumb, but he did write down what he thought were the most important sounds Grandfather made, and it only took a couple of days for Momik to notice that what Grandfather was saying wasn't all gibberish, in fact he was telling somebody a story, just as Momik had thought all along. Momik tried hard to remember what Grandma Henny used to tell him about Anshel (that was a long, long time ago, before Momik understood things like an alter kopf, before he ever heard about Over There), but all he could remember was that she said Grandfather wrote poems for grownups too, and that he had a wife and daughter who were killed Over There, and he also tried to find hints in the story from the old magazine, but he didn't come up with anything. Then Momik went to the school library and asked Mrs. Govrin the librarian if she had any books by a writer called Anshel Wasserman, and Mrs. Govrin peered at him over her glasses and said she never heard of him, and she knows everyone. Okay, so Momik didn't say anything, he just smiled to himself inside.

He went over to Bella's to share his discovery (that Grandfather was telling a story), but she only looked at him with that expression he doesn't like, pitying him and shaking her head from side to side and unbuttoning his top button, and she said, Sport, yingaleh, you're going to have to start pulling yourself together now, you're pale and scrawny, a real little fertel,[6] how will they ever take you into the army, tell me, but Momik was stubborn and he explained that Grandfather Anshel was telling a story. Grandma Henny also used to like to tell stories when she still had her mind, and Momik remembered her special story voice and the way she stretched the words out and how her stomach filled with the words, and the peculiar way his palms would start sweating and the back of his knees, which is just how it felt when Grandfather talked now. And then he explained to Bella that he understood now that his poor grandfather was locked up in the story like the farmer with the sad face and the mouth open to scream that Aunt Idka and Uncle Shimmik brought from Switzerland, and this farmer lived his whole life in a glass ball where the snow fell if you shook it, and Mama and Papa put it on the living-room buffet, and Momik couldn't stand that mouth so one day he accidentally broke the glass and freed the farmer, and meanwhile Momik continues to record Grandfather's gibberish in the spy notebook slyly labeled *Geography,* and little by little he makes out a word here and there like Herrneigel, for instance, or Scheherazade, for instance, which he doesn't find in the *Hebrew Encyclopedia,* so he asks Bella for no particular reason what does Scheherazade mean, and Bella's just glad to hear he's stopped thinking about Over There, and she says she'll ask her son Joshua, the major, and two days later she answers Momik that Scheherazade was an Arab princess who lived in Baghdad, which is a little strange since if you read the papers you know there isn't any princess in Baghdad, there's a prince, Prince Kassem, pshakrev, who hates us like all the goyim, may-their-memory-be-blotted-out, but

---

6. A quarter of a chicken.

Momik doesn't know the meaning of the word "surrender," he
has the patience of an elephant, and he understands that a thing
may seem mysterious and scary and confused today, but it will
clear up by tomorrow, because it's just a question of logic,
there's always an explanation, that's how it is in arithmetic, and
that's how it is in everything else, but till the truth comes out,
you just do things normally as if nothing happened, you go to
school every morning and sit there for hours, and you don't let
it hurt your feelings when the children say you walk like a
camel, the way you slouch, oh, what do they know, and you
don't feel bad when they call you Helen Keller because you wear
glasses and have braces which is why he tries not to talk, and
you don't give in when they try to butter you up so you'll tell
them when the next surprise quiz in arithmetic will be, and on
top of this Momik has to worry about the deal he made with
Laizer the Crook who swipes his sandwich every morning and
then there's the distance home from school every day which you
use arithmetic to figure out, seven-hundred-and-seventy-seven
steps, no more, no less, from the school gate to the lottery booth
where Mama and Papa sit squeezed together all day long not
saying one word, and they see him turn the corner, all the way
up the street, for this they possess animal instincts, and when he
gets there Mama comes out with the house keys. Mama is very
squatty, and looks something like a kilo bag of flour, and she
wets her fingers with spit to comb the hair of Motl Ben Paisee
the Chazzan, he should look tidy, and she wipes a speck of dirt
off his cheek and his sleeve too, though Momik knows very well
there isn't any dirt there, she just likes to touch him, and he,
poor orphan, patiently faces her fingernails, gazing anxiously
into her eyes, because if there's anything wrong with her eyes
they won't grant us papers to get into America, and Mama, who
doesn't know she's Motl's mother just now, says quickly under
her breath, Your papa is becoming impossible, and she can't
stand those krechtzes one more minute, like an old man ninety
years old he sounds, and she swings around to look at Papa who
just stares up in the air like there's nothing there and doesn't

budge, and Mama tells Momik Papa hasn't washed in a week, it's the way he stinks that keeps the customers away, no one's stopped at the booth for two days now except the three regulars, why should the lottery people let us keep the booth with no customers and where are we supposed to get money to eat I'd like to know, and the only reason she stays here with him all day long like a sardine is because you can't trust him with money, he might go off and sell the tickets at a discount, or he could get a heart attack from the hooligans, God forbid, why is God punishing me like this, let Him kill me right now instead of a little at a time, she says, and her face falls exhausted, but then she suddenly gazes at him, and for just a minute her eyes are pretty and young-looking, not frightened or angry, the opposite, you might say she seems to be trying out some new chendelach[7] on Momik to make him smile, to make him special to her, and her eyes light up, but it only lasts about a half a minute and she changes back into the way she was before, and Momik sees her eyes change, and Motl whispers softly to her, in the voice of My Brother Elijah, Hush, nu, hush, Mama, weep no more, the doctor said it isn't good for you to cry, please, Mama, for our sake, and Momik makes a vow, tfu, may he die in Hitler's black tomb unless he finds a green stone that cures diseases of the eye and other cholerias, and this is what Momik is thinking so hard to help him not hear the seventh-grade hooligans shouting a safe distance away from big fat Papa: "Lottery little, lottery big, turns a pauper into a pig," a kind of ditty they made up, but Momik and Mama hear nothing, and Momik sees Papa, the sad giant of an Emperor, staring down at his enormous hands, no, all three of them are deaf to the hooligans, because they hear only their own secret language which is Yiddish, which soon the beautiful Marilyn Monroe will understand because she married Mr. Miller, a Jew, and every day she learns three new words, and these hooligans, let them drop dead, amen, and Mama touches Momik here and there while he says the magic word

---

7. Coquettish, ingratiating behavior.

"Chaimova" seven times to himself, which is what you're supposed to say to infidels at the border tavern in the Motl Ben
Paisee book, because when you say "Chaimova," they drop
everything and obey you, especially if you ask them to help you
cross the border to America, not to mention a simpler thing
like handling a gang of seventh graders whom Momik will
only refrain from throwing to the infidels out of the goodness
of his heart.

"There's a drumstick in the refrigerator for you and one for
him," says Mama, "and be careful with the small bones, you
shouldn't swallow any, God forbid, and he shouldn't either. Be
careful." "Okay." "And be careful with the gas too, Shleimeleh,
and blow the match out right away, so there won't be a fire,
God forbid." "Okay." "And don't forget to make sure you turn
off the gas knob when you're done, and the little tap behind the
stove too. The one behind is the most important." "Yes." "And
don't drink soda water out of the refrigerator. Yesterday I
noticed at least one glass less in the bottle. You drank it, and it's
winter now. And as soon as you're inside lock the door twice.
The top lock and the bottom lock. Just once is no good."
"Okay." "And make sure he goes to sleep as soon as lunch is
over. Don't let him go out like a shlumper." "Okay." She carries
on talking to herself a little longer, making sure with her tongue
that there are no words left over, because if she's left out a single word, then everything she said will be wasted, but it's all
right, there's nothing left out, nothing bad will happen to
Momik, God forbid, so Mama can make her last speech, like
this: "Don't open the door to anyone. We're not expecting company. And Papa and I will be home at seven as usual, don't
worry. Do your homework. Don't turn the heater on even if it
gets cold. You can play after you do your homework, but no
wildness, and don't read too much, you'll ruin your eyes. And
don't get into any fights. If anyone hits you, you come here
to us right away." Her voice sounded weaker and farther
away. "Goodbye, Shleimeleh, say goodbye to Papa. Goodbye,
Shleimeleh. You be careful."

This must be how she bade him goodbye when he was a baby in the royal nursery. His father, who was still the Emperor and a commando fighter in those days, summoned the royal hunter and, with tear-choked voice, ordered him to take this infant deep into the forest and leave him there, prey to the birds of the sky, as they say. It was a kind of curse on children they had in those days. Momik didn't quite understand it yet. But anyway, luckily the royal hunter took pity on him and raised him secretly as his own, and many years later Momik returned to the castle as an unknown youth and became secret adviser to the Emperor and Empress, and that way, unbeknownst to anyone, he protected the poor Emperor and Empress who had banished him from their kingdom, and of course this is all imaginary, Momik is a truly scientific, arithmetically gifted boy, there's no one like him in fourth grade, but meanwhile, till the truth will out, Momik has to use imaginary things and hints and hunches and the talking that stops the minute he walks into the room, that's how it was when Mama and Papa sat talking with Idka and Shimmik about the compensation money from Germany, and Papa said angrily, Take a man like me, for instance, who lost a child Over There, which is why Momik isn't so sure it's only imaginary, and sometimes when he's really feeling low, it makes him so happy just to think how glad they'll be the day he can finally tell Mama and Papa that he's the boy they gave away to the hunter, it will be exactly like Joseph and his brothers. But sometimes he imagines it a different way, that he's the boy who lost his twin brother, because Momik has this feeling that he used to have a Siamese twin, and when they were born, they were cut in two like in *Believe It or Not*: "300 astonishing cases that shook the world," and maybe someday they'll meet and be joined together again (if they want).

And from the lottery booth he makes his way home at a precise and scientific pace, they call it the camel walk because they don't understand that he's directing his footsteps through the secret passages and shortcuts only he knows, and there are some trees you have to brush against accidentally, because he has this feeling maybe there's somebody inside and you have to show him he hasn't been forgotten, and then he crosses the dump behind the deserted synagogue where old Munin lives all by himself and you have to hurry past on account of Munin but also on account of the saintly martyrs waiting there impatiently for someone to release them from holy extermination, and from here it's just ten steps to the gate of Momik's yard, and you can see the house already, a kind of concrete block perched on four wobbly legs, under which is a small cellar, they should have gotten only one apartment in the house actually, not two, but they signed Grandma Henny up as a separate family, like Uncle Shimmik told them to, and that's how they got the whole building to themselves, so even though nobody lives in the other half of the house or ever goes in there, it's theirs, they suffered enough Over There, and it's a mitzvah to cheat this government, choleria, and in the yard there's a big old pine tree that keeps out the sun and twice Papa went out with an ax to chop it down, but he scared himself each time and came back quietly, and Mama stormed at him because he had mercy on a tree but not on this child who was going to grow up in the dark without the vitamins you get from the sun, and Momik has a room all to himself, with a portrait of Prime Minister David Ben-Gurion and a picture of Vultures with their wings spread like steel birds boldly defending our nation's skies, and it's too bad Mama and Papa won't let him hang any more pictures on the wall because it ruins the plaster, but except for the pictures, which really do ruin the plaster a little, his room is neat and tidy, everything in its place, and this room could definitely be a model for other children, if they would ever come over, that is.

It's a very quiet street, more like a lane really. There are only six houses on it, and it's always quiet, except when Hannah Zeitrin insults Our Lord. Momik's house is pretty quiet too. His mama and papa don't have many friends. In fact they don't have any friends at all except for Bella naturally, whom Mama goes to see on Saturday afternoons when Papa sits by the window in his undershirt and stares out, and except for Aunt Idka and

Uncle Shimmik, who come twice a year for a whole week, and then everything changes. They're different from Mama and Papa. More like Bella really. And even though Idka has a number on her arm, they go to restaurants and to the theater and to Gigan and Schumacher, the comedians, and they laugh so hard, Mama glances sideways and kisses her fingertips and touches her forehead, and Idka says, What harm is there in a little laughter, Gisella, and Mama smiles a foolish smile like she's been caught and says, Don't mind me, laugh, laugh, there's no harm, I do it just to be safe. Idka and Shimmik play cards too and go to the seashore, and Shimmik even knows how to swim. Once they sailed on a luxury ship, the *Jerusalem,* for a whole month because Shimmik owns a big garage in Natanya, and also he knows how to cheat on his income tax really well, pshakrev, and there's only one small problem, which is that they don't have any children, because Idka did all sorts of scientific experiments Over There.

Momik's mama and papa never go away on trips, not even out of town, except once a year, a few days after Passover, when they spend three days at a small pension in Tiberias. This is sort of strange because they even take Momik out of school for the three days. In Tiberias they're different. Not so different, but a little different somehow. For instance, they sit at a café and order sodas and cake for three. One morning of the vacation they all go to the beach and sit under Mama's yellow umbrella which you could call a parasol, with everybody dressed very lightly. Then they rub Vaseline on their legs so they won't burn, and on their noses all three of them wear little white plastic shades. Momik doesn't have a swimming suit, because it'd be silly to spend all that money on something you use only once a year and shorts are good enough. They allow him to run on the beach then as far as the water, and you can bet he knows things like the exact depth, length, and breadth of the Sea of Galilee and what kinds of fish live in it better than any of those hooligans swimming out there. In the past when Momik and his parents went to Tiberias, Aunt Idka would come up to Jerusalem alone to take care of Grandma Henny. She always brought a stack of Polish newspapers with her from Natanya which she left with Bella when she went home. Momik used to clip out pictures of Polish soccer players from the newspapers (especially *Pshegelond*) like Shimkoviak, the fantastic goalkeeper with the catlike leaps, but the year Grandfather Anshel arrived, Idka didn't want to stay with him on her own because he's so difficult, so Mama and Papa went by themselves, and Momik stayed with his aunt and with Grandfather, because only Momik knows how to handle him.

That was the year he discovered his parents were running away from home and the city on account of Holocaust Day. He was already nine and a quarter by then. Bella used to call him the neighborhood mizinik,[8] but actually he was the only kid around. It had been that way since the day he arrived in his baby carriage, and the neighborhood women leaned over him and cooed, "Oy, Mrs. Neuman, vas far ein mieskeit," what an ugly thing, and the ones who knew better looked away and spat three times to save him from what they carry inside them like a disease, and for nine-and-a-quarter years after that, every time he walked down the street he heard the same greeting and spitting, and Momik is always nice and well mannered, because he knows what they think of the other children in the neighborhood, they're rude and wild and shvartzers, all of them, so you can see Momik has a lot of responsibility for the grownups on the street.

His full name, it should be mentioned, was Shlomo Efraim Neuman, in So-and-so's and So-and-so's memory. They'd have liked to give him a hundred names. Grandma Henny did it all the time. She would call him Mordechai Leibeleh, and Shepseleh and Mendel and Anshel and Shulam and Chumak, and Shlomo Haim, and that's how Momik got to know who they all were, Mendel who ran off to Russia to be a Communist nebuch, and disappeared, and Shulam the Yiddishist who sailed for America and the ship sank, and Isser who played the violin and died with

---

8. The child of one's old age; the youngest child in the family.

the Nazis, may-their-name-be-blotted-out, and tiny Leibeleh and Shepseleh there was no more room for at the table, the family was so big by then, and Grandma Henny's father told them to eat like the gentry, and they believed him and ate on the floor under the table, and Shlomo Haim grew up to be a sports champion and Anshel Efraim wrote the saddest, loveliest poems and then he went to live in Warsaw and became a Hebrew writer nebuch, and they all met their end with the Nazis, may-their-name-be-blotted-out, one fine day they closed in on the shtetl and gathered everyone together by the river—aiii, little Leibeleh and Shepseleh, forever laughing under the table, and Shlomo Haim who was half paralyzed and recovered by a miracle and became a Samson the Hero, forever flexing his muscles at the Jewish Olympics with the Prut River in the background, and little Anshel, the delicate one, they wondered how he would ever get through the winter, and they put hot bricks under his bed at night so he wouldn't freeze, there he sits in his sailor suit with his hair parted in the middle looking so serious with his big eyeglasses; Goodness me, Grandma clapped her hands, you look just like him. She told him all about them long long ago, in the days when she could still remember, and they thought he was too young to understand, but once when Mama saw that his eyes weren't staring blankly anymore, she told Grandma Henny to stop right away, and she also hid the book with the amazing pictures (she probably sent it to Aunt Idka). And now Momik is trying as hard as he can to remember what was in the pictures and the stories. He writes down every new thing he remembers, even the little things that don't seem important, because this is war, and in war we use everything we have. That's what the State of Israel does when it fights against the Arabs, pshakrev.

Bella helps him sometimes too, of course, but not so willingly, and the main part he has to do for himself. He isn't angry with her or anything, no, of course not, obviously anyone from Over There can't give him real clues, and they also can't ask him to help in a simple, straightforward way. It seems they have all these laws of secrecy in the kingdom. But hardships like these don't worry Momik, who has no choice, because he's got to take charge once and for all. And over the past few weeks an awful lot of crooked lines have gone into his spy notebook which he now writes in under the covers where he can't see. He isn't always exactly sure how you're supposed to write those words in Hebrew that Papa screams out in his sleep every night. Anyway, Papa seemed to have calmed down a little and he'd stopped with the nightmares for a while till Grandfather arrived and then everything started up again. The screaming is certainly weird, but what do we have logic and brains and Bella for? When we examine the screaming in the light of day, it turns out to be quite simple. It was like this, there was a war in that kingdom, and Papa was the Emperor and also the chief warrior, a commando fighter. One of his friends (his lieutenant?) was called Sondar. This strange name may have been his name in the underground, like in the days of the Etzel and Lehi. They all lived in a big camp with a complicated name. There they were trained to go on daring missions, which were so secret even today you have to keep mum about them. Also there were some trains around, but that part isn't so clear. Maybe those trains are like the ones his secret brother Bill tells him about, the trains attacked by savage Indians. Everything is so mixed up. And there were also these big campaigns in Papa's kingdom called Aktions, and sometimes (probably to make the people feel proud) they would have really incredible parades, like we have on Independence Day. Left, right, left, right, Papa screams in his sleep, Links recht, he screams in the German language Bella will positively not translate for Momik, till he practically shouts at her and she gets angry and tells him it means left, right, to the left, to the right. Is that it, Momik wonders, then why didn't she want to translate it? Mama wakes up at night from Papa's screaming and she pokes him and shakes him, and cries, Nu, Tuvia, sha, be still, the child can hear you, Over There is gone, it's the middle of the night, a klag zal im trefin, you'll wake the boy, Tuvia! And then Papa wakes up scared and starts with the big krechtzes that sound like a frying pan sizzling under the

faucet, and Momik in his room meanwhile has shut the notebook under the covers, but he still hears Papa sort of sighing
into his hands, and now he thinks carefully, the way Amos
Chacham does before answering a very interesting question,
Supposing Papa touched his eyes and went on seeing as usual,
would that mean that the death in his hands is gone?

Well, he must touch Mama sometimes when they're jammed
together in the lottery booth. And he always used to lift
Grandma Henny in his arms and carry her to the table and back
to bed again. And every Thursday he bathes Grandfather
Anshel with a washrag and a little basin, because Mama is disgusted.

Okay, okay, they're from Over There, so maybe that's why he
can't hurt them. But here's one important thing to think about:
when he's selling tickets in the lottery booth he wears little rubber thimble things on each finger!

Not to mention the most conclusive scientific evidence of all,
the thing that happened with the leeches the time Madame
Miranda Bardugo came to cure Papa when he had eczema all
over his hands. Momik has worked out various theories like a
serious investigator: a boiling kettle? To look at them, if you
didn't know, you'd think they were just ordinary hands. Or
sandpaper maybe? Porcupine quills? Momik was having a hard
time falling asleep. For a long time now, ever since Grandfather
Anshel showed up, he hadn't been able to fall asleep at night.
Dry ice? A needle?

In the morning, before breakfast (Mama and Papa always
leave first), he quickly jots down another guess: "Boldly charg-
ing from the camp, our valiant heroes surprised the savage
Indians with Red Slipper, who had attacked the mail train. The
Emperor galloped ahead on his faithful steed, bursting with
splendor, also shooting his rifle in every direction. Sondar of the
Commandos covered him from behind. The mighty Emperor
shouted to me, his bold roar resounding through the frozen
kingdom." Momik paused to read what he had written so far.

This was definitely an improvement over what usually came out. But it still wasn't good enough. So much was missing. The main thing was missing, he felt sometimes. But what was this main thing? No, the writing should have more power, more biblical splendor, like Grandfather Anshel's writing. Only how? He would have to be bolder. Because whatever it was that happened Over There must have really been something for everyone to try so hard not to talk about it. Momik also started including some things they were learning about in school just then, like Orde Wingate and the Night Platoons, and also the Super Mystère jets we'll soon have, God willing, from our friends and eternal allies the French, and he even used the first Israeli nuclear reactor currently under construction in the sands of Nahal Rubin, and in next week's issue, a sensation-something article with exclusive photographs of thc pool where they actually do the atomic thing! Momik felt he was getting closer to solving the riddle. (Momik always remembered what Sherlock Holmes said in "The Adventure of the Dancing Men," that what one man invents another can discover, so he's sure he will succeed.) It's a fight for his parents and for the others too. Of course they know nothing about it, why should they know. He's fighting like a partisan. Undercover. All alone. So that they'll finally be able to forget and relax a little, and stop being so scared for once in their lives. He's found a way. It is dangerous, to tell the truth, but Momik isn't scared. That is, he's scared, but there's just no other way. Bella unknowingly gave him the biggest clue of all when she mentioned the Nazi Beast. That was a very long time ago though, and he hadn't quite understood it then, but the day Grandfather arrived and Momik went down to the cellar to look for the sacred old magazine with his story in it, he understood exactly. And in a way that was when Momik made up his mind to find the Beast and tame it and make it good, and persuade it to change its ways and stop torturing people and get it to tell him what happened Over There and what it did to those people, and it's been about a month now, almost a whole month since Grandfather Anshel arrived that Momik has been busy up to his ears, in complete secrecy, down in the small dark cellar under the house, raising the Nazi Beast.

That was a winter they would remember for years. Not because of the rain, it didn't rain in the beginning, but because of the wind. The winter of '59, said the old people of Beit Mazmil, and no one had to say any more. Momik's father walked around the house at night with yellow gatkes showing under his trousers, and a big wad of cotton in each ear, and he would stuff pieces of torn-up newspaper into the keyholes to stop the wind from getting in (which could get in even through there). At night Mama worked on the sewing machine Shimmik and Idka gave her. Bella fixed it so lots of ladies would bring Mama their quilt covers to mend and their old sheets to patch up and she could earn a little extra for the house. It was a sec-ondhand Singer sewing machine, and when Mama sat working at it and the wheel turned and creaked, Momik felt as if she were controlling the weather outside. The noise from the machine made Papa jumpy, but he didn't say anything, because he also needed the little extra, and besides he didn't want to get into trouble with Mama and her mouth, so he would pace around the house, krechtzing and switching the radio on and off, saying, This wind and all the other troubles are from the government, choleria. He always voted for the Orthodox Party, not because he was Orthodox, he wasn't one bit, but because he hated Ben-Gurion for being in power, and the General Zionists for being in the Opposition, and Ya'ari for being a Communist, pshakrev. And the winter with the winds and the drought began when the Orthodox Party left the Coalition, which is a sign from God that He is not pleased with the way things are going around here, Papa said, with a brave and careful look at Mama, who just kept sewing and said to herself out loud, Oich mir a politikacker—Dag Hammarskjöld.

But Momik was pretty worried, because he noticed that the whistling winds were confusing the people he'd become friendly with lately, and he had this feeling, not that he believed it could actually happen, but things were sure weird and a little scary too. Mrs. Hannah Zeitrin for instance. She got another install-ment of her compensation for the tailor shop her family used to own in Danzig, but instead of spending it on food or stuffing it into an old shoe in the storeroom, she went out and bought her-self new clothes, aza yar oif mir, may such a year befall me, and the wardrobe of that woman, says Mama to Bella, her eyes burning with rage, the way she wiggles like a boat, the slut, what did she lose out in the street? And Bella, who is pure gold, and who gives even Hannah a free glass of tea, just laughs and says, What do you care, Gisella, tell me, did you give birth to her at the age of seventy that you should worry so much about her? You know why a woman buys herself a fur coat, don't you, she wants to keep herself warm and the neighbors boiling. And Momik listens and sees that Bella and Mama don't understand, Hannah just wants to look beautiful, that's all, not to make Mama mad, and not even for mating, but because she has a new idea which only Momik knows about from listening to her when she talks to herself and scratches on the bench with the old people. But Hannah Zeitrin isn't the only one around here who's overdoing it lately. Mr. Munin is acting stranger than ever. Actually, with Munin it started even before Grandfather arrived, but now he's really gone too far. Sometime around the beginning of the year, Mr. Munin heard that the Russians sent Lunik 1 to the moon, and he started to be very interested in space things and became so impatient he made Momik come and tell him anything new he heard about Sputniks, right away, and even promised to pay Momik two piasters for listening to *New World of Science* on the radio Saturday mornings, and for bringing him a report on everything they say about Our Friend, that's what he calls Lunik 1, as if they know each other. So on Saturday morning after the program Momik runs outside and crawls through the hole in the fence to the back yard of the deserted synagogue where Mr. Munin lives as caretaker. Straightaway he tells him everything they said on the program, and Munin gives him a note on which he wrote in advance on

Friday: "In exchange for this note I will pay bearer the sum of 2 (two) piasters after the Holy Sabbath." The deal has been working out pretty well for a couple of weeks now. When Momik brings really good news about space and the latest discoveries, Munin is very happy. He bends down and draws the moon like a round ball in the dirt with a stick, and beside it all nine planets whose names he knows by heart, and next to that, proud as a baleboos,[9] he draws a picture of his friend, Lunik 1, who didn't quite make it to the moon and so became, nebuch, planet number ten. Munin is very knowledgeable, and he explains all about rockets and jet propulsion, and about an inventor called Zaliukov Munin wrote to once about an idea that could get him the Nobel Prize, but then the war broke out and everything went kaput, and the time is not yet ripe to discuss this but someday the whole world will understand who Munin is, and then they'll envy him, oh yes, that's all they'll be able to do, because they will never know what the good life is, the true life, true happiness, yes, he isn't ashamed to say it, the word is happiness, Momo, happiness, it must exist somewhere, right? Ah, nu, here I go, talking your head off. He drew in the dust as he talked, and Momik stood by, not understanding any of this, facing the bald spot with the dirty black yarmulke on it, and the two pairs of glasses tied together with a yellow rubber band, and the long white whiskers on his cheeks. Munin almost always had an unlit cigarette dangling from his lips that had a strange, sharp smell, not like anything he'd ever smelled before, kind of like the smell of carobs on a tree, and in a way Momik does enjoy standing close to Munin and smelling that smell, and Munin doesn't mind too much either. And once when the Americans launched Pioneer 4 and Momik went over before school to tell Munin, he found him sitting in the sun as usual, on an old car seat, warming himself like a cat, and beside him, on an old newspaper, were pieces of wet bread for the birds he always feeds, and the birds know

9. Landlord or master of the house.

him now and they fly around with him wherever he goes, and Mr. Munin had just been reading a holy book with a picture of a naked prophetess on the cover, and it seemed to Momik he'd seen that book somewhere before maybe at Lipschitz's in the shopping center, but how could that be, Mr. Munin wouldn't be interested in things like that, Momik knows the kind of ladies he looks for in the ads. Munin quickly hid the book away and said, Nu, Momo, what news dost thou bring? (he always talks like that, in the language of Our Sages of Blessed Memory), and Momik tells him about Pioneer 4 and Munin jumps up from the car seat and lifts Momik high in the air, and hugs him with all his might, to his prickly whiskers, and his coat and the stink, and he dances wildly all around the yard, a strange and frightening dance under the sky and the treetops and the sun, and Momik is afraid that someone passing by will see him like this, and Munin's two black coattails fly up in the air behind him, and he doesn't let Momik down until he's all worn out, and then he takes a crumpled piece of paper out of his pocket and looks around to see if anyone's watching, and then he crooks his finger for Momik to come closer, and Momik who's still pretty dizzy comes closer and sees it's a kind of map with names written on it in a language he doesn't understand and a lot of little Mogen Davids everywhere, and Munin whispers in his face, "The Lord redeemeth in the twinkling of an eye, and the sons of light soar high," and then he imitates a flying leap with his big hand and says, "Feeeiiiww!!" so loud and furiously that Momik who is still dizzy trips over a stone and falls down, and that's when Momik with his very own eyes saw stinky black hilarious Munin taking off diagonally in a strong wind to the sky like the Prophet Elijah in his chariot maybe, and at that moment, a moment he would never-ever-black-and-blue forget, he understood at long last that Munin was actually a kind of secret magician like the Lamed Vavim, the way Hannah Zeitrin isn't just a woman but a witch too, and Grandfather Anshel is a kind of prophet in reverse who tells what used to be, and maybe Max and Moritz and Mr. Marcus are also playing secret roles and they aren't just here by chance, they're here to help Momik, because before he started fighting for his parents and raising the Nazi Beast, he rarely even noticed them. Okay, maybe he noticed them, but he never used to talk to any of them before except Munin, and he always tried to keep as far away from them as possible, and now he hangs around with them all the time, and when he isn't hanging around with them he's thinking about them and what they say about Over There, and what a dope he was not to understand it before, and the truth is, he did use to sort of make fun of them sometimes because of how they look and stink and things like that, but now Momik hopes for one thing only, that they'll pass him all their secret clues so he'll be able to figure them out before this crazy wind gets them.

And at noon when Momik and Grandfather walk home together they have to lean so far against the wind they can hardly see the way, and they're afraid because they hear weird noises that sound like many tongues and Momik is sure there's something hiding inside the tree and in the pavement cracks, that it was probably there for ages till the wind blew it out, and Momik digs deeper in his pockets, and he's sorry now he didn't eat more last summer and put on a little weight, and Grandfather uses his crazy movements to cut through the wind, only suddenly he forgets where he's going, and he stops and looks around, and holds his hands up like a baby waiting for someone to pick him up, and this could turn into something dangerous because what if the wind grabbed him just then, but thank goodness Momik has Chodorov instincts and he always gets there just in time to catch Grandfather and to squeeze his hand, which is so soft on the inside, and they walk on together, and by then you can tell the wind is absolutely furious and it pounces on them out of the Ein Kerem Valley and the Malcha Valley, and sails wet newspapers at their faces and old campaign posters from the walls, and the wind howls like a jackal, and the cypress trees go stark raving mad from the howling, and they bow and writhe as if somebody were tickling their bellies, and it takes Momik and Grandfather forever to get home, and Momik finally unlocks the two locks and locks the bottom lock again right away, and only then does the wind stop howling in their ears, and they can start to hear something.

Now Momik can throw his schoolbag down and help Grandfather off with Papa's big, old overcoat, and sniff him quickly and sit him down at the table, and warm up the food for both of them. Grandma Henny used to have lunch in her room because she couldn't get out of bed without help, but Grandfather keeps him company, which is nice, like having a real grandfather you can talk to and all that.

Momik loved Grandma Henny very much. To this day it makes his heart ache to think of her. And all the suffering she suffered when she died too. But anyway, Grandma Henny had a special language she used when she was seventy-nine after she forgot her Polish and Yiddish and the little bit of Hebrew she learned here. When Momik came home from school he used to run in to see how she was, and she would get all excited and turn red and talk in that language of hers. Momik would bring her food in and sit down to look at her. She pecked at her plate like a bird. She had a permanent smile on her little face, a kind of faraway smile, and she talked to him through her smile. It usually started with her getting angry at him, Mendel, for leaving the family like that and going to do poor people's work in a place called Borislav, and from there he wandered off to Russia where he vanished, how could you do such a thing and break our mother's heart, and then she begs him, Sholem, never, ever, even when he reaches America where the streets are paved with gold, to forget that he's a Jew, and to wear tefillin and pray in the synagogue, and then she would ask him, Isser, to play "Sheraleh" on the violin, and she would close her eyes and you could tell she actually heard that violin, yes, and Momik watched not daring to disturb her. This was better and more exciting than any movie or book, and sometimes he had real tears in his eyes, and Mama and Papa asked what he liked about sitting with Grandma Henny in her room so long, listening to her talk that language no one understands, and Momik said he understood everything. That was a fact. Because Momik has this gift, a gift for all kinds of languages no one understands, he can even understand the silent kind that people who say maybe three words in their whole life talk, like Ginzburg who says, Who am I who am I, and Momik understands that he's lost his memory and that now he's looking for who he is everywhere even in the garbage cans, and Momik has decided to suggest (they've been spending a lot of time on the bench together lately) that he should send a letter to the radio program *Greetings from New Immigrants,* and maybe someone would recognize him and remind him who he is and where he got lost, oh yes, Momik can translate just about anything. He is the translator of the royal realm. He can even translate nothing into something. Okay, that's because he knows there's no such thing as nothing, there must be something, nu, that's exactly how it is with Grandfather Anshel, who also eats like a bird, peck and gulp, only slightly more frightenedly than Grandma Henny, probably because they had to eat very very fast Over There like the Jews in Egypt on the eve of Passover. And Momik has also finally managed to crack Grandfather's code, and he knows now that Grandfather is telling the story to a man or boy by the name of Herrneigel, and he calls his name in different ways, sometimes angrily, sometimes flatteringly, or sometimes a little sadly, but three days ago while Momik was listening to Grandfather talk to himself in his room, he distinctly heard him say "Fried," and Momik had come across that name before in the sacred magazine, and his hands started to tremble with excitement, but he told himself, Look, those are old stories, why would Grandfather tell the same stories over and over and get all excited like that? But naturally he had to check it out now, so when he brought Grandfather home from the green bench and sat him down at the table, he blurted out, "Fried! Paula! Otto! Harotian!" Okay, that was pretty risky, and suddenly he had a feeling Grandfather might do something bad to him. He did give him a very spooky look as a matter of fact, but he didn't do anything, and after sitting still for almost a whole minute, Grandfather said softly and very clearly, "Herrneigel," pointing back over his shoulder with his crooked thumb, as if there were some big or little Herrneigel standing behind him, and then he whispered, "Nazikaput!" but suddenly he smiled a real smile at Momik, the smile of a person who understands, and he leaned over his plate till his face was very close to Momik's and said, "Kazik," kind of gently, as if he had a present to give him, and he formed a little man with his hands, a dwarf or baby or something, and rocked it to his heart the way you rock a baby, and the whole time he kept smiling that sweet smile at Momik, and suddenly Momik saw that Grandfather did resemble Grandma Henny, which is no wonder since they were brother and sister, but then Grandfather's face closed up again, as if someone inside ordered him to stop everything on the outside and come back as quickly as possible because there's no time, and then the mumbling started again with the stupid tunes and the jerky movements and the white spit squirting out of the sides of his mouth, and Momik leaned back, very proud of his commando invasion into the heart of Grandfather's story, like a real Captain Meir Har-Zion alter kopf, and although maybe he didn't know a whole lot just yet, he was absolutely positive that Grandfather Anshel and this Herrneigel had something to do with the war Momik had been waging for a while against the Nazi Beast, and that even though Grandfather came from Over There, maybe he refused to stop fighting, maybe he was the only one from Over There who wouldn't surrender, and that's why he and Momik have a secret pact.

And Momik just sat there looking at Grandfather, his eyes filled with admiration, and now Grandfather seemed to him exactly like an ancient prophet, Isaiah or Moses, and suddenly he realized that all his past plans about what to be when he grew up had been one big mistake, that there was only one thing worth being in life and that's a writer, like Grandfather Anshel, and the thought puffed him up so much that he almost started flying around the room like a balloon, which is why he had to dash to the toilet, but this time it was different, he didn't have to pee after all, and in bewilderment he ran to his room and pulled out his secret notebook, which is also his diary and a truly scientific catalogue of things from Over There, the emperors and kings, the soldiers and the Yiddishists and the athletes from the Jewish Olympics, and the stamps and currency, and precise drawings of all plants and animals, and across the page in great big letters he wrote IMPORTANT DECISION!!! and under this heading he wrote the important decision, which was to become a writer like Grandfather, and then he looked at the writing and saw how good it looked, much better than it usually came out, and now he wanted to find a really terrific finish to match his great decision, and thought of writing "Chazak Chazak Venitchazek" like it says when you come to the end of a book in the Holy Bible, but his hand took over and boldly scrawled sportscaster Nechemia Ben-Avraham's heroic battle cry, "Our boys will do or die!" and no sooner had he written these words than he was filled with a sense of duty and maturity too, and he walked back to the kitchen, slowly and responsibly, and gently wiped the drumstick grease from Grandfather's chin, and led him by the hand to his room, and helped him undress, and caught a peek of his thingy though he tried to look away, and then he went back to the kitchen muttering, No time, no time.

First he switched on the big radio with the glass panel showing the names of capital cities around the world, and he waited for the green eye to warm up; it looked as if he had already missed the beginning of *Greetings from New Immigrants and Locating Lost Relations,* and he did hope none of his names had been called out meanwhile. He picked up the list Papa wrote in big letters like a first grader, and lip-read together with the radio announcing that Rochaleh, daughter of Paula and Avraham Seligson from Phashmishul, is trying to locate her little sister Lealeh who lived in Warsaw between the years . . . Eliahu Frumkin, son of Yocheved and Herschel Frumkin from Stri, is trying to locate his wife Elisheva née Eichler and his two sons

Jacob and Meir . . . Momik doesn't even have to glance at the paper to check, he knows his names by heart. Mrs. Esther Neuman née Shapira, and the child, Mordechai Neuman, and Zvi Hirsch Neuman, and Sarah-Bella Neuman, a lot of lost Neumans wandering around Over There, and Momik is only half listening now, pronouncing the names like the woman on the radio, in a sad singsong that sort of sinks into despair which he has been listening to every lunchtime since he first learned how to read and they gave him the list with the names, Yizhak son of Avraham Neuman, and Arieh Leib Neuman, and Gitel daughter of Hirschel Neuman, all the Neumans, Papa's family, very, very distantly related, he's been told so many times, and he traces circles on the paper which is stained with the grease of a thousand lunches, and in each circle there's a name, but suddenly Momik notices that this is like the singsong of the old people telling their stories about Over There.

It's 1:30 now, time to get going. He wipes the table meticulously, and washes the dishes in his own special way (soap, rinse, soap and rinse again) till the forks and plates glisten and give him naches,[10] because he can't stand dirty silverware lying in the sink, as they very well know, and then he puts the quarter of a chicken he didn't touch into a brown paper bag and looks through the refrigerator to see what he can take for the Beast. He pokes around the bottles of medicines old and new, and the jars of red horseradish and the plate of jellied calf's leg left over from the Sabbath among the pots full of food for the big supper that lies ahead, and for the thousandth time he peers behind the bottle of rosé wine they got as a present a few years ago from the anonymous person who bought a lottery ticket from their booth and won a thousand pounds, the biggest prize anyone ever won from them, and Momik printed on a piece of cardboard: *From this booth, ticket number such and such won 1,000 pounds,* and the man was a mensch and came around to

---

10. Pleasure, particularly the satisfaction Jewish offspring are supposed to afford their parents
    so they can brag to the neighbors.

say thank you and brought the bottle of wine with him, that was really nice, but nobody around here drinks crap like that, still it isn't nice to throw it away, and Momik took out the jar of yogurt (he could always tell Mama he ate it), and a cucumber and an egg, and after listening behind Grandfather's door to make sure he was asleep or talking to himself as usual, Momik went outside and locked the door behind him, the bottom lock too, and he ran down the steps under the wobbly concrete pillars, right into the wind, and forced the creaky cellar door open with all his might, and breathing hard, now or never, he walked in, and his face and back broke out in a cold sweat, and he stood there leaning heavily against the wall with his fist between his teeth to keep from screaming, but inwardly he was screaming, Get out get out get out or it will eat you up, but he doesn't, he mustn't, this is war, and it's stuffy and it stinks in there, like must and mildew, and animals and animal doo-doo, and there are weird noises in the dark, rasping and sputtering and cooing, and a big claw scraping the cage, and a wing spreading slowly, and a beak snapping open and shut somewhere, Get out get out, but he doesn't, and one spot of light breaks through the tiny window also covered with cardboard, and this light helps his eyes get used to the dark little by little, and even then he can hardly see the wooden crates lined up against the wall; not all of them are full yet actually, because the hunt is still on.

So far so good though. He's had some great catches. A big hedgehog he found in the back yard with a pointy black face, sad-looking like a little person, and there's a turtle he found down in Ein Kerem that's still in hibernation, and there's a toad that wanted to cross the road but Momik saved its life and brought it down here, and a lizard that unhitched its tail the instant Momik caught it, but Momik couldn't resist so he scooped up the tail with a piece of paper (it was pretty disgusting) and put the tail in a separate cage with a sign saying: *An as yet unfamiliar animal. May be venomous.* But then he had a scientific conscience about it and added a correction that looked more honest: *Tail may be venomous,* because you never can tell.

And there was also a kitten that most likely went crazy in the dark cage, and then—this is what you could call the crowning touch of the collection—there was the young raven that fell out of its nest in the pine tree kerplunk onto the little balcony. The young raven's parents are very suspicious of Momik, and they swoop down at him whenever they see him in the yard; a few weeks ago they even pecked his back and his arm and there was blood and a big commotion, but they can't prove anything, and the young raven gets the drumstick every day and tears it to pieces with its claws and crooked beak, and Momik watches it and thinks, How cruel, maybe this is the Beast, but you can't really tell who it's going to come out of in the end, and we won't know till they all get the right kind of nourishment and care.

A few days ago he saw a gazelle. He saw her on his way down the Ein Kerem path, a light brown patch on the rocks sweeping by suddenly. She stopped in her tracks and turned toward him looking beautiful and frightened and wild. A gazelle. She stretched forward to sniff him, and Momik held his breath. He wanted a good smell to come out of him, a friendly smell. She raised one hoof off the ground and checked the smell. Then she jumped back and stared at him with wide-open eyes, not lovingly, she was afraid of him and she ran away. Momik searched the rocks for about an hour, but he didn't find her. He was angry and he couldn't understand why. He asked himself if she might have the Beast in her too, because Bella said it could come out of any animal. Any animal? He'd better check with Bella again.

Momik took crates labeled TNUVA PRODUCE and REFRESHING TEMPO SODA from behind Bella's grocery store. He padded them with rags and old newspapers, and made little locks for them out of wire. He lugged all the stuff in the cellar off to one side, Grandma Henny's kifat, the big Jewish Agency beds, the straw mattresses that stank of pee, and the suitcases practically bursting with shmattes[11] that were tied up with rope to keep them

---

11. Rags.

from springing open, and two big sacks full of shoes, because
you never throw out old shoes, as anyone who's ever walked
barefoot for twenty kilometers in the snow can tell you, Papa
said, which was about the only clue he ever got from Papa, and
he wrote it down right away. The snow did pretty much fit in
with that business about the Snow Queen who freezes everybody. And from the kitchen cupboard he stole a couple of old
plates and half-broken cups for the food in the cages, and
Mama noticed right away of course, and he screamed that he
didn't do it, and he saw she didn't believe him, and he threw
himself on the floor, kicking and pounding, and he even said
something mean—that she should leave him alone already and
stop butting into his business, which he never said before he
started fighting the Beast, not to her or to anyone, and Mama
was really frightened, and she shut up, and her hand trembled
over her mouth, and her eyes popped open so wide he was
afraid they would burst, okay, so what could he do, the words
came out. He never guessed he had words like that inside him.
But she shouldn't have made such a big fuss about it. Maybe
they can't help because they aren't allowed to, okay, but do they
have to butt in?

After that he stopped taking things from the house. It's risky
to take anything because Mama has eyes in the back of her
head, and she even sleeps with her eyes open, and she can
always tell what he's thinking, that's happened several times.
She knows about everything in the house. When she's drying the
forks and soup spoons and knives after supper, she counts them
quietly, humming a kind of tune. She knows how many tassels
there are on the living-room carpet, and she always but always
knows exactly what time it is, even when she doesn't have her
watch on. Prophecy must run in the family, because it seems to
have started with Grandfather Anshel and passed down to
Mama and now Momik. The way diseases pass down.

And another thing worth mentioning is that Momik never
slouches on the prophecy job, and he always tries to be a genius
like Shaya Weintraub who calculated the minutes till Passover,

and for the past few days Momik has been experimenting with numbers, not something really big, but fairly interesting all the same—it goes like this: he counts the number of letters in words people say on his fingers, and it could be that Momik Neuman of Beit Mazmil, Jerusalem, is the inventor of a spectacular new method of counting on your fingers, faster than a robot, and no one could ever guess how it works, because it looks as if Momik is just listening to what the person is saying, his teacher for instance, or Mama for instance, but in his head and on his fingers something else is going on. Not every word though, every word, what, is he crazy? Only words with a certain ring to them, if he hears that kind of word, his fingers start running up and down as if they were playing the piano, and they count at Super Mystère speed as if they were jet-propelled and could break the sound barrier. For instance, if someone says the word "infiltrators" on the radio, right away his fingers start running automatically, and he makes a fist which means five fingers and another fist which means five fingers and another two fingers which makes twelve letters all together. Or "national league coach," and the fingers calculate it right away, nineteen letters, or how about the magic word "uranium" which is the most important element in the atomic reactor, bzzz! One fist, two fingers, that's seven letters altogether. And Momik's had so much practice now that he can calculate whole sentences on his fingers, especially juicy ones like "Our forces returned safely," four fists, three fingers; it's really fun too, a very interesting, quiet game, and it also strengthens your hand and finger muscles, which is important because Momik's a little on the short side, and even skinnier than he is short, but—(1) short people can be strong, look at Ernie Tyler who's a dwarf (a midget, that is) and he saved Manchester United, and this year they traded him off again to save Sunderland, and (2) with the help of finger exercises and willpower like Raphael Halperin, Momik may soon become stronger, God willing, than the famous Jewish wrestler Over There, the one and only Zisha Breitbart, feared even by the goyim, may-their-name-be-blotted-out, which must be what they call a deterrent, one fist, four fingers, and by the way, according to the rules of Momik's new game, a word that ends with the middle finger is a word that brings good luck, and that's why he sometimes adds on a "the" to a word to make it come out on the middle finger. Why not? You're allowed to use strategy. In war you have to use strategy.

He waits in the cellar a little while longer. Maybe it's not long enough for the Beast, but it's still pretty hard to stay down there the way you really have to if you want to make it come out. But then he has to go so bad he wets his pants like a baby, and runs home to change. He still hasn't found a way to keep it from happening. The raven flutters its black wings—and before you know it, his pants are wet. And his undershirt is damp too, and it stinks like sweat after two hours of gym class, and meanwhile the cat is yowling, and Momik's eyes are half closed. The first night they could hear the cat all the way up in the house, and Papa wanted to go look for it down there and throw it to the devil, but Mama wouldn't let him go out by himself in the dark, and they just got used to it eventually and didn't even hear it anymore, and pretty soon the yowling got softer, as if it was coming from the cat's stomach. Momik does feel kind of bad about that cat, and he even considered setting it free, only the trouble is, Momik is scared of opening the cage door because the cat might spring at him, so the cat stays, but Momik feels more like the cat's prisoner than the other way around.

So he forces himself to stand there with his eyes shut, his body tense with battle alert, two fists, one finger, in case, God forbid, something happens, and the raven and the cat are watching and all of a sudden the raven opens its beak and makes a terrible croaking sound, and in less than no time Momik finds himself outside with his leg wet all the way down.

And then he runs upstairs and opens the door and locks the bottom lock too and shouts, "Grandfather, I'm here," and changes his pants and washes the disgusting pee from his leg, and sits down to do his homework, but first he has to wait till his hands stop shaking. Okay. Now he can draw an equilateral

triangle and answer the who-said-what-to-whom questions in
the Bible homework, and things like that. This he finishes pretty fast, because homework is never a problem for Momik, and
he also hates to put off doing homework so he does it the same
day, because why should he let it burden his mind? Then he sits
down and times his breathing with his watch (a real watch that
used to belong to Shimmik), and he practices so that someday
he'll be able to enter a contest and sing in one breath against Lee
Gaines, the Negro singer from the Delta Rhythm Boys, who are
currently performing in our country bringing us their new kind
of music called jazz, and just then he remembers that he forgot
as usual to ask Bella for a recipe for sugar cubes to give to
Blacky, the horse that belongs to his secret brother Bill, and he
decides to do the homework his science teacher is going to
assign three lessons from now, the questions are at the back of
each chapter and he likes to be three chapters ahead, too bad he
can't do that in the other subjects, and he finishes his homework
now and wanders around the house, has he forgotten anything,
yes: what do you feed baby hedgehogs, because the hedgehog
seems to be getting fatter so maybe it's a female and you have
to be prepared, because the Beast can come from anywhere.

He ran his fingers over the large volumes of the *Hebrew
Encyclopedia* Papa subscribed to with the special discount offer
and installment payments for employees of the National
Lottery. These were the only books they bought, you can always
find books to read in the library. Momik wants to save up his
money to buy some books, but books are very expensive and
Mama won't allow him to buy any, even with his own money.
She says books attract dust. But Momik simply must have
books, and when there's enough money saved up in his hiding
place from presents and what he gets from Mr. Munin sometimes, he hurries down to Lipschitz's to buy a book, and on the
way home he writes in the jacket in deliberately crooked handwriting: *To my good friend Momik, from Uri*, or in big,
grown-up-looking letters like Mrs. Govrin's he writes: *Property
of Beit Mazmil Elementary School*. This way, if Mama should

ever happen to notice a new book with his school things, Momik has a cover. But the encyclopedia was no use this time, because they weren't up to P for pregnancy yet, and there was nothing under Cubs either. There seemed to be an awful lot of things the encyclopedia was trying to ignore, as if they didn't exist, some of the most interesting things of all in fact, like the thing Mr. Munin has been talking about more and more lately, "Happiness," the encyclopedia doesn't even mention it, or maybe there's some good reason for this because usually it's very very smart. Momik loves to hold the big books in his hands, and it makes him feel good all over to run his fingers down the smooth pages that seem to have a protective covering that keeps your fingers away, so you won't get too close, because who are you, what are you compared to the encyclopedia, with all the little letters crowded in long, straight columns and mysterious abbreviations like secret signals for a big, strong, silent army boldly marching out to conquer the world, all-knowing, all-righteous, and a couple of months ago Momik vowed he would read an entry a day in alphabetical order, because he's a very methodical little boy, and so far he hasn't missed once, except for the time Grandfather Anshel arrived, so the next day to make up for it he read two entries, and even though he doesn't always understand what they're talking about, he likes to touch the pages and feel deep in his stomach and his heart all the power and the silence, and the seriousness, and the scientificness that makes everything so clear and simple, and best of all he likes Volume VI, which is all about Israel, and from the cover you might think it was an ordinary volume like the others, because it looks serious and smart and scientific, but in this volume, right before the end, you suddenly see a burst of fantastic colors, two fantastic whole pages of pictures of all the stamps issued by the State of Israel, and Momik gasps when he turns the pages in this volume slowly and all the beautiful colors leap out at him and take him completely by surprise like huge bouquets of flowers or a peacock's tail fanning out in his face and all those pictures and colors and the wildness of it, and the one thing that reminds him a little of this is the red lining that looks like fire in Mama's black evening bag.

And another secret which can be told now is that those were the stamps that gave Momik the idea of drawing his stamps from Over There. In the past few days, thanks to everything the old people have been teaching him about Over There, he managed to fill nearly a whole album. Once, he had to make do with what he knew already, which wasn't that much, and which wasn't that interesting either, why not admit it; for instance, he used to draw Papa the way they draw Chaim Weizmann our first President on a blue three-piaster stamp, and he drew Mama holding a peace dove, one fist, four fingers, wearing a white dress as in the 1952 Holiday Greetings stamp, and Bella as Baron Edmond de Rothschild, she's a famous philanthropist too, with a bunch of grapes on one side, just like the real stamp. There didn't use to be that much to draw before, but now everything has changed. Momik draws lots of stamps with Grandfather Anshel as Dr. Herzl, Seer of the Nation at the Twenty-third Zionist Congress (because Grandfather Wasserman is a seer and a prophet like that), and little Aaron Marcus as Maimonides with the beads and the funny hat on the brown stamp, and Max and Moritz like the two people carrying the pole of grapes on their shoulders, Ginzburg in front, with his head bowed, and a little balloon coming out of his mouth with his three words, and behind him, Zeidman, small and pink and polite, carrying a tiny briefcase in one hand, with Ginzburg's words coming out of his mouth too in a balloon, because he always does what he sees someone else doing. But the best idea of all is the one with Munin. It's like this: on the Holiday Greetings stamp for 1953 there's a picture of a white dove flying nobly in the air and it says on the stamp, *My dove in the mountain clefts,* and for three days Momik sat down and drew maybe twenty sketches till it came out the way he wanted, a picture of Mr. Munin flying in the air with a bunch of other little birds that always fly around with him because of the bread he crumbles, and Momik drew Munin just like he is in real life, with his black hat and his big red nose like a kartofeleh,[12] only in the picture Momik gave him white wings too like a dove, and in the corner he drew a little white star and wrote *Happiness,* because that's where Munin wants to go so much, isn't it? And there were a lot of other pretty and interesting stamps in his collection, like Marilyn Monroe with her blond hair, as pretty as Hannah Zeitrin's wig, and in the margin he wrote (Bella helped him translate), *Marilyn Monroe redst Yiddish,* because she did promise, but the one with Marilyn is just for fun, and the important stamps in the collection were the new ones from Over There and all the places and historical things like the Old Klauiz (he drew it like the new Cultural Center), and the annual fair at Neustadt which the Prophet Elijah in person used to attend, they said, disguised as a poor farmer, and the hanging pole in Plonsk with the terrible criminal Bobo hanging from it, and he also drew the Jewish Olympics, and even Elijah Leib the miser from Hannah Zeitrin's shtetl who they said wouldn't give his wife any lunch to eat (he was such a miser), and in the stamp you could see where the miser drew a Mogen David with his knife on a loaf of bread so no one would take any while he was out, and then Momik made another series, very well drawn, with all the animals from Over There. He was pretty lucky with that series because by chance he found statues of all the animals on the glass buffet in Bella's living room. He'd been there a thousand times and he never understood what they were till Grandfather Anshel arrived and Momik started to fight and then suddenly he realized that those tiny colored glass figures were obviously the kind of animals they used to have Over There, because that's where Bella brought them from! On Bella's buffet there were blue gazelles, green elephants, purple eagles, and fish with long, bright, delicate fins, and a kangaroo, and lions, all dainty and tiny and transparent, trapped inside the glass, and you're not allowed to touch them because they're breakable, and they look as if they froze in motion, which is just what happened to everyone from Over There.

---

12. Potato.

Anyway, that afternoon Momik drew a picture of Shaya Weintraub with a head like an ear of corn, with a wrinkled forehead from thinking so much, and over him he drew a bottle of Passover wine and matzo, and then he drew good old Motl as the parachutist on the Tenth Anniversary of Hebrew Parachuting stamp, and he cut out little teeth on the new stamps and pasted them in his stamp notebook, and looked at his watch and saw that it was six already, and then he turned the radio on because it was time for *Children's Corner,* and they told the story of King Matt I, and Momik listened, but he jumped up every other minute because he remembered something or other he'd forgotten to do, like sharpening his pencils till they were sharp as a pin, or shining Mama's and Papa's shoes and his own shoes too on a piece of newspaper till they glistened and gave him naches, or making a note in his geography notebook, the secret one, about what he read in the paper yesterday, that the first two mares at the Hebrew Agricultural Exhibit at Beit Dagan are already pregnant, and everyone's waiting, and after the program was over he turned the radio off and picked up *Emil and the Detectives* which he likes to read because of the suspense but also because of the five printing errors he enjoys finding and then he can check to see if he's entered them in his notebook of printing errors from books and newspapers (he's collected almost a hundred and seventy errors already), and even though he knows those mistakes from *Emil and the Detectives* have been in his notebook for a long time, it's 6:33 already, and now Momik goes over to the living-room couch and lies down under the picture his parents got from Idka and Shimmik, a big oil painting of a forest and snow and a stream and a bridge, which must be what Neustadt looked like or Dinov where his old friend once lived, and if you lie down in a certain way, kind of curled up on the couch, you can see when you look up through the branches of the tree in the corner there's a face almost like a child's face which only Momik knows about, and maybe that's his Siamese twin, but you can't tell for sure, and Momik looks at it very hard but the truth is that today he can't concentrate because his head's been hurting badly for a few days now, his eyes too, but don't get tired yet, because today's war has not even begun.

And then Momik suddenly remembered that it was a couple of hours already since he'd decided to become a writer and so far he hadn't written anything, and the reason was that he hadn't found anything to write about. What did he know about dangerous criminals like in *Emil and the Detectives,* or about submarines like in Jules Verne, and his own life seemed so ordinary and boring, all he was was a nine-year-old kid, what's there to tell about that, and he checked his big yellow watch again, and slid off the couch and walked around in circles saying comically, It makes my head ache to watch you krechtzing and spinning like a top, Tuvia, as a certain person we know says to another person, but it wasn't really so comical, though at least when he looked at his watch again it was twenty-one minutes to seven already, and in his head he started broadcasting the final minutes of the big game soon to take place in Yaroslav, Poland, between us and the Polish team, and he let them win by four goals, and then with only five minutes to go and the situation looking kaput, our coach, Giula Mandy, raised his sad eyes to the bleachers full of cheering Poles, when who should he see there but a boy! And one look is enough to tell him that this boy is a born soccer player, the player who will save the day, and if only they had let the boy play at school he would have shown them too, oh well, and Giula Mandy stops the game and whispers something to the referee, and the referee agrees, and a hush falls over the crowd, and Momik wends his way down the stairs to the playing field where he plans a really spectacular defense and offense (he had some experience training Alex Tochner), and in less than four minutes Momik has turned the tide, as they say, and our team wins 5 to 4, please God, amen, and the time was now fourteen minutes to seven, nu, pretty soon now, and Momik went to the bathroom and washed his face with warm water and held his head exactly where the long crack runs down the middle of the mirror, and he heard the rain start falling outside and the police car that went around the block warning people to drive slowly, and all of a sudden Momik remembered he forgot to give Grandfather his tea and laxative at four o'clock, and he felt a sting of conscience, you could do just about anything to Grandfather and he wouldn't even notice, like a baby, and lucky for him Momik was so goodhearted, because other children might take advantage of a dodo like Grandfather and do mean things to him, and Momik stuck his head out the bathroom door and heard Grandfather waking up and talking to himself as usual, and with nine minutes to go, Momik removes his braces and brushes his teeth with ivory toothpaste which is made from special elephants they grow at the Health Clinic, and meanwhile he practices saying words that have the letter *S* because when they put braces on you, it ruins your *S* and you have to make sure you don't lose it, and then finally the living-room clock strikes seven, and in the distance, from Bella's house maybe, comes the sound of news beeps, and Momik's heart races and he counts the steps from the lottery booth to the house but more slowly because they have trouble walking, and the sweat behind his knees and elbows itches, and exactly when he predicted it (almost), he heard the gate creaking in the yard and Papa's cough, and a moment later the door opened and there stood Mama and Papa who quietly said hello, and with their coats still on, and their gloves and the boots lined with nylon bags, their eyes devoured him, and even though Momik could actually feel himself being devoured, he just stood there quietly and let them do it because he knew that was what they needed, and then Grandfather Anshel came out of his room all confused in the big coat and Papa's old shoes on backward, and he tried to go outside in his pajamas but Papa stopped him gently and said, We're going to eat now, Papa; he's always gentle with poor things like him and Max and Moritz, he's nice to them and he feels sorry for them, and Grandfather doesn't understand what's holding him back and he puts up a fight, but in the end he just gives in and lets himself be seated at the table, but he doesn't let them take his coat away.

Supper:

It goes like this: first Mama and Momik set the table very fast, and Mama warms up the big pots from the refrigerator, and then she brings supper in. This is when it starts getting dangerous. Mama and Papa chew with all their might. They sweat and their eyes bulge out of their heads and Momik pretends to be eating while he watches them carefully, wondering how a woman as fat as Mama could come out of Grandma Henny, and how the two of them could have had a scarecrow boy like him. He only tastes what's on the tip of his fork, but it sticks in his throat because he's so nervous. This is just how it is—his parents have to eat a lot of food every night to make them strong. Once they escaped from death, but it isn't going to let them get away a second time, that's for sure. Momik crumbles his bread into little wads which he arranges in squares. Then he makes an even bigger ball of dough, and breaks it exactly in half, and then in half again. And again. You need the hands of a heart surgeon for this kind of precision. And again in half. They won't get angry with him for doing things like this at supper, he knows, because they're not paying any attention to him. Grandfather, in his big woolly overcoat, tells himself the Herrneigel story, sucking on a piece of bread. Mama is all red now and puffing with effort. She chews so hard you can't see her neck. The sweat runs down Papa's forehead. They mop the pots with big chunks of bread and gobble them up. Momik swallows spit and his glasses steam. Mama and Papa vanish then and return behind the pots and frying pans. Their shadows dance on the wall behind them. Suddenly they seem to be floating away on the warm steam from the soup pot and he almost shrieks in fear; God help them, he says in Hebrew in his heart, and translates it into Yiddish so God will understand, Mir zal zein far deine beindelach, Do something to me instead and have mercy on their little bones, as Mama always says about him.

And then comes the big moment when Papa lays his fork aside and gives a long krechtz, and looks around as if he only just noticed he was home, and that he has a son, and that there's a grandfather sitting there. The battle is over. They've earned another day. Momik jumps up and runs to the kitchen faucet and drinks and drinks. Now comes the talking and the annoying questions, but how can you get angry with someone whose life has just been saved by a miracle? Then Momik tells them that he did his homework and that tomorrow he'll start preparing for the Bible test, and that his teacher asked again why his parents won't let him go on the class trip to Mt. Tabor with everybody else (a new teacher who doesn't know), and meanwhile Papa stands up and goes over to the coffee table in the living room, and unbuckles his belt, and his body floods over like a river that fills the room and just about pushes Momik into the kitchen, and Papa sticks his hand out and starts fiddling with the radio. He always does it like that. He waits for the radio to warm up and then starts turning the dial. Warsaw Berlin Prague London Moscow, not really listening, he hears a word or two and turns it some more, Paris Bucharest Budapest, no patience at all, from country to country he moves like that, from city to city, he never stops moving and only Momik guesses that he's waiting for a message from Over There, a message calling him back from exile so that he can be the Emperor he really is again, not like he is here, but so far they haven't called.

And then Papa just gives up and turns the dial back to the Voice of Israel, and listens to the program about Knesset committees, and closes his eyes and you might think he was sleeping, but he hears every single word, and to whatever they say there he makes nasty remarks, and anyway, politics is something that makes him furious and dangerous, and Momik stands in the doorway to the kitchen, and hears Mama counting the forks and knives in her singsong as she dries them, secretly watching Papa's arms falling limply on both sides of the chair. His fingers are puffy, with gray hair on the joints, and you can't tell how they feel when they touch you because they don't.

In bed at night, Momik lies awake thinking. Over There must have been a lovely land with forests everywhere and shiny railroad tracks, and bright, pretty trains, and military parades, and the brave Emperor and the royal hunter, and the Klauiz and the animal fair, and transparent jewel-like animals that shine in the mountains like raisins on a cake. The only trouble is, there's a curse on Over There. And this is where it starts getting kind of blurry. There's this spell that was put on all the children and grownups and animals, and it made them freeze. The Nazi Beast did it. It roamed the country, freezing everything with its icy breath like the Snow Queen in the story Momik read. Momik lies in bed imagining, while Mama works at her machine in the hallway. Her foot goes up and down. Shimmik adjusted the pedal a little higher up because otherwise her foot wouldn't reach it. Over There everyone is covered in a very thin layer of glass that keeps them motionless, and you can't touch them, and they're sort of alive but sort of not, and there's only one person in the whole world who can save them and that's Momik. Momik is almost like Dr. Herzl, only different. He made a blue and white flag for Over There, and between the two blue stripes he drew an enormous drumstick tied to the back of a Super Mystère and below it he wrote the words *If so you will, it is no fairy tale,* but he knows he doesn't have the least idea yet about what he's supposed to do, and that kind of worries him.

Sometimes they come into his room at night and stand next to his bed. They just want to take one last look at him before they start with the nightmares. That's when Momik strains every muscle to look as if he's asleep, to look like a healthy, happy boy, just as cheerful as he can be, always smiling, even in his sleep, ai-li-luli-luli, we have the most hilarious dreams around here, and sometimes he has a really Einsteiny idea, like when he pretends to be talking in his sleep and says, Kick it to me, Joe, we're going to win this game, Danny, and things like that to make them happy, and once on a really horrible day when Grandfather wanted to go outside after supper and they had to lock him up in his room and he started hollering and

Mama cried, well, that horrible day Momik pretended to be asleep and he sang them the national anthem and got so carried away he wet his bed, and all to make them understand they didn't have to get so upset, they didn't have to waste their fears on him or anything, they ought to be saving their strength for the really important things, like supper and their dreams and all the silences, and then just as he was finally falling asleep he heard as if in the distance, or maybe he was dreaming already, Hannah Zeitrin calling God to come already, and also the quiet yowling of the cat who was going crazy in the cellar, and Momik promised to try even harder from now on.

He had two brothers.

Or put it this way, once he had a friend.

The friend's name was Alex Tochner. Alex came from Rumania last year and he knew only a little Hebrew. Netta the teacher sat him next to Momik, because Momik would be a good example, and also because he knows Hebrew best in the whole class, and also maybe because she knew Momik wouldn't make fun of Alex. And when Alex sat down next to Momik, the whole class started laughing at them because they were two four-eyes.

Alex Tochner was short but very strong. Whenever he wrote something his arm muscles popped out. He had bristly yellow hair, and even though he wore glasses, they didn't look as if they were for reading. He was always fidgeting and he didn't talk much. When he did talk though he rolled his *r's,* like the old people. The children called them "the two Polacks," and Momik and Alex hardly spoke a word to each other. But then Momik decided to do something, and one day during General Science he passed Alex a note asking if maybe he could come over after school tomorrow. Alex shrugged his shoulders and said yeah, he guessed so. Momik could hardly sit still for the rest of the day. After supper he asked Mama and Papa if it

would be all right to bring home a friend, and Mama and Papa
gave each other a look and started asking him a bunch of questions like Who is this friend, what does he want from Momik,
and is he one of us or one of them, and is he the kind that steals
things and would he go snooping around the house,
and what do his parents do? Momik told them everything
and in the end they said it was all right if he wanted to bring
him over, but to keep an eye on him. That night Momik was
too excited to sleep. He thought about how he and Alex would
get along together, and how they would be a two-man team,
how this, and how that, and the next morning he was at
school by 7:30.

After school Alex came over and they went out for a falafel
at the shopping center; Alex liked falafel, Momik didn't, but it
was exciting to pay and eat out for once, and in the end he gave
his half to Alex; Alex used so much hot sauce the falafel man
said he'd have to charge him double. Then they went home and
did their homework and then they played checkers. It was definitely more fun to play with another person. Momik made up
his mind that night to be a man from now on and keep his
mouth shut like Alex, but he couldn't not talk, because what are
friends for? What, were they supposed to just keep quiet like a
couple of blockheads? And he went on asking Alex questions
about Alex and Alex's homework and about where Alex came
from, and Alex gave him short answers and Momik was afraid
Alex was getting bored and that he'd leave, and he ran to the
kitchen and climbed up on a chair and reached into Mama's
hiding place and took out the bar of chocolate which isn't for
company, but this was an emergency, as they say, and when he
offered it to Alex he told him that Grandma Henny died not
long ago and Alex took one square of chocolate and then another square and said his father died too, and Momik was excited
because he knows about things like that, and he asked if his
father was killed by Them, and Alex didn't understand what he
meant by Them and said that his father was killed in an accident, he was a boxer and he was knocked out, and now Alex

was the man of the house. Momik was silent thinking, What an interesting life this Alex has, and Alex said, "Over There I was the best runner in my class."

Momik, who knew the record times of all Olympic runners and class champions by heart, said that to be on the team here you had to run sixty meters in 8.5, and Alex said maybe he wasn't in condition right now, but if he started working out he'd make the team for sure. He liked to talk big, and he never smiled at Momik, and he ate up square after square of the chocolate bar that would normally have lasted a month. "They called me an Ashkenazi Bech Bech," said Alex woodenly, "and that's why I'm gonna make the team." Momik said, "They're Ashkenazim too, you know, not all of them, but the ones who called you that." "Nobody calls Alex a Bech Bech."

Alex had so much confidence that Momik was sure he would win, but at the same time he felt kind of glum and he didn't know why. Alex hung around for a little while longer, shamelessly touching everything in sight. He twirled the sewing machine wheel roughly, asked questions guests aren't supposed to ask, and then he said he was sick of being in the house, so Momik jumped up and asked if maybe he wanted a nice cup of tea, because that's what you say when the guests (like Bella or Idka and Shimmik) say they'd better be going now, but Alex made a face and said, There's nothing to do around here, and Momik thought a minute and said maybe they could go hang out at Bella's café because she always had very interesting things to tell, and Alex made another face and asked Momik was he always like this, and Momik didn't understand and asked, Like what? and Alex asked, Aren't there any kids on this street? and Momik said, No, it's not a very big street. He was surprised because he'd thought that Alex, since he was a new immigrant, wouldn't want to play with the other children, that's why Momik hoped he and Alex could be buddies, because Momik is well behaved and nice and he doesn't make fun of people or cuss and things like that, but Momik thought, Well, Alex is still a new immigrant and he doesn't know what's what yet exactly, and it might take a little while for him to catch on that Momik has more in his little finger than all those hooligans and ruffians who laugh and run the sixty at 8.5. So anyway, they walked down the street together, and it was autumn, and the old pear tree in Bella's yard was full of half-rotten fruit, and Alex looked up and said, What?! You've gotta be crazy to let this go! and he sneaked into the yard and swiped a couple of pears and gave one to Momik, and Momik, whose heart was pounding, took a bite and chewed but didn't swallow, because that's stealing, and look who from, too. They walked in the direction of Mt. Herzl, and Alex again said that he was going to make the team, and suddenly Momik had a really brainy idea, and he told Alex that he would be his coach, and Alex said, "You?! You don't know noth—" but Momik quickly explained that he would be an excellent coach, that he'd read things about all the coaches in the world, that at home he had sports pictures and clippings from the newspapers ("And I mean newspapers from all over the world," he said, which wasn't exactly a lie because of *Pshegelond*), and that he could draw up an Olympic training schedule, and that his watch had a second hand, which is the main thing a running coach needs. Alex wanted to see the watch, and Momik showed it to him, and Alex said, Let's try it out, I'll run over to that pole and you time me, and Momik said, Ready Set Go, and Alex ran and Momik timed him and said 10.9, and maybe we shouldn't wave our hands around like that because it wastes energy, and Alex said maybe he wouldn't mind a little coaching, but he didn't feel like coming over to Momik's house anymore. That's how the great friendship began, but Momik doesn't like to think about it anymore.

And he has a pair of brothers too.

The older one's name is Bill. Every month the magazine with the latest adventure comes in at Lipschitz's in the shopping center. Momik stands in the corner and reads and Lipschitz doesn't say anything, because he and Mama come from the same shtetl. And the stories are suspenseful and educational too. His brother Bill is pretty tough. He's so tough he's not allowed to stick up for Momik if someone in Momik's class bothers him, because one blow from Bill and you're dead, and that's why Momik made Bill promise never ever to stick up for him, not even when that business with Laizer the Crook started, and at least twice a week Momik picks himself up off the schoolyard full of blood and dirt but smiling a mysterious smile, because he has mastered his impulses once again, as they say, and held Bill in check.

Bill calls him Johnny, and when they talk together they use short sentences with a lot of exclamation marks, like Punch him in the jaw, Bill!! Good work, Johnny!! etc. Bill has a silver star on his chest which means he's a sheriff. Momik doesn't have a star yet. Together they own a horse called Blacky. Blacky understands every word you say, and he loves to gallop wildly through the countryside, but in the end he always comes back and nuzzles Momik's chest with his head, and it's great, and just then Netta the teacher asks, Just what are we smiling about, Shlomo Neuman? and Momik hides Blacky away. He steals sugar from the kitchen and experiments with different ways of making sugar cubes which is what Blacky likes best, but so far no luck, and the *Hebrew Encyclopedia* isn't up to Sugar yet, and meanwhile he'll just have to find some way to feed this horse of his, won't he. At least three times a week they go galloping through the Ein Kerem Valley in search of missing children or children whose parents lost them, and they set Orde Wingate ambushes for train robbers. Sometimes as Momik lies on his stomach in ambush, he sees the tall smokestack of the new building they just finished over on Mt. Herzl, which they call Yad Vashem, a funny sort of name, and he pretends it's a ship sailing by, full of illegal immigrants from Over There that nobody wants to take in, like in the days of the British Mandate pshakrev, and he's going to have to rescue that ship somehow, with Blacky or Bill or with mindpower or with his animals or the atomic reactor or with Grandfather Anshel's story and the Children of the Heart, anything, and when he asked his old people what the smokestack is for, they looked at each other, and finally Munin told him that there's a museum there, and Aaron

Marcus, who hadn't been out of his house for a couple of years, asked, Is it an art museum? and Hannah Zeitrin smiled crookedly and said, Oh sure it is, a museum of human art, that's what kind of art.

And the whole time they're there in ambush Momik has to keep making sure Bill's star isn't flashing light, so that the criminals won't spot them, but anyway Bill gets killed at least twenty times a day by the bullets and knives of the villains, and in the end he always comes back to life, thanks to Momik who gets really scared when Bill dies, and maybe it's the fear, his very hopelessness, you might say, that brings Bill back to life, and he sits up and smiles and says, "Thanks, Johnny, you saved my life!!" And meanwhile Blacky gorges himself on sugar cubes stuck together with mud and spit, and sugar cubes made out of plastic glue, and sugar cubes Momik freezes between the ice blocks in Eizer the milkman's ice chest, and Bill died and came back to life and died and came back to life again and again, and that was the best part of the game, only it wasn't really a game at all, a game, ha! Momik didn't enjoy it one bit, but he could never dream of stopping it because he has to practice, because there are so many people waiting for him to become a leading world expert, just as everyone waited for Professor Jonas Salk to invent the polio vaccine, and Momik knows someone's got to be the first to volunteer to enter the frozen kingdom and fight the Beast and rescue all the people and take them away, and you just have to have a plan, that's all, something that hero Captain Meir Har-Zion would do if he were fighting it, a bold, daring stunt maybe only Giula Mandy the coach we brought here all the way from Hungary could devise to make his parents better both now and backward in time, only the Beast doesn't seem to want to take off its disguises yet, and there hasn't been that much progress with the animals lately either, and it made him feel bad to think maybe he was keeping all those poor animals in the dark for nothing, but then he would tell himself, In war there's suffering and sometimes the innocent suffer too (these are the words that came to him), like Laika the dog who sacri-

ficed herself on the scientific altar of Sputnik 2, so he was just
going to have to try harder and sleep less, never forgetting the
example of Grandfather Anshel, who tells his story in the hope
of someday beating Herrneigel once and for all, and sometimes
Momik has a feeling Grandfather is getting so mixed up in his
story that Herrneigel must be losing patience too.

And one time at lunch there was a terrible rumpus.
Grandfather started screaming at the top of his lungs, and then
he cupped his hand over his ear and listened, and his face turned
red and his lips were trembling, and Momik jumped up and
went over to the door because suddenly he understood all the
things he hadn't understood before, stupid him, that Herrneigel
himself was the Nazikaput, because *kaput* means finished, as
Momik knew from Hebrew, and a Nazi is a beast and now it
was clear to him that Herrneigel was angry with Grandfather
because of the story, because he didn't want to be kaput and so
he was trying to force Grandfather to change the story the way
he wanted it, but Grandfather is no weakling, that's for sure,
you touch his story and he turns into a different man! Yes,
Grandfather grabbed a drumstick and waved it wildly, hollering
in old-fashioned Hebrew that he would not let Herrneigel inter-
fere with his story because his story was his whole life, and
Momik, whose heart sank all the way down to his underpants,
saw by the look on Grandfather's face that Nazikaput was getting a little worried now and he must have decided to give in to
Grandfather because Grandfather was so convincingly in the
right, but suddenly Grandfather turned away from the wall and
stared blankly at Momik, and Momik knew that if Grandfather
wanted to, he could pull him right into his story just the way he
did Herrneigel, and Momik would have run away only he
couldn't move, and he tried to scream but no sound came out,
and then Grandfather motioned with his finger for Momik to
come closer, and it was like a magic spell, Momik moved
toward him thinking, This is it, he would get into Grandfather's
story now and nobody would ever find him, and he was just
lucky Grandfather didn't want to do that to him, he wouldn't

do a thing like that to Momik, Momik was such a good little boy; okay, maybe he tortures the animals in the cellar a little but that's because of the war, and then when he got up close to Grandfather, Grandfather said in a low, clear voice, like a completely normal person, Nu, did you see that goy? Oich mir a chucham, and Grandfather smiled a normal smile at Momik, like a smart and ancient man, and he put his hand on Momik's shoulder like a real grandfather and whispered in his ear that he was going to turn this goy around and send him back to Chelm, and Momik didn't want to miss his big chance to ask Grandfather what the story was about, and find out if he was right that the Children of the Heart were after Herrneigel, and by the way, what did they need that baby for (Momik does know something about suspense stories and when there's danger, babies are big trouble), but then the usual thing happened: Grandfather stepped back and stared at Momik as though he'd never seen him before in his life, and he started talking very fast, saying those things he always says in that tune, and Momik was all alone again.

Then as he slipped his untouched lunch into a brown paper bag for the animals, he started thinking that maybe it would be a good idea to consult this expert he read about in the newspaper, the expert who's in the same profession as Momik. Wiesenthal, they call him, and he lives in Vienna, which is where he sets off from to hunt them. Momik hoped that if he wrote him a letter, the hunter would give him some information about important matters, like where they hide and what their habits are in food and prey, and also if they run in herds, and how can it be that out of one single beast comes a whole army of people, and whether there's some magic word (Momik thinks there isn't) like "Chaimova" or "uranium" that if you say it to them makes them obey you and follow you everywhere, and maybe the hunter has a picture of them, alive or dead, so that Momik will be able to see what he's looking for. Momik was pretty busy for a few days planning what to write to him. He tried to imagine the hunter's house, with big rugs made from the fur of the Beast, and a special shelf for rifles and bows and pipes, and heads of Nazi Beasts hunted down in the jungles hanging from the wall, with glassy eyes, and Momik tried to write the letter, but it didn't come out right, he tried maybe twenty times but it still didn't come out right, and that week it said in Bella's newspaper that the hunter was setting off on another trip to South America, and they showed a picture, a man with nice, sad eyes, with a bald forehead, not at all as Momik imagined, so Momik was left alone again with no one to help him, and now he was getting a little nervous.

But he told himself that the hunter wouldn't be able to help him anyway, because the weird thing about this war against the Beast is that each person has to fight it alone, and even people who really need his help can't ask straight out, because of this secret oath it seems they've taken, and Momik keeps telling himself that he isn't trying hard enough and that he isn't concentrating hard enough, and it was also around this time that he had a couple of hunting accidents, starting when an abandoned jackal cub bit him under the knee and he had to have twelve agonizing rabies shots. And after that he accidentally fell on top of a little porcupine that was hiding under a bush in the valley, and his knee began to look like a sieve. Momik had always liked reading about animals, but it wasn't until he started fighting the Beast that he'd ever had to actually touch one, and the truth is, it kind of disgusted him, though in a way it didn't. He had a real instinct for animals, he guessed, and maybe when it was all over, he would get himself a pet dog. A regular dog. Not for the war, for fun. But meanwhile the injured pigeon he found in the backyard practically pecked his eye out, and another cat he tried to catch by the garbage cans as a replacement for his crazy cat scratched his arm all over. Momik was certainly being brave in this war. He never knew he could be so brave, but it was bravery out of fear, and he knew it. Because he was afraid. And what about the ravens, the parents of the raven that was his prisoner, who now knew for sure that Momik was the one who snatched their kid, and every time he went out of the house they swooped down on him like a pair of Egyptian MiGs, and the first time it happened, by the way, one of the ravens actually jabbed his neck and arm and he almost had a fit, as they say, and he ran all the way to the lottery booth and told Mama and Papa about the attack, but he didn't explain it too well, and also he didn't know the word for raven in Yiddish, and Mama didn't quite understand seeing the blood and the rip in his shirt, and she rushed him over to the health clinic and shrieked and fainted as she tried to explain to Dr. Erdreich that something terrible happened, an eagle tried to take my child away, and some people in Beit Mazmil remember Momik to this day as the child the eagle tried to snatch.

But it was no use. The cellar was turning blacker and more suffocating every day, and Momik didn't dare make a move. The animals grew wild and voracious, and flung themselves against the walls of their cages, and hurt themselves and howled and shrieked. The injured pigeon died, and it was too sickening to take the body out, and it started to stink and the ants came in, choleria. Momik always had this feeling that the cellar was full of big, sticky old cobwebs just waiting to grab him if he made a move. He'd never felt so dirty and smelly in his whole life. These little animals were a lot stronger than he was, he could see that now, because they hated him and they knew what it meant to be wild and to fling themselves and shriek in their cages, and he thought maybe that was a sign that the war had begun and the Beast wasn't kidding around anymore, that it was sneaking up on him now, paralyzing him with a polio Jonas Salk had never dreamed of, and this was serious, because Momik couldn't tell where the Beast was going to pounce from, he didn't know what to do if it decided to show itself, maybe it would pounce out of two animals at the same time, how would he be able to say something like "Chaimova" before it tore him to shreds?

He rubbed some kerosene from the heater all over his arms and legs so that maybe the smell would make it sick, and he also put a mothball in each pocket of his shirt and trousers, but that still didn't seem like enough, so then he decided to write a welcoming address. It took him at least a week to write it, and he knew that it would have to be the best speech in the whole world to have an effect on the Beast the split second before it attacked. First he wrote how you should always be good and think of the other person, and that you have to learn how to forgive like on Yom Kippur, but when he read it out loud, he knew the Beast would never believe this kind of thing. It had to be stronger. He tried to figure out how the Beast feels things, what affects it. He tried to draw a picture of it, but it came out looking like a lonely little polar bear, full of anger and hating the whole world, and he understood now that the speech was going to have to wipe out all the hatred and loneliness in one stroke, because there are things even a frozen polar bear longs for in its heart, so then Momik wrote a long speech about friendship between two friends who love each other, and about nice, simple conversations between a mother and father and a father and son. And he told the Beast about how sweet little brothers and sisters are, and how much fun it is to pick them up and put them in their strollers and show them off at the shopping center, and other silly things; he had a feeling this was the kind of thing that would really get the Beast, like a soccer tournament when you score and everyone cheers and no one calls you names, or like a Saturday morning walk with Mama and Papa when they both hold him by the hand and say, "Little bird, little bird, fly a-wayyy!" and toss him in the air, or like the school trip to Mt. Tabor, when the whole class goes hiking and they sing songs, and at night they whoop it up in the hostel, but when he saw it written down, he knew it was a stupid speech, a sickening speech, it was a crummy stinking speech, and he tore it to pieces and burned it in the kitchen sink, and decided to give up on the speech idea and just sit and wait and see what it would do when it turned up, and it was clear to Momik now that the Beast was only stalling like this to get him mad and bring him down even more, and he made up his mind to show the Beast it could never-ever-black-and-blue do that to him.

And for two weeks it did look as if there was going to be a chance for a surprise victory, because a third brother had now joined the other two: Motl Ben Paisee, the Chazzan. Momik would never forget those days. In school they read this story by Sholem Aleichem, and Momik had a strong feeling about it and decided to say something sort of casually after supper. Nu, Papa opened his mouth and started to talk! He talked in complete sentences, and Momik listened and almost cried for joy. Papa's eyes, which are blue with red rims, turned a little brighter, as if the Beast had left them for a second. Momik was as sly as a young fox! Like the fox in the story about the cheese and the raven! He told Papa (casually) about My Brother Elijah, and Manny the calf, and the river they poured barrels of kvass into, and with your own eyes you could see the Beast open its mouth a little, to let Papa tumble right out to Momik.

Little by little Papa told him all about his tiny village and the muddy lanes and the chestnut trees we don't have in this country, and the old fishmonger and the water drawer and the lilac blossoms, and the heavenly taste of bread Over There, and the cheder, which was the schoolroom, and the rebbe, who earned a little extra money mending broken pottery with the help of a wire he would wind around the pots, and how at the age of three he used to walk home from cheder all by himself on snowy nights, lighting his way with a special lamp made out of a radish with a candle stuck inside it, and then Mama said, There was a kind of bread there they don't have in this country, now when you mention it, yes I remember: we used to bake it at home, where else, and it lasted the week, if I could taste that taste once more in my life, and Papa said, Where we used to live, between our village and Chodorov, there was a big forest. A real forest, not like these toothless combs the National Smashional Fund plants around here, in that forest we had big pojomkes[13] they don't have in this country, like great big cherries, and Momik was amazed to hear that there was a village called Chodorov

---

13. A raspberry-like fruit.

just like the name of the goalkeeper on the Tel Aviv Ha Poel team, but he didn't want to interrupt so he kept quiet, and Mama gave a little krechtz full of memories and said, Yes, but where I come from we called them yagedes,[14] and Papa said, No, yagedes is something else, yagedes is smaller. Ach, the fruit there, a mechayeh,[15] and the grass, you remember the grass? And Mama said, Remember, what do you mean remember, oy, how can I forget, zal ich azoy haben koach tzu leben, may I have the strength to live, how I remember all those things, such green you never saw, and strong, not like the grass in this country that looks half dead, you call that grass, it's a leprosy of the earth, and Over There when they mowed the wheat and stacked it in the fields, remember, Tuvia? Ach! says Papa inhaling, and the way it smelled! Where we lived people used to be afraid to fall asleep on a fresh bale, God forbid they shouldn't be able to wake up again . . .

They talked like this to each other and they both talked to Momik. This was why Momik read some other stories by Sholem Aleichem (what a funny name for a writer!), which they didn't even tell you to read in school. He borrowed the stories about Menachem Mendel and Tevye the Dairyman from the school library, and read them chapter by chapter, quickly and thoroughly the way he does. The village was becoming very familiar to him. In the first place, he realized that there were a lot of things he knew about already from his friends on the bench, and whatever he didn't understand Papa was glad to explain, words like *gabai, galach, melamed dardakai,* and things like that. And each time Papa would start explaining, he thought of something else and would tell a little more, and Momik remembered everything, and afterward he would run to his room and write it down in his geography notebook (he was up to notebook 3 by now!), and on the last pages of the notebook he made a little dictionary with the translation of the

---

14. Blackberries.

15. Something tangible or intangible that refreshes or revives.

words in the language of Over There into our language Hebrew, and so far he had eighty-five words. In geography class at school, with the atlas open on his desk, Momik carried out experiments, substituting Boibrik for Tel Aviv, and Haifa for Katrielibka with Mt. Carmel for the Hill of the Jews, the hill where miracles happen, and Jerusalem is Yahoupitz, and Momik made little pencil marks like an army commander makes on a battle map: Menachem Mendel goes from here to there, from Odessa to Yahoupitz and Zamrinka, and the Menashe Forest is where Tevye rides his old horse, and the Jordan is the San River which demanded a fresh victim every year, they believed, till one day the rabbi's son drowned and the rabbi cursed the river and it shrank to the size of a little creek, and on Mt. Tabor Momik writes *Goldeneh Bergel,* and pencils in the little barrels of gold that the King of Sweden left there when he was running away from the Russians, and on Mt. Arbel he draws a small cave, like the one Dobush the terrible robber dug in the mountain near Mama's town, Bolichov, to hide in and plot his crimes. Momik has no end of ideas.

And down in Ein Kerem, three brothers galloped their horse Blacky, wildly and fiercely, holding each other by the waist. Bill the strong one sat in front, Momik the responsible one sat in the middle, and Motl sat in the rear, his payes[16] curled behind his ears, his eyes gleaming, and his muscles getting stronger by the day, and soon they would be able to take him out on a real mission.

Okay, so there were a lot of things you had to explain to him that he never knew before like what the sound barrier is, which is broken by the jets given to us by our Eternal Allies the French, and who Nathaniel Balsberg the religious runner on the Elizur track team is, who beat the five-kilometer record, with-the-help-of-God, and what the Suleiman Fire Gang is, and what exactly they use the swimming pool at the new atomic reactor in Nahal Soreq for, and how you should always have a piece of cardboard

---

16. The earlocks of religious Jews.

folded in your shirt pocket wherever you go, to stop bullets aimed at your heart, and what a reprisal is, one fist three fingers, and Motl nearly botched things up because he just didn't know how to sit still in an ambush and wait quietly, or what an Uzi is, and a Super Mystère and an EMX, because in his shtetl they probably had different names for guns and airplanes.

One time Momik dawdled in the school library waiting for it to get dark outside, and Mrs. Govrin told him to go home, so he hung around a little while longer in the playground, and when the coast was clear, he took the big surprise out of his schoolbag, the radish he had cut in two and scooped out with his jackknife, and he stuck a candle into the radish and lit it, and walked all the way home like this in a very gentle rain that didn't blow the candle out, through the snowdrifts of the chestnut forest and the lilac groves and the big pojomkes which might in fact be yagedes, but who cares, and the good smell of the bread they baked at home, and the big river with the tadpoles and the tiny leeches, and the animal fair where they sold the good horse they loved dearly because they didn't have enough money for food, and so the three-year-old child made his way home from Rabbi Itzla's cheder to a house full of boys and girls, brothers and sisters, where he would sit and eat under the table like the gentry, and Mama and Papa came out to meet him because they were worried sick and they saw him walking through the streets of Borochov, slowly and carefully, shielding the candle with his hand to make sure it wouldn't blow out, striding responsibly with the emotion of the torch runner at the Maccabean Games, all the way here from a foreign land, and Mama and Papa huddled together not knowing what to do, and he looked up at them and wanted to say something beautiful, but all of a sudden Papa's face changed and shrank as if he were disgusted or something, and he raised his enormous hand and smacked the candle with all his might (his fingers didn't touch Momik), and the candle fell into a little puddle and was extinguished, and Papa said in a choked voice, Enough of this nonsense. You pull yourself together now, and be normal, and never again did he tell Momik about his village and how he was a boy there, and Motl never returned again either, maybe he didn't want to, or maybe Momik felt funny because of what had happened, and so, Momik was left alone once more to face the Beast, but the Beast wasn't ready to appear yet.

At night Mama leans over his bed and sniffs his feet which smell of kerosene and then suddenly she says something really hilarious in Yiddish, she says, God, maybe you could play with some other family?

And don't forget there were other things besides the search and the hunter and the sweat to think about, there were regular things too, and no one was allowed to suspect anything was wrong so they wouldn't start asking questions and butting in, and he had tests to study for and there was school every day from eight to one, which is pretty unbearable unless you keep telling yourself that all the kids around you go to a secret school we established in the underground, and whenever you hear footsteps outside you have to get your guns and prepare to die, and there was Grandfather who was becoming grouchier and jumpier than ever to look after, his Nazi must have really been upsetting him, and Momik had strategies and special oaths to think about every time Nasser pshakrev says he's going to stop one of our ships in the Suez Canal, and what about those stupid postcards somebody stuck Momik's name on, and he had to send off more and more postcards with names of people he didn't even know, you erase the top name on the list and add the name of another boy at the bottom, or God forbid something terrible will happen to him, like the banker from Venezuela who didn't take it seriously and lost all his money and his wife died, poor man, and don't even ask how much those postcards cost him, though luckily Mama didn't skimp on this and gave him whatever he needed to mail them all, so anyway besides all the regular things there was that kid Laizer from seventh grade, who'd been snatching Momik's sandwich every day now for three months. At first it really scared him, because how could a boy only three years older than him be such a crook and a shvartzer and desperate enough maybe to commit a terrible crime like extortion which you can go to jail for. But Momik realized that since this was how things stood, he'd better not think about it too much because he had to save his energy for more important things, and since Laizer was stronger than him anyhow, what good would it do to think about it all the time and feel insulted and want to die and start crying, right? And since Momik is a scientific boy who is very good at making decisions, he walked right up to Laizer and explained to him in a logical way that if the other children saw him give his sandwich away, they'd tell the teacher on him, and therefore he had a more spylike method to propose. The extortionist criminal who lived in a hut and had a big scar on his forehead was about to get angry and say something, but then he thought over what Momik told him and just kept quiet. Momik took a piece of paper from his right pocket with a list of the six safest places in school where you could hide a sandwich which someone else could pick up later without getting into trouble. Momik detected as he read the list out that Laizer was beginning to regret the whole thing, but he was just beginning to develop a little confidence now. From his left pocket he took out a second list he'd made for Laizer. This was a list of all the days of our first trial month (he told Laizer), noting where the sandwich would be on each particular day. Laizer was clearly sorry about the whole thing now. He started to say, Cut the crap, Helen Keller, I was only fooling, who needs your stinkin' sandwich anyway, but Momik wouldn't hear of it, he felt stronger than the criminal now, and though he could have just said okay then, no more extortion, he didn't want to stop, and he practically shoved the papers at Laizer, telling him, We start tomorrow, and the next day he put the sandwich in the appointed place and sat waiting in ambush according to plan, and watched as Laizer walked up, glanced at the paper, looked both ways, and picked up the goods, though he didn't look very happy about it to Momik; in fact, when he peered into the little bag Momik had packed so nicely, he looked thoroughly revolted but there was no choice, like it or lump it, he had to do what Momik said so as not to spoil this devious plan which was more than he and maybe Momik too could handle. And to top it off, Momik had the Beast to fight in various ways he thought up from day to day, because it was clearer than ever now that he must not fail, this was really serious, too many people and things were involved and everything depended on him, and if the Beast wouldn't take off its disguise, it was just being trickier than him, that's all, it had more combat experience than he had, but if it ever did decide to show itself, it would show itself to Momik and no one else, because who else but Momik would challenge it like this, with so much daring, chutzpah, and the devotion of soldiers who charge ahead and fling themselves on the barbed-wire fence so the others can climb over them. And by the end of winter, when the wind was having one last fling at wrecking Beit Mazmil, Momik reversed his tactics, figuring that what he needed in order to fight the Beast was the very thing that most scared it, the thing he'd been avoiding all along, which was to get to know more about the Beast and its crimes, because otherwise he'd just be wasting energy no matter what he did, because the fact of the matter is, he didn't have a clue about how to fight it. And that's the truth. Which is how he got involved with the Holocaust and all that. In total secrecy, Momik joined the public library (his parents wouldn't allow him to be a member of two libraries) and he would take the Number 18 bus to town some afternoons and read everything the library had on it. The library had a big shelf with a sign saying LIBRARY OF THE HOLOCAUST AND VALOR, and Momik started going through it book by book. He read incredibly fast because he was afraid that time was running out, and though he didn't understand most of it, he knew that someday he would. He read *Mysteries of Fate* and *The Diary of Anne Frank; Let Me Stay the Night, Feifel; The Doll House; The Cigarette Vendors of Three-Cross Square;* and many other books. The children he met in the library were kind of like him, like he'd always felt deep inside all these years. They spoke Yiddish at home with

their parents and didn't have to hide it, and they were also fighting the Beast, which is the main thing.

On the days Momik didn't go to the library, he would spend
hours in the gloomy cellar. From a quarter to two in the afternoon till it got dark, and even a few minutes after sometimes, he
would sit on the cold floor in front of the animals with their
shiny eyes and nasty noises, and the way they tried to act as if
they didn't care when he was around, but he knew it could happen any minute, because obviously even the Beast would crack
up if you made it nervous enough by studying its crimes in a scientific way, and by sitting and staring at it so maddeningly day
after day, and it took all Momik's effort to sit there one minute
more, two minutes more, with his feet firmly planted to keep
him from beating it out of there, and he started making weird
noises like wheezing or like a kitten squealing, he was beginning
to remind himself of Grandfather with all these noises, but he
stayed put even after the light coming through the tiny slit in the
window faded and it was pitch-dark, and he was doing this
because of what seemed to be a very important clue which he
found tucked slyly away in *Mysteries of Fate* where it said distinctly, "From utter 'darkness' sprang the Nazi beast."

Day after day. In the adult reading room at the public library
Momik sat on a high-backed chair, with his feet dangling down.
He told Hillel the librarian that he was working on a special
report for school about the Holocaust, and no one asked any
questions. He read history books with tiny print about what the
Nazis did, and stumbled over a lot of words and expressions
that weren't used anymore. He puzzled over some peculiar photographs, he couldn't figure out what was going on and what
went where, but deep down inside he began to sense that these
photographs might reveal the first part of the secret everyone
had tried to keep from him. There were pictures of a mother
and father forced to choose between two children, to choose
which one would stay with them and which one would go away
forever, and he tried to figure out how they would choose,
according to what, and he saw a picture of a soldier forcing an

old man to ride another old man like a horse, and he saw pictures of executions in ways he never knew existed, and he saw pictures of graves where a lot of dead people lay in the strangest positions, on top of each other, with somebody's foot stuck in somebody else's face, and somebody's head on so crooked Momik couldn't twist his head around like that, and so little by little Momik started to understand new things, like how weak the human body is, for instance, and how it can break in so many shapes and directions if you want to break it, and how weak a thing a family is if you want to break it, just like that it happens and it's all over. At six in the evening Momik would leave the library, tired and quiet. On the bus home, he didn't see or hear anything.

Almost every day at recess he would sneak out of school and detour around the street where the lottery booth is to Bella's grocery store. He would get there all out of breath, pull her by the hand to the corner (if there happened to be a customer in the store just then), and start firing questions at her in a whisper that was more like a roar: What was the death train, Bella? Why did they kill little children? What do people feel when they have to dig their own graves? Did Hitler have a mother? Did they really use the soap they made out of human beings? Where do they kill people nowadays? What's a Jude? What are experiments with human beings? What and how and why and why and how and what? Bella, who could see for herself by now how important and serious it was, answered his every question and didn't cover anything up, only her face looked miserable and grim. Momik was also a little worried. Not nervous, just very worried. It was getting harder all the time, the Beast was winning, that much was certain, and though he knew everything about it now and wasn't a little nine-and-a-quarter-year-old ninny anymore who believed the Beast would come out of a hedgehog or some poor cat or even a raven, he was still in one terrible mess; he'd found out where the Beast actually was, though he couldn't tell how it happened, or how it could appear from just thinking and imagining it, but this much was clear, the

Beast did exist, he could feel it in his bones the way Bella could tell when it was going to rain, and it was also clear that Momik had been the one who stupidly woke it out of its long sleep, the one who challenged it to come out, the way Judah Ken-Dor challenged the Egyptians at the Mitla Pass to shoot at him, so they'd give themselves away; only Judah Ken-Dor had his buddies covering him from behind, while Momik was all alone, and now he had to fight to the finish, though nobody cared whether he wanted to or not, and he knew only too well that if he ever tried to run away, the Beast would chase him to the ends of the earth (it has spies and supporters everywhere), and little by little, it would do to him what it did to all the others, only this time in an even slyer, more diabolical way, and who could say how many years it would torture him like that and what would happen in the end.

But then single-handedly Momik discovered how to bring the Beast out of the animals in the cellar, and it was so simple really, it was amazing he hadn't thought of it sooner, since even the sleepy turtle knows it's a turtle when it catches a whiff of cucumber peels, and the raven ruffles its feathers when Momik comes with the drumstick, so quite simply, all Momik had to do now was show the Beast the food it liked best—a Jew.

So then he started to put a plan together, cleverly and very carefully. First he copied out pictures from the library books into his notebook, and made notes to remind him what a Jew looks like, how a Jew looks at a soldier, how a Jew looks when he's frightened, how he looks in a convoy, and how he digs a grave. He also made notes from his own store of experience with Jews, like how a Jew krechtzes, how he screams out in his sleep, and how he chews on a drumstick, etc. Momik worked like a combination scientist and detective. Take the boy in this picture, for instance, the one with the visor cap and his hands up. Momik tried to figure things from the boy's eyes, like what the beast in front of him looked like just then, and whether he knew how to whistle with two fingers, and whether he'd ever heard that Chodorov isn't just the name of a town but the name of a great goalie, and what his parents had done to make him have to stick his hands up like that, and where they were when they ought to have been taking care of him, and whether he was religious or not and had a collection of real stamps from Over There, and whether he'd ever imagined that someday in the State of Israel, in Beit Mazmil in Jerusalem, there would be a boy called Momik Neuman. There were so many things to find out about how to be a real Jew, about how to have the kind of expression a Jew has, and to give off the exact same smell, like Grandfather, for instance, and Munin, and Max and Moritz, a smell that's known to drive the Beast insane, so that day after day as Momik sits in the dark cellar facing the cages not doing anything much, just staring blindly ahead, trying not to fall asleep, because lately, he doesn't know why, he's sort of exhausted all the time, he can hardly move or concentrate, and sometimes he has these not very nice thoughts, like what does he need this for, and why does he have to do all the fighting himself, and why does no one step in to help him or take notice of what's going on around here, not Mama or Papa, not Bella or the children in his class or his teacher Netta who only screams at him that his grades are going down down down, and not Dag Hammarskjöld from the United Nations who today arrived in Israel and went all the way to Sedeh Boker just to eat supper with Ben-Gurion, this Dag Hammarskjöld who founded UNICEF for the children of the world and worries about saving the children of Africa and India from malaria and other cholerias, the only thing he doesn't have time for is the war on the Beast. And to tell the truth, there are days when Momik sits in the cellar half awake and half asleep and he envies the Beast. Yes, he envies it for being so strong that it never suffers from pity, and that it can sleep soundly at night even after all those things it did, and that it even seems to enjoy being cruel, the way Uncle Shimmik enjoys it when you scratch his back, and maybe the Beast is right and it isn't so terrible to be cruel, but really cruel, and to tell the truth, Momik has also been kind of enjoying it lately when he does something really bad, it happens

mostly after dark, when he starts being more afraid and hating
the Beast more than ever and hating the whole world, it suddenly happens, he gets this feeling as if he has fever all over but
especially in his head and his heart, and he almost explodes with
power and cruelty, and that's when he could almost fling himself against the cages and shatter them and smash every head on
the Beast without mercy, and could even let it wound him with
its claws and teeth and all its beaks, before jamming into it as
hard as he can so the Beast will know once and for all what
Momik feels, or maybe not, maybe it would be better to kill it
without jamming into it, just to smash it and bash it and kick it
and stomp on it and torture it and blow it to bits, and you could
even throw an atom bomb in its face now because that article
finally came out about our atomic reactor which is huge and
awesome rising out of the golden sand dunes of Nahal Rubin
near Rishon Le-Zion, towering proudly over the shore and the
roaring blue waves, the builders' hammers gaily tapping its
splendid dome, that's what it said in the newspaper, and even
though the newspaper says "for peaceful purposes," Momik
can read between the lines, as they say, and he catches the meaning behind those smiles of Bella's, whose son is a very high
ranking major in the army, peaceful purposes, yeah sure, sure,
let them blast the Arabs away pshakrev, but he had to admit the
Beast didn't seem too worried by his threats, and sometimes
Momik even suspected that whenever he started feeling this
way, wild and hateful that is, the Beast was smiling slyly to itself
in the dark, and then he would get even more frightened and not
know what to do and tell himself, Calm down, but how much
longer would he have the strength to calm down all by himself,
and he would get frightened like this and wake up from his
dream and look around and smell the stench of the animals
which clings to him so strongly he sometimes feels as if it's coming out of his mouth, and he doesn't get up even though it's
pitch-dark now and his parents are probably worried to death
about where he is, and please don't let them think of coming
down here to look for him, no they wouldn't come down here,

they better not, and he sits a while longer, dozing on the cold stone floor, wrapped in Papa's big old overcoat to which Momik had pinned a lot of yellow cardboard stars, and sometimes when he wakes up and remembers, he reaches out to show the animals what he's glued on his arms with plastic glue, numbers cut out of old lottery tickets he collected by the lottery booth, and if that wasn't enough, he would sit up and pause for a refreshing cough or krechtz, and before he stood to leave, he would challenge the Beast one last time in a really disgusting way, by turning his back on it in the pitch-dark and copying a few passages from the diary of Anne Frank, who also hid from it, into his Geography Notebook #4, and whenever he finished copying out a really sad line from the book (which he stole from the public library), his pen would tremble a little, and then he would have to add a few words of his own about a boy called Momik Neuman who's also hiding like that and fighting and afraid, and the amazing thing is that what he wrote came out sounding just like her, like Anne that is.

And sometimes after lunch, when Momik wants to get Grandfather out of the way and put him to sleep so he can go down to the cellar right away, Grandfather stares at him strangely and begs with his eyes to let him go out for a while, and even though sometimes it's raining and cold outside, Momik can feel how much Grandfather is suffering in the house, and he takes him along, they put their coats on and go out, and lock the bottom lock too, and Momik holds Grandfather's hand and feels the warm currents of Grandfather's story flow into his own hand and up to his head, and he draws strength from Grandfather, unbeknownst to him, and squeezes and squeezes the strength out for himself till finally Grandfather lets out a kind of howl and pulls his hand away and looks at Momik as if he understands something.

They sit down on the wet green bench and watch the gray street that seems slanted on account of the rain, and the fog changes the shapes of things, and everything looks so different, everything is so sad, and out of the wind and the whirling leaves comes a black coat with two tails, or a blond wig, or the two dodos hand in hand, scrounging through the garbage pails, and so Grandfather's friends gather at the bench, though no one told them he was there, and then the door at Bella's opens and cute little Aaron Marcus steps out even though Bella begs him not to, and when she sees that Momik is there too, boy does she ever open her mouth and tell him to take Grandfather home this minute, but Momik just stares at her and doesn't answer, and in the end she slams the door.

Mr. Aaron Marcus walked over and sat down with a krechtz, and they all made room for him and gave a krechtz, and Momik gave one too and it felt good. Momik wasn't afraid anymore of Marcus's twitches which made his face look a hundred years old, may-he-live-to-be-a-hundred-and-twenty. Once he asked Bella whether Marcus made faces on account of some disease, God forbid, or something like that, and Bella said, The father of my Hezkel, may-he-rest-in-peace, deserves more than the inquisitiveness of rude little children who must know everything and what will there be left to learn when they're ten years old, but of course Momik didn't give up—we know Momik and the type of person he is—he went off to think it over, and returned to Bella a little while later and told her he knew the answer. That was funny because meanwhile Bella had forgotten the question, but Momik reminded her and said probably Mr. Marcus makes those faces because he escaped from a certain place (Momik did not want to spell out that it was Over There) and he wants to keep people from recognizing his real face and capturing him, and Bella pursed her lips as if she was getting angry, but you could see that she was holding back a smile, and she said, Maybe it's the other way around, smarty, maybe Mr. Marcus is trying to keep alive the faces of all the people who were with him in a certain place, and it isn't at all that he wants to run away from them, he wants to stay with them, nu, what do you say to that, Einstein? And this answer knocked Momik for a loop, as they say, and he looked at Mr. Marcus in a completely different way after that, in fact he discovered the faces of a lot of people he never met before in Mr. Marcus's face, old people, men, women, and children and even babies, not to mention the fact that everyone around here made faces all the time, which was a sure sign that Marcus like the others was fighting a secret war.

The rain fell and the old people talked. You could never tell exactly when the noises and the krechtzes turned into real talking all of a sudden. They told their usual stories which Momik knew by heart already but loved to hear over and over. Red Sonya and Black Sonya, and Chaim Eche the cripple who played "Sheraleh" at weddings, and that meshuggeneh they called Job who sucked lavender candy and the children dragged him around everywhere like a dog and made him do whatever they wanted by promising him candy, and the big, beautiful mikva[17] they built, and how everyone put the cholent[18] in the bakery on Thursday to cook overnight, and the whole shtetl smelled of it, and this way you could rest from the war and the Beast and the stink in the cellar, you could forget everything and sort of not exist, and just then, for some reason, oftzeluchus[19] as they said around here, he thinks of something annoying and troubling, the memory of a big fat palm slapping the candle, and the candle fell and the flame went *tsss* in the puddle, and Papa's face, and the word he said, and suddenly Momik sits up and moves his head away from Hannah Zeitrin's shoulder where he was leaning a little without noticing, and he said in a hard, loud voice that in the big game coming up in Yaroslav we're going to beat those Poles 10 to 0, Stelmach alone will score five, and at once the old ones grew quiet and looked at him blankly, and Hannah Zeitrin said sadly and clearly, Alter kopf, and Yedidya Munin on his other side reached his skinny hand with the black hairs out to him, and for once he wasn't going to pinch his

---

17. A ritual bath.

18. Meat stew with potatoes, beans, and eggs.

19. Out of sheer spite.

cheek but gently cup his chin and draw it closer very slowly, who would have believed Momik would let Munin do such a thing to him, and in public too, but now Momik is a little tired and he doesn't mind feeling his face against the black coat with the strange smell, and he thinks it's a good thing he isn't alone and that he has these secret warriors with him here, they're like a band of partisans who fought together for a long long time, and the big battle is about to begin and they've sat down to rest a while in the forest, and though to look at them you'd think they were just a bunch of meshuggeners, who cares, it's so nice to lie here on Munin's coat beside his friends and hear the wool rustling and the quiet ticking of the pocket watch and the heart-beats that seem to come from far away, it's nice like this.

That night something terrible happened, which started like this: they heard terrible screams coming from the street, and it was fourteen minutes past eleven o'clock at night by Momik's watch, and the shutters rolled open and the lights went on, and in his heart Momik felt uh-oh now the Beast is coming out of the cellar, and he hid under the covers, but it was a woman screaming, not a Beast, so he jumped out of bed, ran to the window, and raised the shutters, and Mama and Papa called from the other room to close the shutters, but he'd stopped listening to them a long time ago, and he looked out the window and saw a real live naked woman running up and down the street screaming terrible screams, and you couldn't understand her, and even though the moon was almost full, it took Momik a couple of minutes to see that it was Hannah Zeitrin, because her pretty blond wig had fallen, and her hair was bald underneath and she had great big breasts that were flopping all over, and it was a good thing she had on a kind of small, triangle thing, like black fur down below, and Hannah Zeitrin who only this after-noon had been sitting on the bench next to him like a good friend raised her arms and screamed in Yiddish: God, God, how long must I wait for you, God, and people started screaming, Quiet, go home and sleep, you're crazy, it's the middle of the night, and somebody on the second floor where the uppity

young couple live threw a whole bucketful of cold water down
and drenched her, but she didn't stop running and tearing out
her hair, and when she ran under the streetlamp, you could see
the makeup she always smears on her face dripping, and suddenly the lights went on at Bella's and wouldn't you know it,
Bella ran down the stairs and hugged Hannah with a big blan-
ket, and Hannah stood still at first, trembling a little from the
cold with her head drooping and Bella led her very slowly, but
suddenly she stopped and shrieked, "Brutes!" and when she
passed the house of the uppity couple she shrieked, "You're
worse than they are! God will pay you double for this!" and
then she and Hannah disappeared between the black cypress
trees next to Hannah's house, and one by one the lights went
out in all the houses, and Momik rolled down the shutters
and went back to bed. But he had seen something no one
else noticed, that while Hannah was running naked, Mr.
Munin came out of the synagogue next door to Momik's and
stood there in the shadows but also a little in the moonlight. He
wasn't wearing his glasses and his whole body jerked back and
forth, and his eyes looked at Hannah and shone, and his hands
were down in the darkness, and Momik saw his shoulders shake
and his lips move, but he couldn't tell what he was saying
though he had the feeling it was probably something very
important, that Munin may have been revealing a great secret
about the Beast and how to fight it, and Momik wanted to
scream out the window, I can't hear you, but Munin's eyes suddenly popped open, and his mouth opened together with his
eyes, and his body fell forward and backward as if somebody
were shaking him with all his might, and then he raised his arms
like a big black bird and started jumping and screaming, but
without a voice, as if somebody above were pulling him up by
a string, and suddenly the string broke and Munin fell down in
a heap and lay there for a long time, and Momik could still hear
him krechtzing quietly to himself like the crazy cat for a long
time after it was over, and in the morning Munin wasn't lying
there anymore.

But the Beast knew it was a trick and it wouldn't come out.
None of Momik's tricks was any use. The Beast could probably
tell the difference between a real Jew and Momik suddenly trying to act like a Jew, and if Momik could tell the difference he'd
do the right thing, but he doesn't. He's become like his own
shadow lately, dragging his feet when he walks, and he has this
new chendeleh, as Bella called it, krechtzing like an old person,
even at school, and everybody made fun of him—and the only
good thing that happened around that time is that he came in
fifth in his class in the sixty-meter dash, which never happened
before, why now all of a sudden when he didn't have the
strength to do anything, and everyone said he ran like Zatopek
the Czech Locomotive, and they only laughed because he ran
the whole race with his eyes shut tight and made faces as if a
monster were after him, but at least now they saw he could do
it if he really wanted to, and even Alex Tochner who was a
friend of his once for two weeks and Momik coached him every
day in the Ein Kerem Valley till Alex broke the class record and
made the team like nothing, even Alex came up to him and said,
Nice going, Helen Keller, but even these words of praise made
no difference to Momik.

Bill and Motl had disappeared long ago, and he couldn't
bring them back. It was as if the Beast had frozen his brains, and
everyone noticed now. Bella wouldn't answer his questions anymore, and when he pleaded with her she told him she could eat
herself for the harm she'd done by telling him what she'd told
him already, and that she'd had it up to here with his investigations, that he should go play with children his own age please,
and she didn't say it in an angry way but pityingly, which is
worse. His parents had also been giving him funny looks lately,
and you could see that they were just waiting for a chance to
explode because of him. They'd started acting really strange:
first they cleaned the house like crazy, washing and scrubbing
everything each day (including windows and panels), and there
wasn't a speck of dust anywhere, but they just kept cleaning and
cleaning, and one night when Momik got up to pee he saw that

all the lights in the house were on and Mama and Papa were down on their knees scraping the cracks between the tiles with kitchen knives, and when they saw him they smiled like children caught red-handed, and Momik didn't say anything, and in the morning he pretended he'd forgotten. A few days later, on Saturday, Bella said something to Mama, and Mama turned white as this wall, and early Sunday morning Mama took Momik to the health clinic to see Dr. Erdreich who examined him thoroughly from head to toe and told Mama no no it wasn't the Disease, that's how they talk about polio, which in our country is contracted by several children each year even after vaccinations and shots, and the doctor prescribed vitamins and cod-liver oil twice a day, but nothing helped, how could it, and though Mama and Papa started eating bigger suppers than ever and forced Momik to swallow more and more food, they knew the child was breaking down before their very eyes, and that there was nothing they could do about it, they tried everything, you have to admit, they brought over a little bearded rabbi from Mea Shearim who rolled a hard-boiled egg all over Momik and whispered, and they even went to see Madame Miranda Bardugo who was practically the queen of Beit Mazmil, and she used leeches on people and cured everything, but she refused to come on account of what happened to her leeches the time she used them on Papa's hands, and Mama and Bella sat in the kitchen together drinking tea, and Bella said crying tears of pity for the boy, Something must be done, look at him, there's nothing left but his eyes, and as usual Mama started to cry with her saying, If only we knew what to do, if you tell me the name of a doctor we'll take him to that doctor, but I don't need a doctor to see what this is, Bella, I should be a doctor, a doctor of tsuris, and what Shlomo has, no doctor can help, I tell you, we brought it with us from Over There, and it sits on us here and here and here, and only God can help, and Bella gave a krechtz and blew her nose and said, Oy, God help us till God helps us.

These were very bad days. Everyone around Momik was scared and didn't know what to do. They were waiting for him to get better, and meanwhile they wouldn't move or breathe. It all depended on him. When he moved they moved, and when he screamed they screamed. And it felt like the street was different too, as if you were hearing the voices of people who were already dead and stories that only people around here remembered and names and words that only people around here understood and hungered for, and Hannah Zeitrin came out naked almost every night now and shouted at God, and people just waited patiently for Bella to come and take her away, and sometimes when you looked up you could see, between the tree-tops and the clouds, a fast-moving shadow, something that resembled black coattails flying, and the glint of glasses, and a minute later Munin landed next to Momik who couldn't drag himself any farther, and glanced cautiously around (because he isn't allowed to come close to children for some reason) and put his hand on Momik's shoulder and walked that strange walk of his (because of the hernia) and whispered things in his ear about the stars and God and thrust and where the happy life awaits us, not here not here, and the burned-out cigarette danced from his upper lip, while he muttered words from the Bible and synagogue prayers, and he laughed and laughed the weird laughter of someone who's about to hoodwink the world, and Momik didn't have the patience for him anymore.

All day long Momik's head burned, but the thermometer showed nothing. He felt as if his mind were doing an oftzeluchus on him and making him think thoughts that weren't good. Momik had been starting with the nightmares himself lately and crying out in his sleep at night, and Mama and Papa would come running, and beg him with their eyes to stop this please, to go back to being what he was before only a few short months ago, but enough, he hasn't got the strength to pretend to be happy in his sleep for them anymore, aililuliii, what's happening to him, what's happening, everything is breaking down, the Beast is beating him, beating him before ever coming out of its disguise, and he punched his pillow which was wet all over and saw that his fingers were cramped and crooked with fear or whatever, and again and again he punched his pillow and screamed at his parents who huddled together and cried, and then he fell asleep but he woke up right away with a new nightmare: Motl was walking down the street of a city Momik didn't know, Motl was small and scrawny and he walked funny, and Momik was glad to see him and screamed, Motl! But Motl didn't hear him or pretended not to, and Momik saw a booth on the corner like the lottery booth, and in it sat Mama and Papa crowded together and sad, right in the corner where the Golden Ray of Fortune is painted on the lottery sign, and then he saw that it wasn't a street at all, it was a river, maybe the San, and maybe not, and the lottery booth was floating in it like a little boat, and Motl was walking toward this boat, he was walking in the water but he wasn't getting wet and he never reached the boat, because the closer he came, the farther away it moved, and suddenly a couple of boys were there, and a grown-up man was walking with them, and they were walking in circles around Motl, and suddenly for no reason at all one of them boxed him in the face, and they all jumped on him and started kicking him and punching him and yelling at each other, Bash him in the teeth, Emil, Punch him in the belly, Gustav, and Momik almost fainted when he realized it was Emil and the detectives, grown up now in Germany, and the man watching them and laughing to himself must have been Yashkeh the policeman who sometimes went to Emil's mother's house for a cup of tea, and Motl lay there bloody and half dead, and Momik looked up and saw Mama and Papa in the booth rowing their boat away, and Mama looked at Momik and said, God will help him, there's nothing I can do to help him now, and Bella suddenly slipped out of her window (how did she get there anyway?) and screamed at his parents, Brutes, at least someone should stay home with him in the afternoon, if you knew the company he keeps, and Mama shrugged her shoulders and said, We don't have the strength anymore, Mrs. Bella, we ran out a long time ago, that's life, and everyone is alone in the end, and on they rowed till finally they were gone, and when Momik looked at Motl again, he saw that the river wasn't really a river but a crowd of people streaming in from the side streets, and when he looked again he saw some people and children he recognized, from the famous Fives and secret Sixes, and Captain Nemo's children, and Sherlock Holmes was there with Watson, and they were all yelling and laughing and rolling these strange little bundles, and when they came close to him he saw that all the bundles were his good friends, Yotam the Sorcerer, and My Brother Elijah, and Anne Frank, and the Children of the Heart from Grandfather's story, and even baby Kazik was there, and Momik started to scream and he woke up, and this kept happening all night long, and next morning as Momik lay more dead than alive in his bed which stank of sweat, he realized he'd been making a huge mistake, that he'd been wasting his efforts, because obviously the Beast knew he wasn't Jewish enough, so all he had to do now was to get hold of a real Jew, someone who actually came from Over There who'd be able to taunt the Beast till it showed itself, and then we'll see, and Momik knew of just the person.

Grandfather Anshel wasn't at all surprised when Momik shared his secret and asked him to help. Momik of course knew Grandfather didn't understand any of this, but he wanted to be completely fair so he frankly explained the pitfalls and dangers, while also pointing out that his parents had to be rescued from their fears once and for all, and when he said this, he didn't quite believe it himself anymore because it wasn't his parents he had to save, and who needs that Beast anyhow, let it go to sleep and leave us alone, but there was no choice, and he had to keep talking and arguing. At the end of the speech Momik told Grandfather that for such a major decision Grandfather was entitled to have three days to think it over, but he was only saying that of course.

Grandfather didn't need three days, he made his mind up there and then. He shook his head so hard Momik was afraid his neck would snap, God forbid, and you'd have thought he understood something after all, that the whole time he'd only been waiting for Momik to ask him, and maybe this was the real reason he came to them in the first place, and Momik started to feel a little better.

As he was getting the cellar ready for Grandfather's first visit, he felt almost cheerful. First he brought down the little duster with the colored feathers Mama had for dusting, and he used it to sweep the filthy floor. Then under a pile of junk he found the little bench they called a benkaleh and he put it in the middle of the room and decided this would be Grandfather's benkaleh. He also hung Papa's overcoat with the yellow stars from the nails that stuck out of the wall, and he ripped the empty sleeves, and then he tore out all the pictures he'd copied from library books into his fake Geography Notebook #3 and taped them to the wall, and when he looked around he said twice in Yiddish, Zer shoin, very pretty, and rubbed his palms together and said Whew over them as if he were blowing on a little fire, and then he went up to the house, and inside he locked the bottom lock too, and saw that Grandfather had fallen asleep after lunch with his head resting on the table next to the plate with the drumstick on it, and a fine thread of spit dribbling from his mouth. Momik woke him gently and they went outside and Momik locked the bottom lock too and they walked carefully down the stairs and Momik opened the cellar door and went in first to make sure everything was all right, and quickly, quietly he said, Here, I brought him to you, and then he stepped aside (his heart was pounding) and let Grandfather in, and only then did he dare open his eyes because nothing was happening as far as he could tell, and he led Grandfather to the middle of the room and turned him a little to the right and to the left so his smell would spread in all directions, and the whole time he kept watching the animals, thinking they seemed a little more alert than usual but nothing else, and Grandfather didn't even notice the animals, he just wandered around muttering like a dodo.

Okay, Momik reminded himself that he couldn't really expect anything to happen so fast. Maybe the Beast forgot what a real

Jew smells like and Momik would just have to wait patiently for it to remember. He sat Grandfather down on the benkaleh in the middle of the floor. Grandfather did try to resist a little, to tell the truth, but Momik had lost patience with this kind of non-sense, so he put his hands around Grandfather's neck and pressed slowly till he gave in and sat down. Momik sat before him on the floor and said, Now start talking, and Grandfather gave him a funny look as if he was afraid of him or something, and why should he be afraid now, all he had to do was to obey Momik with no nonsense, there was nothing to be afraid of, and suddenly Momik shouted as loud as he could, Talk, you hear? Start talking or else, but he didn't know why he was shouting or what he meant by "or else," and Grandfather started talking very fast, and that disgusting spit squirted out of his mouth, which is exactly what Momik had hoped would happen, and he said, Wave your hands too! And Grandfather waved his hands the way he does, and Momik watched him closely to make sure he was really trying hard and doing what he was supposed to do, and he also glanced at the cages and the suitcases and the torn mattresses and silently cried, Jude! Jude! Here, I brought you the kind you like, a real Jude that looks like a Jude and talks like a Jude and smells like a Jude, a Jude grandfather with a Jude grandson, so come on out . . .

In the days that followed, Momik did some pretty desperate things. They would sit on the floor together, eating pieces of dry bread, as Momik softly sang partisan songs, in both Hebrew and Yiddish, and recited prayers from Papa's High Holiday prayer book. He even covered the far wall of the cellar with pages torn out of Anne's book, but the Beast would not come out. It simply would not come out.

The poor animals howled and shrieked and scratched, and the cat was dying now, but Momik wasn't afraid of the animals, he was afraid of the Beast which was here in the cellar, you could really feel it flexing its huge muscles, ready to pounce, only how could you tell where it was going to pounce from, darn it, and Momik sat looking at Grandfather Anshel and didn't know what to do. He was fed up with this stupid grandfather who did nothing but drawl out his crummy story in a whiny voice. Sometimes Momik felt like going over to him and snapping his mouth shut. Once when Grandfather made a sign that he had to pee, Momik didn't get up to take him out but sat staring into his eyes instead, and he saw how confused Grandfather was, howling like some crazy cat and grabbing himself there and writhing desperately and then he wet his pants and they smelled revolting, but Momik wasn't the least bit sorry for him anymore, on the contrary, when Grandfather looked up at him with a dazed and pitiful expression on his face, Momik just got up and walked out, leaving Grandfather all alone in the dark, and he went back to the house and locked himself in and listened to the radio and heard how our team lost the game against the Poles in Yaroslav 7 to 2, while the Poles jeered at our boys, and Nechemia Ben-Avraham the sportscaster described how Yanush Achurak and Liberda and Shershinsky are walking all over our boys Goldstein and Stelmach, so Momik could see he was losing right down the line, as they say, though on the other hand, as everyone knows, Momik isn't the kind of boy who cares about losing or jeering or harassment or extortion, but there is one thing he will never allow himself to lose at, because there is no other way, and that's why he had a new plan, more daring than anything up to now, which he worked out because Grandfather Anshel was apparently too small to bring out the Beast wherever it was, and as always, Momik had to think this through like a good shopkeeper (Bella was the one who taught him this even though she herself was a regular shlimazel when it comes to business things), and get some more Jews in, enough to make the Beast think it was worth coming out, and this seemed so funny to him that he laughed a weird laugh which startled him and he shut up and listened to the game on the radio, and thought about Grandfather who might be gobbled up any moment down there, and in his mind, which he could no longer control, Momik planned to ask his classmates to lend him their grandmothers and grandfathers for a little while and bring them down to the Beast in a big group, and he let out another laugh like a high-pitched squeak on the radio, and then stifled it and looked around to see if anyone had heard.

And he didn't even wait to hear the end of the game because he stopped believing a miracle would happen and some wonder boy of a soccer player would leap down from the stands past the jeering crowds and join our eleven-man team on the field and show those Poles a thing or two, and run circles around them and save the day and clobber them 8 to 7 (the last goal with the final whistle), and he stomped out of the house and locked the bottom lock and went down the stairs and waited at the door for a second, listening for the victim's screams, but all he heard was Grandfather's tune, and then Momik went in and sat down facing Grandfather, feeling all tired out; he must really have been tired out because sometime later he found himself stretched out at Grandfather's feet, and decided that maybe it wouldn't be such a good idea to bring any more Jewish grandfathers in, because it sure was getting harder to put up with people lately, they were simply impossible, with their secrets and ideas and the craziness darting out of their eyes, and how come there's the other type of people, like the kids in his class, everything seems so simple to, only Momik knows how not simple it is, because once is enough; once you know how not simple it is and how frightening it is, you can never believe in anything again, oh what an act it is, but even though he was asleep now he couldn't stop fighting, and he heard someone calling, Get up, get up, if you fall asleep now, you're done for, and maybe it was this voice that kept him from falling asleep, no, it was something else too, hard to remember what exactly, maybe he got up, yes, and he walked out of the cellar, and wandered around in a fog, dragging his feet, till he got to the green bench where he stopped awhile; he just sat there and waited, thinking of nothing, watching a big brown autumn leaf that had fallen from some tree long ago, and he saw the veins sticking out of the leaf like the veins on Mama's legs, and down the middle there was a long line that split the leaf in two, and he thought what would happen now if he tore the leaf in two and threw each half in a different direction, would they miss each other or what, and as he sat there his old people approached, and they didn't have to ask any questions, they knew, they looked at his face and saw it was time to do what they'd planned all along, and Momik waited another minute till they all had the same smell, and then he said, Ah well, nu, and they all followed him, Hannah and Munin and Marcus and Ginzburg and Zeidman, like sheep they followed wherever he led, they traipsed down the street forever along the paths with the snowdrifts and the black forests and the churches and haystacks with the fresh smell, and someone who saw them on their way asked Momik, Where to? but Momik didn't look up to see who it was, and he didn't answer, he led his Jews onward to the cellar, and heard Grandfather talking to himself inside, and Momik opened the door for them and beckoned them in and shut the door.

They waited patiently inside for their eyes to get used to the dark, till gradually they could make Grandfather out on his benkaleh, and the white pages on the walls, and Mr. Munin was the first who had enough nerve to go to the wall and look at one of the pictures up close, and it took him a while to figure out what he was looking at but when he did understand he stiffened and backed away and he must have been frightened because you could feel his fear run through them like an electric current, and they huddled together, but then slowly they spread out through the cellar and started to file past the walls, looking at the pictures as if they were at an exhibition, and the more they looked at the pictures like that, the more they gave off the sharp, old smell which nearly suffocated Momik, but he knew this smell was probably his last chance, and inwardly he screamed, Show it, show it, go on, be Jews and show it, and he crouched down with his hands on his knees as if he were coaching the players on the soccer field and inwardly shouted, Now, now, go on, be wizards and prophets and witches and let's give it one more battle, one last fight, be so Jewish it won't know what to do with itself, and even if the Beast was never here before, now it's got to come out, but nothing happened, except that his poor animals were getting even jumpier; the raven flapped its wings and made swooshing sounds, and the cat yowled horribly, and Momik went down on his hands and knees and drew his head in and thought what an idiot he'd been to believe in wizards and witches and all that, a nechtiger tog,[20] as Bella would say, there's no such thing, look at them, this poor bunch of crazy Jews who stuck to him and ruined everything, his whole life they ruined, and what made him think they could ever help him, huh, he could teach them a few things, come to think of it, every single one of them, what you do in an emergency, one fist four fingers, how to run circles around the world, but what do they care anyway, they seem to like it even when you hurt them and when you laugh at them and they're miserable, they've never done anything in their whole lives to fight back, they just sit there bickering about those stories no one gives a darn about, what the rabbi said to the widow and how a piece of meat fell into the milk soup, and meanwhile more and more of them were killed, and they always have to get the last word in too, as if the one who gets the last word in stays alive, and all those stupid exaggerations which are a pack of lies, the genius in Warsaw everyone supposedly knew, and the nobleman Munin claims kissed him and hugged him like a brother! and the Polish government minister who bowed to Mr. Marcus once, oh yeah, sure, sure! And even Bella, believing she's prettier than Marilyn Monroe, really! And even when they talk about what the goyim put them through, the pogroms and expulsions and tortures, they talk about it with a kind of krechtz, forgiving it all, like someone who makes fun of himself for being weak and a nebuch, and anyone who laughs at himself gets laughed at by

---

20. Literally, "a nocturnal day"; used to designate something which is unreasonable or impossible.

others, everyone knows that, and slowly Momik raised his head from the floor and felt himself fill with hatred and rage and revenge, and his head was on fire and the room danced before his eyes, and these Jews were scurrying along the walls and pictures so fast he could hardly tell what was real and what was a picture and he wanted to stop them but he didn't know how, once he had a magic word but he couldn't remember it, and he raised his arms and begged, Enough, stop it now, he raised his arms as if to surrender, like a boy he saw in a picture once, but a terrible scream escaped him, the cry of a Beast, and it was so frightening that everything stood still and the room stopped dancing and the Jews fell down and lay panting on the floor, and then he got up and stood over them, and his legs wobbled and everything was fuzzy, and then he heard Grandfather humming his tune in the silence like an electric pole, only this time the story sounded clear and he told it nicely with biblical expression, and Momik held his breath and listened to the story from start to finish, and swore he would never-ever-black-and-blue forget a single word of the story, but he instantly forgot because it was the kind of story you always forget and have to keep going back to the beginning to remember, it was that kind of story, and when Grandfather finished telling it, the others started telling their stories, and they were all talking at once and they said things no one would ever believe, and Momik remembered them forever and ever and instantly forgot them, and sometimes they fell asleep in the middle of a word and their heads drooped down on their chest and when they woke up they started where they left off and Momik went over the pictures he'd copied in pencil once out of those books, and he remembered that each time he'd copied a picture he felt he had to draw it a little differently, like the one with the child they forced to scrub the street with a toothbrush, well Momik drew the toothbrush bigger than it was in the photograph, and the old man they forced to ride on the other old man, Momik drew him half standing so he wouldn't be so heavy, yes, he felt he had to make these changes, but now he couldn't remember why exactly, and he was kind of angry with himself for not being precise and scientific enough, because if he had been, maybe his latest problems would be over by now, and he leaned against the wall, because he couldn't stand up anymore, and his Jews were still talking and bobbing around as if they were praying, and sometimes it seemed to him that he was imagining all this, and his eyes kept darting around in search of where it would pounce from, and then Grandfather Anshel started telling his story from the beginning again, and Momik squeezed his head because he didn't think he could stand it anymore, he wanted to vomit everything, everything he'd eaten for lunch and everything he'd learned about lately, including himself, and now these stinky Jews here too, the kind the goyim called Jude, before he thought that was just an insult, but now he saw it suited them perfectly, and he whispered, Jude, and felt a warm thrill in his stomach and felt his muscles filling out all over, and he said it again out loud, Jude, and it made him feel strong, and he shook himself and stood over Grandfather Wasserman, sneering, Shut up already, enough already, we're sick of your story, you can't kill the Nazikaput with a story, you have to beat him to death, and for that you need a naval commando unit to break into the room and take him hostage till Hitler comes to save him, and then they catch Hitler and kill him too with terrible tortures, they yank his nails out one by one, shrieks Momik, leaving Grandfather and approaching the cages, and you gouge his eyes out without an anaesthetic, and then you bomb Germany and wipe out every trace of Over There, every good trace and every evil trace, and you liberate the six million with a spy mission the likes of which have never been seen, you turn back the clock like a time machine, sure, there must be someone at the Weizmann Institute who could invent something like that, and they'll bring the whole world down on their knees, pshakrev, and spit in their faces, and we'll fly overhead in our jet planes, war is what we need, screamed Momik, and his eyes were like the eyes of his cat, and his hands ran down the cages and opened the metal latches, and once again he turned and saw his little shtetl, and he stood there motionless, watching the raven and the cat and the lizard and the others slowly leave their cages; they didn't understand what was going on, they didn't believe this was it, that it was over now, but the Jews understood all right, and got up from the floor and huddled together with their backs to the animals and whispered fearfully, and the animals made noises at each other and wouldn't let each other move, when anyone moved even the teensiest bit, there was shrieking and howling and feathers standing on end, and the cellar was filled with the sounds of danger and fear, and it seemed incredible that only half a minute from here there was a city and people and books, and Momik who thought he might be dead or something, closed his eyes, and, risking his life, passed the raven and the cat and didn't feel them scratching and pecking him, what was that to him after all he'd been through, and he went over to his Jews, and they looked at him with sad, worried faces, but they moved over all the same and made way for him, and he was still laughing at them in his heart for their willingness to forgive him so soon after what he'd done to them, but it felt good when they closed in around him and he was standing in the ring, and he thought the Beast would never be able to get him in the ring, it would never try to get in, because it knows it wouldn't stand a chance, but when he opened his eyes and saw them all around him, tall and ancient, gazing at him with pity, he knew with all his nine-and-a-half-year-old alter kopf intelligence that it was too late now.

There are just a few things more worth mentioning here in the interest of scientific accuracy: Momik couldn't say goodbye to his cellar just like that, and though he never brought Grandfather or any of the others with him, he still went in sometimes to be alone in the days that followed. The animals he let go, but their smell lingered on and the smell of the Jews did too. His teacher Netta came over to talk to Mama and Papa, and they agreed about certain things. Momik didn't care. He didn't even ask. He didn't make a note that Yair Pantilat broke the record for the 800-meter dash, or that Flora and Alinka, the two mares at the Beit Dagan Agricultural Fair, foaled, and the foals were given Hebrew names, Dan and Dagan. At the end of the school year Momik's report card said *Promoted,* but not at our school, and Mama told him that the following year he would attend a special school near Natanya, and he wouldn't be living at home, but this was for his own good, because there would be fresh air and healthy food there, and once a week he could visit Idka and Shimmik who lived nearby. Momik said nothing. That summer, when he went away to visit his new school, Grandfather walked out of the house and never returned. This happened exactly five months after he arrived in the ambulance. The police searched awhile but they never found him. Momik used to lie in bed at night in boarding school, wondering where Grandfather was now and who he was telling his story to. At home Grandfather was never mentioned again, except one time when Mama thought of him and said to Idka angrily, "If there was at least a grave to visit, but to disappear like that?" ∿

INTERPRETIVE QUESTIONS
FOR DISCUSSION

Why does reading Grandfather Anshel's *Children of the Heart* story make Momik decide to fight the Nazi Beast?

1. Why does Momik think that he is the only one who can save Mama and Papa from their fears and silences and krechtzes? (243)

2. Why does Momik at first try to rescue his parents and Grandfather Anshel by spying on them and writing facts about Over There in his secret notebook? Why does Momik decide that there is only one thing worth being in life and "that's a writer, like Grandfather Anshel"? (265)

3. Why does Momik think that Grandfather Anshel's *Children of the Heart* story is not only the most exciting story ever written, but the origin of every book and work of literature? (234–235)

4. Why does Momik think that, by being systematic and having a plan for "a bold, daring stunt," he would be able to vanquish the Beast and make his parents "better both now and backward in time"? (288)

5. Why does Momik think that the best way to give his animals the kind of nourishment and care that will make the Nazi Beast show itself is to keep them caged up in the dark cellar of his house?

6. Why do Mama and Papa devour Momik with their eyes when they return home at night? (279)

7. Why does Momik almost shriek in fear, and silently ask God to do something to him instead, when he watches his parents frantically gobble their dinner? (280)

8. Why does Momik fantasize that he has a brother Bill who could kill schoolyard bullies like Laizer the Crook with one blow? Why would he rather master his impulses—hold Bill in check and get beaten up—than fight back? (286)

9. Why does Momik consider it a chance for victory over the Nazi Beast when his calculated mention of a Sholem Aleichem story causes Papa to tell him all about life in his tiny Polish village? Why does Momik think that the Beast opened its mouth a little, "to let Papa tumble right out" to him? (294)

10. Why does Momik try to reenter his parents' past in Poland by carrying a radish lantern, like the one Papa had as a boy, as he walks home from school? (297)

11. Why does Papa angrily smack the radish lantern out of Momik's hand, telling him, "Enough of this nonsense"? Why does Motl, Momik's imaginary brother from the story by Sholem Aleichem, disappear after this incident? (297)

12. Why is Momik able to draw strength from Grandfather's Herrneigel story? (306)

Suggested textual analyses
Pages 251–258: beginning, "It's a very quiet street," and ending, "raising the Nazi Beast."

Pages 294–298: beginning, "And for two weeks," and ending, "but the Beast wasn't ready to appear yet."

Why does Momik become increasingly alienated from his family and schoolmates as he learns more about the Holocaust?

1. Why does Momik feel that he has a responsibility to all of the grownups in the neighborhood to be nice and well mannered? (253)

2. Why does Momik fantasize that his father is an Emperor and a commando fighter who had tearfully ordered that the infant Momik be taken into the forest to die? Why does Momik imagine that many years later he served and protected the Emperor and Empress as their secret adviser? (250)

3. Why does Momik stop obeying Mama and Papa when he starts fighting the Beast? (270, 300)

4. Why does Momik believe that "if Grandfather wanted to, he could pull him right into his story just the way he did Herrneigel"? Why does he think that, if this happened, he would be lost and "nobody would ever find him"? (289)

5. Why is Momik, after twenty attempts, still unable to write the letter asking for help from the Viennese man who is an expert in hunting Nazi Beasts? (291)

6. Why does Momik feel that the hatred and wildness of the animals in the cellar make them stronger than he is? When Momik tries to figure out "how the Beast feels things," why does his drawing of it come out looking "like a lonely little polar bear, full of anger and hating the whole world"? (292–293)

7. Why does Momik's fight against the Beast remain solitary, even though he realizes that the other children he meets in the library are "kind of like him"—that they feel like he does, speak Yiddish at home, and are also fighting the Beast? (300–301)

8. Why does Momik continue to visit his caged animals in the cellar even though he no longer believes that the Beast will "come out

of a hedgehog or some poor cat or even a raven"? Why does he instead believe that the Beast could appear from "just thinking and imagining it"? (302)

9. Why does Momik begin to believe that the Beast is winning? Why does he feel the existence of the Beast "in his bones"? (302–303)

10. Why does Momik imagine smashing and tormenting the Beast and even letting it "wound him with its claws and teeth and all its beaks"? (305)

11. Why does Momik almost begin to enjoy feeling wild and hateful? (304–305)

12. Why does Momik try to lure the Beast out of hiding by masquerading as a Jewish Holocaust survivor—"the food it liked best"? (303, 306)

Suggested textual analyses
Pages 289–290: beginning, "And one time at lunch," and ending, "and Momik was all alone again."

Pages 300–306: beginning, "And by the end of winter," and ending, "and looks at Momik as if he understands something."

Why does Momik, who wants to destroy the Nazi Beast, end up torturing and humiliating Jews?

1. When he feels bad about torturing his animals, why does Momik tell himself, "In war there's suffering and sometimes the innocent suffer too"? (288) Why does Momik envy the Beast for "being so strong that it never suffers from pity"? (304)

2. Why does Momik feel that he has no choice but to fight the Beast, even though he no longer believes that he is fighting it in order to save his parents from their fears? (315)

3. Why does Momik laugh "a weird laugh" when he decides that he must bring more Jews into the cellar—"enough to make the Beast think it was worth coming out"? (318)

4. Why does Momik feel suffocated by the smell of fear that "his Jews" give off? Why does Momik believe that it is this smell that will make the Nazi Beast show itself? (320)

5. Why does Momik feel himself fill with "hatred and rage and revenge" when nothing happens in the cellar filled with the old Jews from his neighborhood? (322)

6. Why does a terrible scream, "the cry of a Beast," escape Momik when he wants to tell the old people to stop looking at the pictures? (322)

7. After Momik screams, why is Grandfather able to tell his story clearly and "nicely with biblical expression"? Why is it the kind of story that "you always forget and have to keep going back to the beginning to remember"? (322)

8. Why does Momik want to vomit "everything he'd learned about lately, including himself"? (323)

9. Why does calling the old people "Jude" make Momik feel strong? (323)

10. Why does Momik free the animals from their cages, screaming, "war is what we need"? (323)

11. Why does Momik move inside the circle of old people and think that the Beast will "never be able to get him . . . because it knows it wouldn't stand a chance"? (324)

12. When he sees the old people gazing at him with pity, why does Momik know that it is "too late now" and that the Beast will destroy him? (324)

Suggested textual analysis
Pages 317–325: from "In the days that followed," to the end of the selection.

FOR FURTHER REFLECTION

1. What does it take in order for a person to respond with an open heart, as Bella does, to the horrible suffering that is the legacy of the Holocaust?

2. Is it possible to escape the past of one's ethnic group? Can we overcome the histories of our parents' suffering?

3. What enables some people, like Aunt Idka and Uncle Shimmik, to start a new life, while others are unable to recover?

4. How *does* one best fight the Nazi Beast that, under the right conditions, can emerge anywhere?

An American Childhood

Childhood

Annie Dillard

ANNIE DILLARD (1945–   ) was born in
Pittsburgh, Pennsylvania. An essayist, poet,
and fiction writer, she won the Pulitzer Prize
in 1975 for *Pilgrim at Tinker Creek,* a book
of poetic-theological essays. *An American
Childhood* was nominated for a National
Book Critics Circle Award in 1987.
She published her first novel, *The Living,*
in 1992. Since 1979, Dillard has been
distinguished visiting professor and more
recently writer in residence at Wesleyan
University in Middletown, Connecticut.

WHEN EVERYTHING ELSE has gone from my brain—the President's name, the state capitals, the neighborhoods where I lived, and then my own name and what it was on earth I sought, and then at length the faces of my friends, and finally the faces of my family—when all this has dissolved, what will be left, I believe, is topology: the dreaming memory of land as it lay this way and that.

I will see the city poured rolling down the mountain valleys like slag, and see the city lights sprinkled and curved around the hills' curves, rows of bonfires winding. At sunset a red light like housefires shines from the narrow hillside windows; the houses' bricks burn like glowing coals.

The three wide rivers divide and cool the mountains. Calm old bridges span the banks and link the hills. The Allegheny River flows in brawling from the north, from near the shore of Lake Erie, and from Lake Chautauqua in New York and eastward. The Monongahela River flows in shallow and slow from the south, from West Virginia. The Allegheny and the Monongahela meet and form the westward-wending Ohio.

Where the two rivers join lies an acute point of flat land from which rises the city. The tall buildings rise lighted to their tips. Their lights illumine other buildings' clean sides, and illumine the narrow city canyons below, where people move, and shine reflected red and white at night from the black waters.

When the shining city, too, fades, I will see only those forested mountains and hills, and the way the rivers lie flat and moving among them, and the way the low land lies wooded among them, and the blunt mountains rise in darkness from the rivers' banks, steep from the rugged south and rolling from the north, and from farther, from the inclined eastward plateau where the high ridges begin to run so long north and south unbroken that to get around them you practically have to navigate Cape Horn.

In those first days, people said, a squirrel could run the long length of Pennsylvania without ever touching the ground. In those first days, the woods were white oak and chestnut, hickory, maple, sycamore, walnut, wild ash, wild plum, and white pine. The pine grew on the ridgetops where the mountains' lumpy spines stuck up and their skin was thinnest.

The wilderness was uncanny, unknown. Benjamin Franklin had already invented his stove in Philadelphia by 1753, and Thomas Jefferson was a schoolboy in Virginia; French soldiers had been living in forts along Lake Erie for two generations. But west of the Alleghenies in western Pennsylvania, there was not even a settlement, not even a cabin. No Indians lived there, or even near there.

Wild grapevines tangled the treetops and shut out the sun. Few songbirds lived in the deep woods. Bright Carolina parakeets—red, green, and yellow—nested in the dark forest. There were ravens then, too. Woodpeckers rattled the big tree trunks, ruffed grouse whirred their tail feathers in the fall, and every long once in a while a nervous gang of empty-headed turkeys came hustling and kicking through the leaves—but no one heard any of this, no one at all.

In 1753, young George Washington surveyed for the English this point of land where rivers met. To see the forest-blurred lay of the land, he rode his horse to a ridgetop and climbed a tree. He judged it would make a good spot for a fort. And an English fort it became, and a depot for Indian traders to the Ohio country, and later a French fort and way station to New Orleans.

But it would be another ten years before any settlers lived there on that land where the rivers met, lived to draw in the flowery scent of June rhododendrons with every breath. It would be another ten years before, for the first time on earth, tall men and women lay exhausted in their cabins, sleeping in the sweetness, worn out from planting corn.

In 1955, when I was ten, my father's reading went to his head.

My father's reading during that time, and for many years before and after, consisted for the most part of *Life on the Mississippi*. He was a young executive in the old family firm, American Standard; sometimes he traveled alone on business. Traveling, he checked into a hotel, found a bookstore, and chose for the night's reading, after what I fancy to have been long deliberation, yet another copy of *Life on the Mississippi*. He brought all these books home. There were dozens of copies of *Life on the Mississippi* on the living-room shelves. From time to time, I read one.

Down the Mississippi hazarded the cub riverboat pilot, down the Mississippi from St. Louis to New Orleans. His chief, the pilot Mr. Bixby, taught him how to lay the boat in her marks and dart between points; he learned to pick a way fastidiously inside a certain snag and outside a shifting shoal in the black dark; he learned to clamber down a memorized channel in his head. On tricky crossings the leadsmen sang out the soundings, so familiar I seemed to have heard them the length of my life: "Mark four! . . . Quarter-less-four! . . . Half three! . . . Mark three! . . . Quarter-less . . . " It was an old story.

When all this reading went to my father's head, he took action. From Pittsburgh he went down the river. Although no one else that our family knew kept a boat on the Allegheny River, our father did, and now he was going all the way with it. He quit the firm his great-grandfather had founded a hundred years earlier down the river at his family's seat in Louisville, Kentucky; he sold his own holdings in the firm. He was taking off for New Orleans.

New Orleans was the source of the music he loved: Dixieland jazz, O Dixieland. In New Orleans men would blow it in the air and beat it underfoot, the music that hustled and snapped, the music whose zip matched his when he was a man-about-town at home in Pittsburgh, working for the family firm; the music he tapped his foot to when he was a man-about-town in New York for a few years after college working for the family firm by day and by night hanging out at Jimmy Ryan's on Fifty-second Street with Zutty Singleton, the black drummer who befriended him, and the rest of the house band. A certain kind of Dixieland suited him best. They played it at Jimmy Ryan's, and Pee Wee Russell and Eddie Condon played it too—New Orleans Dixieland chilled a bit by its journey up the river, and smoothed by its sojourns in Chicago and New York.

Back in New Orleans where he was headed they would play the old stuff, the hot, rough stuff—bastardized for tourists maybe, but still the big and muddy source of it all. Back in New Orleans where he was headed the music would smell like the river itself, maybe, like a thicker, older version of the Allegheny River in Pittsburgh, where he heard the music beat in the roar of his boat's inboard motor; like a thicker, older version of the wide Ohio River at Louisville, Kentucky, where at his family's summer house he'd spent his boyhood summers mucking about in boats.

Getting ready for the trip one Saturday, he roamed around our big brick house snapping his fingers. He had put a record on:

338

Sharkey Bonano, "Li'l Liza Jane." I was reading Robert Louis Stevenson on the sunporch: *Kidnapped.* I looked up from my book and saw him outside; he had wandered out to the lawn and was standing in the wind between the buckeye trees and looking up at what must have been a small patch of wild sky. Old Low-Pockets. He was six feet four, all lanky and leggy; he had thick brown hair and shaggy brows, and a mild and dreamy expression in his blue eyes.

When our mother met Frank Doak, he was twenty-seven: witty, boyish, bookish, unsnobbish, a good dancer. He had grown up an only child in Pittsburgh, attended Shady Side Academy, and Washington and Jefferson College in Pennsylvania, where he studied history. He was a lapsed Presbyterian and a believing Republican. "Books make the man," read the blue bookplate in all his books. "Frank Doak." The bookplate's woodcut showed a square-rigged ship under way in a steep following sea. Father had hung around jazz in New York, and halfheartedly played the drums; he had smoked marijuana, written poems, begun a novel, painted in oils, imagined a career as a riverboat pilot, and acted for more than ten seasons in amateur and small-time professional theater. At American Standard, Amstan Division, he was the personnel manager.

But not for long, and never again; Mother told us he was quitting to go down the river. I was sorry he'd be leaving the Manufacturers' Building downtown. From his office on the fourteenth floor, he often saw suicides, which he reported at dinner. The suicides grieved him, but they thrilled us kids. My sister Amy was seven.

People jumped from the Sixth Street bridge into the Allegheny River. Because the bridge was low, they shinnied all the way up the steel suspension cables to the bridge towers before they jumped. Father saw them from his desk in silhouette, far away. A man vigorously climbed a slanting cable. He slowed near the top, where the cables hung almost vertically; he paused on the stone tower, seeming to sway against the sky, high over the bridge and the river below. Priests, firemen, and others—presumably family members or passersby—gathered on the bridge. In about half the cases, Father said, these people talked the suicide down. The ones who jumped kicked off from the tower so they'd miss the bridge, and fell tumbling a long way down.

Pittsburgh was a cheerful town, and had far fewer suicides than most other cities its size. Yet people jumped so often that father and his colleagues on the fourteenth floor had a betting pool going. They guessed the date and time of day the next jumper would appear. If a man got talked down before he jumped, he still counted for the betting pool, thank God; no manager of American Standard ever wanted to hope, even in the smallest part of himself, that the fellow would go ahead and jump. Father said he and the other men used to gather at the biggest window and holler, "No! Don't do it, buddy, don't!" Now he was leaving American Standard to go down the river, and he was a couple of bucks in the hole.

While I was reading *Kidnapped* on this Saturday morning, I heard him come inside and roam from the kitchen to the pantry to the bar, to the dining room, the living room, and the sunporch, snapping his fingers. He was snapping the fingers of both hands, and shaking his head, to the record—"Li'l Liza Jane"—the sound that was beating, big and jivey, all over the house. He walked lightly, long-legged, like a soft-shoe hoofer barely in touch with the floor. When he played the drums, he played lightly, coming down soft with the steel brushes that sounded like a Slinky falling, not making the beat but just sizzling along with it. He wandered into the sunporch, unseeing; he was snapping his fingers lightly, too, as if he were feeling between them a fine layer of Mississippi silt. The big buckeyes outside the glass sunporch walls were waving.

A week later, he bade a cheerful farewell to us—to Mother, who had encouraged him, to us oblivious daughters, ten and seven, and to the new baby girl, six months old. He loaded his twenty-four-foot cabin cruiser with canned food, pushed off from the dock of the wretched boat club that Mother hated, and pointed his bow downstream, down the Allegheny River. From there it was only a few miles to the Ohio River at Pittsburgh's point, where the Monongahela came in. He wore on westward down the Ohio; he watched West Virginia float past his port bow and Ohio past his starboard. It was 138 river miles to New Martinsville, West Virginia, where he lingered for some races. Back on the move, he tied up nights at club docks he'd seen on the charts; he poured himself water for drinks from dockside hoses. By day he rode through locks, twenty of them in all. He conversed with the lockmasters, those lone men who paced silhouetted in overalls on the concrete lock-chamber walls and threw the big switches that flooded or drained the locks: "Hello, up there!" "So long, down there!"

He continued down the river along the Kentucky border with Ohio, bumping down the locks. He passed through Cincinnati. He moved along down the Kentucky border with Indiana. After 640 miles of river travel, he reached Louisville, Kentucky. There he visited relatives at their summer house on the river.

It was a long way to New Orleans, at this rate another couple of months. He was finding the river lonesome. It got dark too early. It was September; people had abandoned their pleasure boats for the season; their children were back in school. There were no old salts on the docks talking river talk. People weren't so friendly as they were in Pittsburgh. There was no music except the dreary yacht-club jukeboxes playing "How Much Is That Doggie in the Window?" Jazz had come up the river once and for all; it wasn't still coming, he couldn't hear it across the water at night rambling and blowing and banging along high and tuneful, sneaking upstream to Chicago to get educated. He wasn't free so much as loose. He was living alone on beans in a boat and having witless conversations with lockmasters. He mailed out sad postcards.

From phone booths all down the Ohio River he talked to Mother. She told him that she was lonesome, too, and that three children—maid and nanny or no—were a handful. She said, further, that people were starting to talk. She knew Father couldn't bear people's talking. For all his dreaminess, he prized respectability above all; it was our young mother, whose circumstances bespoke such dignity, who loved to shock the world. After only six weeks, then—on the Ohio River at Louisville—he sold the boat and flew home.

I was just waking up then, just barely. Other things were changing. The highly entertaining new baby, Molly, had taken up residence in a former guest room. The great outer world hove into view and began to fill with things that had apparently been there all along: mineralogy, detective work, lepidopterology, ponds and streams, flying, society. My younger sister Amy and I were to start at private school that year: the Ellis School, on Fifth Avenue. I would start dancing school.

Children ten years old wake up and find themselves here, discover themselves to have been here all along; is this sad? They wake like sleepwalkers, in full stride; they wake like people brought back from cardiac arrest or from drowning: *in medias res,* surrounded by familiar people and objects, equipped with a hundred skills. They know the neighborhood, they can read and write English, they are old hands at the commonplace mysteries, and yet they feel themselves to have just stepped off the boat, just converged with their bodies, just flown down from a trance, to lodge in an eerily familiar life already well under way.

I woke in bits, like all children, piecemeal over the years. I discovered myself and the world, and forgot them, and discovered them again. I woke at intervals until, by that September when Father went down the river, the intervals of waking tipped the scales, and I was more often awake than not. I noticed this process of waking, and predicted with terrifying logic that one of these years not far away I would be awake continuously and never slip back, and never be free of myself again.

Consciousness converges with the child as a landing tern touches the outspread feet of its shadow on the sand: precisely, toe hits toe. The tern folds its wings to sit; its shadow dips and spreads over the sand to meet and cup its breast.

Like any child, I slid into myself perfectly fitted, as a diver meets her reflection in a pool. Her fingertips enter the fingertips on the water, her wrists slide up her arms. The diver wraps herself in her reflection wholly, sealing it at the toes, and wears it as she climbs rising from the pool, and ever after.

I never woke, at first, without recalling, chilled, all those other waking times, those similar stark views from similarly lighted precipices: dizzying precipices from which the distant, glittering world revealed itself as a brooding and separated scene—and so let slip a queer implication, that I myself was both observer and observable, and so a possible object of my own humming awareness. Whenever I stepped into the porcelain bathtub, the bath's hot water sent a shock traveling up my bones. The skin on my arms pricked up, and the hair rose on the back of my skull. I saw my own firm foot press the tub, and the pale shadows waver over it, as if I were looking down from the sky and remembering this scene forever. The skin on my face tightened, as it had always done whenever I stepped into the tub, and remembering it all drew a swinging line, loops connecting the dots, all the way back. You again.

I walked. My mother had given me the freedom of the streets as soon as I could say our telephone number. I walked and memorized the neighborhood. I made a mental map and located myself upon it. At night in bed I rehearsed the small world's scheme and set challenges: Find the store using backyards only. Imagine a route from the school to my friend's house. I mastered chunks of town in one direction only; I ignored the other direction, toward the Catholic church.

On a bicycle I traveled over the known world's edge, and the ground held. I was seven. I had fallen in love with a red-haired fourth-grade boy named Walter Milligan. He was tough, Catholic, from an iffy neighborhood. Two blocks beyond our school was a field—Miss Frick's field, behind Henry Clay Frick's mansion—where boys played football. I parked my bike on the sidelines and watched Walter Milligan play. As he ran up and down the length of the field, following the football, I ran up and down the sidelines, following him. After the game I rode my bike home, delirious. It was the closest we had been, and the farthest I had traveled from home.

(My love lasted two years and occasioned a bit of talk. I knew it angered him. We spoke only once. I caught him between classes in the school's crowded hall and said, "I'm sorry." He looked away, apparently enraged; his pale freckled skin flushed. He jammed his fists in his pockets, looked down, looked at me for a second, looked away, and brought out gently, "That's okay." That was the whole of it: beginning, middle, and end.)

Across the street from Walter Milligan's football field was Frick Park. Frick Park was 380 acres of woods in residential Pittsburgh. Only one trail crossed it; the gravelly walk gave way to dirt and led down a forested ravine to a damp streambed. If you followed the streambed all day you would find yourself in a distant part of town reached ordinarily by a long streetcar ride. Near Frick Park's restful entrance, old men and women from other neighborhoods were lawn bowling on the bowling green. The rest of the park was wild woods.

My father forbade me to go to Frick Park. He said bums lived there under bridges; they had been hanging around unnoticed since the Depression. My father was away all day; my mother said I could go to Frick Park if I never mentioned it.

I roamed Frick Park for many years. Our family moved from house to house, but we never moved so far I couldn't walk to Frick Park. I watched the men and women lawn bowling—so careful the players, so dull the game. After I got a bird book I found, in the deep woods, a downy woodpecker working a tree trunk; the woodpecker looked like a jackhammer man banging Edgerton Avenue to bits. I saw sparrows, robins, cardinals, juncos, chipmunks, squirrels, and—always disappointingly, emerging from their magnificent ruckus in the leaves—pedigreed dachshunds, which a woman across the street bred.

I never met anyone in the woods except the woman who walked her shiny dachshunds there, but I was cautious, and hoped I was braving danger. If a bum came after me I would disarm him with courtesy ("Good afternoon"). I would sneak him good food from home; we would bake potatoes together under his bridge; he would introduce me to his fellow bums; we would all feed the squirrels.

The deepest ravine, over which loomed the Forbes Avenue bridge, was called Fern Hollow. There in winter I searched for panther tracks in snow. In summer and fall I imagined the woods extending infinitely. I was the first human being to see these shadowed trees, this land; I would make my pioneer clearing here, near the water. Mine would be one of those famously steep farms: "How'd you get so beat up?" "Fell out of my cornfield." In spring I pried flat rocks from the damp streambed and captured red and black salamanders. I brought the salamanders home in a bag once and terrified my mother with them by mistake, when she was on the phone.

In the fall I walked to collect buckeyes from lawns. Buckeyes were wealth. A ripe buckeye husk splits. It reveals the shining brown sphere inside only partially, as an eyelid only partially discloses an eye's sphere. The nut so revealed looks like the calm brown eye of a buck, apparently. It was odd to imagine the settlers who named it having seen more male deer's eyes in the forest than nuts on a lawn.

Walking was my project before reading. The text I read was the town; the book I made up was a map. First I had walked across one of our side yards to the blackened alley with its buried dime. Now I walked to piano lessons, four long blocks north of school and three zigzag blocks into an Irish neighborhood near Thomas Boulevard.

I pushed at my map's edges. Alone at night I added newly memorized streets and blocks to old streets and blocks, and imagined connecting them on foot. From my parents' earliest injunctions I felt that my life depended on keeping it all straight—remembering where on earth I lived, that is, in relation to where I had walked. It was dead reckoning. On darkening evenings I came home exultant, secretive, often from some exotic leafy curb a mile beyond what I had known at lunch, where I had peered up at the street sign, hugging the cold pole, and fixed the intersection in my mind. What joy, what relief, eased me as I pushed open the heavy front door!—joy and relief because, from the very trackless waste, I had located home, family, and the dinner table once again.

An infant watches her hands and feels them move. Gradually she fixes her own boundaries at the complex incurved rim of her skin. Later she touches one palm to another and tries for a game to distinguish each hand's sensation of feeling and being felt. What is a house but a bigger skin, and a neighborhood map but the world's skin ever expanding?

Some boys taught me to play football. This was fine sport. You thought up a new strategy for every play and whispered it to the others. You went out for a pass, fooling everyone. Best, you got to throw yourself mightily at someone's running legs. Either you brought him down or you hit the ground flat out on your chin, with your arms empty before you. It was all or nothing. If you hesitated in fear, you would miss and get hurt: you would take a hard fall while the kid got away, or you would get kicked in the face while the kid got away. But if you flung yourself wholeheartedly at the back of his knees—if you gathered and joined body and soul and pointed them diving fearlessly—then you likely wouldn't get hurt, and you'd stop the ball. Your fate, and your team's score, depended on your concentration and courage. Nothing girls did could compare with it.

Boys welcomed me at baseball, too, for I had, through enthusiastic practice, what was weirdly known as a boy's arm. In winter, in the snow, there was neither baseball nor football, so the boys and I threw snowballs at passing cars. I got in trouble throwing snowballs, and have seldom been happier since.

On one weekday morning after Christmas, six inches of new snow had just fallen. We were standing up to our boot tops in snow on a front yard on trafficked Reynolds Street, waiting for cars. The cars traveled Reynolds Street slowly and evenly; they were targets all but wrapped in red ribbons, cream puffs. We couldn't miss.

I was seven; the boys were eight, nine, and ten. The oldest two Fahey boys were there—Mikey and Peter—polite blond boys who lived near me on Lloyd Street, and who already had four brothers and sisters. My parents approved Mikey and Peter Fahey. Chickie McBride was there, a tough kid, and Billy Paul and Mackie Kean too, from across Reynolds, where the boys grew up dark and furious, grew up skinny, knowing, and skilled. We had all drifted from our houses that morning looking for action, and had found it here on Reynolds Street.

It was cloudy but cold. The cars' tires left behind them on the snowy street a complex trail of beige chunks like crenellated castle walls. I had stepped on some earlier; they squeaked. We could have wished for more traffic. When a car came, we all popped it one. In the intervals between cars we reverted to the natural solitude of children.

I started making an iceball—a perfect iceball, from perfectly white snow, perfectly spherical, and squeezed perfectly translucent so no snow remained all the way through. (The Fahey boys and I considered it unfair actually to throw an iceball at somebody, but it had been known to happen.)

I had just embarked on the iceball project when we heard tire chains come clanking from afar. A black Buick was moving toward us down the street. We all spread out, banged together some regular snowballs, took aim, and, when the Buick drew nigh, fired.

A soft snowball hit the driver's windshield right before the driver's face. It made a smashed star with a hump in the middle.

Often, of course, we hit our target, but this time, the only time in all of life, the car pulled over and stopped. Its wide black door opened; a man got out of it, running. He didn't even close the car door.

He ran after us, and we ran away from him, up the snowy Reynolds sidewalk. At the corner, I looked back; incredibly, he was still after us. He was in city clothes: a suit and tie, street shoes. Any normal adult would have quit, having sprung us into flight and made his point. This man was gaining on us. He was a thin man, all action. All of a sudden, we were running for our lives.

Wordless, we split up. We were on our turf; we could lose ourselves in the neighborhood backyards, everyone for himself. I paused and considered. Everyone had vanished except Mikey Fahey, who was just rounding the corner of a yellow brick house. Poor Mikey, I trailed him. The driver of the Buick sensibly picked the two of us to follow. The man apparently had all day.

He chased Mikey and me around the yellow house and up a backyard path we knew by heart: under a low tree, up a bank, through a hedge, down some snowy steps, and across the grocery store's delivery driveway. We smashed through a gap in another hedge, entered a scruffy backyard and ran around its back porch and tight between houses to Edgerton Avenue; we ran across Edgerton to an alley and up our own sliding woodpile to the Halls' front yard; he kept coming. We ran up Lloyd Street and wound through mazy backyards toward the steep hilltop at Willard and Lang.

He chased us silently, block after block. He chased us silently over picket fences, through thorny hedges, between houses, around garbage cans, and across streets. Every time I glanced back, choking for breath, I expected he would have quit. He must have been as breathless as we were. His jacket strained over his body. It was an immense discovery, pounding into my hot head with every sliding, joyous step, that this ordinary adult evidently knew what I thought only children who trained at football knew: that you have to fling yourself at what you're doing, you have to point yourself, forget yourself, aim, dive.

Mikey and I had nowhere to go, in our own neighborhood or out of it, but away from this man who was chasing us. He impelled us forward; we compelled him to follow our route. The air was cold; every breath tore my throat. We kept running, block after block; we kept improvising, backyard after backyard, running a frantic course and choosing it simultaneously, failing always to find small places or hard places to slow him down, and discovering always, exhilarated, dismayed, that only bare speed could save us—for he would never give up, this man—and we were losing speed.

He chased us through the backyard labyrinths of ten blocks before he caught us by our jackets. He caught us and we all stopped.

We three stood staggering, half blinded, coughing, in an obscure hilltop backyard: a man in his twenties, a boy, a girl. He had released our jackets, our pursuer, our captor, our hero: he knew we weren't going anywhere. We all played by the rules. Mikey and I unzipped our jackets. I pulled off my sopping mittens. Our tracks multiplied in the backyard's new snow. We had been breaking new snow all morning. We didn't look at each other. I was cherishing my excitement. The man's lower pants legs were wet; his cuffs were full of snow, and there was a prow of snow beneath them on his shoes and socks. Some trees bordered the little flat backyard, some messy winter trees. There was no one around: a clearing in a grove, and we the only players.

It was a long time before he could speak. I had some difficulty at first recalling why we were there. My lips felt swollen; I couldn't see out of the sides of my eyes; I kept coughing.

"You stupid kids," he began perfunctorily.

We listened perfunctorily indeed, if we listened at all, for the chewing out was redundant, a mere formality, and beside the point. The point was that he had chased us passionately without giving up, and so he had caught us. Now he came down to earth. I wanted the glory to last forever.

But how could the glory have lasted forever? We could have run through every backyard in North America until we got to Panama. But when he trapped us at the lip of the Panama Canal, what precisely could he have done to prolong the drama of the chase and cap its glory? I brooded about this for the next few years. He could only have fried Mikey Fahey and me in boiling oil, say, or dismembered us piecemeal, or staked us to anthills. None of which I really wanted, and none of which any adult was likely to do, even in the spirit of fun. He could only chew us out there in the Panamanian jungle, after months or years of exalting pursuit. He could only begin, "You stupid kids," and continue in his ordinary Pittsburgh accent with his normal righteous anger and the usual common sense.

If in that snowy backyard the driver of the black Buick had cut off our heads, Mikey's and mine, I would have died happy, for nothing has required so much of me since as being chased all over Pittsburgh in the middle of winter—running terrified, exhausted—by this sainted, skinny, furious red-headed man who wished to have a word with us. I don't know how he found his way back to his car.

While Father was motoring down the river, my reading was giving me a turn.

At a neighbor boy's house, I ran into Kimon Nicolaides' *The Natural Way to Draw*. This was a manual for students who couldn't get to Nicolaides' own classes at New York's Art Students League. I was amazed that there were books about things one actually did. I had been drawing in earnest, but at random, for two years. Like all children, when I drew I tried to reproduce schema. The idea of drawing from life had astounded me two years previously, but I had gradually let it slip, and my drawing, such as it was, had sunk back into facile sloth. Now this book would ignite my fervor for conscious drawing, and bind my attention to both the vigor and the detail of the actual world.

For the rest of August, and all fall, this urgent, hortatory book ran my life. I tried to follow its schedules: every day, sixty-five gesture drawings, fifteen memory drawings, an hour-long contour drawing, and "The Sustained Study in Crayon, Clothed" or "The Sustained Study in Crayon, Nude."

While Father was gone, I outfitted an attic bedroom as a studio, and moved in. Every summer or weekend morning at eight o'clock I taped that day's drawing schedule to a wall. Since there was no model, nude or clothed, I drew my baseball mitt.

I drew my baseball mitt's gesture—its tense repose, its expectancy, which ran up its hollows like a hand. I drew its contours—its flat fingertips strung on square rawhide thongs. I drew its billion grades of light and dark in detail, so the glove weighed vivid and complex on the page, and the trapezoids small as dust motes in the leather fingers cast shadows, and the pale palm leather was smooth as a belly and thick. "Draw anything," said the book. "Learning to draw is really a matter of learning to see," said the book. "Imagine that your pencil point is touching the model instead of the paper." "All the student need concern himself with is reality."

With my pencil point I crawled over the mitt's topology. I slithered over each dip and rise; I checked my bearings, admired the enormous view, and recorded it like Meriwether Lewis mapping the Rockies.

One thing struck me as odd and interesting. A gesture drawing took forty-five seconds; a Sustained Study took all morning. From any still-life arrangement or model's pose, the artist could produce either a short study or a long one. Evidently, a given object took no particular amount of time to draw; instead the artist took the time, or didn't take it, at pleasure. And, similarly, things themselves possessed no fixed and intrinsic amount of interest; instead things were interesting as long as you had attention to give them. How long does it take to draw a baseball mitt? As much time as you care to give it. Not an infinite amount of time, but more time than you first imagined. For many days, so long as you want to keep drawing that mitt, and studying that mitt, there will always be a new and finer layer of distinctions to draw out and lay in. Your attention discovers— seems thereby to produce—an array of interesting features in any object, like a lamp.

By noon, all this drawing would have gone to my head. I slipped into the mitt, quit the attic, quit the house, and headed up the street, looking for a ball game.

My friend had sought permission from his father for me to borrow *The Natural Way to Draw*; it was his book. Grown men and growing children rarely mingled then. I had lived two doors away from this family for several years, and had never clapped eyes on my good friend's father; still, I now regarded him as a man after my own heart. Had he another book about drawing? He had; he owned a book about pencil drawing. This book began well enough, with the drawing of trees. Then it devoted a chapter to the schematic representation of shrubbery. At last it dwindled into its true subject, the drawing of buildings.

My friend's father was an architect. All his other books were about buildings. He had been a boy who liked to draw, according to my friend, so he became an architect. Children who drew, I learned, became architects; I had thought they became painters. My friend explained that it was not proper to become a painter; it couldn't be done. I resigned myself to architecture school and a long life of drawing buildings. It was a pity, for I disliked buildings, considering them only a stiffer and more ample form of clothing, and no more important.

I began reading books, reading books to delirium. I began by vanishing from the known world into the passive abyss of reading, but soon found myself engaged with surprising vigor because the things in the books, or even the things surrounding the books, roused me from my stupor. From the nearest library I learned every sort of surprising thing—some of it, though not much of it, from the books themselves.

The Homewood branch of Pittsburgh's Carnegie Library system was in a Negro section of town—Homewood. This branch was our nearest library; Mother drove me to it every two weeks for many years, until I could drive myself. I only very rarely saw other white people there.

I understood that our maid, Margaret Butler, had friends in Homewood. I never saw her there, but I did see Henry Watson.[1]

I was getting out of Mother's car in front of the library when Henry appeared on the sidewalk; he was walking with some other old men. I had never before seen him at large; it must have been his day off. He had gold-rimmed glasses, a gold front tooth, and a frank, open expression. It would embarrass him, I thought, if I said hello to him in front of his friends. I was wrong. He spied me, picked me up—books and all—swung me as he always did, and introduced Mother and me to his friends. Later, as we were climbing the long stone steps to the library's door, Mother said, "That's what I mean by good manners."

The Homewood Library had graven across its enormous stone facade: FREE TO THE PEOPLE. In the evenings, neighborhood people—the men and women of Homewood—browsed in the library, and brought their children. By day, the two vaulted rooms, the adults' and children's sections, were almost empty. The kind Homewood librarians, after a trial period, had given me a card to the adult section. This was an enormous silent room with marble floors. Nonfiction was on the left.

---

1. Dillard's grandmother's chauffeur and gardener.

Beside the farthest wall, and under leaded windows set ten feet from the floor, so that no human being could ever see anything from them—next to the wall, and at the farthest remove from the idle librarians at their curved wooden counter, and from the oak bench where my mother waited in her camel's-hair coat chatting with the librarians or reading—stood the last and darkest and most obscure of the tall nonfiction stacks: NEGRO HISTORY and NATURAL HISTORY. It was in Natural History, in the cool darkness of a bottom shelf, that I found *The Field Book of Ponds and Streams.*

The Field Book of Ponds and Streams was a small, blue-bound book printed in fine type on thin paper, like *The Book of Common Prayer.* Its third chapter explained how to make sweep nets, plankton nets, glass-bottomed buckets, and killing jars. It specified how to mount slides, how to label insects on their pins, and how to set up a freshwater aquarium.

One was to go into "the field" wearing hip boots and perhaps a head net for mosquitoes. One carried in a "rucksack" half a dozen corked test tubes, a smattering of screw-top baby-food jars, a white enamel tray, assorted pipettes and eyedroppers, an artillery of cheesecloth nets, a notebook, a hand lens, perhaps a map, and *The Field Book of Ponds and Streams.* This field—unlike the fields I had seen, such as the field where Walter Milligan played football—was evidently very well watered, for there one could find, and distinguish among, daphnia, planaria, water pennies, stonefly larvae, dragonfly nymphs, salamander larvae, tadpoles, snakes, and turtles, all of which one could carry home.

That anyone had lived the fine life described in Chapter 3 astonished me. Although the title page indicated quite plainly that one Ann Haven Morgan had written *The Field Book of Ponds and Streams,* I nevertheless imagined, perhaps from the authority and freedom of it, that its author was a man. It would be good to write him and assure him that someone had found his book, in the dark near the marble floor at the Homewood

Library. I would, in the same letter or in a subsequent one, ask him a question outside the scope of his book, which was where I personally might find a pond, or a stream. But I did not know how to address such a letter, of course, or how to learn if he was still alive.

I was afraid, too, that my letter would disappoint him by betraying my ignorance, which was just beginning to attract my own notice. What, for example, was this noisome-sounding substance called cheesecloth, and what do scientists do with it? What, when you really got down to it, was enamel? If candy could, notoriously, "eat through enamel," why would anyone make trays out of it? Where—short of robbing a museum— might a fifth-grade student at the Ellis School on Fifth Avenue obtain such a legendary item as a wooden bucket?

The Field Book of Ponds and Streams was a shocker from beginning to end. The greatest shock came at the end.

When you checked out a book from the Homewood Library, the librarian wrote your number on the book's card and stamped the due date on a sheet glued to the book's last page. When I checked out *The Field Book of Ponds and Streams* for the second time, I noticed the book's card. It was almost full. There were numbers on both sides. My hearty author and I were not alone in the world, after all. With us, and sharing our enthusiasm for dragonfly larvae and single-celled plants, were, apparently, many Negro adults.

Who were these people? Had they, in Pittsburgh's Homewood section, found ponds? Had they found streams? At home, I read the book again; I studied the drawings; I reread Chapter 3; then I settled in to study the due-date slip. People read this book in every season. Seven or eight people were reading this book every year, even during the war.

Every year, I read again *The Field Book of Ponds and Streams*. Often, when I was in the library, I simply visited it. I sat on the marble floor and studied the book's card. There we all were. There was my number. There was the number of someone else who had checked it out more than once. Might I contact this person and cheer him up? For I assumed that, like me, he had found pickings pretty slim in Pittsburgh.

The people of Homewood, some of whom lived in visible poverty, on crowded streets among burned-out houses—they dreamed of ponds and streams. They were saving to buy microscopes. In their bedrooms they fashioned plankton nets. But their hopes were even more vain than mine, for I was a child, and anything might happen; they were adults, living in Homewood. There was neither pond nor stream on the streetcar routes. The Homewood residents whom I knew had little money and little free time. The marble floor was beginning to chill me. It was not fair.

I had been driven into nonfiction against my wishes. I wanted to read fiction, but I had learned to be cautious about it.

"When you open a book," the sentimental library posters said, "anything can happen." This was so. A book of fiction was a bomb. It was a land mine you wanted to go off. You wanted it to blow your whole day. Unfortunately, hundreds of thousands of books were duds. They had been rusting out of everyone's way for so long that they no longer worked. There was no way to distinguish the duds from the live mines except to throw yourself at them headlong, one by one.

The suggestions of adults were uncertain and incoherent. They gave you Nancy Drew with one hand and *Little Women* with the other. They mixed good and bad books together because they could not distinguish between them. Any book which contained children, or short adults, or animals, was felt to be a children's book. So also was any book about the sea— as though danger or even fresh air were a child's prerogative— or any book by Charles Dickens or Mark Twain. Virtually all British books, actually, were children's books; no one understood children like the British. Suited to female children were love stories set in any century but this one. Consequently one had read, exasperated often to fury, *Pickwick Papers, Désirée,*

Wuthering Heights, Lad, a Dog, Gulliver's Travels, Gone with the Wind, Robinson Crusoe, Nordhoff and Hall's *Bounty* trilogy, *Moby Dick, The Five Little Peppers, Innocents Abroad, Lord Jim, Old Yeller.*

The fiction stacks at the Homewood library, their volumes alphabetized by author, baffled me. How could I learn to choose a novel? That I could not easily reach the top two shelves helped limit choices a little. Still, on the lower shelves I saw too many books: Mary Johnson, *Sweet Rocket;* Samuel Johnson, *Rasselas;* James Jones, *From Here to Eternity.* I checked out the last because I had heard of it; it was good. I decided to check out books I had heard of. I had heard of *The Mill on the Floss.* I read it, and it was good. On its binding was printed a figure, a man dancing or running; I had noticed this figure before. Like so many children before and after me, I learned to seek out this logo, the Modern Library colophon.

The going was always rocky. I couldn't count on Modern Library the way I could count on, say, *Mad* magazine, which never failed to slay me. *Native Son* was good, *Walden* was pretty good, *The Interpretation of Dreams* was okay, and *The Education of Henry Adams* was awful. *Ulysses,* a very famous book, was also awful. *Confessions* by Augustine, whose title promised so much, was a bust. *Confessions* by Jean-Jacques Rousseau was much better, though it fell apart halfway through.

In fact, it was a plain truth that most books fell apart halfway through. They fell apart as their protagonists quit, without any apparent reluctance, like idiots diving voluntarily into buckets, the most interesting part of their lives, and entered upon decades of unrelieved tedium. I was forewarned, and would not so bobble my adult life; when things got dull, I would go to sea.

Jude the Obscure was the type case. It started out so well. Halfway through, its author forgot how to write. After Jude got married, his life was over, but the book went on for hundreds of pages while he stewed in his own juices. The same thing happened in *The Little Shepherd of Kingdom Come,* which Mother brought me from a fair. It was simply a hazard of reading. Only a heartsick loyalty to the protagonists of the early chapters, to the eager children they had been, kept me reading chronological narratives to their bitter ends. Perhaps later, when I had become an architect, I would enjoy the latter halves of books more.

This was the most private and obscure part of life, this Homewood Library: a vaulted marble edifice in a mostly decent Negro neighborhood, the silent stacks of which I plundered in deep concentration for many years. There seemed then, happily, to be an infinitude of books.

I no more expected anyone else on earth to have read a book I had read than I expected someone else to have twirled the same blade of grass. I would never meet those Homewood people who were borrowing *The Field Book of Ponds and Streams;* the people who read my favorite books were invisible or in hiding, underground. Father occasionally raised his big eyebrows at the title of some volume I was hurrying off with, quite as if he knew what it contained—but I thought he must know of it by hearsay, for none of it seemed to make much difference to him. Books swept me away, one after the other, this way and that; I made endless vows according to their lights, for I believed them.

What can we make of the inexpressible joy of children? It is a kind of gratitude, I think—the gratitude of the ten-year-old who wakes to her own energy and the brisk challenge of the world. You thought you knew the place and all its routines, but you see you hadn't known. Whole stacks at the library held books devoted to things you knew nothing about. The boundary of knowledge receded, as you poked about in books, like Lake Erie's rim as you climbed its cliffs. And each area of knowledge disclosed another, and another. Knowledge wasn't a body, or a tree, but instead air, or space, or being—whatever pervaded, whatever never ended and fitted into the smallest cracks and the widest space between stars.

Any way you cut it, colors and shadows flickered from multiple surfaces. Just enough work had already been done on everything—moths, say, or meteorites—to get you started and interested, but not so much there was nothing left to do. Often I wondered: was it being born just now, in this century, in this country? And I thought: no, any time could have been like this, if you had the time and weren't sick; you could, especially if you were a boy, learn and do. There was joy in concentration, and the world afforded an inexhaustible wealth of projects to concentrate on. There was joy in effort, and the world resisted effort to just the right degree, and yielded to it at last. People cut Mount Rushmore into faces; they chipped here and there for years. People slowed the spread of yellow fever; they sprayed the Isthmus of Panama puddle by puddle. Effort alone I loved. Some days I would have been happy to push a pole around a threshing floor like an ox, for the pleasure of moving the heavy stone and watching my knees rise in turn.

I was running down the Penn Avenue sidewalk, revving up for an act of faith. I was conscious and self-conscious. I knew well that people could not fly—as well as anyone knows it—but I also knew the kicker: that, as the books put it, with faith all things are possible.

Just once I wanted a task that required all the joy I had. Day after day I had noticed that if I waited long enough, my strong unexpressed joy would dwindle and dissipate inside me, over many hours, like a fire subsiding, and I would at last calm down. Just this once I wanted to let it rip. Flying rather famously required the extra energy of belief, and this, too, I had in superabundance.

There were boxy yellow thirties apartment buildings on those Penn Avenue blocks, and the Evergreen Café, and Miss Frick's house set back behind a wrought-iron fence. There were some side yards of big houses, some side yards of little houses, some streetcar stops, and a drugstore from which I had once tried to heist a five-pound box of chocolates, a Whitman sampler, confusing "sampler" with "free sample." It was past all this that I ran that late fall afternoon, up old Penn Avenue on the cracking cement sidewalks—past the drugstore and bar, past the old and new apartment buildings and the long dry lawn behind Miss Frick's fence.

I ran the sidewalk full tilt. I waved my arms ever higher and faster; blood balled in my fingertips. I knew I was foolish. I knew I was too old really to believe in this as a child would, out of ignorance; instead I was experimenting as a scientist would, testing both the thing itself and the limits of my own courage in trying it miserably self-conscious in full view of the whole world. You can't test courage cautiously, so I ran hard and waved my arms hard, happy.

Up ahead I saw a business-suited pedestrian. He was coming stiffly toward me down the walk. Who could ever forget this first test, this stranger, this thin young man appalled? I banished the temptation to straighten up and walk right. He flattened himself against a brick wall as I passed flailing—although I had left him plenty of room. He had refused to meet my exultant eye. He looked away, evidently embarrassed. How surprisingly easy it was to ignore him! What I was letting rip, in fact, was my willingness to look foolish, in his eyes and in my own. Having chosen this foolishness, I was a free being. How could the world ever stop me, how could I betray myself, if I was not afraid?

I was flying. My shoulders loosened, my stride opened, my heart banged the base of my throat. I crossed Carnegie and ran up the block waving my arms. I crossed Lexington and ran up the block waving my arms.

A linen-suited woman in her fifties did meet my exultant eye. She looked exultant herself, seeing me from far up the block. Her face was thin and tanned. We converged. Her warm, intelligent glance said she knew what I was doing—not because she herself had been a child but because she herself took a few loose aerial turns around her apartment every night for the hell of it, and by day played along with the rest of the world and took the streetcar. So Teresa of Avila checked her unseemly joy and hung on to the altar rail to hold herself down. The woman's smiling, deep glance seemed to read my own awareness from my face, so we passed on the sidewalk—a beautifully upright woman walking in her tan linen suit, a kid running and flapping her arms— we passed on the sidewalk with a look of accomplices who share a humor just beyond irony. What's a heart for?

I crossed Homewood and ran up the block. The joy multiplied as I ran—I ran never actually quite leaving the ground—and multiplied still as I felt my stride begin to fumble and my knees begin to quiver and stall. The joy multiplied even as I slowed bumping to a walk. I was all but splitting, all but shooting sparks. Blood coursed free inside my lungs and bones, a light-shot stream like air. I couldn't feel the pavement at all.

I was too aware to do this, and had done it anyway. What could touch me now? For what were the people on Penn Avenue to me, or what was I to myself, really, but a witness to any boldness I could muster, or any cowardice if it came to that, any giving up on heaven for the sake of dignity on earth? I had not seen a great deal accomplished in the name of dignity, ever.

The French and Indian War was a war of which I, for one, reading stretched out in the bedroom, couldn't get enough. The names of the places were a litany: Fort Ticonderoga on the Hudson, Fort Vincennes on the Wabash. The names of the people were a litany: the Sieur de Contrecoeur; the Marquis de Montcalm; Major Robert Rogers of the Rangers; the Seneca Chief Half-King.

How witless in comparison were the clumsy wars of Europe: on this open field at nine o'clock sharp, soldiers in heavy armor, dragged from their turnip patches in feudal obedience to Lord

So-and-So, met in long ranks the heavily armored men owned or paid for by Lord So-and-So, and defeated them by knocking them over like ninepins. What was at stake? A son's ambition, or an earl's pride.

In the French and Indian War, and the Indian wars, a whole continent was at stake, and it was hard to know who to root for as I read. The Indians were the sentimental favorites, but they were visibly cruel. The French excelled at Indian skills and had the endearing habit of singing in boats. But if they won, we would all speak French, which seemed affected in the woods. The Scotch-Irish settlers and the English army were very uneasy allies, but their cruelties were invisible to me, and their partisans wrote all the books that fell into my hands.

It all seemed to take place right here, here among the blossoming rhododendrons outside the sunporch windows just below our bedroom, here in the Pittsburgh forest that rose again from every vacant lot, every corner of every yard the mower missed, every dusty crack in the sidewalk, every clogged gutter on the roof—an oak tree, a sycamore, a mountain ash, a pine.

For here, on the tip of the point where the three rivers met, the French built Fort Duquesne. It linked French holdings on the Great Lakes to their settlement at New Orleans. It was 1754; the forest was a wilderness. From Fort Duquesne the French set their Indian allies to raiding far-flung English-speaking settlements and homesteads. The Indians burned the farms and tortured many farm families. From Fort Duquesne the French marched out and defeated George Washington at nearby Fort Necessity. From Fort Duquesne the French marched out and defeated General Edward Braddock: Indian warriors shot from cover, which offended those British soldiers who had time to notice before they died. It was here in 1758 that General John Forbes established British hegemony over the Mississippi watershed, by driving the French from the point and building Fort Pitt.

Here our own doughty provincials in green hunting shirts fought beside regiments of rangers in buckskins, actual Highlanders in kilts, pro-English Iroquois in warpaint, and

British regulars in red jackets. They came marching vividly through the virgin Pittsburgh forest; they trundled up and down the nearby mountain ridges by day and slept at night on their weapons under trees. Pioneer scouts ran ahead of them and behind them; messengers snuck into their few palisaded forts, where periwigged English officers sat and rubbed their foreheads while naked Indians in the treetops outside were setting arrows on fire to burn down the roof.

Best, it was all imaginary. That the French and Indian War took place in this neck of the woods merely enhanced its storied quality, as if that fact had been a particularly pleasing literary touch. This war was part of my own private consciousness, the dreamlike interior murmur of books.

Costumed enormous people, transparent, vivid, and bold as decals, as tall and rippling as people in dreams, shot at each other up and down the primeval woods, race against race. Just as people in myths travel rigidly up to the sky, or are placed there by some great god's fingers, to hold still forever in the midst of their loving or battles as fixed constellations of stars, so the fighting cast of the French and Indian War moved in a colorful body—locked into position in the landscape but still loading muskets or cowering behind the log door or landing canoes on a muddy shore—into books. They were fabulous and morally neutral, like everything in history, like everything in books. They were imagination's playthings: toy soldiers, toy settlers, toy Indians. They were a part of the interior life; they were private; they were my own.

In books these wars played themselves out ceaselessly; the red-warpainted Indian tomahawked the settler woman in calico, and the rangy settler in buckskin spied out the Frenchman in military braid. Whenever I opened the book, the war struck up again, like a record whose music sounded when the needle hit. The skirling of Highlanders' bagpipes came playing again, high and thin over the dry oak ridges. The towheaded pioneer schoolchildren were just blabbing their memorized psalms when from right outside the greased parchment window sounded the wild and fatal whoops of Indian warriors on a raid.

The wild and fatal whoops, the war whoops of the warriors, the red warriors whooping on a raid. It was a delirium. The tongue diddled the brain. Private life, book life, took place where words met imagination without passing through world.

I could dream it all whenever I wanted—and how often I wanted to dream it! Fiercely addicted, I dosed myself again and again with the drug of the dream.

Parents have no idea what the children are up to in their bedrooms: They are reading the same paragraphs over and over in a stupor of violent bloodshed. Their legs are limp with horror. They are reading the same paragraphs over and over, dizzy with gratification as the young lovers find each other in the French fort, as the boy avenges his father, as the sound of muskets in the woods signals the end of the siege. They could not move if the house caught fire. They hate the actual world. The actual world is a kind of tedious plane where dwells, and goes to school, the body, the boring body which houses the eyes to read the books and houses the heart the books enflame. The very boring body seems to require an inordinately big, very boring world to keep it up, a world where you have to spend far too much time, have to *do* time like a prisoner, always looking for a chance to slip away, to escape back home to books, or escape back home to any concentration—fanciful, mental, or physical—where you can lose your self at last. Although I was hungry all the time, I could not bear to hold still and eat; it was too dull a thing to do, and had no appeal either to courage or to imagination. The blinding sway of their inner lives makes children immoral. They find things good insofar as they are thrilling, insofar as they render them ever more feverish and breathless, ever more limp and senseless on the bed.

Throughout these long, wonderful wars, I saw Indian braves behind every tree and parked car. They slunk around, fairly bursting with woodcraft. They led soldiers on miraculous escapes through deep woods and across lakes at night; they paddled their clever canoes noiselessly; they swam underwater without leaving bubbles; they called to each other like owls. They nocked their arrows silently on the brow of the hill and snuck up in their soft moccasins to the camp where the enemy lay sleeping under heavy guard. They shrieked, drew their osage bows, and never missed—all the while communing deeply with birds and deer.

I had been born too late. I would have made a dandy scout, although I was hungry all the time, because I had taught myself, with my friend Pin, to walk in the woods silently: without snapping a twig, which was easy, or stepping on a loud leaf, which was hard. Experience taught me a special, rolling walk for skulking in silence: you step down with your weight on the ball of your foot, and ease it to your heel.

The Indians who captured me would not torture me, but would exclaim at my many abilities, and teach me more, all the while feeding me handsomely. Soon I would talk to animals, become invisible, ride a horse naked and shrieking, shoot things.

I practiced traveling through the woods in Frick Park without leaving footprints. I practiced tracking people and animals, such as the infamous pedigreed dachshunds, by following sign. I knew the mark of Walter Milligan's blunt heel and the mark of Amy's sharp one. I practiced sneaking up on Mother as she repotted a philodendron, Father as he washed the car, saying, as I hoped but doubted the Indians said, "Boo."

What does it feel like to be alive?

Living, you stand under a waterfall. You leave the sleeping shore deliberately; you shed your dusty clothes, pick your barefoot way over the high, slippery rocks, hold your breath, choose your footing, and step into the waterfall. The hard water pelts your skull, bangs in bits on your shoulders and arms. The strong water dashes down beside you and you feel it along your calves and thighs rising roughly back up, up to the roiling surface, full of bubbles that slide up your skin or break on you at full speed. Can you breathe here? Here where the force is greatest and only the strength of your neck holds the river out of your face? Yes, you can breathe even here. You could learn to live like this. And you can, if you concentrate, even look out at the peaceful far bank where maples grow straight and their leaves lean down. For a joke you try to raise your arms. What a racket in your ears, what a scattershot pummeling!

It is time pounding at you, time. Knowing you are alive is watching on every side your generation's short time falling away as fast as rivers drop through air, and feeling it hit.

Who turned on the lights? You did, by waking up: you flipped the light switch, started up the wind machine, kicked on the flywheel that spins the years. Can you catch hold of a treetop, or will you fly off the diving planet as she rolls? Can you ride out the big blow on a coconut palm's trunk until you fall asleep again, and the winds let up? You fall asleep again, and you slide in a dream to the palm tree's base; the winds die off, the lights dim, the years slip away as you idle there till you die in your sleep, till death sets you cruising down the Tamiami Trail.[2]

Knowing you are alive is feeling the planet buck under you, rear, kick, and try to throw you; you hang on to the ring. It is riding the planet like a log downstream, whooping. Or, conversely, you step aside from the dreaming fast loud routine and feel time as a stillness about you, and hear the silent air asking in so thin a voice, Have you noticed yet that you will die? Do you remember, remember, remember? Then you feel your life as a weekend, a weekend you cannot extend, a weekend in the country.

O Augenblick verweile.

---

2. The road between Tampa and Miami.

My friend Judy Schoyer was a thin, messy, shy girl whose thick blond curls lapped over her glasses. Her cheeks, chin, nose, and blue eyes were round; the lenses and frames of her glasses were round, and so were her heavy curls. Her long spine was supple; her legs were long and thin so her knee socks fell down. She did not care if her knee socks fell down. When I first knew her, as my classmate at the Ellis School, she sometimes forgot to comb her hair. She was so shy she tended not to move her head, but only let her eyes rove about. If my mother addressed her, or a teacher, she held her long-legged posture lightly, alert, like a fawn ready to bolt but hoping its camouflage will work a little longer.

Judy's family were members of the oldest, most liberal, and best-educated ranks of Pittsburgh society. They were Unitarians. I visited her Unitarian Sunday school once. There we folded paper to make little geese; it shocked me to the core. One of her linear ancestors, Edward Holyoke, had been president of Harvard University in the eighteenth century, which fact paled locally before the greater one, that her great-grandfather's brother had been one of the founding members of Pittsburgh's Duquesne Club. She was related also to Pittsburgh's own Stephen Foster.

Judy and her family passed some long weekends at a family farmhouse in the country on a little river, the nearest town to which was Paw Paw, West Virginia. When they were going to the farm, they said they were going to Paw Paw. The trip was a four-hour drive from Pittsburgh. Often they invited me along.

There in Paw Paw for the weekend I imagined myself in the distant future remembering myself now, twelve years old with Judy. We stood on the high swinging plank bridge over the river, in early spring, watching the first hatch of small flies hover below us.

The river was a tributary of the distant Potomac—a tributary so stony, level, and shallow that Judy's grandmother regularly drove her old Model A Ford right through it, while we hung out over the running boards to try and get wet. From above the river, from the hanging center of the swinging bridge, we could see the forested hill where the big house stood. There at the big house we would have dinner, and later look at the Gibson girls in the wide, smelly old books in the cavernous living room, only recently and erratically electrified.

And from the high swinging bridge we could see in the other direction the log cabin, many fields away from the big house, where we children stayed alone: Judy and I, and sometimes our friend Margaret, who had a dramatic, somewhat morbid flair and who wrote poetry, and Judy's good-natured younger brother. We cooked pancakes in the cabin's fireplace; we drew water in a bucket from the well outside the door.

By Friday night when we'd carried our duffel and groceries from the black Model A at the foot of the hill, or over the undulating bridge if the river was high, when we children had banged open the heavy log-cabin door, smelled the old logs and wood dust, found matches and lighted the kerosene lanterns, and in the dark outside had drawn ourselves a bucket of sweet water (feeling the rope go slack and hearing the bucket hit, then feeling the rope pull as the bucket tipped and filled), and hunted up wood for a fire, smelled the loamy nighttime forest again, and heard the whippoorwill—by that time on Friday night I was already grieving and mourning, only just unpacking my nightgown, because here it was practically Sunday afternoon and time to go.

"What you kids need," Mrs. Schoyer used to say, "is more exercise."

How exhilarating, how frightening to ride the tippy Model A over the shallow river to the farm at Paw Paw, to greet again in a new season the swaying bridge, the bare hills, the woods behind the log cabin, the hayloft in the barn—and know I had just so many hours. From the minute I set foot on that land across the river, I started ticking like a timer, fizzing like a fuse.

On Friday night in the log cabin at Paw Paw I watched the wild firelight on Judy's face as she laughed at something her cheerful brother said, laughed shyly even here. When she laughed, her cheeks rose and formed spheres. I loved her spherical cheeks and knocked myself out to make her laugh. I could hardly see her laughing eyes behind her glasses under hanging clumps of dark-blond curls. She was nimble, sway-backed, long-limbed, and languid as a heron, and as abrupt. In Pittsburgh she couldn't catch a ball—nearsighted; she perished of bashfulness at school sports. Here she could climb a tree after a kitten as smoothly as a squirrel could, and run down her nasty kicking pony with authority, and actually hit it, and scoop up running hens with both swift arms. She spoke softly and not often.

Judy treated me with amused tolerance. At school I was, if not a central personage, at least a conspicuous one; and I had boyfriends all along and got invited to the boys' school dances. Nevertheless, Judy put up with me, not I with Judy. She possessed a few qualities that, although they counted for nothing at school, counted, I had to admit, with me. Her goodness was both intrinsic and a held principle. This thin, almost speechless child had moral courage. She intended her own life—starting when she was about ten—to be not only harmless but good. I considered Judy's goodness, like Judy's farm, a nice place to visit. She put up with my fast-talking avoidance of anything that smacked of manual labor. That she was indulging me altogether became gradually clear to both of us—though I pretended I didn't know it, and Judy played along.

On Saturday mornings in Paw Paw we set out through the dewy fields. I could barely lay one foot before the other along the cowpath through the pasture, I was so nostalgic for this scene already, this day just begun, when Judy and I were twelve. With Margaret we boiled and ate blue river mussels; we wrote and staged a spidery melodrama. We tried to ride the wretched untrained pony, which scraped us off under trees. We chopped down a sassafras tree and made a dirty tea; and we started to clean a run-over snake, in order to make an Indian necklace from its delicate spine, but it smelled so bad we quit.

After Saturday-night dinner in the big-house dining room—its windows gave out on the cliffside treetops—Mr. Schoyer told us, in his calm, ironic voice, Victor Hugo's story of a French sailor who was commended for having heroically captured a cannon loose on the warship's deck, and then hanged for having loosed the cannon in the first place. There were usually a dozen or more of us around the table, rapt. When the household needed our help, Mrs. Schoyer made mild, wry suggestions, almost diffidently.

I would have liked going to prison with the Schoyers. My own family I loved with all my heart; the Schoyers fascinated me. They were not sharply witty but steadily wry. In Pittsburgh they invited foreigners to dinner. They went to art galleries, they heard the Pittsburgh Symphony. They weren't tan. Mr. Schoyer, who was a corporation lawyer, had majored in classical history and literature at Harvard. Like my father, he had studied something that had no direct bearing on the clatter of coin. He was always the bemused scholar, mild and democratic, posing us children friendly questions as if Pittsburgh or Paw Paw were Athens and he fully expected to drag from our infant brains the Pythagorean theorem. What do you make of our new President? Your position on capital punishment? Or, conversationally, after I had been branded as a lover of literature, "You recall that speech of Pericles, don't you?" or "Won't you join me in reading 'A Shropshire Lad' or 'Ballad of East and West'?" At Paw Paw the Schoyers did every wholesome thing but sing. None of them could carry a tune.

If there was no moon that night, we children took a flashlight down the steep dirt driveway from the big house and across the silvery pastures to the edge of the woods where the log cabin stood. The log cabin stayed empty, behind an old vine-hung gate, except when we came. In front of the cabin we drew water from the round stone well; under the cabin we put milk and butter in the old cellar, which was only a space dug in the damp black dirt—dirt against which the butter's wrap looked too thin.

That was the farm at Paw Paw, West Virginia. The farm lay far from the nearest highway, off three miles of dirt road. When at the end of the long darkening journey from Pittsburgh we turned down the dirt road at last, the Schoyers' golden retriever not unreasonably began to cry, and so, unreasonably, invisibly, did I. Some years when the Schoyers asked me to join them I declined miserably, refused in a swivet, because I couldn't tolerate it, I loved the place so.

I knew what I was doing at Paw Paw: I was beginning the lifelong task of tuning my own gauges. I was there to brace myself for leaving. I was having my childhood. But I was haunting it as well, practically reading it, and preventing it. How much noticing could I permit myself without driving myself round the bend? Too much noticing and I was too self-conscious to live; I trapped and paralyzed myself, and dragged my friends down with me, so we couldn't meet each other's eyes, my own loud awareness damning us both. Too little noticing, though—I would risk much to avoid this—and I would miss the whole show. I would wake on my deathbed and say, What was that?

Everywhere, things snagged me. The visible world turned me curious to books; the books propelled me reeling back to the world.

At school I saw a searing sight. It turned me to books; it turned me to jelly; it turned me much later, I suppose, into an early version of a runaway, a scapegrace. It was only a freshly hatched Polyphemus moth crippled because its mason jar was too small.

The mason jar sat on the teacher's desk; the big moth emerged inside it. The moth had clawed a hole in its hot cocoon and crawled out, as if agonizingly, over the course of an hour, one leg at a time; we children watched around the desk, tranfixed.

After it emerged, the wet, mashed thing turned around walking on the green jar's bottom, then painstakingly climbed the twig with which the jar was furnished.

There, at the twig's top, the moth shook its sodden clumps of wings. When it spread those wings—those beautiful wings—blood would fill their veins, and the birth fluids on the wings' frail sheets would harden to make them tough as sails. But the moth could not spread its wide wings at all; the jar was too small. The wings could not fill, so they hardened while they were still crumpled from the cocoon. A smaller moth could have spread its wings to their utmost in that mason jar, but the Polyphemus moth was big. Its gold furred body was almost as big as a mouse. Its brown, yellow, pink, and blue wings would have extended six inches from tip to tip, if there had been no mason jar. It would have been big as a wren.

The teacher let the deformed creature go. We all left the classroom and paraded outside behind the teacher with pomp and circumstance. She bounced the moth from its jar and set it on the school's asphalt driveway. The moth set out walking. It could only heave the golden wrinkly clumps where its wings should have been; it could only crawl down the school driveway on its six frail legs. The moth crawled down the driveway toward the rest of Shadyside, an area of fine houses, expensive apartments, and fashionable shops. It crawled down the driveway because its shriveled wings were glued shut. It crawled down the driveway toward Shadyside, one of several sections of town where people like me were expected to settle after college, renting an apartment until they married one of the boys and bought a house. I watched it go.

I knew that this particular moth, the big walking moth, could not travel more than a few more yards before a bird or a cat began to eat it, or a car ran over it. Nevertheless, it was crawling with what seemed wonderful vigor, as if, I thought at the time, it was still excited from being born. I watched it go till the bell rang and I had to go in. I have told this story before, and may yet tell it again, to lay the moth's ghost, for I still see it

crawl down the broad black driveway, and I still see its golden
wing clumps heave.

I had not suspected, among other things, that moths came so
big. From a school library book I learned there were several
such enormous American moths, all wild silk moths which spun
cocoons, and all common.

Gene Stratton Porter's old *Moths of the Limberlost* caught
my eye; for some years after I read it, it was my favorite book.
From one of its queer painted photographs I learned what the
Polyphemus moth would have looked like whole: it was an
unexpected sort of beauty, brown and wild. It had pink stripes,
lavender crescents, yellow ovals—all sorts of odd colors no one
would think to combine. Enormous blue eye-spots stared eerily
from its hind wings. Coincidentally, it was in the Polyphemus
chapter that the book explained how a hatched moth must
spread its wings quickly, and fill them with blood slowly, before
it can fly.

Gene Stratton Porter had been a vigorous, loving kid who
grew up long ago near a swampy wilderness of Indiana, and had
worked up a whole memorable childhood out of insects, of all
things, which I had never even noticed, and my childhood was
half over.

When she was just a tot, she learned how entomologists carry
living moths and butterflies without damaging them. She commonly carried a moth or butterfly home from her forest and
swamp wanderings by lightly compressing its thorax between
thumb and index finger. The insect stops moving but is not hurt;
when you let it go, it flies away.

One day, after years of searching, she found a yellow swallowtail. This is not the common tiger swallowtail butterfly, but
Papilio turnus: "the largest, most beautiful butterfly I had ever
seen." She held it carefully in the air, its wings high over the
back of her fingers. She wanted to show the fragile, rare creature to her father and then carry it back to precisely where she
found it. But she was only a child, and so she came running

home with it instead of walking. She tripped, and her fingers pinched through the butterfly's thorax. She broke it to pieces. And that was that. It was like one of Father's bar jokes.

⌒

I intended to live the way the microbe hunters lived. I wanted to work. Hard work on an enormous scale was the microbe hunters' stock-in-trade. They took a few clear, time-consuming steps and solved everything. In those early days of germ theory, large disease-causing organisms, whose cycles traced straight-forward patterns, yielded and fell to simple procedures. I would know just what to do. I would seize on the most casual remarks of untutored milkmaids. When an untutored milkmaid remarked to me casually, "Oh, everyone knows you won't get the smallpox if you've had the cowpox," I would perk right up.

Microbe Hunters sent me to a biography of Louis Pasteur. Pasteur's was the most enviable life I had yet encountered. It was his privilege to do things until they were done. He established the germ theory of disease; he demonstrated convincingly that yeasts ferment beer; he discovered how to preserve wine; he isolated the bacillus in a disease of silkworms; he demonstrated the etiology of anthrax and produced a vaccine for it; he halted an epidemic of cholera in fowls and inoculated a boy for hydrophobia. Toward the end of his life, in a rare idle moment, he chanced to read some of his early published papers and exclaimed (someone overheard), "How beautiful! And to think that I did it all!" The tone of this exclamation was, it seemed to me, astonished and modest, for he had genuinely forgotten, moving on.

Pasteur had not used up all the good work. Mother told me again and again about one of her heroes, a doctor working for a federal agency who solved a problem that arose in the late for-ties. Premature babies, and only premature babies, were turning up blind, in enormous numbers. Why? What do premature babies have in common?

"Look in the incubators!" Mother would holler, and knock the side of her head with the heel of her hand, holler outraged, glaring far behind my head as she was telling me this story, holler, "Look in the incubators!" as if at her wit's end facing a roomful of doctors who wrung their useless hands and accepted this blindness as one of life's tough facts. Mother's hero, like all of Mother's heroes, accepted nothing. She rolled up her sleeves, looked in the incubators, and decided to see what happened if she reduced the oxygen in the incubator air. That worked. Too much oxygen had been blinding them. Now the babies thrived; they got enough oxygen, and they weren't blinded. Hospitals all over the world changed the air mixture for incubators, and prematurity no longer carried a special risk of blindness.

Mother liked this story, and told it to us fairly often. Once she posed it as a challenge to Amy. We were all in the living room, waiting for dinner. "What would you do if you noticed that all over the United States, premature babies were blind?" Without even looking up from her homework, Amy said, "Look in the incubators. Maybe there's something wrong in the incubators." Mother started to whoop for joy before she realized she'd been had.

Problems still yielded to effort. Only a few years ago, to the wide-eyed attention of the world, we had seen the epidemic of poliomyelitis crushed in a twinkling, right here in Pittsburgh.

We had all been caught up in the polio epidemic: the early neighbor boy who wore one tall shoe, to which his despairing father added another two soles every year; the girl in the iron lung reading her schoolbook in an elaborate series of mirrors while a volunteer waited to turn the page; my friend who limped, my friend who rolled everywhere in a wheelchair, my friend whose arm hung down, Mother's friend who walked with crutches. My beloved dressed-up aunt, Mother's sister, had come to visit one day and, while she was saying hello, flung herself on the couch in tears; her son had it. Just a touch, they said, but who could believe it?

When Amy and I had asked, Why do we have to go to bed so early? Why do we have to wash our hands again? we knew Mother would kneel to look us in the eyes and answer in a low, urgent voice, So you do not get polio. We heard polio discussed once or twice a day for several years.

And we had all been caught up in its prevention, in the wild ferment of the early days of the Salk vaccine, the vaccine about which Pittsburgh talked so much, and so joyously, you could probably have heard the crowd noise on the moon.

In 1953, Jonas Salk's Virus Research Laboratory at the University of Pittsburgh had produced a controversial vaccine for polio. The small stories in the Pittsburgh *Press* and the *Post-Gazette* were coming out in *Life* and *Time*. It was too quick, said medical colleagues nationwide: Salk had gone public without first publishing everything in the journals. He rushed out a killed-virus serum without waiting for a safe live-virus one, which would probably be better. Doctors walked out of professional meetings; some quit the foundation that funded the testing. Salk was after personal glory, they said. Salk was after money, they said. Salk was after big prizes.

Salk tested the serum on five thousand Pittsburgh schoolchildren, of whom I was three, because I kept changing elementary schools. Our parents, like ninety-five percent of all Pittsburgh parents, signed the consent forms. Did the other mothers then bend over the desk in relief and sob? I don't know. But I don't suppose any of them gave much of a damn what Salk had been after.

When Pasteur died, near a place wonderfully called Saint-Cloud, he murmured to the devoted assistants who surrounded his bed, *"Il faut travailler."*

Il faut indeed *travailler*—no one who grew up in Pittsburgh could doubt it. And no one who grew up in Pittsburgh could doubt that the great work was ongoing. We breathed in optimism—not coal dust—with every breath. What couldn't be done with good hard *travail*?

The air in Pittsburgh had been dirty; now we could see it was clean. An enormous, pioneering urban renewal was under way; the newspapers pictured fantastic plans, airy artists' water-colors, which we soon saw laid out and built up in steel and glass downtown. The Republican Richard King Mellon had approached Pittsburgh's Democratic, Catholic mayor, David L. Lawrence, and together with a dozen business leaders they were razing the old grim city and building a sparkling new one; they were washing the very air. The Russians had shot Sputnik into outer space. In Shippingport, just a few miles down the Ohio River, people were building a generating plant that used atomic energy—an idea that seemed completely dreamy, but there it was. A physicist from Bell Laboratories spoke to us at school about lasers; he was about as wrought up a man as I had ever seen. You could not reasonably believe a word he said, but you could see that he believed it.

We knew that "Doctor Salk" had spent many years and many dollars to produce the vaccine. He commonly worked sixteen-hour days, six days a week. Of course. In other laboratories around the world, other researchers were working just as hard, as hard as Salk and Pasteur. Hard work bore fruit. This is what we learned growing up in Pittsburgh, growing up in the United States.

Salk had isolated seventy-four strains of polio virus. It took him three years to verify the proposition that a workable vaccine would need samples of only three of these strains. He grew the virus in tissues cultured from monkey kidneys. The best broth for growing the monkey tissue proved to be Medium Number 199; it contained sixty-two ingredients in careful proportion.

This was life itself: the big task. Nothing exhilarated me more than the idea of a life dedicated to a monumental worthwhile task. Doctor Salk never watched it rain and wished he had never been born. How many shovelfuls of dirt did men move to dig the Panama Canal? Two hundred and forty million cubic yards. It took ten years and twenty-one thousand lives and $336,650,000, but it was possible.

I thought a great deal about the Panama Canal, and always contemplated the same notion: You could take more time, and do it with teaspoons. I saw myself and a few Indian and Caribbean coworkers wielding teaspoons from our kitchen: Towle, Rambling Rose. And our grandchildren, and their grandchildren. Digging the canal across the isthmus at Panama would tear through a good many silver spoons. But it could be done, in theory and therefore in fact. It was like Mount Rushmore, or Grand Coulee Dam. You hacked away at the landscape and made something, or you did not do anything, and just died.

How many filaments had Thomas Edison tried, over how many years, before he found one workable for incandescence? How many days and nights over how many years had Marie Curie labored in a freezing shed to isolate radium? I read a biography of George Washington Carver: so many years on the soybean, the peanut, the sweet potato, the waste from ginning cotton. I read biographies of Abraham Lincoln, Thomas Edison, Daniel Boone.

It was all the same story. You have a great idea and spend grinding years at dull tasks, still charged by your vision. All the people about whom biographies were not written were people who failed to find something that took years to do. People could count the grains of sand. In my own life, as a sideline, and for starters, I would learn all the world's languages.

What if people said it could not be done? So much the better. We grew up with the myth of the French Impressionist painters, and its queer implication that rejection and ridicule guaranteed, or at any rate signaled, a project's worth. When little George Westinghouse at last figured out how to make air brakes, Cornelius Vanderbilt of the New York Central Railroad said to him, "Do you mean to tell me with a straight face that a moving train can be stopped with wind?" "They laughed at Orville," Mother used to say when someone tried to talk her out of a wild scheme, "and they laughed at Wilbur."

I had small experience of the evil hopelessness, pain, starvation, and terror that the world spread about; I had barely seen people's malice and greed. I believed that in civilized countries, torture had ended with the Enlightenment. Of nations' cruel options I knew nothing. My optimism was endless; it grew sky-high within the narrow bounds of my isolationism. Because I was all untried courage, I could not allow that the loss of courage was a real factor to be reckoned in. I put my faith in willpower, that weak notion by which children seek to replace the loving devotion that comes from intimate and dedicated knowledge. I believed that I could resist aging by willpower.

I believed then, too, that I would never harm anyone. I usually believed I would never meet a problem I could not solve. I would overcome any weakness, any despair, any fear. Hadn't I overcome my fear of the ghosty oblong that coursed round my room, simply by thinking it through? Everything was simple. You found good work, learned all about it, and did it.

Questions of how to act were also transparent to reason. Right and wrong were easy to discern: I was right, and Amy was wrong. Many of my classmates stole things, but I did not. Sometimes, in a very tight spot, when at last I noticed I had a moral question on my hands, I asked myself, What would Christ have done? I had picked up this method (very much on the sly—we were not supposed really to believe these things) from Presbyterian Sunday school, from summer camp, or from any of the innumerable righteous orange-bound biographies I read. I had not known it to fail in the two times I had applied it.

As for loss, as for parting, as for bidding farewell, so long, thanks, to love or a land or a time—what did I know of parting, of grieving, mourning, loss? Well, I knew one thing; I had known it all along. I knew it was the kicker. I knew life pulled you in two; you never healed. Mother's emotions ran high, and she suffered sometimes from a web of terrors, because, she said, her father died when she was seven; she still missed him.

My parents played the Cole Porter song "It's All Right with Me." When Ella Fitzgerald sang, "There's someone I'm trying so hard to forget—don't you want to forget someone too?," these facile, breathy lyrics struck me as an unexpectedly true expression of how it felt to be alive. This was experience at its most private and inarticulate: longing and loss. "It's the wrong time, it's the wrong place, though your face is charming, it's the wrong face." I was a thirteen-year-old child; I had no one to miss, had lost no one. Yet I suspect most children feel this way, probably all children feel this way, as adults do; they mourn this absence or loss of someone, and sense that unnameable loss as a hole or hollow moving beside them in the air.

Loss came around with the seasons, blew into the house when you opened the windows, piled up in the bottom desk and dresser drawers, accumulated in the back of closets, heaped in the basement starting by the furnace, and came creeping up the basement stairs. Loss grew as you did, without your consent; your losses mounted beside you like earthworm castings. No willpower could prevent someone's dying. And no willpower could restore someone dead, breathe life into that frame and set it going again in the room with you to meet your eyes. That was the fact of it. The strongest men and women who had ever lived had presumably tried to resist their own deaths, and now they were dead. It was on this fact that all the stirring biographies coincided, concurred, and culminated.

Time itself bent you and cracked you on its wheel. We were getting ready to move again. I knew I could not forever keep riding my bike backward into ever-older neighborhoods to look the ever-older houses in the face. I tried to memorize the layout of this Richland Lane house, but I couldn't force it into my mind while it was still in my bones.

I saw already that I could not in good faith renew the increasingly desperate series of vows by which I had always tried to direct my life. I had vowed to love Walter Milligan forever; now I could recall neither his face nor my feeling, but only this quondam urgent vow. I had vowed to keep exploring Pittsburgh by bicycle no matter how old I got, and planned an especially sweeping tour for my hundredth birthday in 2045. I had vowed to keep hating Amy in order to defy Mother, who kept prophesying I would someday not hate Amy. In short, I always vowed, one way or another, not to change. Not me. I needed the fierceness of vowing because I could scarcely help but notice, visiting the hatchling robins at school every day, that it was mighty unlikely.

As a life's work, I would remember everything—everything, against loss. I would go through life like a plankton net. I would trap and keep every teacher's funny remark, every face on the street, every microscopic alga's sway, every conversation, configuration of leaves, every dream, and every scrap of overhead cloud. Who would remember Molly's infancy if not me? (Unaccountably, I thought that only I had noticed—not Molly, but time itself. No one else, at least, seemed bugged by it. Children may believe that they alone have interior lives.)

Some days I felt an urgent responsibility to each change of light outside the sunporch windows. Who would remember any of it, any of this our time, and the wind thrashing the buckeye limbs outside? Somebody had to do it, somebody had to hang on to the days with teeth and fists, or the whole show had been in vain. That it was impossible never entered my reckoning. For work, for a task, I had never heard the word.

As a child I read hoping to learn everything, so I could be like my father. I hoped to combine my father's grasp of information and reasoning with my mother's will and vitality. But the books were leading me away. They would propel me right out of Pittsburgh altogether, so I could fashion a life among books somewhere else. So the Midwest nourishes us (Pittsburgh is the Midwest's eastern edge) and presents us with the spectacle of a land and a people completed and certain. And so we run to our bedrooms and read in a fever, and love the big hardwood trees outside the windows, and the terrible Midwest summers, and the terrible Midwest winters, and the forested river valleys with the blue Appalachian Mountains to the east of us and the broad great plains to the west. And so we leave it sorrowfully, have grown strong and restless by opposing with all our will and mind and muscle its simple, loving, single will for us: that we stay, that we stay and find a place among its familiar possibilities. Mother knew we would go; she encouraged us.

I had awakened again, awakened from my drawing and reading, from my exhilarating game playing, from my intense collecting and experimenting, and my cheerful friendships, to see on every side of me a furious procession of which I had been entirely unaware. A procession of fast-talking, keen-eyed, high-stepping, well-dressed men and women of all ages had apparently hoisted me, or shanghaied me, some time ago, and were bearing me breathless along I knew not where. This was the startling world in which I found that I had been living all along. Packed into the procession, I pedaled to keep up, but my feet only rarely hit the ground.

The pace of school life quickened, its bounds tightened, and a new kind of girl emerged from the old. The old-style girl was obedient and tidy. The new-style girl was witty and casual. It was a small school, twenty in a class. We all knew who mattered, not only in our class but in the whole school. The teachers knew, too.

In summer we girls commonly greeted each other, after a perfunctory hello, by extending our forearms side by side to compare tans. We were blond, we were tan, our teeth were white and straightened, our legs were brown and depilated, our blue eyes glittered pale in our dark faces; we laughed; we shuffled the cards fast and dealt four hands. It was not for me. I hated it so passionately I thought my shoulders and arms, swinging at the world, would split off from my body like loose spinning blades, and fly wild and slice everyone up. With all my heart, sometimes, I longed for the fabled Lower East Side of

Manhattan, for Brooklyn, for the Bronx, where the thoughtful and feeling people in books grew up on porch stoops among seamstress intellectuals. There I belonged if anywhere, there where the book people were—recent Jewish immigrants, everybody deep every livelong minute. I could just see them, sitting there feeling deeply. Here, instead, I saw polished fingernails clicking, rings flashing, gold bangle bracelets banging and ringing together as sixteen-year-old girls like me pushed their cuticles back, as they ran combs through their just-washed, just-cut, just-set hair, as they lighted Marlboros with hard snaps of heavy lighters, and talked about other girls or hair. It never crossed my mind that you can't guess people's lives from their chatter.

This was the known world. Women volunteered, organized the households, and reared the kids; they kept the traditions, and taught by example a dozen kinds of love. Mother polished the brass, wiped the ashtrays, stood barefoot on the couch to hang a picture. Margaret Butler washed the windows, which seemed to yelp. Mother dusted and polished the big philodendrons, tenderly, leaf by leaf, as if she were washing babies' faces. Margaret came sighing down the stairs with an armful of laundry or wastebaskets. Mother inspected the linens for a party; she fetched from a closet the folding felted boards she laid over the table. Margaret turned on the vacuum cleaner again. Mother and Margaret changed the sheets and pillowcases.

Then Margaret left. I had taken by then to following her from room to room, trying to get her to spill the beans about being black; she kept moving. Nothing changed. Mother wiped the stove; she ran the household with her back to it. You heard a staccato in her voice, and saw the firm force of her elbow, as she pressed hard on a dried tan dot of bean soup, and finally took a fingernail to it, while quizzing Amy about a car pool to dancing school, and me about a ride back from a game. No page of any book described housework, and no one mentioned it; it didn't exist. There was no such thing.

A woman at our country club, a prominent figure at our church, whose daughters went to Ellis, never washed her face all summer, to preserve her tan. We rarely saw the pale men at all; they were off pulling down the money on which the whole scene floated. Most men came home exhausted in their gray suits to scantily clad women smelling of Bain de Soleil, and do-nothing tanned kids in Madras shorts.

There was real beauty to the old idea of living and dying where you were born. You could hold a place in a kind of eternity. Your grandparents took you out to dinner Sunday nights at the country club, and you could take your own grandchildren there when that time came: more little towheads, as squint-eyed and bony-legged and Scotch-Irish as hillbillies. And those grandchildren, like figures in a reel endlessly unreeling, would partake of the same timeless, hushed, muffled sensations.

They would join the buffet line on Sunday nights in winter at the country club. I remember: the club lounges before dinner dimly lighted and opulent like the church; the wool rugs absorbing footsteps; the lined damask curtains lapping thickly across tall, leaded-glass windows. The adults drank old-fashioneds. The fresh-haired children subsisted on bourbon-soaked maraschino cherries, orange slices, and ice cubes. They roved the long club corridors in slippery shoes; they opened closet doors, tried to get outside, laughed so hard they spit their ice cubes, and made sufficient commotion to rouse the adults to dinner. In the big dining room, layers of fine old unstarched linen draped the tables as thickly as hospital beds. Heavy-bottomed glasses sank into the tablecloths soundlessly.

And sempiternal too were the summer dinners at the country club, the sun-shocked people somnambulistic as angels. The children's grandchildren could see it. Space and light multiplied the club rooms; the damask curtains were heaved back; the French doors now gave out onto a flagstone terrace overlooking the swimming pool, near the sixth hole. On the terrace, men and women drank frozen daiquiris, or the unvarying Scotch, and their crystal glasses clicked on the glass tabletops, and then stuck in pools of condensation as if held magnetically, so they had to skid the glasses across the screeching tabletops to the edges in order to raise them at all. The cast-iron chair legs, painted white, marked and chipped the old flagstones, and dug up the interstitial grass.

The dressed children on the terrace looked with longing down on the tanned and hilarious children below. The children below wouldn't leave the pool, although it was seven-thirty; they knew no parent would actually shout at them from the flagstone terrace above. When these poolside children jumped in the water, the children on the terrace above could see their shimmering gray bodies against the blue pool. The water knit a fabric of light over their lively torsos and limbs, a loose gold chain mail. They looked like fish swimming in wide gold nets.

The children above were sunburnt, and their cotton dresses scraped their shoulders. The outsides of their skins felt hot, and the insides felt cold, and they tried to warm one arm with another. In summer, no one drank old-fashioneds, so there was nothing for children to eat till dinner.

This was the world we knew best—this, and Oma's. Oma's world was no likely alternative to ours; Oma had a chauffeur and her chauffeur had to drink from his own glass.

When I was fifteen, I felt it coming; now I was sixteen, and it hit.

My feet had imperceptibly been set on a new path, a fast path into a long tunnel like those many turnpike tunnels near Pittsburgh, turnpike tunnels whose entrances bear on brass plaques a roll call of those men who died blasting them. I wandered witlessly forward and found myself going down, and saw the light dimming; I adjusted to the slant and dimness, traveled further down, adjusted to greater dimness, and so on. There wasn't a whole lot I could do about it, or about anything. I was going to hell on a handcart, that was all, and I knew it and everyone around me knew it, and there it was.

I was growing and thinning, as if pulled. I was getting angry, as if pushed. I morally disapproved most things in North America, and blamed my innocent parents for them. My feelings deepened and lingered. The swift moods of early childhood—each formed by and suited to its occasion—vanished. Now feelings lasted so long they left stains. They arose from nowhere, like winds or waves, and battered at me or engulfed me.

When I was angry, I felt myself coiled and longing to kill someone or bomb something big. Trying to appease myself, during one winter I whipped my bed every afternoon with my uniform belt. I despised the spectacle I made in my own eyes—whipping the bed with a belt, like a creature demented!— and I often began halfheartedly, but I did it daily after school as a desperate discipline, trying to rid myself and the innocent world of my wildness. It was like trying to beat back the ocean.

Sometimes in class I couldn't stop laughing; things were too funny to be borne. It began then, my surprise that no one else saw what was so funny.

I read some few books with such reverence I didn't close them at the finish, but only moved the pile of pages back to the start, without breathing, and began again. I read one such book, an enormous novel, six times that way—closing the binding between sessions, but not between readings.

On the piano in the basement I played the maniacal "Poet and Peasant Overture" so loudly, for so many hours, night after night, I damaged the piano's keys and strings. When I wasn't playing this crashing overture, I played boogie-woogie, or something else, anything else, in octaves—otherwise, it wasn't loud enough. My fingers were so strong I could do push-ups with them. I played one piece with my fists. I banged on a steel-stringed guitar till I bled, and once on a particularly piercing rock-and-roll downbeat I broke straight through one of Father's snare drums.

I loved my boyfriend so tenderly, I thought I must transmogrify into vapor. It would take spectroscopic analysis to locate my molecules in thin air. No possible way of holding him was close enough. Nothing could cure this bad case of gentleness except, perhaps, violence: maybe if he swung me by the legs and split my skull on a tree? Would that ease my insane wish to kiss too much his eyelids' outer corners and his temples, as if I could love up his brain?

I envied people in books who swooned. For two years I felt myself continuously swooning and continuously unable to swoon; the blood drained from my face and eyes and flooded my heart; my hands emptied, my knees unstrung, I bit at the air for something worth breathing—but I failed to fall, and I couldn't find the way to black out. I had to live on the lip of a waterfall, exhausted.

When I was bored I was first hungry, then nauseated, then furious and weak. "Calm yourself," people had been saying to me all my life. Since early childhood I had tried one thing and then another to calm myself, on those few occasions when I truly wanted to. Eating helped; singing helped. Now sometimes I truly wanted to calm myself. I couldn't lower my shoulders; they seemed to wrap around my ears. I couldn't lower my voice although I could see the people around me flinch. I waved my arm in class till the very teachers wanted to kill me.

I was what they called a live wire. I was shooting out sparks that were digging a pit around me, and I was sinking into that pit. Laughing with Ellin at school recess, or driving around after school with Judy in her jeep, exultant, or dancing with my boyfriend to Louis Armstrong across a polished dining-room floor, I got so excited I looked around wildly for aid; I didn't know where I should go or what I should do with myself. People in books split wood.

When rage or boredom reappeared, each seemed never to have left. Each so filled me with so many years' intolerable accumulation it jammed the space behind my eyes, so I couldn't see. There was no room left even on my surface to live. My rib cage was so taut I couldn't breathe. Every cubic centimeter of atmosphere above my shoulders and head was heaped with last straws. Black hatred clogged my very blood. I couldn't peep, I couldn't wiggle or blink; my blood was too mad to flow.

For as long as I could remember, I had been transparent to myself, unselfconscious, learning, doing, most of every day. Now I was in my own way; I myself was a dark object I could not ignore. I couldn't remember how to forget myself. I didn't want to think about myself, to reckon myself in, to deal with myself every livelong minute on top of everything else—but swerve as I might, I couldn't avoid it. I was a boulder blocking my own path. I was a dog barking between my own ears, a barking dog who wouldn't hush.

So this was adolescence. Is this how the people around me had died on their feet—inevitably, helplessly? Perhaps their own selves eclipsed the sun for so many years the world shriveled around them, and when at last their inescapable orbits had passed through these dark egoistic years it was too late, they had adjusted.

Must I then lose the world forever, that I had so loved? Was it all, the whole bright and various planet, where I had been so ardent about finding myself alive, only a passion peculiar to children, that I would outgrow even against my will?

∞

I quit the church. I wrote the minister a fierce letter. The assistant minister, kindly Dr. James H. Blackwood, called me for an appointment. My mother happened to take the call.

"Why," she asked, "would he be calling you?" I was in the kitchen after school. Mother was leaning against the pantry door, drying a crystal bowl.

"What, Mama? Oh. Probably," I said, "because I wrote him a letter and quit the church."

"You—what?" She began to slither down the doorway, weak-kneed, like Lucille Ball. I believe her whole life passed before her eyes.

As I climbed the stairs after dinner I heard her moan to Father, "She wrote the minister a letter and quit the church."

"She—what?"

Father knocked on the door of my room. I was the only person in the house with her own room. Father ducked under the doorway, entered, and put his hands in his khakis' pockets. "Hi, Daddy." Actually, it drove me nuts when people came in my room. Mother had come in just last week. My room was getting to be quite the public arena. Pretty soon they'd put it on the streetcar routes. Why not hold the U.S. Open here? I was on the bed, in uniform, trying to read a book. I sat up and folded my hands in my lap.

I knew that Mother had made him come—"She listens to you." He had undoubtedly been trying to read a book, too.

Father looked around, but there wasn't much to see. My rock collection was no longer in evidence. A framed tiger swallowtail, spread and only slightly askew on white cotton, hung on a yellowish wall. On the mirror I'd taped a pencil portrait of Rupert Brooke; he was looking off softly. Balanced on top of the mirror were some yellow-and-black FALLOUT SHELTER signs, big aluminum ones, which Judy had collected as part of her antiwar effort. On the pale maple desk there were, among other books and papers, an orange thesaurus, a blue three-ring binder with a boy's name written all over it in every typeface, a green assignment notebook, and Emerson's *Essays*.

Father began, with some vigor: "What was it you said in this brilliant letter?" He went on: But didn't I see? That people did these things—quietly? Just—quietly? No fuss? No flamboyant gestures. No uncalled-for letters. He was forced to conclude that I was deliberately setting out to humiliate Mother and him.

"And your poor sisters, too!" Mother added feelingly from the hall outside my closed door. She must have been passing at that very moment. Then, immediately, we all heard a hideous shriek ending in a wail; it came from my sisters' bathroom. Had Molly cut off her head? It set us all back a moment—me on the bed, Father standing by my desk, Mother outside the closed door—until we all realized it was Amy, mad at her hair. Like me, she was undergoing a trying period, years long; she, on her part, was mad at her hair. She screeched at it in the mirror; the sound carried all over the house, kitchen, attic, basement, everywhere, and terrified all the rest of us, every time.

Funny how badly I'd turned out. Now I was always in trouble. It felt as if I was doing just as I'd always done—I explored the neighborhood, turning over rocks. The latest rocks were difficult. I'd been in a drag race, of all things, the previous September, and in the subsequent collision, and in the hospital; my parents saw my name in the newspapers, and their own names in the newspapers. Some boys I barely knew had cruised by that hot night and said to a clump of us girls on the sidewalk, "Anybody want to come along for a drag race?" I did, absolutely. I loved fast driving.

It was then, in the days after the drag race, that I noticed the ground spinning beneath me, all bearings lost, and recognized as well that I had been loose like this—detached from all I saw and knowing nothing else—for months, maybe years. I whirled through the air like a bull-roarer spun by a lunatic who'd found his rhythm. The pressure almost split my skin. What else can you risk with all your might but your life? Only a moment ago I was climbing my swing set, holding one cold metal leg between my two legs tight, and feeling a piercing oddness run the length of my gut—the same sensation that plucked me when my tongue touched tarnish on a silver spoon. Only a moment ago I was gluing squares of paper to rocks; I leaned over the bedroom desk. I was drawing my baseball mitt in the attic, under the plaster-stain ship; a pencil study took all Saturday morning. I was capturing the flag, turning the double play, chasing butterflies by the country-club pool. Throughout these many years of childhood, a transparent sphere of timelessness contained all my running and spinning as a glass paperweight holds flying snow. The sphere of this idyll broke; time unrolled before me in a line. I woke up and found myself in juvenile court. I was hanging from crutches; for a few weeks after the drag race, neither knee worked. (No one else got hurt.) In juvenile court, a policeman wet all ten of my fingertips on an ink pad and pressed them, one by one, using his own fingertips, on a form for the files.

Turning to the French is a form of suicide for the American who loves literature—or, as the joke might go, it is at least a cry for help. Now, when I was sixteen, I had turned to the French. I flung myself into poetry as into Niagara Falls. Beauty took away my breath. I twined away; I flew off with my eyes rolled up; I dove down and succumbed. I bought myself a plot in Valéry's marine cemetery, and moved in: cool dirt on my eyes, my brain smooth as a cannonball. It grieves me to report that I tried to see myself as a sobbing fountain, apparently serene, tall and thin among the chill marble monuments of the dead. Rimbaud wrote a lyric that gently described a man sleeping out in the grass; the sleeper made a peaceful picture, until, in the poem's last line, we discover in his right side two red holes. This, and many another literary false note, appealed to me.

I'd been suspended from school for smoking cigarettes. That was a month earlier, in early spring. Both my parents wept. Amy saw them weeping; horrified, she began to cry herself. Molly cried. She was six, missing her front teeth. Like Mother and me, she had pale skin that turned turgid and red when she cried; she looked as if she were dying of wounds. I didn't cry, because, actually, I was an intercontinental ballistic missile, with an atomic warhead; they don't cry.

Why didn't I settle down, straighten out, shape up? I wondered, too. I thought that joy was a childish condition that had forever departed; I had no glimpse then of its return the minute I got to college. I couldn't foresee the pleasure—or the possibility—of shedding sophistication, walking away from rage, and renouncing French poets.

While I was suspended from school, my parents grounded me. During that time, Amy began to visit me in my room.

When she was thirteen, Amy's beauty had grown inconspicuous; she seemed merely pleasant-looking and tidy. Her green uniform jumper fit her neatly; her thick hair was smoothly turned under; her white McMullen collars looked sweet. She had a good eye for the right things; people respected her for it. I think that only we at home knew how spirited she could get. "Oh, no!" she cried when she laughed hard. "Oh, no!" Amy adored our father, rather as we all did, from afar. She liked boys whose eyebrows met over their noses. She liked boys, emphatically; she followed boys with her big eyes, awed.

In my room, Amy listened to me rant; she reported her grade's daily gossip, laughed at my jokes, cried, "Oh, no!" and told me about the book she was reading, Wilkie Collins, *The Woman in White*. I liked people to tell me about the books they were reading. Next year, Amy was going to boarding school in Philadelphia; Mother had no intention of subjecting the family to two adolescent maelstroms whirling at once in the same house.

Late one night, my parents and I sat at the kitchen table; there was a truce. We were all helpless, and tired of fighting. Amy and Molly were asleep.

"What are we going to do with you?"

Mother raised the question. Her voice trembled and rose with emotion. She couldn't sit still; she kept getting up and roaming around the kitchen. Father stuck out his chin and rubbed it with his big hands. I covered my eyes. Mother squeezed white lotion into her hands, over and over. We all smoked; the ashtray was full. Mother walked over to the sink, poured herself some ginger ale, ran both hands through her short blond hair to keep it back, and shook her head.

She sighed and said again, looking up and out of the night-black window, "Dear God, what are we going to do with you?" My heart went out to them. We all seemed to have exhausted our options. They asked me for fresh ideas, but I had none. I racked my brain, but couldn't come up with anything. The U.S. Marines didn't take sixteen-year-old girls.

Enervated, fanatic, filled long past bursting with oxygen I couldn't use, I hunched skinny in the school's green uniform, etiolated, broken, bellicose, starved, over the back-breaking desk. I sighed and sighed but never emptied my lungs. I said to myself, "O breeze of spring, since I dare not know you,/Why part the silk curtains by my bed?" I stuffed my skull with poems' invisible syllables. If unauthorized persons looked at me, I hoped they'd see blank eyes.

On one of these May mornings, the school's headmistress called me in and read aloud my teachers' confidential appraisals. Madame Owens wrote an odd thing. Madame Owens was a sturdy, affectionate, and humorous woman who had lived through two world wars in Paris by eating rats. She had curly black hair, rouged cheeks, and long, sharp teeth. She swathed her enormous body in thin black fabrics; she sat at her desk with her tiny ankles crossed. She chatted with us; she reminisced.

Madame Owens's kind word on my behalf made no sense. The headmistress read it to me in her office. The statement began, unforgettably, "Here, alas, is a child of the twentieth century." The headmistress, Marion Hamilton, was a brilliant and strong woman whom I liked and respected; the school's small-minded trustees would soon run her out of town on a rail. Her black hair flared from her high forehead. She looked up at me significantly, raising an eyebrow, and repeated it: "Here, alas, is a child of the twentieth century."

I didn't know what to make of it. I didn't know what to do about it. You got a lot of individual attention at a private school.

Outside the study hall the next fall, the fall of our senior year, the Nabisco plant baked sweet white bread twice a week. If I sharpened a pencil at the back of the room I could smell the baking bread and the cedar shavings from the pencil. I could see the oaks turning brown on the edge of the hockey field, and see the scoured silver sky above shining a secret, true light into everything, into the black cars and red brick apartment buildings of Shadyside glimpsed beyond the trees. Pretty soon all twenty of us—our class—would be leaving. A core of my classmates had been together since kindergarten. I'd been there eight years. We twenty knew by bored heart the very weave of each other's socks. I thought, unfairly, of the Polyphemus moth crawling down the school's driveway. Now we'd go, too.

Back in my seat, I repeated the poem that began, "We grow to the sound of the wind playing his flutes in our hair." The poems I loved were in French, or translated from the Chinese, Portuguese, Arabic, Sanskrit, Greek. I murmured their heart-breaking syllables. I knew almost nothing of the diverse and energetic city I lived in. The poems whispered in my ear the password phrase, and I memorized it behind enemy lines: There is a world. There is another world.

I knew already that I would go to Hollins College in Virginia; our headmistress sent all her problems there, to her alma mater. "For the English department," she told me. William Golding was then writer in residence; before him was Enid Starkie, who wrote the biography of Rimbaud. But, "To smooth off her rough edges," she had told my parents. They repeated the phrase to me, vividly.

I had hopes for my rough edges. I wanted to use them as a can opener, to cut myself a hole in the world's surface, and exit through it. Would I be ground, instead, to a nub? Would they send me home, an ornament to my breed, in a jewelry bag?

I was in no position to comment. We had visited the school; it was beautiful. It was at the foot of Virginia's Great Valley, where the Scotch-Irish had settled in the eighteenth century, following the Alleghenies south.

EPILOGUE

A dream consists of little more than its setting, as anyone knows who tells a dream or hears a dream told:

We were squeezing up the stone street of an Old World village.

We were climbing down the gangway of an oceangoing ship, carrying a baby.

We broke through the woods on the crest of a ridge and saw water; we grounded our blunt raft on a charred point of land.

We were lying on boughs of a tree in an alley.

We were dancing in a darkened ballroom, and the curtains were blowing.

The setting of our urgent lives is an intricate maze whose blind corridors we learn one by one—village street, ocean vessel, forested slope—without remembering how or where they connect in space.

You travel, settle, move on, stay put, go. You point your car down the riverside road to the blurred foot of the mountain. The mountain rolls back from the floodplain and hides its own height in its trees. You get out, stand on gravel, and cool your eyes watching the river move south. You lean on the car's hot hood and look up at the old mountain, up the slope of its green western flank. It is September, the goldenrod is out, and the asters. The tattered hardwood leaves darken before they die. The mountain occupies most of the sky. You can see where the route ahead through the woods will cross a fire scar, will vanish behind a slide of shale, and perhaps reemerge there on that piny ridge now visible across the hanging valley—that ridge apparently inaccessible, but with a faint track that fingers its greenish spine. You don't notice starting to walk; the sight of the trail has impelled you along it, as the sight of the earth moves the sun.

Before you the mountain's body curves away backward like a gymnast; the mountain's peak is somewhere south, rolled backward, too, and out of sight. Below you lies the pale and widening river; its fat bank is forest now, and hills, and more blue hills behind them, hiding the yellow plain. Overhead and on the mountain's side, clouds collect and part. The clouds soak the ridges; the wayside plants tap water on your legs.

Now: if here while you are walking, or there when you've attained the far ridge and can see the yellow plain and the river shining through it—if you notice unbidden that you are afoot on this particular mountain on this particular day in the company of these particular changing fragments of clouds,—if you pause in your daze to connect your own skull-locked and interior mumble with the skin of your senses and sense, and notice you are living,—then will you not conjure up in imagination a map or a globe and locate this low mountain ridge on it, and find on one western slope the dot which represents you walking here astonished?

You may then wonder where they have gone, those other dim dots that were you: you in the flesh swimming in a swift river, swinging a bat on the first pitch, opening a footlocker with a screwdriver, inking and painting clowns on celluloid, stepping out of a revolving door into the swift crowd on a sidewalk, being kissed and kissing till your brain grew smooth, stepping out of the cold woods into a warm field full of crows, or lying awake in bed aware of your legs and suddenly aware of all of it, that the ceiling above you was under the sky—in what country, what town?

You may wonder, that is, as I sometimes wonder privately, but it doesn't matter. For it is not you or I that is important, neither what sort we might be nor how we came to be each where we are. What is important is anyone's coming awake and discovering a place, finding in full orbit a spinning globe one can lean over, catch, and jump on. What is important is the moment of opening a life and feeling it touch—with an electric hiss and cry—this speckled mineral sphere, our present world.

On your mountain slope now you must take on faith that those apparently discrete dots of you were contiguous: that little earnest dot, so easily amused; that alien, angry adolescent; and this woman with loosening skin on bony hands, hands now fifteen years older than your mother's hands when you pinched their knuckle skin into mountain ridges on an end table. You must take on faith that those severed places cohered, too—the dozens of desks, bedrooms, kitchens, yards, landscapes—if only through the motion and shed molecules of the traveler. You take it on faith that the multiform and variously lighted latitudes and longitudes were part of one world, that you didn't drop chopped from house to house, coast to coast, life to life, but in some once comprehensible way moved there, a city block at a time, a highway mile at a time, a degree of latitude and longitude at a time, carrying a fielder's mitt and the Penguin *Rimbaud* for old time's sake, and a sealed envelope, like a fetish, of untouchable stock certificates someone one hundred years ago gave your grandmother, and a comb. You take it on faith, for the connections are down now, the trail grown over, the highway moved; you can't remember despite all your vowing and memorization, and the way back is lost.

Your very cells have been replaced, and so have most of your feelings—except for two, two that connect back as far as you can remember. One is the chilling sensation of lowering one foot into a hot bath. The other, which can and does occur at any time, never fails to occur when you lower one foot into a hot bath, and when you feel the chill spread inside your shoulders, shoot down your arms and rise to your lips, and when you remember having felt this sensation from always, from when your mother lifted you down toward the bath and you curled up your legs: it is the dizzying overreal sensation of noticing that you are here. You feel life wipe your face like a big brush.

You may read this in your summer bed while the stars roll westward over your roof as they always do, while the constellation Crazy Swan nosedives over your steaming roof and into the tilled prairie once again. You may read this in your winter chair while Orion vaults over your snowy roof and over the hard continent to dive behind a California wave. "O'Ryan," Father called Orion, "that Irishman." Any two points in time, however distant, meet through the points in between; any two points in our atmosphere touch through the air. So we meet.

I write this at a wide desk in a pine shed as I always do these recent years, in this life I pray will last, while the summer sun closes the sky to Orion and to all the other winter stars over my roof. The young oaks growing just outside my windows wave in the light, so that concentrating, lost in the past, I see the pale leaves wag and think as my blood leaps: Is someone coming?

Is it Mother coming for me, to carry me home? Could it be my own young, my own glorious Mother, coming across the grass for me, the morning light on her skin, to get me and bring me back? Back to where I last knew all I needed, the way to her two strong arms?

And I wake a little more and reason, No, it is the oak leaves in the sun, pale as a face. I am here now, with this my own dear family, up here at this high latitude, out here at the farthest exploratory tip of this my present bewildering age. And still I break up through the skin of awareness a thousand times a day, as dolphins burst through seas, and dive again, and rise, and dive. ∾

INTERPRETIVE QUESTIONS
FOR DISCUSSION

Why does the author say that she will retain "the dreaming memory" of Pittsburgh's topology when everything else is gone from her mind?

1. Why does the author see her development as a person as inextricably tied up with the topology and history of Pittsburgh?

2. Why was Frank Doak's aborted journey down the Mississippi River a defining period in the author's personal history?

3. Why does the author characterize walking the neighborhood as her "project before reading"? (345)

4. Why is the author drawn to read *The Field Book of Ponds and Streams* every year and to "visit" it in the library? Why does the author believe that reading and thinking about this book from the Homewood branch library awakened her social consciousness? (354–356)

5. Why can't the author as a young girl "get enough" of the French and Indian War? Why does she call the war "all imaginary" and consider it "part of my own private consciousness"? (361–365)

6. What does the author mean when she says that the cast of characters in the French and Indian War were "morally neutral, like everything in history, like everything in books"? Why does the author see history as a work of literature? (363)

7. Why does the adolescent author refuse to revisit the Schoyers' farm at Paw Paw, the place she loved so much? (371)

8. Why has the author told before, and believe that she will tell again, the story of the crippled Polyphemus moth walking vigorously toward the affluent neighborhood of Shadyside? Why does she say that this "searing sight" turned her into "an early version of a runaway, a scapegrace"? (371)

9. Why does the author say that the Midwest nourished her optimistic sense of America and its people? Why does she see books as having led her to leave her beloved Pittsburgh forever? (381)

Suggested textual analyses

Pages 335–337: from the beginning of the selection to "worn out from planting corn."

Pages 343–346: beginning, "I walked," and ending, "but the world's skin ever expanding?"

Is the author claiming that hers is a unique story of privilege and intellectualism or that it is representative of her generation's "American Childhood"?

1. Why has the author found "joy in effort" and not frustration? Why has the author learned from books that "with faith all things are possible"? (359; cf. 376–378)

2. Why does the author remember her experience of being chased by the man at whom she had thrown snowballs as one of the happiest and most exhilarating of her life? Why did the young author brood for several years after this incident about how the glory of the chase could have been prolonged and capped? (347–350)

3. Why did the ten-year-old author consider her attempt to fly a test of her courage? Why is she "a free being" when she allows herself to appear foolish in the eyes of a stranger? (359–361)

4. Why does the author remember so clearly and fondly the woman who met her "exultant eye" during her flying experiment, and see her as an accomplice who had shared "a humor just beyond irony"? (360, 361)

5. Why is the author's optimism "endless" when she is a girl? (379) Does it come from her youth, her parents' example, or the culture of the 1950s?

6. Why does the author, who loves her parents, hate so passionately the affluent world that she has been brought up in? (382) Why are the author's parents so baffled about what to do about their daughter, even though they have fostered her values of independence, experimentation, and social consciousness? (392)

7. Why, in telling the story of her "American Childhood," does the author spend relatively little time describing her adolescent angst, even though this stage makes her typical of her time? (390–393)

8. What is the meaning of Madame Owen's comment about the author, "Here, alas, is a child of the twentieth century"? (393)

Suggested textual analysis
Pages 374–381: beginning, "I intended to live," and ending, "I had never heard the word."

Why does the author conclude that what is important is not our past or our aspirations for the future, but only our present world?

1. Why does the author see herself as beginning to "wake up" to the world when she was ten years old? (342–343)

2. Why does the author ask, "is this sad?" when she observes that ten-year-olds "find themselves here, discover themselves to have been here all along"? (342)

3. Why does her father's trip down the Mississippi River make the author "more often awake than not" toward her surroundings? (342)

4. Why did the author's self-directed drawing course bind her attention "to both the vigor and the detail of the actual world"? (351)

5. Why does the twelve-year-old author imagine herself in the distant future remembering herself at Paw Paw? Why does the author insist that she knew what she was doing at Paw Paw— "beginning the lifelong task of tuning my own gauges"? (367, 371)

6. Why does the young author vow to make it her "life's work" to remember everything? (381)

7. Why does the author see herself at fifteen as awakening again, realizing that she had been living all along in the country club society of affluent Pittsburgh? (382)

8. Why does the author conclude that it doesn't matter where the child in each of us has gone? Why does she feel that what is most important is finding "the moment of opening a life and feeling it touch . . . our present world"? (396)

9. Why as she writes her memoir does the author wonder whether her young, glorious mother is coming to bring her back "to where I last knew all I needed"? (398)

10. Why does her consciousness of the world seem to the author as if she were breaking "through the skin of awareness a thousand times a day, as dolphins burst through seas, and dive again, and rise, and dive"? (398)

Suggested textual analyses
Pages 342–343: beginning, "Children ten years old," and ending, "You again."

Pages 395–398: from "A dream consists of," to the end of the selection.

FOR FURTHER REFLECTION

1. Did the 1950s nurture more optimism and hope for children growing up then than our world does today?

2. Are we all products of our local history and topology, or does it take a person of curiosity, vision, and intellect to see one's development in this way?

3. Has recent history undermined the maxim that baby boomers grew up learning: "hard work bears fruit"?

4. Is it rare for children today to have heroes like Pasteur, Salk, and the builders of the Panama Canal?

5. Does the author's analysis of the secret to football—"forget yourself, aim, dive"—capture what is unique about the American spirit?

6. Would Dillard regard Proust as someone who was "too self-conscious to live," or would she sympathize with his method of endeavoring to recapture the past?

POETRY

William Wordsworth

Adrienne Rich

Robert Lowell

WILLIAM WORDSWORTH (1770–1850) was born in the "Lake Country" of northern England. In 1798, Wordsworth—together with Samuel Coleridge—published *Lyrical Ballads,* which heralded the beginning of English literary Romanticism. Wordsworth became poet laureate in 1843.

∾

ADRIENNE RICH (1929–   ) published her first book of poems, *A Change of World,* in 1951. That same year her book was chosen by W. H. Auden for the prestigious Yale Younger Poets Award. *Diving into the Wreck: Poems 1971–72,* from which our selection comes, won the 1974 National Book Award. Rich has also won the 1991 Common Wealth Award in Literature, the 1992 William Whitehead Award for lifetime achievement, and the Academy of American Poets' 1992 fellowship for "distinguished poetic achievement."

ROBERT LOWELL (1917–1977) was born
into an old and prominent Boston family
that included John Lowell, member of the
Continental Congress, and poets James
Russell Lowell and Amy Lowell. Lowell won
the 1947 Pulitzer Prize for poetry for *Lord
Weary's Castle* and the National Book
Award in 1960 for *Life Studies*.

Ode

INTIMATIONS OF IMMORTALITY FROM RECOLLECTIONS OF EARLY CHILDHOOD

The Child is father of the Man;
And I could wish my days to be
Bound each to each by natural piety.

1

THERE WAS a time when meadow, grove, and stream,
The earth, and every common sight,
    To me did seem
    Appareled in celestial light,
The glory and the freshness of a dream.
It is not now as it hath been of yore—
    Turn whereso'er I may,
    By night or day,
The things which I have seen I now can see no more.

2

    The Rainbow comes and goes,
    And lovely is the Rose,
    The Moon doth with delight
Look round her when the heavens are bare,
    Waters on a starry night
    Are beautiful and fair;
  The sunshine is a glorious birth;
  But yet I know, where'er I go,
That there hath passed away a glory from the earth.

3

Now, while the birds thus sing a joyous song,
  And while the young lambs bound
    As to the tabor's sound,
To me alone there came a thought of grief:
A timely utterance gave that thought relief,
    And I again am strong:
The cataracts blow their trumpets from the steep;
No more shall grief of mine the season wrong;
I hear the Echoes through the mountains throng,
The Winds come to me from the fields of sleep,
    And all the earth is gay;
      Land and sea
   Give themselves up to jollity,
    And with the heart of May
  Doth every Beast keep holiday—
    Thou Child of Joy,
Shout round me, let me hear thy shouts, thou happy Shepherd-boy!

4

Ye blessèd Creatures, I have heard the call
  Ye to each other make; I see
The heavens laugh with you in your jubilee;
   My heart is at your festival,
   My head hath its coronal,
The fullness of your bliss, I feel—I feel it all.
    Oh, evil day! if I were sullen
    While Earth herself is adorning,
     This sweet May morning,
    And the Children are culling
     On every side,
  In a thousand valleys far and wide,
   Fresh flowers; while the sun shines warm,
And the Babe leaps up on his Mother's arm—
    I hear, I hear, with joy I hear!
    —But there's a Tree, of many, one,

A single Field which I have looked upon,
Both of them speak of something that is gone:
      The Pansy at my feet
      Doth the same tale repeat:
Whither is fled the visionary gleam?
Where is it now, the glory and the dream?

5

Our birth is but a sleep and a forgetting:
The Soul that rises with us, our life's Star,
      Hath had elsewhere its setting,
      And cometh from afar:
      Not in entire forgetfulness,
      And not in utter nakedness,
But trailing clouds of glory do we come
      From God, who is our home:
Heaven lies about us in our infancy!
Shades of the prison-house begin to close
      Upon the growing Boy
      But he
Beholds the light, and whence it flows,
      He sees it in his joy;
The Youth, who daily farther from the east
      Must travel, still is Nature's Priest,
      And by the vision splendid
      Is on his way attended;
At length the Man perceives it die away,
And fade into the light of common day.

6

Earth fills her lap with pleasures of her own;
Yearnings she hath in her own natural kind,
And, even with something of a Mother's mind,
      And no unworthy aim,
    The homely Nurse doth all she can
To make her foster child, her Inmate Man,
     Forget the glories he hath known,
And that imperial palace whence he came.

7

Behold the Child among his newborn blisses,
A six-years' Darling of a pygmy size!
See, where 'mid work of his own hand he lies,
Fretted by sallies of his mother's kisses,
With light upon him from his father's eyes!
See, at his feet, some little plan or chart,
Some fragment from his dream of human life,
Shaped by himself with newly-learnèd art;
     A wedding or a festival,
     A mourning or a funeral;
       And this hath now his heart,
     And unto this he frames his song;
       Then will he fit his tongue
To dialogues of business, love, or strife;
     But it will not be long
     Ere this be thrown aside,
     And with new joy and pride
The little Actor cons another part;
Filling from time to time his "humorous stage"[1]
With all the Persons, down to palsied Age,
That Life brings with her in her equipage;
     As if his whole vocation
     Were endless imitation.

---

1. [I.e., playing the parts of characters with various temperaments, called "humors"
by Elizabethan poets and playwrights.]

8

Thou, whose exterior semblance doth belie
     Thy Soul's immensity;
Thou best Philosopher, who yet dost keep
Thy heritage, thou Eye among the blind,
That, deaf and silent, read'st the eternal deep,
Haunted forever by the eternal mind—
     Mighty Prophet! Seer blest!
     On whom those truths do rest,
Which we are toiling all our lives to find,
In darkness lost, the darkness of the grave;
Thou, over whom thy Immortality
Broods like the Day, a Master o'er a Slave,
A Presence which is not to be put by;
Thou little Child, yet glorious in the might
Of heaven-born freedom on thy being's height,
Why with such earnest pains dost thou provoke
The years to bring the inevitable yoke,
Thus blindly with thy blessedness at strife?
Full soon thy Soul shall have her earthly freight,
And custom lie upon thee with a weight,
Heavy as frost, and deep almost as life!

9

     O joy! that in our embers
     Is something that doth live,
     That nature yet remembers
     What was so fugitive!
The thought of our past years in me doth breed
Perpetual benediction; not indeed
For that which is most worthy to be blest;
Delight and liberty, the simple creed
Of Childhood, whether busy or at rest,
With new-fledged hope still fluttering in his breast—
     Not for these I raise
     The song of thanks and praise;

But for those obstinate questionings
  Of sense and outward things,
  Fallings from us, vanishings;
  Blank misgivings of a Creature
Moving about in worlds not realized,
High instincts before which our mortal Nature
Did tremble like a guilty Thing surprised;
  But for those first affections,
  Those shadowy recollections,
 Which, be they what they may,
Are yet the fountain light of all our day,
Are yet a master light of all our seeing;
 Uphold us, cherish, and have power to make
Our noisy years seem moments in the being
Of the eternal Silence: truths that wake,
  To perish never;
Which neither listlessness, nor mad endeavor,
  Nor Man nor Boy,
Nor all that is at enmity with joy,
Can utterly abolish or destroy!
  Hence in a season of calm weather
  Though inland far we be,
Our Souls have sight of that immortal sea
  Which brought us hither,
  Can in a moment travel thither,
And see the Children sport upon the shore,
And hear the mighty waters rolling evermore.

10

Then sing, ye Birds, sing, sing a joyous song!
  And let the young Lambs bound
  As to the tabor's sound!
We in thought will join your throng,
  Ye that pipe and ye that play,
  Ye that through your hearts today
  Feel the gladness of the May!

What though the radiance which was once so bright
Be now forever taken from my sight,
    Though nothing can bring back the hour
Of splendor in the grass, of glory in the flower;
        We will grieve not, rather find
        Strength in what remains behind;
        In the primal sympathy
        Which having been must ever be;
        In the soothing thoughts that spring
        Out of human suffering;
        In the faith that looks through death,
In years that bring the philosophic mind.

11

And O, ye Fountains, Meadows, Hills, and Groves,
Forebode not any severing of our loves!
Yet in my heart of hearts I feel your might;
I only have relinquished one delight
To live beneath your more habitual sway.
I love the Brooks which down their channels fret,
Even more than when I tripped lightly as they;
The innocent brightness of a newborn Day
        Is lovely yet;
The clouds that gather round the setting sun
Do take a sober coloring from an eye
That hath kept watch o'er man's mortality;
Another race hath been, and other palms are won.
Thanks to the human heart by which we live,
Thanks to its tenderness, its joys, and fears,
To me the meanest flower that blows can give
Thoughts that do often lie too deep for tears.

William Wordsworth

Diving into the Wreck

FIRST having read the book of myths,
and loaded the camera,
and checked the edge of the knife-blade,
I put on
the body-armor of black rubber
the absurd flippers
the grave and awkward mask.
I am having to do this
not like Cousteau with his
assiduous team
aboard the sun-flooded schooner
but here alone.

There is a ladder.
The ladder is always there
hanging innocently
close to the side of the schooner.
We know what it is for,
we who have used it.
otherwise
it is a piece of maritime floss
some sundry equipment.

I go down.
Rung after rung and still
the oxygen immerses me
the blue light
the clear atoms
of our human air.
I go down.
My flippers cripple me,
I crawl like an insect down the ladder
and there is no one
to tell me when the ocean
will begin.

First the air is blue and then
it is bluer and then green and then
black I am blacking out and yet
my mask is powerful
it pumps my blood with power
the sea is another story
the sea is not a question of power
I have to learn alone
to turn my body without force
in the deep element.

And now: it is easy to forget
what I came for
among so many who have always
lived here
swaying their crenellated fans
between the reefs
and besides
you breathe differently down here.

I came to explore the wreck.
The words are purposes.
The words are maps.
I came to see the damage that was done
and the treasures that prevail.
I stroke the beam of my lamp
slowly along the flank
of something more permanent
than fish or weed

the thing I came for:
the wreck and not the story of the wreck
the thing itself and not the myth
the drowned face always staring
toward the sun
the evidence of damage
worn by salt and sway into this threadbare beauty
the ribs of the disaster
curving their assertion
among the tentative haunters.

This is the place.
And I am here, the mermaid whose dark hair
streams black, the merman in his armored body.
We circle silently
about the wreck
we dive into the hold.
I am she: I am he

whose drowned face sleeps with open eyes
whose breasts still bear the stress
whose silver, copper, vermeil cargo lies
obscurely inside barrels
half-wedged and left to rot
we are the half-destroyed instruments
that once held to a course
the water-eaten log
the fouled compass

We are, I am, you are
by cowardice or courage
the one who find our way
back to this scene
carrying a knife, a camera
a book of myths
in which
our names do not appear.

Adrienne Rich

For the Union Dead

Relinquunt Omnia Servare Rem Publicam.[1]

THE OLD South Boston Aquarium stands
in a Sahara of snow now. Its broken windows are boarded.
The bronze weathervane cod has lost half its scales.
The airy tanks are dry.

Once my nose crawled like a snail on the glass;
my hand tingled
to burst the bubbles
drifting from the noses of the cowed, compliant fish.

My hand draws back. I often sigh still
for the dark downward and vegetating kingdom
of the fish and reptile. One morning last March,
I pressed against the new barbed and galvanized

fence on the Boston Common. Behind their cage,
yellow dinosaur steamshovels were grunting
as they cropped up tons of mush and grass
to gouge their underworld garage.

Parking spaces luxuriate like civic
sandpiles in the heart of Boston.
A girdle of orange, Puritan-pumpkin colored girders
braces the tingling Statehouse,

---

1. [They gave up everything to serve the State.]

shaking over the excavations, as it faces Colonel Shaw
and his bell-cheeked Negro infantry
on St. Gaudens' shaking Civil War relief,
propped by a plank splint against the garage's earthquake.

Two months after marching through Boston,
half the regiment was dead;
at the dedication,
William James could almost hear the bronze Negroes breathe.

Their monument sticks like a fishbone
in the city's throat.
Its Colonel is as lean
as a compass-needle.

He has an angry wrenlike vigilance,
a greyhound's gentle tautness;
he seems to wince at pleasure,
and suffocate for privacy.

He is out of bounds now. He rejoices in man's lovely,
peculiar power to choose life and die—
when he leads his black soldiers to death,
he cannot bend his back.

On a thousand small town New England greens,
the old white churches hold their air
of sparse, sincere rebellion; frayed flags
quilt the graveyards of the Grand Army of the Republic.

The stone statues of the abstract Union Soldier
grow slimmer and younger each year—
wasp-waisted, they doze over muskets
and muse through their sideburns . . .

Shaw's father wanted no monument
except the ditch,
where his son's body was thrown
and lost with his "niggers."

The ditch is nearer.
There are no statues for the last war here;
on Boyleston Street, a commercial photograph
shows Hiroshima boiling

over a Mosler Safe, the "Rock of Ages"
that survived the blast. Space is nearer.
When I crouch to my television set,
the drained faces of Negro schoolchildren rise like balloons.

Colonel Shaw
is riding on his bubble,
he waits
for the blessèd break.

The Aquarium is gone. Everywhere,
giant finned cars nose forward like fish;
a savage servility
slides by on grease.

Robert Lowell

INTERPRETIVE QUESTIONS
FOR DISCUSSION

In Wordsworth's "Ode," why does the poet look upon "those first affections, / Those shadowy recollections" of childhood as the "fountain light of all our day"?

1. Why does the poet draw strength from his memories of childhood even though he looks upon it as a lost paradise?

2. Why, according to the poet, do we lose our awareness of eternal things as we grow older?

3. Why in the middle of nature's splendor does "a thought of grief" come to the poet "alone"? Why does "a timely utterance" relieve the poet's sorrow and give him strength?

4. Why do the "Tree, of many, one" and the "single Field" interrupt the poet's joy in the May celebration, and make him wonder instead "Whither is fled the visionary gleam? / Where is it now, the glory and the dream?"

5. Why does Earth—"with something of a Mother's mind, / And no unworthy aim"—do all she can to make us forget heaven?

6. Why is a child our "best Philosopher" and "Eye among the blind," while the rest of us are toiling in the darkness? Why, despite this natural wisdom, do children rush the "inevitable yoke"?

7. Why does the poet give thanks and praise, not for "Delight and liberty, the simple creed / Of Childhood," but for "those obstinate questionings / Of sense and outward things"?

8. According to the poet, why should we not grieve, "Though nothing can bring back the hour / Of splendor in the grass, of glory in the flower"?

9. Why has the poet only "relinquished one delight" to live beneath nature's "more habitual sway"? Why does he now love the brooks even more than when he "tripped lightly as they"?

10. Why, according to the poet, does nature become even more beautiful and moving to an eye that has "kept watch o'er man's mortality"?

11. Why can "the meanest flower that blows" give the poet "Thoughts that do often lie too deep for tears"?

12. Are we meant to think that acquiring "the philosophic mind" is preferable to recapturing the spirit of a child, or is it just the best we can hope for?

Why does the person speaking in "Diving into the Wreck" want to "explore" the wreck, "to see the damage that was done / and the treasures that prevail"?

1. Why does the speaker read the book of myths before diving into the wreck?

2. Why must the speaker dive into the wreck alone?

3. Why is the ladder described as "always there / hanging innocently"? Why are we told that those who have used it know what it is for?

4. Why does the speaker contrast her "powerful" mask with the sea, which is "not a question of power"?

5. Why is it easy for the speaker to forget what she came for among "so many who have always / lived here"?

6. Why are words "purposes" and "maps" for exploring the wreck?

7. Why does the speaker come for "the wreck and not the story of the wreck / the thing itself and not the myth"?

8. Why does the speaker change from an "I" to a "we" as she explores the wreck? Why does she go from being alone to being both a "she" and a "he"?

9. Why does the speaker say "we are the half-destroyed instruments / that once held to a course"?

10. Why is it either by cowardice or courage that those who explore the wreck find their way back to it? Why are the names of those who explore the wreck not in the book of myths?

In "For the Union Dead," is the author attempting to honor those who died fighting for the Union?

1. Why does the poet connect Colonel Shaw and his troops with the demise of the old South Boston Aquarium and with the new "underworld garage" on the Boston Common?

2. Why does the poet "often sigh still / for the dark downward and vegetating kingdom / of the fish and reptile"?

3. According to the poem, why does the monument to Colonel Shaw and his black soldiers stick "like a fishbone / in the city's throat"?

4. Why, according to the poet, does Colonel Shaw seem to "wince at pleasure, / and suffocate for privacy"? Why does the Colonel rejoice in man's "lovely, / peculiar power to choose life and die"?

5. Does the poet think that the Union dead are more fittingly honored on small town New England greens than on the Boston Common? Why does he describe the churches as holding "their air / of sparse, sincere rebellion"?

6. Why does the poet tell us that Shaw's father "wanted no monument / except the ditch, / where his son's body was thrown / and lost with his 'niggers' "? Why does the poet say that "The ditch is nearer"?

7. Why are we told that there are no statues for the last war here, but only a commercial photograph of Hiroshima boiling over a Mosler safe that survived the blast?

8. Why does the poet tell us that the "drained faces of Negro schoolchildren" on television "rise like balloons"?

9. Why is Colonel Shaw said to be "riding on his bubble" and waiting "for the blessèd break"?

10. Why are we told that the Aquarium has been replaced by fish-like cars, "a savage servility" that "slides by on grease"?

For Further Reflection

1. Is revisiting the past more like remembering heaven or diving into a wreck?

2. Are children our best philosophers?

3. Is our country in danger of losing touch with the meaning of its history?

4. To what extent is our understanding of the past based on myth?

5. Is it possible to live with the joy and openness of childhood throughout our lives?

SONG OF SOLOMON

Toni Morrison

TONI MORRISON (1931–   ), born in
Lorain, Ohio, is the author of six novels as
well as *Playing in the Dark: Whiteness and
the Literary Imagination,* a work of literary
criticism. *Song of Solomon* was chosen as
winner of the National Book Critics Circle
Award for fiction in 1978; the novel *Beloved*
won the 1988 Pulitzer Prize for fiction.
Morrison is Robert F. Goheen Professor,
Council of the Humanities, at Princeton
University. She was awarded the Nobel Prize
for literature in 1993.

NOTE: All page references are
from the Plume/Penguin edition of
Song of Solomon (first printing 1987).

INTERPRETIVE QUESTIONS
FOR DISCUSSION

Why is Milkman still a boy at the age of thirty-one?

1. Why does Milkman feel an urgent need to escape his parents' past, "which was threatening to become his present"? (180)

2. Why does Ruth take secret pleasure in nursing her son even when he is old enough to stand up and wear knickers? (13–14)

3. Why is Milkman known by a nickname that recalls his mother's infantalization of him, while Guitar has a name originating in something he wanted to do? (15, 45)

4. Why does Macon Dead believe that the one important thing his son needs to know is that he must "own things," so that he can own himself and "other people too"? (55) Why does Macon think that money is "the only real freedom there is"? (163)

5. Why does Ruth repeatedly provoke her husband's anger and violence? (64–67)

6. Why is Milkman's first real act of independence caused by his father's violence toward his mother? Why do Milkman's sisters give him a startling, new "look of hatred" after he knocks his father down and cock-walks to his mother to ask how she is? (68; cf. 120)

7. After "decking" his father, why is Milkman unable to take advantage of or accept the "infinite possibilities and enormous responsibilities" that lay before him? (68)

8. Why does Milkman sleep with Hagar even though he has been warned off her by Pilate, who calls her Milkman's sister? Why does Milkman lose interest in Hagar because sex with her is "so free, so abundant"? (91)

9. Why does Milkman feel so disconnected from his father as Macon relates his story about Ruth and her possibly incestuous relationship with her father? Why does Macon's story cause Milkman to see his mother for the first time as a person with a life apart from his own? (74–75)

10. Why does Guitar say that Milkman is not a "serious person"? (104)

11. Why is Milkman bored with life at the age of thirty-one, and especially bored with the racial politics that absorb Guitar? Why does Milkman believe that he could thrive in the presence of someone who inspired fear, such as his father, Pilate, or Guitar? (107, 177)

12. Why does Guitar's "clarion call" to live life and steal Pilate's gold cause Milkman to feel "a self inside himself emerge"? (183–184) Why do both Milkman and Guitar believe that Pilate's gold promises "complete power, total freedom, and perfect justice"? (185)

Suggested textual analyses

Pages 98–106 (from Chapter 4): beginning, "After about three years or so of Hagar's on-again-off-again passion," and ending, "ask him where he was going or tell him to wait."

Pages 176–186 (from Chapter 8): beginning, "They met again on Sunday," and ending, "and put it in her mouth."

Why does figuring out the puzzle of his ancestry leave Milkman feeling as "eager and happy as he had ever been in his life"?

1. Why is Milkman angry when he hears Reverend Cooper describe the murder of his grandfather? Why hadn't he felt angry when he heard the story from his father? (232)

2. What is the "something" Milkman misses in his life when he listens to the old men in Danville reminisce about his father, grandfather, and Pilate, and the life they made for themselves on their farm, Lincoln's Heaven? (234–235)

3. Why does Milkman grow fierce with pride as he talks with the old men about his father, the son of the fabulous Macon Dead? (235–236)

4. Why does Milkman decide to stop "sliding through, over, and around difficulties" after his knife fight with Saul in Solomon's General Store? (271)

5. Why must Milkman feel his personality give way before he can understand that his watch and money are of no use in the woods? Why does this experience enable Milkman to understand what Guitar missed about the South and how he was maimed by it? (277–278)

6. When returning from the hunt, why does Milkman feel for the first time that he belongs to the earth—that his legs are tree trunks extending deep into the rock and soil? Why does Milkman laugh "hard, loud, and long" and lose his limp? (280–281)

7. Why do the hunters offer Milkman the heart of the bobcat? Why does Milkman, "quickly, before any thought could paralyze him," reach into the animal's rib cage and pull its heart out? (282)

8. Why is Milkman's relationship with Sweet reciprocal in a way that his relationship with Hagar never was? (285)

9. When sleeping with Sweet, why does Milkman dream of flying in a "relaxed" way, like "a man lying on a couch reading a newspaper"? Why does he dream that he is alone in the sky, but that somebody is "watching him and applauding"? (298)

10. Why does Milkman learn the truth about his family's real names from a children's chant?

11. Why does learning his family's history make Milkman eager to go home, when before he had yearned to escape? (329)

12. Why does Milkman, who earlier willed Hagar dead, get his wish? Why is Pilate able to forgive Milkman for the death of her "baby girl"? (318, 334)

Suggested textual analyses

Pages 269–281 (from Chapter 11): beginning, "You pretty good with a bottle," and ending, "And he did not limp."

Pages 326–331 (from Chapter 15): beginning, "The fan belt didn't last long enough," and ending, "To both questions he could answer yes."

Why does the novel end with Milkman "flying" into the arms of his "brother," Guitar?

1. Before he leaps, why does Milkman offer Guitar his life, saying, "You need it? Here"? (337)

2. Why does Milkman tell himself that Guitar is exceptional because he would both save Milkman's life and take it? (331)

3. Why has Guitar come to believe that every white person is "a potential nigger-killer" and that white people are unnatural? (155–156) Why does Guitar insist that he is not angry at

anybody even though he is killing innocent white people to balance the ratio of black people killed by whites? (157)

4. Why is Milkman attracted to Guitar's killing work, imagining how he would ask Guitar, "Did it change you? And if I do it, will it change me too?" (176)

5. Why does Guitar glare at Pilate after they leave the police station? (208) Why does the look of "jeweled hatred" in Guitar's eyes make Milkman suddenly realize that Guitar "could kill, would kill, and probably had killed"? (210)

6. Why does Guitar tell Milkman, "Wanna fly, you got to give up the shit that weighs you down"? (179; cf. 184)

7. Why does the ghost of Pilate's father tell her, "You just can't fly on off and leave a body"? (208) Why are we told that Solomon abandoned his wife and children in order to fly away to freedom? (322–323)

8. Why does Milkman share Pilate's sense of peace when they are driving back to Shalimar to bury the bones of Milkman's grandfather, the first Macon Dead? (334)

9. What does Milkman mean when he says that Pilate could fly "without ever leaving the ground"? (336)

10. Why does Milkman's discovery that he can "ride" the air mean that it doesn't matter whether he kills Guitar or vice versa? (337)

11. What does it mean, at the end of the novel, that Milkman "now knew what Shalimar knew: If you surrendered to the air, you could *ride* it"? (337)

12. Is Milkman's suicide a triumphant act of self-actualization or an abdication of responsibility for self and community? Is he embracing or rejecting Pilate's values of kinship and love through his suicide?

Suggested textual analyses
Pages 152–161 (Chapter 6): beginning, "I took her home," and ending, "That's funny. I'm scared for you too."

Pages 331–337 (from Chapter 15): from "Should I go home first," to the end of the novel.

FOR FURTHER REFLECTION

1. Is the notion that an awareness of family history is central to a person's identity an outmoded idea in today's world?

2. Is it possible to grow up without in some way "decking" your father?

3. How can parents teach their children to "fly without leaving the ground"?

4. Does Morrison provide a vision of how African Americans can overcome the legacy of slavery?

5. Should we want and expect children to understand the past suffering of their parents or grandparents?

ONE HUNDRED YEARS
OF SOLITUDE

Gabriel García Márquez

GABRIEL GARCÍA MÁRQUEZ (1928–)
grew up in Azacataca, a small town in a
tropical region of Colombia that—
imaginatively transformed and reborn as
Macondo—provides the setting for many of
his novels and short stories. After attending
the University of Bogotá, he worked as a
reporter and as a foreign correspondent in
Rome, Paris, Barcelona, Caracas, and
New York. Márquez was awarded the
Nobel Prize for literature in 1982.

NOTE: All page references are from the
HarperPerennial edition of *One Hundred Years
of Solitude* (first printing 1991).

Interpretive Questions
for Discussion

Why are both the village of Macondo and the Buendía clan condemned to one hundred years of solitude and then to be "exiled from the memory of men"?

1. Why does the author have the founding of Macondo come about as the result of the killing of Prudencio Aguilar? (20–23) After his conversation with the ghost of Prudencio Aguilar, why does José Arcadio Buendía destroy his alchemy lab and lose his mind, lapsing into "a state of total innocence"? (81)

2. Why are we told that in the beginning Macondo was a "truly happy village where no one was over thirty years of age and where no one had died," and whose inhabitants believed they had "lost the evil of original sin"? (9, 85)

3. Why does the author have the Buendía family tempted by incest and plagued by the fear of incest throughout its history?

4. Why does the author have the people of Macondo suffer from an insomnia plague that eliminates fatigue but results in a loss of memory, an "idiocy that had no past"? (45)

5. Why is Macondo unable to derive lasting benefit from contact with the outside world? Why does the arrival of the banana company cause "a colossal disturbance" in Macondo, disturbing even the pattern of the rains and the cycle of harvests? (233)

6. Why does José Arcadio Buendía, a "youthful patriarch" and "the most enterprising man ever to be seen in the village," become lazy and careless as a result of his "urge to discover the wonders of the world"? (9–10)

7. Why does the author have the wise Catalonian abandon Macondo, saying that "the past was a lie"? (408) Why does the true history of Macondo come to seem like a hallucination in comparison with the history in the schoolbooks? (355, 415)

8. Why do Aureliano and Amaranta Úrsula achieve the insight that "dominant obsessions can prevail against death"? Why is their child "the only one in a century who had been engendered with love"? (417)

9. Why does the last Aureliano—who seems "predisposed to begin the race again . . . and cleanse it of its pernicious vices and solitary calling"—have the tail of a pig, finally realizing Úrsula's fears of one hundred years earlier? (417)

10. Why are Melquíades' keys revealed to Aureliano Babilonia at the moment that he sees his son being dragged off by ants? (420)

11. Why does the author have the Buendía family die out at the moment its last living member finally deciphers Melquíades' parchments? (422)

12. In Márquez' mythic world, are human beings without hope of redemption? Is Macondo an Eden destroyed by the loss of its solitude?

Suggested textual analyses
Pages 1–18: the entire first chapter.

Pages 298–319: the entire chapter.

Pages 404–422: the entire last chapter.

Why does the politically active Colonel Aureliano Buendía end his days making little gold fishes?

1. Why does Colonel Aureliano Buendía not only fail in his effort to bring about a revolution, but wish to destroy "all trace of his passage through the world"? (178)

2. Why does Colonel Aureliano Buendía become "lost in the solitude of his immense power" and "lose direction"? (171)

3. Why, whenever he is facing death, does the Colonel recall the experience of going with his father to see ice? (1, 272)

4. Why does Colonel Aureliano Buendía decide that he is fighting the revolution because of pride, whereas Colonel Gerineldo Márquez is fighting "for something that doesn't have any meaning for anyone"? (139)

5. According to the author, why can't Colonel Aureliano Buendía and General Moncada carry out their plan to set up "a humanitarian regime that would take the best from each doctrine" of the liberal and conservative parties? (150)

6. After defeating the army forces occupying Macondo, why does Colonel Aureliano Buendía give strict orders that no one, not even Úrsula, should come closer to him than ten feet? (160)

7. Why does Colonel Aureliano Buendía refuse to commute the death sentence of his friend General Moncada? (162) Why does he sack the General's widow's house when she refuses to let him in after the execution? (169)

8. When Colonel Aureliano Buendía decides that his party has compromised so much that it is now fighting only for power, why does he say, "Since that's the way it is . . . we have no objection to accepting"? Why does he first condemn Colonel Gerineldo Márquez to death for calling it "a betrayal," then relent and spare him, saying, "the farce is over"? (173, 174)

9. Why is Colonel Aureliano Buendía destined to lose all thirty-two of his uprisings and have none of the seventeen Aurelianos—"all skillful craftsmen, the men of their houses, peace-loving people"—survive? (222)

10. When the Colonel makes "one last effort to search in his heart for the place where his affection had rotted away," why is he unable to find it? (177) Why can he "understand only that the secret of a good old age is simply an honorable pact with solitude"? (205)

11. Why is Úrsula the only human being who succeeds in penetrating Colonel Aureliano Buendía's misery? (177) Why does Úrsula say that he "had not lost his love for the family because he had been hardened by the war, as she had thought before, but that he had never loved anyone"? (254)

12. Before he dies, why does the Colonel fall into the "trap of nostalgia" and see "the face of his miserable solitude"? (272–273)

Suggested textual analysis
Pages 165–185: the entire chapter.

Are we meant to think that Úrsula, rather than her husband or her son the colonel, represented the best hope for the Buendía family to survive and succeed in the modern world?

1. Why is it Úrsula, "with the secret and implacable labor of a small ant," who thwarts the plan to move Macondo? Why does she insist she is willing to die if that's what it takes for the rest of her family to remain? (13–14)

2. Why does the author have José Arcadio Buendía's killing of Prudencio Aguilar and his decision to leave the peaceful Indian village come about as a result of Úrsula's fear of begetting a child with a pig's tail? (20–22)

3. Why does the author make Úrsula the titular matriarch and moral leader of the Buendía clan, but perpetuate the family through Pilar Ternera?

4. Why does Úrsula not hesitate to abandon Macondo to search for her son José Arcadio? Why does the author have the connection between Macondo and the outside world discovered accidentally by Úrsula after José Arcadio Buendía's efforts to find it had failed "in his frustrated search for the great inventions"? (37)

5. Why is José Arcadio destroyed by his guilt over Prudencio Aguilar's death, while Úrsula is not? (79–81)

6. Why is Úrsula able to restrain the cruel despotism of her nephew Arcadio, but not that of her son the Colonel? (108, 162, 173–174)

7. Why does Úrsula connect names with personalities in the Buendía family, concluding that "while the Aurelianos were withdrawn, but with lucid minds, the José Arcadios were impulsive and enterprising, but they were marked with a tragic sign"? Why is she disturbed by the mixing up of the identity of the twins? (186–187)

8. Why does Úrsula almost "go mad" when she realizes that "it was as if the defects of the family and none of the virtues had been concentrated" in both Aureliano Segundo and José Arcadio Segundo? Are we meant to think that her plan for José Arcadio to become Pope in order to "restore the prestige of the family" is harebrained? (194)

9. Are we meant to agree with Úrsula's insights about her family— that the Colonel "was simply a man incapable of love," that Amaranta "was the most tender woman who had ever existed," and that Rebeca "was the only one who had the unbridled courage that Úrsula had wanted for her line"? (254–255)

10. Why does Úrsula ask God, "without fear, if he really believed that people were made of iron in order to bear so many troubles and mortifications"? Why is she tempted to draw "out of her heart the infinite stacks of bad words that she had been forced to swallow over a century of conformity"? (256–257)

Suggested textual analyses

Pages 19–37: the entire chapter.

Pages 250–257: from the beginning of the chapter to, " 'Here,' she said."

FOR FURTHER REFLECTION

1. Is it important for the citizens of a country to share an accepted version of its history?

2. Is the history we have been taught in school a myth?

3. Is Márquez' imaginative world amoral or does it present an implicit set of values to guide us?

4. Is solitude—for a person or a culture—a blessing or a curse?

5. Do you agree with the wise Catalonian that the wildest and most tenacious love is an ephemeral truth in the end?

6. Which do you think is more important: openness to exuberant love and passion, or developing a sense of order and responsibility?

ACKNOWLEDGMENTS

All possible care has been taken to trace ownership and secure permission for each selection in this anthology. The Great Books Foundation wishes to thank the following authors, publishers, and representatives for permission to reprint copyrighted material.

Overture, from REMEMBRANCE OF THINGS PAST, VOLUME 1, by Marcel Proust. Translated by C. K. Scott Moncrieff and Terence Kilmartin. Translation copyright 1981 by Random House, Inc. and Chatto & Windus. Reprinted by permission of Random House, Inc.

The Rat Man, from "Notes upon a Case of Obsessional Neurosis," in THE COLLECTED PAPERS, VOLUME 3, by Sigmund Freud. Translated by Alix and James Strachey. Published by Basic Books, Inc. by arrangement with the Hogarth Press, Ltd. and the Institute of Psycho-Analysis, London. Reprinted by permission of BasicBooks, a division of HarperCollins Publishers, Inc.

The Island, from THE ISLAND: THREE TALES, by Gustaw Herling. Translated by Ronald Strom. Translation copyright 1967 by Ronald Strom. Reprinted by permission of Viking Penguin, a division of Penguin Books USA, Inc.

Momik, from SEE UNDER: LOVE, by David Grossman. Translated by Betsy Rosenberg. Translation copyright 1989 by Betsy Rosenberg. Reprinted by permission of Farrar, Straus & Giroux, Inc.